THE ARCH OF EXPERIENCE

Ian W. Mills
Judith H. Mills

I am a part of all that I have met;

Yet all experience is an arch wherethrough

Gleams that untravel'd world, whose margin fades

For ever and for ever when I move.

from "Ulysses," by Alfred, Lord Tennyson

Executive Editor: MAGGIE GOH
Developmental Editor: DAVID FRIEND
Production Editor: PAM YOUNG
Art Director: MARY OPPER
Designer: AVRIL ORLOFF
Cover Illustration: TOMIO NITTO
Drawings: GAIL GELTNER

Canadian Cataloguing in Publication Data
Main entry under title:
The Arch of experience
ISBN 0-03-922032-X
1. English literature.   2. Canadian literature
(English).*   3. Readers (Secondary).   I. Mills,
Ian W. (Ian William), 1943-   .   II. Mills.
Judith H., 1939-   .

PN6014.A72 1986   820'.8   C86-093993-6

Holt, Rinehart and Winston of Canada, Limited is grateful for the evaluations and suggestions of these educators:

Elaine Baker
Conception Bay South Integrated
  Board
Manuels,
Conception Bay, Newfoundland

Gertrude Bohan
Edmonton Separate School Board
Edmonton, Alberta

Mark Brubacher
York Board of Education
Toronto, Ontario

Terence Comeau
Board of School Trustees District #20
St. John, New Brunswick

Denise Cummings
Protestant School Board
Côte St. Luc, Québec

Frances Davis
Vanier College, Saint-Laurent Campus
Saint-Laurent, Québec

Robert Dawe
Avalon Consolidated Integrated
Mount Pearl, Newfoundland

Peter Fergus
Ottawa Board of Education
Ottawa, Ontario

Don Gale
Port au Port Roman Catholic
  School Board
Stephensville, Newfoundland

Nigel Gough
Perth County Board of Education
Stratford, Ontario

Roman Kopchuk
St. James–Assiniboia School
  Division #2
Winnipeg, Manitoba

Allan McPherson
London & Middlesex County
  Roman Catholic Separate
  School Board
London, Ontario

Joan Newton
River East School Division #9
Winnipeg, Manitoba

Maureen Ross
Edmonton, Alberta

Audrey Young
St. James–Assiniboia School
  Division #2
Winnipeg, Manitoba

Printed in Canada   2 3 4 5   91 90 89 88 87

THE ARCH OF EXPERIENCE

Ian W. Mills
Judith H. Mills

Holt, Rinehart and Winston of Canada, Ltd.

CONTENTS

Note: For detailed information about the genre, source, and date of
publication of each of the selections, see **Acknowledgments**, p. 410.

I am a part of all that I have met;

Yet all experience is an arch wherethrough

Gleams that untravel'd world, whose margin fades

For ever and for ever when I move.

from "Ulysses," by Alfred, Lord Tennyson

Introduction

n "Ulysses," Tennyson likens the desire for understanding to a journey. He calls Ulysses a "gray spirit yearning in desire/ To follow knowledge, like a sinking star,/Beyond the utmost bound of human thought." Think of this anthology, *The Arch of Experience*, as though it were a landscape for you to travel in and to explore, a landscape of ideas and issues, of human emotions and concerns, expressed in a variety of literary forms: short stories, memoirs, biographies, speeches, editorials, newspaper and magazine articles, and essays.

The six units of the book contain selections presenting differing perspectives on a theme or topic. (You can further enrich the reading process by drawing up your own groupings.) The selections will introduce you to new ideas and experiences and also challenge you with interesting, and even peculiar, viewpoints. Like any traveller in unfamiliar territory, you may be perplexed as well as entertained by what you encounter, but your language skills will serve as a guide.

In the activities following each selection you will use language to formulate and clarify your thoughts and to communicate them to others. There are opportunities for personal response, for formal critical writing, and for self-expression in a number of formats. The activities also encourage you to extend your understanding through small group discussions and peer editing and evaluation.

Bear in mind that speaking and writing are processes; you will not have a perfect product at first attempt. Competent speaking depends on constant practice. Competent writing depends on constant revision, editing, and proofreading. Your writing folder will help you keep track of the progression of your work: from inception and planning, through one or more drafts, to polishing and completion.

The six units are separated by short pieces of writing on different aspects of language. We hope that you will find them amusing and informative, and that they will prompt you to reflect on your own use of language.

As part of your senior English program, you may be required to complete an independent project. At the end of the book (p. 404), you will find activities that extend the readings in *The Arch of Experience*. You may wish to take one of these activities as the basis of your independent study, or to use it for a starting point only.

"I am a part of all that I have met," says Ulysses. You will meet many writers and many characters as you read through this book: some will speak for you; others will argue positions that run counter to your vision of the world. Read critically, remembering that the writers, like you, are products of a particular time and place in human history. Their views, whether you accept or reject them, may help you to build your own arch of experience.

LOOK TO THE ESSENCE

Look to the essence of a thing, whether it be a
point of doctrine, of practice, or of interpretation.
Marcus Aurelius Antoninus

We are all problem solvers and decision makers, although
we rarely consider how we go about those processes.
How do we make a judgment; what steps are involved?
The question defies a simple answer, but Marcus
Aurelius' injunction – "Look to the essence . . . " – is a
good place to begin. Each of the selections in this unit
deals in some sense with evaluating, or making
judgments. In the essays, the writers present their
opinions, and the reader must judge the reasonableness
of their arguments. The authors of the short stories leave
it to the reader to determine what characters and actions
are good and bad, right and wrong. In both the essays
and the stories, the reader must first identify the essence
of the writer's communication; that is the origin of critical
thinking.

Before you read Marya Mannes's personal
essay on making aesthetic judgments,
consider how you might respond to the central
question she poses: how do you know a novel,
a painting, a piece of music, or any other work
of art is good? What are your personal
standards for judgment? How did you arrive at
them?

HOW DO YOU KNOW IT'S GOOD?

Marya Mannes

uppose there were no critics to tell us how to react to a picture, a play, or a new composition of music. Suppose we wandered innocent as the dawn into an art exhibition of unsigned paintings. By what standards, by what values would we decide whether they were good or bad, talented or untalented, successes or failures? How can we ever know that what we think is right?

For the last fifteen or twenty years the fashion in criticism or appreciation of the arts has been to deny the existence of any valid criteria and to make the words "good" or "bad" irrelevant, immaterial, and inapplicable. There is no such thing, we are told, as a set of standards, first acquired through experience and knowledge and later imposed on the subject under discussion. This has been a popular approach, for it relieves the critic of the responsibility of judgment and the public of the necessity of knowledge. It pleases those resentful of disciplines, it flatters the empty-minded by calling them open-minded, it comforts the confused. Under the banner of democracy and the kind of equality which our forefathers did *not* mean, it says, in effect, "Who are you to tell us what is good or bad?" This is the same cry used so long and so effectively by the producers of mass media who insist that it is the public, not they, who decides what it wants to hear and see, and that for a critic to say that *this* program is bad and *this* program is good is purely a reflection of personal taste. Nobody recently has expressed this philosophy more succinctly than Dr. Frank Stanton, the highly intelligent president of CBS television. At a hearing before the Federal Communications Commission, this phrase escaped him under questioning: "One man's mediocrity is another man's good program."

There is no better way of saying, "No values are absolute." There is another important aspect to this philosophy of *laissez faire*: It is the fear, in all observers of all forms of art, of guessing wrong. This fear is well come by, for who has not heard of the contemporary outcries against artists who later were called great? Every age has its arbiters who do not grow with their times, who cannot tell evolution from revolution or the difference between frivolous faddism, amateurish experimentation, and profound and necessary change. Who wants to be caught *flagrante delicto* with an error of judgment as serious as this? It is far safer, and certainly easier, to look at a picture or a play or a poem and to say "This is hard to understand, but it may be good," or simply to welcome it as a new form. The word "new" – in our country especially – has magical connotations. What is new must be good; what is old is probably bad. And if a critic can describe the new in language that nobody can understand, he's safer still. If he has mastered the art of saying nothing with exquisite complexity, nobody can quote him later as saying anything.

But all these, I maintain, are forms of abdication from the responsibility of judgment. In creating, the artist commits himself; in appreciating, you have a commitment of your own. For after all, it is the audience which makes the arts. A climate of appreciation is essential to its flowering, and the higher the expectations of the public, the better the performance of the artist. Conversely, only a public ill-served by its critics could have accepted as art and as literature so much in these last years that has been neither. If anything goes, everything goes; and at the bottom of the junkpile lie the discarded standards too.

But what are these standards? How do you get them? How do you know they're the right ones? How can you make a clear pattern out of so many intangibles, including that greatest one, the very private I?

Well for one thing, it's fairly obvious that the more you read and see and hear, the more equipped you'll be to practise that art of association which is at the basis of all understanding and judgment. The more you live and the more you look, the more aware you are of a consistent pattern – as universal as the stars, as the tides, as breathing, as night and day – underlying everything. I would call this pattern and this rhythm an order. Not order – *an* order. Within it exists an incredible diversity of forms. Without it lies chaos. I would further call this order – this incredible diversity held within one pattern – health. And I would call chaos – the wild cells of destruction – sickness. It is in the end up to you to distinguish between the diversity that is health and the chaos that is sickness, and you can't do this without a process of association that can link a bar of Mozart with the corner of a Vermeer painting, or a Stravinsky score with a Picasso abstraction; or that can relate an aggressive cat with a Franz Kline painting and a fit of coughing with a John Cage composition.

There is no accident in the fact that certain expressions of art live for all time and that others die with the moment, and although you may not always define the reasons, you can ask the questions. What does an artist say that is timeless; how does he say it? How much is fashion, how much is merely reflection? Why is Sir Walter Scott so hard to read now, and Jane Austen not? Why is baroque right for one age and too effulgent for another?

Can a standard of craftsmanship apply to art of all ages, or does each have its own, and different, definitions? You may have been aware, inadvertently, that craftsmanship has become a dirty word these years because, again, it implies standards – something done well or done badly. The result of this convenient avoidance is a plenitude of actors who can't project their voices, singers who can't phrase their songs, poets who can't communicate emotion, and writers who have no vocabulary – not to speak of painters who can't draw. The dogma now is that craftsmanship gets in the way of expression. You can do better if you don't know *how* you do it, let alone *what* you're doing.

I think it is time you helped reverse this trend by trying to rediscover craft: the command of the chosen instrument, whether it is a brush, a word, or a voice. When you begin to detect the difference between freedom and sloppiness, between serious experimentation and ego-therapy, between skill and slickness, between strength and violence, you are on your way to separating the sheep from the goats, a form of segregation denied us for quite a while. All you need to restore it is a small bundle of standards and a Geiger counter that detects fraud.

Purpose and craftsmanship – end and means – these are the keys to your judgment in all the arts. What is this painter trying to say when he slashes a broad band of black across a white canvas and lets the edges dribble down? Is it a statement of violence? Is it a self-portrait? If it is *one* of these, has he made you believe it? Or is this a gesture of the ego or a form of therapy? If it shocks you, what does it shock you into?

And what of this tight little painting of bright flowers in a vase? Is the painter saying anything new about flowers? Is it different from a million other canvases of flowers? Has it any life, any meaning, beyond its statement? Is there any pleasure in its forms or texture? The question is not whether a thing is abstract or representational, whether it is "modern" or conventional. The question, inexorably, is whether it is good. And this is a decision which only you, on the basis of instinct, experience, and association, can make for yourself. It takes independence and courage. It involves, moreover, the risk of wrong decision and the humility, after the passage of time, of recognizing it as such. As we grow and change and learn, our attitudes can change too, and what we once thought obscure or "difficult" can later emerge as coherent and illuminating. Entrenched prejudices, obdurate opinions are as sterile as no opinions at all.

Yet standards there are, timeless as the universe itself. And when you have committed yourself to them, you have acquired a passport to that elusive but immutable realm of truth. Keep it with you in the forests of bewilderment. And never be afraid to speak up.

───────────────────────────◆•◆•───────────────────────────

1. With a classmate, make a list of the popular shibboleths Mannes attacks and summarize the alternatives she presents.

2. In a few sentences of your own words, explain what Mannes means by the following statements:
   a) " . . . it is the audience which makes the arts."
   b) "It is in the end up to you to distinguish between the diversity that is health and the chaos that is sickness . . . ."

3. In order to persuade the reader to accept her views, Mannes employs certain stylistic techniques. In a small group, evaluate the effect on the reader of:
   a) clusters of interrogative sentences;
   b) rhetorical questions;
   c) the switch in mid-essay from the use of *we* to the use of *I* and *you*;
   d) the concluding imperative sentences.

4. Mannes implies that many artists today have forfeited craftsmanship because it "gets in the way of expression." If you were invited to participate with Mannes in a panel discussion about the relationship between craftsmanship and expression, would you take her side? Jot down the points you would raise, making specific reference to works of art you are familiar with. Trade notes with a classmate and discuss the similarities and differences in your views.

5. By the convention of her time, Mannes sometimes uses masculine pronouns (*he, him, his*) and the word *man* when she is referring to people in general. Today, that convention is considered to be sexist. Find examples of sexist language in her essay and rewrite

them in non-sexist language. Before you begin, you may wish to read the excerpt from "*Man* as a False Generic" (p. 67). You might be interested in keeping a list, as you read this book, of other instances of what are now considered to be sexist expressions or assumptions. (Look at p.106 in "Nurses' New Role: Patients' Advocate," for one example.)

6. a) Select two works of art (musical, literary, or visual): one that in your opinion is good and one that is bad. Explain the reasons for your judgments in a short piece of writing. Bring the works of art to class and, without revealing your own views, give two or three classmates a chance to make their own analyses and judgments. Afterward, read your criticism aloud and discuss together the similarities and differences in your evaluations.

b) Mannes wants people to make their own well-reasoned judgments about art. Consider the extent to which you used her suggestions or referred to her essay when you worked on 6(a). Write a critique of "How Do You Know It's Good?" in which you assess the strength of her arguments and the usefulness of her essay, expressing your judgments in the form of a letter to Mannes.

ESSENCE OF MARIGOLD
Elizabeth Brewster

I am sitting here at my dining-room table staring at a large yellow marigold that I bought this morning in the Farmers' Market. Only ten cents, but beautiful and crinkly, undeniably real. Marigolds have almost no scent, it's true, but if I press my nose right up against it, this one gives off a faint spicy odour, like some kind of kitchen herb. Not at all sweet, mildly medicinal in fact, but pleasant. I have put it in a little brown pottery vase and set it in the centre of the table. Geraniums also: a double red geranium in a tin container. Exactly the shade of red geranium my mother would have liked.

Should I paint one of them? A still life, say – marigold and transistor radio? Geranium on window-sill, with prairie city beyond it? (The geranium must stay in the tin container, which must not be camouflaged in any way.) No. I don't feel like painting them. I have painted flowers from time to time (pale narcissi in a brown pot set against a blue background; also those deep red, semi-purplish gladioli now framed on my living-room wall). I think I was trying to hold on to them, but these flowers I intend to let go. I couldn't catch their scent, anyway. (The geranium, some people would say, has no scent. Except in the leaves.) And anyhow I have gone on to other things than flowers. Prairie landscapes. Crowd scenes. I am a good painter. Maybe not great, but good. Too conscientious, maybe? Not experimental enough? A failure in imagination? My fans (and I have fans, bless them) wouldn't say so. They think of me as a female prairie Alex Colville – or maybe that Alex Colville is a male Maritime Daisy Lister. If I don't have quite Colville's reputation, I have the excuse that I'm a few years younger.

I'm a few years younger than Marguerite Chrystal, too. An admirable painter, though unlike Alex Colville. The magic without the realism. If she painted the marigold, she would paint its essence. One might think of the heart of the sun, or of the ruffled flight of a ballerina. (I have a fleeting image of a ballerina as I might paint her: I would concentrate, I think, on the muscles. Ballerinas are really tough ladies. I like that combination of toughness and grace.)

Marguerite is in my mind just now because she has painted my portrait. Oh, not in oils. No, she has written a short story about me. (Marguerite, unfairly, has several talents.) She told me about this story, said she would send me a copy, but forgot to. I ran across it yesterday in the public library, stood reading it at the magazine rack, trying to decide in my mind whether I liked it, as the ballet dancer might stand in front of my portrait of her, objecting to the prominence of her muscles. Has she caught my essence, I wonder?

Really, though, the story is not so much about me as it is about memory. Here are two women, two painters, who have quite different memories of the occasion when they met. Which is telling the truth? Are there two truths?

I have a diary dating from the time I met Marguerite. I have a bundle of letters from her. (She has forgotten she wrote me.) I have clippings about exhibitions, a few sketches. I could look them up, I could document this account, but I don't intend to this time. I'll try to get at the essence.

I arrived in Saskatoon by myself on the train that day, the day I was to collect the prize. (I insist that I arrived by myself, although Marguerite is equally certain that my parents came with me.) My certainty springs from the fact that my arrival by myself was a triumph. I was my parents' only child and too much protected. I had never been separated from my mother for more than a day. On this occasion, however, I had argued (successfully) that I was perfectly able to look after myself. After all, I was almost seventeen. (Marguerite remembers me as younger, a plump, composed child, perhaps twelve, fourteen at most. I was, in fact, rather thin, if not scrawny, and not at all composed.) The trip to Saskatoon from Kasoba was not a difficult one, although rather long, and I was to be met at the railway station by one of the local artists, a Mrs. Curtis, who was putting me up in her house. Lucky that Mrs. Curtis made that offer. If I had been staying at an hotel, for instance, my parents would not have felt I should be alone. But they could not have afforded a good hotel, either for themselves or for me. Once before, I had won a prize for a watercolour, but had not been able to come. If I had I'd have spent all my prize money.

Now, as the train chugged its way through the autumn fields, stopping here and there at small prairie towns, I was torn between delight and fear. I was free, and I was about to encounter the unknown. I ate the egg sandwiches and solid doughnuts that my mother had packed for my lunch, half in a delightful daydream, half in nervous fear that something would go wrong.

Saskatoon station. Much larger than the station at Kasoba, and I have never been here before. I am wearing a navy-blue suit, handed down to me by a cousin in Ontario who is a year or so older than I am. I hate it, but am lucky to have it. Anyhow, I have told Mrs. Curtis that I will be wearing this navy-blue suit. I have no idea what she will be wearing or what she will look like. For some reason I imagine her with white hair, fat like the eldest of my aunts.

While I stand there uncertainly, there rushes up to me a trim little woman in a smart dress – I can't describe it, I just know it is smart – with her coat flung over her shoulders. Her hair is piled up on top of her head in an auburn mass, from which a few wisps have escaped. She is holding a chubby little boy, three or four years old, by the hand. They look as if they have both been running.

"Daisy Lister?" she gasps. "I'm Bea Curtis."

Mrs. Curtis takes charge of me immediately. I am whisked, with my little battered suitcase (my mother's little battered suitcase, that is) out of the station and into a taxi. Taxis are rather outside the range of my experience. In Kasoba everything is within walking distance. I walk to school every day; my father walks to the drugstore where he works for his small wartime salary; my parents and I walk to church together on Sundays. Sometimes one of my uncles who is better off than my father takes us for a drive in his car, but not too often. Mrs. Curtis and the little boy (Binker, he is called) and I all sit together in the back seat of the taxi. I am delighted with Saskatoon. It has trees and a river, as Kasoba hasn't, and a huge hotel that looks like a castle. "Pretty river," Mrs. Curtis says abstractedly to Binker.

I think that she is speaking to me, and say "Yes" a little too fervently. She looks at me with surprise, and I turn a bright pink (I feel the blood rushing into my face) and lapse into silence.

I am to collect the prize for my watercolour that evening, at a meeting of the Group. The Group is trying to encourage talent in improbable places like Kasoba. That is why I am here. It is Marguerite who has written to me before, and I rather wish I could have stayed with her, but she does not have room. She is a genuine artist (I suspect that Mrs. Curtis isn't) and is living in some hand-to-mouth artistic way in a single room.

Mrs. Curtis settles me into a trim little room in her trim little house.

She looks me over thoughtfully. There is time, she thinks, to put a few pin curls in my hair. What do I plan to wear? I have a new dress, bought especially for the occasion, a green flowered dress with a fussy lace collar. I like it myself, and in Kasoba it seemed right, but I see through Mrs. Curtis's eyes that it is all wrong. Perhaps without the lace? It was the lace that I had especially liked, but Mrs. Curtis persuades me (tactfully, tactfully) to allow her to take the collar off while I am having a nap before dinner. Not that I do have a nap before dinner. (Supper, we called it in Kasoba.)

At dinner, I meet Mr. Curtis, who is a business man in the city, rather older than Mrs. Curtis and beginning to go bald. He is a friendly man. "I like your painting, Daisy," he says. "I don't know much about art – Bea's the artist around here – but I thought you should get the prize. That field of black-eyed Susans – I do like that."

I see that his opinion isn't to be taken seriously, but he is kind. I like him, as I like Mrs. Curtis. I am intimidated, however, by the fact that there is a maid who waits on the table and even wears a uniform. Nobody that I know in Kasoba has a maid. I find it difficult to talk in the presence of somebody who is in the room but not part of the company. Anyhow, it is hard for me to keep my mind on dinner or on Mr. and Mrs. Curtis. I am thinking of the evening to come, of meeting Marguerite, of being presented with my prize.

The meeting that night is in an artist's studio (Marguerite and I agree on that). A big attic room without much furniture; burlap curtains at the windows; canvases propped against walls. There are some poets present as well as the painters. (I remember a dentist who told me he wrote a sonnet a day and kept his writings in a barrel.) Marguerite has not yet arrived when Mrs. Curtis and I come in. The studio is like a stage waiting for its leading lady. (Though surely I am the leading lady for that evening, the Promising Young Artist from out there in Kasoba?) There is a handsome young man present with dark hair and brown eyes who seems to me the leading man and who attaches himself to Marguerite as soon as she comes in.

2

It is morning again (Sunday morning), and I look once more at my marigold and the geranium, which have survived the night very well. The marigold has perceptibly more scent today than yesterday. A scent like that of the marigolds in my mother's garden, although hers were the tiny button marigolds rather than large ones like this. There was a thunderstorm last night – one of those thorough-going prairie storms – and the sky is still sullen: but patches of blue show through the clouds, and I hear crows cawing. I drink a cup of coffee and read over what I have written. Why, I wonder, do I delay so long about actually bringing Marguerite onto the scene? Is it because I am afraid I can't possibly paint her essence? Her essence has always seemed to me a mystery, untouchable. I, on the other hand, am not at all mysterious. I have often painted my own portrait, not so much from any great narcissism as from the realization that I look like so many other people I know. My mother told me early on, "You may be talented, but that doesn't make you better than other people." I tend to agree with her: painters, poets, millionaires may have some special ability to handle paints or words or money, but we are really only ordinary people with one highly developed skill, like jugglers or *cordon bleu* chefs.

Nevertheless, I didn't think Marguerite was ordinary. I didn't expect her to be ordinary. There was something extraordinary about her letters, even their appearance on the page. Her handwriting was excited and angular, with high loops that reminded me of bird-wings, quite unlike my own careful schoolgirlish hand. Her sentences were breathless, flying in all directions at once. On the margins there were often quick sketches of creatures on the wing, fabulous birds, butterflies, sometimes weirdly distorted and frightening, but always strangely beautiful.

When I imagined her – created an image of her to go with the letters – I imagined someone small and quick and birdlike, with piercing bright eyes. I saw her in my mind dancing in bare feet with peacock plumes in her hair. The real Marguerite wasn't like that. She was handsome, though – handsome rather than beautiful, I think – a tall, statuesque young woman somewhere in her twenties. She was dark (there I had guessed right) and glowed rather, I fancied, like those spikes of crimson gladioli that I painted later with their purple shadows. I was – and yet was not – disappointed, and stood there readjusting my vision of her while she bent over me (she was so much taller than I). I caught a surprised expression also on her face. "You don't look the way I imagined you," she said, but did not elaborate, and I fancied that she must be disappointed, that she had possibly invented someone more flowerlike as the painter of those black-eyed Susans and red lilies. Years later, she told me, "It was your age. I hadn't expected someone quite so young, a mere child."

"I wasn't a mere child," I said indignantly, remembering my seventeen years, from which she had so absurdly subtracted. (At that point she remembered me as having been only ten. She almost fancied having met me with a doll in my arms.)

Still, I suppose I did seem younger than my age. My parents had babied me, and I was a shy little person without many friends. I had not yet been out with a boy. Even for Kasoba, I guess I was backward. There is some truth, then, in her memory of me as being a mere child. A partial truth.

As far as the presentation with the prize is concerned, I don't remember it at all. I suppose the prize was a cheque. I went home afterwards with money, which I spent rather foolishly in my mother's opinion. (I also sold the painting of black-eyed Susans to Mr. Curtis, who wanted it for his office. My first sale.) I don't remember who handed me the prize. Marguerite, maybe? Mrs. Curtis? Some man or other, more likely. I envisage someone older and dimmer. Marguerite remembers me as very composed at the time of the presentation, pleased but unimpressed. Possibly. She also has distinct memories of both my parents and of their reactions. Quite untrue, of course. My parents were not there. As I keep insisting.

After the presentation, the meeting turned into a party. There were drinks, cocktails possibly, beer possibly. I think I had a ginger ale. My parents, I knew, would not have approved my drinking anything stronger. Perhaps indeed ginger ale was all I was offered.

I sat, I remember, next to Marguerite and the dark young man. I don't remember his name, but I fancy (or fancied) that he and Marguerite were in love. I thought that Marguerite was terribly sophisticated, sitting there with her drink and her cigarette, from which she blew elaborate smoke rings. They talked, she and the dark young man, about painting, about poetry, about the pronunciation of the word "extraordinary." (Why do I remember that?) Marguerite leaned forward intently. She was rapt, caught up in the presence of the dark young man. She quoted Edna St. Vincent Millay, "Euclid alone has gazed on beauty bare." She quoted again, "Only until this cigarette is ended." (Does she remember quoting Millay? Probably not. A poet who has become unfashionable.) The dark young man quoted W.H. Auden in return. I fell in love a little, I think, with both Marguerite and the dark young man. And more deeply in love than I had been before with painting.

That, of course, was the essence. That was what she left out of her story, because she didn't know it. How could she?

I couldn't sleep that night, I remember. I lay awake in the little room in Mrs. Curtis's house, reconstructing the dimly lit studio, inwardly posing Marguerite and the dark young man. I could have painted them. In fact I sketched them together the next day on the back of an envelope in my purse, as I was going home on the train. Maybe the envelope that contained my cheque, I don't know. I never saw the dark young man again (he is dead now, I think) and I did not see Marguerite for over twenty years.

That is not to say, however, that she disappeared from my life. Far from it. There were in the early years her letters, which came from time to time from different cities, from Montreal, Toronto, Vancouver. She learned to type, and her letters came now typed on yellow paper, but still rapid, exclamatory, decorated with those marginal flying creatures. Marguerite doesn't remember the letters. She thinks I have kept them because of some strange passion for documentation – if indeed I have kept them. She wavers between thinking I keep letters, diaries, documents, old sketches because I am unimaginative and need them to lean on, and that other (disquieting?) possibility that I haven't kept them at all, or that I am inventing letters that perhaps never even existed. It's strange that she isn't able to imagine why I kept them, or why I might invent them if I hadn't received them. She can imagine the phoenix, the unicorn, the marriage of heaven and hell, the day of judgment. She can even imagine my parents, though she hasn't got them quite right. (My father didn't have rough, callused hands, as she thinks. He had beautiful hands of which he was rather proud. It's a detail, but important, as physical details so often are.) In spite of her ability to imagine (and I always told her she was the imaginative one) she can't imagine why I kept her letters. I marvel.

We had lost track of each other for a while when I wrote to her again, that year I was home with a back injury. I had been thrown from a horse, and spent six months or so in a cast recovering back home in Kasoba, with my mother fussing over me. A dull space of time, but I did a lot of work that year. I was beginning to get some reputation by then – I suppose that's why I thought I could write her again. She invited me to visit her in Vancouver if I ever reached there: but by the time I went to Vancouver she was somewhere else, New York I think, and I lost track of her again.

I seemed always to be arriving in places after Marguerite had left. Montreal, Toronto, Vancouver, London, Paris. I spent a year in Boston; she spent a year in New York. We shared a number of the same friends at different times. We won the same awards for different reasons. For a short time, in Vancouver, I even had the same lover as Marguerite had had. Not for long, though. I felt, perhaps unreasonably, that comparisons were being made, and looked elsewhere.

It's hard to say what Marguerite meant to me – the idea of Marguerite, that is to say. A Muse, an ideal? Perhaps. A friend, an older sister, a rival? All of those. A model? Definitely not. Influences work in peculiar ways, as I am tempted to tell the young person who is doing a thesis on my work. One may be influenced to go in the same direction or in the opposite direction. If Marguerite insists on painting the phoenix or the day of judgment, I must paint marigolds or geraniums. Or if I paint the phoenix, I must demonstrate that he flies like a crow, or the day of judgment resembles a farm auction in the Depression. I can't, or won't, paint like Marguerite any more than I would dress like Marguerite or talk like Marguerite. I am inexorably, stubbornly myself. Marguerite doesn't need to be stubborn. It has never occurred to her to be anyone but herself. She never kept my letters and doesn't even remember them, or thinks she doesn't. But where has she got that picture of my parents, inaccurate though it is, except from the letters and sketches I sent her?

Marguerite was out of the country for a number of years, in Athens, in Calcutta, in Rio de Janeiro. Her paintings showed the effects of that restless wandering. During that time I came home, after my parents' deaths, to the prairie, dug myself in, settled down, became that painter whose "deliberate ordinariness elevated to the level of myth" pleased some art critics, though definitely not all. During the last ten years or so, since she came back to Ottawa, I have seen Marguerite a number of times. We have visited each other's exhibitions, admire each other's work as much as sisters ever admire each other's work.

"I always knew we would see each other again," she tells me when I visit her that first time in Ottawa. "People who are important to each other always recur in each other's lives. It's part of the pattern."

I see that she envisages us in a tapestry woven by some great celestial artist. She has made tea for me; we drink it ceremoniously, a communion. I look at her doubtfully over the teacup. She has been important to me, oddly, all these years, but if I have been important to her, I am trying to imagine how.

---

1. a) The narrator attempts to explain what Marguerite – or the idea of Marguerite – has meant to her. In a discussion with a classmate, evaluate the nature of her relationship with the older painter. (Check the meaning of *marguerite* in French.)
   b) On your own, summarize in writing your joint assessment of the relationship. Compare your account with your classmate's to confirm that you both have an accurate record of the judgments you reached. Place your summary in your writing folder.

2. "Are there two truths?" Or are there many? Daisy and Marguerite have different memories of the circumstances of their first meeting. Create a third account of the meeting in the form of a diary entry made by the young man who attached himself to Marguerite.

3. In a small group, assess why Brewster might have chosen "Essence of Marigold" as the title for her story. Select a spokesperson to present your judgments to the class; she or he should be prepared to answer any questions about your interpretation.

4. Working with a classmate, write the script of an interview between Marguerite Chrystal and an art reporter conducting background research for a biographical sketch on Daisy Lister. The interview should clarify the question raised in the final sentence of the story.

5. In a short essay, show that the painting styles of the two women reveal their characters. Before you begin writing, compose a thesis statement that indicates the direction of your argument.

Before you read Krauthammer's essay, explore with one or two classmates your own reactions to the placing of a baboon heart into the chest of a human infant. Note down the main ideas and feelings that are expressed during your discussion. Consider also the probable attitudes of the parents of the child, of the doctors and nurses, and of the infant when it becomes old enough to understand what was done.

SINNING BRAVELY: THE CASE OF BABY FAE

Charles Krauthammer

The placing of a baboon heart into the chest of little Baby Fae caused indignation in many quarters. For some, who might safely be called eccentric, the concern was animal rights. Pickets outside Loma Linda University Medical Center and elsewhere protested the use of baboons as organ factories. Dr. Leonard Bailey, the chief surgeon, was not impressed. "I am a member of the human species," he said. Human babies come first. It was unapologetic speciesism. He did not even have to resort to sociology, to the argument that in a society that eats beef, wears mink and has for some time been implanting pigs' valves in human hearts, the idea of weighing an animal's life equally against a human baby's is bizarre.

Others were concerned less with the integrity of the donor than with the dignity of the recipient. At first, before Baby Fae's televised smile had beguiled skeptics, the word ghoulish was heard: some sacred barrier between species had been broken, some principle of separateness between man and animal violated. Indeed, it is a blow to man's idea of himself to think that a piece of plastic or animal tissue may occupy the seat of the emotions and perform perfectly well (albeit as a pump).

It is biological Galileism, and just as humbling. Nevertheless it is fact. To deny it is sentimentality. And to deny life to a child in order to preserve the fiction of man's biological uniqueness is simple cruelty.

Still others were concerned with the observing public, and its proxy, the press. For a while, when Baby Fae was doing well, the big issue was made out to be the public's (read: the press's) right to know. There were reiterated complaints about withheld information, vital forms not made public, too few press conferences. It is true that, in its first encounter with big-time media, Loma Linda proved inept at public relations. But how important can that be? In time the important information will be published and scrutinized in the scientific literature, a more reliable setting for judging this procedure than live television.

Baby Fae brought out defenders of man and beast and press. But who was defending Baby Fae? There *was* something disturbing – subtly, but profoundly disturbing – about the baboon implant. It has nothing to do with animal rights or the Frankenstein factor or full disclosure. It has to do with means and ends.

It turns out that before placing a baboon heart into the chest of Baby Fae, doctors at Loma Linda had not sought a human heart for transplant. That fact betrays their primary aim: to advance a certain line of research. As much as her life became dear to them, Baby Fae was to be their means.

The end – cross-species transplant research – is undoubtedly worthy. Human transplants offer little hope for solving the general problem of children's dying of defective hearts. There simply are not enough human hearts to go around. Baboons grown in captivity offer, in theory, a plausible solution to the problem. To give Baby Fae a human heart would have advanced the cause of children in general very little. But it might have advanced the cause of *this* child more than a baboon's heart, which, given the imperfect state of our knowledge, was more likely to be rejected.

Doctors like to imagine that the therapeutic imperative and the experimental imperative are one and the same. On the contrary. They are almost always in conflict. At the extreme are the notorious cases in which the patient is actually sacrificed on the altar of science: the Tuskegee experiment, in which a group of black men with syphilis were deliberately left untreated for 40 years; the Willowbrook experiment, in which retarded children were injected with hepatitis virus; and the Brooklyn study, in which elderly patients were injected with live cancer cells. Loma Linda was at the other extreme. Here, far from being at war with the therapeutic, the experimental was almost identical with it. But not quite. The baboon heart was ever so slightly more experimental, more useful to science (or so the doctors thought), more risky for Baby Fae. If it were your child, and you had two hearts available, and you cared not a whit for science (perhaps even if you cared quite a bit for science), you would choose the human heart.

The Loma Linda doctors did not. Hence the unease. One does not have to impute venal motives – a desire for glory or a lust for publicity – to wonder about the ethics of the choice. The motive was science, the research imperative. Priority was accorded to the claims of the future, of children not yet stricken, not yet even born.

Is that wrong?

Civilization hangs on the Kantian principle that human beings are to be treated as ends and not means. So much depends on that principle because there is no crime that cannot be, that has not been, committed in the name of the future against those who inhabit the present. Medical experimentation, which invokes the claims of the future, necessarily turns people into means. That is why the Nuremberg Code on human experimentation (established after World War II in reaction to the ghastly Nazi experiments on prisoners) declares that for research to be ethical the subject must give consent. The person is violated if it is unwillingly – even if only uncomprehendingly – used for the benefit of others.

But not if it volunteers, and thus, in effect, joins the research enterprise. Consent is the crucial event in the transition from therapy to experiment. It turns what would otherwise be technological barbarism into humane science. Consent suspends the Hippocratic injunction "First, do no harm." Moreover, it redeems not only the researcher but the researched. To be used by others is to be degraded; to give oneself to others is to be elevated. Indeed, consciously to make one's life a means to some higher end is the essence of the idea of service. If Barney Clark decides to dedicate the last days of his life to the service of humanity, then – and only then – may we operate.

Infants, who can decide nothing, are the difficult case. (If Baby Fae had volunteered for her operation, the ethical questions would evaporate.) Since infants are incapable of giving consent, the parents do so on their behalf. In Baby Fae's case what kind of consent did they give? If her parents thought that the operation might save their child (*i.e.*, that it was therapeutic), then they were misled. There was no scientific evidence to support that claim. The longest previous human survival with a heart xerograft was $3^1/_2$ *days*. (Baby Fae lived 17 more.) The longest *animal* survival in Dr. Bailey's own studies was 165 days.

If, on the other hand, the parents had been told that the purpose was to test a procedure that might help other babies in the future (*i.e.*, that it was experimental), what right did they have to volunteer a child – even their child – to suffer on behalf of humanity?

After Baby Fae died, it was argued, retroactively, that in fact the operation reduced her suffering, that she was pink and breathing instead of blue and gasping. Perhaps. But the cameras were brought in only when she was well. She was not seen when not doing well: enduring respirators, cannulas, injections, stitches, arrhythmias, uremia. Was this really less agonal than a natural death, which would have come mercifully weeks earlier?

No. Baby Fae was a means, a conscripted means, to a noble end. This experiment was undertaken to reduce not her suffering, but, perhaps some day, that of others. But is that really wrong? Don't the suffering babies of the future have any claim on us? How do we reconcile the need to advance our knowledge through research, with the injunction against using innocents for our own ends?

Two serious men have attempted an answer. One is Jonas Salk. "When you inoculate children with a polio vaccine," he said of his early clinical tests, "you don't sleep well for two or three months." So Salk tested the vaccine on himself, his wife and his own children. This is an extraordinary response. It certainly could not have improved his sleep. It did not even solve the ethical dilemma. After all, the Salk children were put at risk, and they were no less innocent than the rest. But by involving his own kin (and himself), Salk arranged to suffer with the others if his science failed. He crossed the line that separates user from used. By joining his fate to the used, he did not so much solve the ethical problem as turn it, heroically, into an existential one.

Princeton philosopher Paul Ramsey offers another version of that response. Ramsey comes from the other side of the great research debate. He argues that children may never be made guinea pigs and that we have no right to "consent" on their behalf. A most stringent Kantian, he would prohibit all experimentation on nonconsenting subjects. But for those of us who see the requirement for research as a moral imperative equal in force to the imperative to respect the individual, he counsels: if you must do it, do it, but do not deny the moral force of the imperative you violate. In a society that grants the future *some* claims, a society that will not countenance the endless destruction of children by polio – or by hypoplastic left-heart syndrome – "research medicine, like politics, [becomes] a realm in which men have to 'sin bravely'."

Baby Fae lived, and died, in that realm. Only the bravery was missing: no one would admit the violation. Bravery was instead fatuously ascribed to Baby Fae, a creature as incapable of bravery as she was of circulating her own blood. Whether this case was an advance in medical science awaits the examination of the record by the scientific community. That it was an adventure in medical ethics is already clear.

---

1. a) In your notebook, write a short definition of Krauthammer's expression "sinning bravely."
   b) Looking closely at the final two paragraphs, explain in writing how the author uses the concept of sinning bravely to answer the ethical dilemma he poses.

2. In your group, review the notes you made during your pre-reading discussion. Record any changes in opinion prompted by

Krauthammer's essay, as well as any new issues you encountered there. Summarize the discrepancies between Krauthammer's view and the various positions held in your group.

3. Write short paragraphs, for inclusion in your writing folder, explaining how Krauthammer makes use of each of the following ideas in building his case:
a) the conflict between the therapeutic imperative and the experimental imperative;
b) the principle that human beings are to be treated as ends and not means;
c) consent as the crucial difference between therapy and experiment.

4. Write a short essay to persuade the reader to accept your judgment concerning one of the following topics:
a) compulsory physical education in senior high school;
b) province-wide examinations in certain subjects to determine entrance into university;
c) raising the drinking age to 21;
d) a topic of your choice approved by your teacher.
Use Krauthammer's essay as a model for your own.

5. "How Do You Know It's Good?" (p. 4) and "Sinning Bravely: The Case of Baby Fae" are similar in that both essays are attempts to convince the reader of the soundness of the essayist's judgment. Reread the essays, noting down the methods each writer uses to persuade his or her audience. (You may wish to prepare for your analysis by consulting your teacher about the basic tools of rhetoric.) Compare your notes with those of a classmate, and together judge which of the two essays is more convincing.

sur•ro•gate *adj.*, deputy, substitute – *Concise Oxford Dictionary*

The brave new world of "new birth technology" offers hope to couples who want children but who are unable to conceive or bear them. At the same time, it brings moral and legal problems. Before you read these two articles on the topic, consider with a classmate the respective rights of the individuals involved in the transaction: the couple receiving the child; the surrogate mother; the infant.

TIME TO BAN SURROGATE MOTHERHOOD
Lynda Hurst

ngland's High Court Justice Sir John Brimstead Latey undoubtedly made the only feasible decision this week when he allowed an American couple to keep the newborn baby it had paid a British woman to bear. He must have wondered, however, how his court ever got caught appearing to sanction such a grim transaction.

The couple had paid $15 000 to a surrogate parent agency which, in turn, had passed on half that amount to a London housewife. She had two children but apparently was not averse to renting out her womb.

When the story broke, British observers split into two camps: one supporting the right of childless couples to "have" a child through any means, including the hiring of a stranger's body; the other objecting to the commercial exploitation of buying and selling babies.

Britain hardly can be said to be intolerant of what's been called the "new birth technology." It was Britain's Drs. Steptoe and Edwards, after all, who pioneered this debatably brave new world back in 1978 when they produced the world's first test-tube baby, Louise Brown.

Destroying Embryos: It was Britain, too, that first demanded a moratorium on further reproductive research when it learned Steptoe and

Edwards were creating and destroying dozens of embryos in an attempt to implant one successfully.

Rumours that the doctors were experimenting on these embryos ultimately proved groundless, but the Thatcher government nevertheless took an unprecedented stand last year and prohibited all research on fertilized eggs after the 11-day stage.

The point here is that in the past decade, Britain has demonstrated considerable open-mindedness and understanding when it comes to the plight of would-be parents who find themselves infertile. Having done so, however, it now finds no contradiction in banning commercial surrogacy.

From what I can gather, it intends to do so without any ifs, ands, or buts, believing that the practice is socially unethical and subject to wild abuse.

What is obvious to the British is not, however, so obvious here. Both Canada and the United States continue to waffle on this issue. On paper, the buying of babies is still illegal but, nevertheless, the practice – in its euphemistically named surrogate form – flourishes.

At least half a dozen lawyers in the United States specialize in this profitable sideline, the most notorious being Noel Keane of Dearborn, Michigan, who processes several dozen such births a year, charging $5000 on top of the standard $10 000 surrogate fee.

Keane was involved in what is probably the most infamous instance of surrogacy abuse. It involved a handicapped infant born to a Lansing woman who'd been paid to bear it by a New York man. When the degree of the baby's retardation became known, the man refused to take custody, claiming it was not his.

Indeed, it was not. Blood tests proved the woman's own husband was in fact the parent.

Televised Battle: Keane, the couple, and the New York man fought it out on The Phil Donahue Show, of all places, and when last heard from were still involved in a series of lawsuits while the baby lingered with foster parents.

Despite this case and at least a dozen others in which the surrogate mother refused to hand over the contracted child when it was born, U.S. legislators continue to look the other way.

In Canada, a 1983 federal Law Reform Commission recommended that anti-abuse surrogate laws be put in place before the practice here extends to U.S. levels. It called for guidelines defining rights and legal status of a child born in this manner, the rights and duties of the biological parents and their spouses, and the enforceability of the contract if the child is born defective.

The recommendations make many of us shiver in distaste. The buying and selling of children is either morally right or morally wrong. This society has always regarded it as patently wrong and to say – as the Commission more or less said – that buying and selling is going to happen *anyway* is no reason to sanctify it by drawing up guidelines.

I think Canada should follow the lead of Britain and state, without qualification, that the bearing of children for commercial gain simply isn't on. I realize that seems hard on those couples who've failed to adopt an infant through traditional channels or who are not appropriate subjects for test-tube reproduction, but perhaps they too can understand that the potential abuse of a babies-for-profit system is too great ever to condone officially.

SURROGATE MOTHERHOOD: WHY IT SHOULD BE PERMITTED
Allan C. Hutchinson

*T*he Ontario Law Reform Commission's recent report on artificial reproduction gives an unofficial green light to surrogate motherhood. Or at least an amber light. In an enlightened discussion, the report rejects the banning of surrogate motherhood in favour of regulating it.

The report's recommendations for legal reforms make good sense.

Surrogacy involves an arrangement whereby a woman agrees to conceive a child on behalf of a couple who will assume sole responsibility for its upbringing. These agreements are usually reached to overcome infertility or genetic impairment; "inconvenience" is not an acceptable reason for surrogacy.

Although there was a powerful dissent, the majority of the law reform commissioners maintained that, as a matter of public policy, surrogacy ought to be permissible. Actual engagement in such an agreement is, of course, a question of individual morality. It is the trappings of the surrogacy agreement, the commissioners argue, that are objectionable.

The exploitation of impoverished women – and a possible tendency to regard babies as commodities – can be dealt with by regulatory devices. Moreover, surrogacy will not disappear if it is prohibited: it will add another dimension to the shadowy world of clandestine agreements.

In place of the present legal uncertainty, the report proposes that all surrogacy agreements be in writing and be approved and supervised by the Family Court. The suitability of all participants, terms of remuneration and the like would be at the discretion of a judge. Upon the birth of the child, the surrogate parent would cease to have any legal relationship with it and the commissioning couple would become its sole legal parents. Private agencies would be permitted to facilitate surrogacy arrangements, but only under strict government regulation. Unapproved agreements would be unenforceable and participants would be punished by a fine.

Within the narrow range of feasible political options, these proposals are to be applauded. The all-male commissioners have refused to be intimidated by reactionary responses in other jurisdictions. Yet, perhaps for good strategic reasons, they do not make explicit the positive rationale in favour of surrogacy arrangements.

A convincing argument must be based on the overriding demands of equality. The case can best be made by focussing on the traditional arguments against surrogacy.

In his dissent, Allan Leal, vice-chairman of the Law Reform Commission, relies on two central claims: that surrogacy undermines "the basic principle of our social ordering" that "the procreation and rearing of children should take place within a marital union" and that such arrangements are "basically exploitive." Both objections draw their force from the dominant male view of sexual roles and family relations.

Regarding the first critical claim, marriage as a life-long relation is no longer the norm in society. Considerations of formal legality ought not to take priority over the existence of stable, supportive, and caring commitments as the best context for child-rearing.

More important, the marital union has historically been the site of female oppression. It is within the home, as a mother, and the bedroom, as a wife, that many women have experienced most acutely the treacherous "security" of legal marriage.

This, of course, ties in with the objection that surrogacy exploits women. The potential for exploiting women in surrogacy agreements is very real. But the moral outrage this occasions is hypocritical in a society that turns a blind eye to wholesale exploitation in other ways. Not only have many women been the objects of male domination in the "natural" organization of sexual relations, but they are the daily victims of economic exploitation.

Support for surrogacy must be firmly based on equality, a quality much talked about but rarely implemented. The freedom of men to control their own sexual lives must be extended to women. This is nowhere more urgent than in procreative decisions. The traditional views of motherhood and sexual exploitation are male. The "natural" has been determined by men and endured by women.

Any improvement must begin with opportunities for women to reclaim and redefine their sexual roles and responsibilities. Motherhood is one place to begin. And surrogacy is a first step. If society is to take its commitment to equality between men and women seriously, the commission's proposals ought to be accepted.

1. Both Lynda Hurst and Allan Hutchinson seek to persuade news-paper readers, Hurst through the medium of a personal opinion column, and Hutchinson through an essay from the editorial pages.

   a) In your notebook, draw up a chart of the stylistic differences between the two articles.

   b) Compare your chart with that of a classmate, resolving if possible any discrepancies in your analyses.

2. Identify in Hurst's column the paragraph that states and explains her position on the legal aspects of the surrogacy issue. Anticipate her reaction to the report of the Ontario Law Reform Commission cited in Hutchinson's essay, and then, in her voice, write a letter to the Commission responding to their recommendations.

3. Like a good debater, Hutchinson anticipates opposing arguments, focussing on them to make his own case. Reread the section of his essay in which he deals with the usual arguments against surrogacy and, using his ideas as a base, write a letter to the editor attacking Hurst's position.

4. a) Neither essay considers what will happen when the children born of surrogate mothers become adults possessed of adult rights. Discuss whether they should be entitled to learn precise details about their biological mother and their family background. (Most adopted people in Canada have not had that right.) Can legislation truly define membership in a family? Talk about these and related issues in a small group.

   b) In a piece of personal writing for your writing folder, explore your own feelings on the subject of surrogate motherhood.

"Melancholy was the dominant note of his temperament," the narrator says of Little Chandler. Jot down the characteristics of a melancholy nature, and identify two or three characters from literature you've read who could be described as melancholy. Compare your work with a classmate's.

A LITTLE CLOUD
James Joyce

Eight years before he had seen his friend off at the North Wall and wished him godspeed. Gallaher had got on. You could tell that at once by his travelled air, his well-cut tweed suit, and fearless accent. Few fellows had talents like his and fewer still could remain unspoiled by such success. Gallaher's heart was in the right place and he had deserved to win. It was something to have a friend like that.

Little Chandler's thoughts ever since lunchtime had been of his meeting with Gallaher, of Gallaher's invitation and of the great city London where Gallaher lived. He was called Little Chandler because, though he was but slightly under the average stature, he gave one the idea of being a little man. His hands were white and small, his frame was fragile, his voice was quiet and his manners were refined. He took the greatest care of his fair silken hair and moustache and used perfume discreetly on his handkerchief. The half-moons of his nails were perfect and when he smiled you caught a glimpse of a row of childish white teeth.

As he sat at his desk in the King's Inns he thought what changes those eight years had brought. The friend whom he had known under a shabby and necessitous guise had become a brilliant figure on the

London Press. He turned often from his tiresome writing to gaze out of the office window. The glow of a late autumn sunset covered the grass plots and walks. It cast a shower of kindly golden dust on the untidy nurses and decrepit old men who drowsed on the benches; it flickered upon all the moving figures – on the children who ran screaming along the gravel paths and on everyone who passed through the gardens. He watched the scene and thought of life; and (as always happened when he thought of life) he became sad. A gentle melancholy took possession of him. He felt how useless it was to struggle against fortune, this being the burden of wisdom which the ages had bequeathed to him.

He remembered the books of poetry upon his shelves at home. He had bought them in his bachelor days and many an evening, as he sat in the little room off the hall, he had been tempted to take one down from the bookshelf and read out something to his wife. But shyness had always held him back; and so the books remained on their shelves. At times he repeated lines to himself and this consoled him.

When his hour had struck he stood up and took leave of his desk and of his fellow-clerks punctiliously. He emerged from under the feudal arch of the King's Inns, a neat modest figure, and walked swiftly down Henrietta Street. The golden sunset was waning and the air had grown sharp. A horde of grimy children populated the street. They stood or ran in the roadway or crawled up the steps before the gaping doors or squatted like mice upon the thresholds. Little Chandler gave them no thought. He picked his way deftly through all that minute vermin-like life and under the shadow of the gaunt spectral mansions in which the old nobility of Dublin had roystered. No memory of the past touched him, for his mind was full of a present joy.

He had never been in Corless's but he knew the value of the name. He knew that people went there after the theatre to eat oysters and drink liqueurs; and he had heard that the waiters there spoke French and German. Walking swiftly by at night he had seen cabs drawn up before the door and richly dressed ladies, escorted by cavaliers, alight and enter quickly. They wore noisy dresses and many wraps. Their faces were powdered and they caught up their dresses, when they touched earth, like alarmed Atalantas. He had always passed without turning his head to look. It was his habit to walk swiftly in the street even by day and whenever he found himself in the city late at night he hurried on his way apprehensively and excitedly. Sometimes, however, he courted the causes of his fear. He chose the darkest and narrowest streets and, as he walked boldly forward, the silence that was spread about his footsteps troubled him, the wandering, silent figures troubled him; and at times a sound of low fugitive laughter made him tremble like a leaf.

He turned to the right towards Capel Street. Ignatius Gallaher on the London Press! Who would have thought it possible eight years before? Still, now that he reviewed the past, Little Chandler could remember many signs of future greatness in his friend. People used to say that Ignatius Gallaher was wild. Of course he did mix with a rakish set of fellows at that time, drank freely and borrowed money on all sides. In the end he had got mixed up in some shady affair, some money transaction: at least, that was one version of his flight. But nobody denied him talent. There was always a certain . . . something in Ignatius Gallaher that impressed you in spite of yourself. Even when he was out at elbows and at his wits' end for money he kept up a bold face. Little Chandler remembered (and the remembrance brought a slight flush of pride to his cheek) one of Ignatius Gallaher's sayings when he was in a tight corner:

"Half time now boys," he used to say lightheartedly. "Where's my considering cap?"

That was Ignatius Gallaher all out; and, damn it, you couldn't but admire him for it.

Little Chandler quickened his pace. For the first time in his life he felt himself superior to the people he passed. For the first time his soul revolted against the dull inelegance of Capel Street. There was no doubt about it: if you wanted to succeed you had to go away. You could do nothing in Dublin. As he crossed Grattan Bridge he looked down the river towards the lower quays and pitied the poor stunted houses. They seemed to him a band of tramps, huddled together along the river-banks, their old coats covered with dust and soot, stupefied by the panorama of sunset and waiting for the first chill of night to bid them arise, shake themselves and be gone. He wondered whether he could write a poem to express his idea. Perhaps Gallaher might be able to get it into some London paper for him. Could he write something original? He was not sure what idea he wished to express but the thought that a poetic moment had touched him took life within him like an infant hope. He stepped onward bravely.

Every step brought him nearer to London, farther from his own sober inartistic life. A light began to tremble on the horizon of his mind. He was not so old – thirty-two. His temperament might be said to be just at the point of maturity. There were so many different moods and impressions that he wished to express in verse. He felt them within him. He tried to weigh his soul to see if it was a poet's soul. Melancholy was the dominant note of his temperament, he thought, but it was a melancholy tempered by recurrences of faith and resignation and simple joy. If he could give expression to it in a book of poems perhaps men would listen. He would never be popular: he saw that. He could not sway the crowd but he might appeal to a little circle of kindred minds. The English critics, perhaps, would recognize him as one of the Celtic school by reason of the melancholy tone of his poems; besides that, he would put in allusions. He began to invent sentences and phrases from the notice which his book would get. *"Mr. Chandler has the gift of easy and graceful verse"* . . . *"A wistful sadness pervades these poems."* . . . *"The Celtic note."* It was a pity his name was not more Irish-looking. Perhaps it would be better to insert his mother's name before the surname: Thomas Malone Chandler, or better still: T. Malone Chandler. He would speak to Gallaher about it.

He pursued his revery so ardently that he passed his street and had to turn back. As he came near Corless's his former agitation began to overmaster him and he halted before the door in indecision. Finally he opened the door and entered.

The light and noise of the bar held him at the doorway for a few moments. He looked about him, but his sight was confused by the shining of many red and green wine-glasses. The bar seemed to him to be full of people and he felt that the people were observing him curiously. He glanced quickly to right and left (frowning slightly to make his errand appear serious), but when his sight cleared a little he saw that nobody had turned to look at him: and there, sure enough, was Ignatius Gallaher leaning with his back against the counter and his feet planted far apart.

"Hallo, Tommy, old hero, here you are! What is it to be? What will you have? I'm taking whisky: better stuff than we get across the water. Soda? Lithia? No mineral? I'm the same. Spoils the flavour. . . . Here, *garçon*, bring us two halves of malt whisky, like a good fellow. . . . Well, and how have you been pulling along since I saw you last? Dear God, how old we're getting! Do you see any signs of aging in me – eh, what? A little grey and thin on the top – what?"

Ignatius Gallaher took off his hat and displayed a large closely cropped head. His face was heavy, pale and clean-shaven. His eyes, which were of bluish slate-colour, relieved his unhealthy pallor and shone out plainly above the vivid orange tie he wore. Between these rival features the lips appeared very long and shapeless and colourless. He bent his head and felt with two sympathetic fingers the thin hair at the crown. Little Chandler shook his head as a denial. Ignatius Gallaher put on his hat again.

"It pulls you down," he said, "press life. Always hurry and scurry, looking for copy and sometimes not finding it: and then, always to have something new in your stuff. Damn proofs and printers, I say, for a few days. I'm deuced glad, I can tell you, to get back to the old country. Does a fellow good, a bit of a holiday. I feel a ton better since I landed again in dear dirty Dublin. . . . Here you are, Tommy. Water? Say when."

Little Chandler allowed his whisky to be very much diluted.

"You don't know what's good for you, my boy," said Ignatius Gallaher. "I drink mine neat."

"I drink very little as a rule," said Little Chandler modestly. "An odd half-one or so when I meet any of the old crowd: that's all."

"Ah, well," said Ignatius Gallaher, cheerfully, "here's to us and to old times and old acquaintance."

They clinked glasses and drank the toast.

"I met some of the old gang today," said Ignatius Gallaher. "O'Hara seems to be in a bad way. What's he doing?"

"Nothing," said Little Chandler. "He's gone to the dogs."

"But Hogan has a good sit, hasn't he?"

"Yes; he's in the Land Commission."

"I met him one night in London and he seemed to be very flush. . . . Poor O'Hara! Boose, I suppose?"

"Other things, too," said Little Chandler shortly.

Ignatius Gallaher laughed.

"Tommy," he said, "I see you haven't changed an atom. You're the very same serious person that used to lecture me on Sunday mornings when I had a sore head and a fur on my tongue. You'd want to knock about a bit in the world. Have you never been anywhere even for a trip?"

"I've been to the Isle of Man," said Little Chandler.

Ignatius Gallaher laughed.

"The Isle of Man!" he said. "Go to London or Paris: Paris, for choice. That'd do you good."

"Have you seen Paris?"

"I should think I have! I've knocked about there a little."

"And is it really so beautiful as they say?" asked Little Chandler.

He sipped a little of his drink while Ignatius Gallaher finished his boldly.

"Beautiful?" said Ignatius Gallaher, pausing on the word and on the flavour of his drink. "It's not so beautiful, you know. Of course, it is beautiful. . . . But it's the life of Paris; that's the thing. Ah, there's no city like Paris for gaiety, movement, excitement. . . ."

Little Chandler finished his whisky and, after some trouble, succeeded in catching the barman's eye. He ordered the same again.

"I've been to the Moulin Rouge," Ignatius Gallaher continued when the barman had removed their glasses, "and I've been to all the Bohemian cafés. Hot stuff! Not for a pious chap like you, Tommy."

Little Chandler said nothing until the barman returned with two glasses: then he touched his friend's glass lightly and reciprocated the former toast. He was beginning to feel somewhat disillusioned. Gallaher's accent and way of expressing himself did not please him. There was something vulgar in his friend which he had not observed before. But perhaps it was only the result of living in London amid the bustle and competition of the Press. The old personal charm was still there under this new gaudy manner. And, after all, Gallaher had lived, he had seen the world. Little Chandler looked at his friend enviously.

"Everything in Paris is gay," said Ignatius Gallaher. "They believe in enjoying life – and don't you think they're right? If you want to enjoy yourself properly you must go to Paris. And, mind you, they've a great feeling for the Irish there. When they heard I was from Ireland they were ready to eat me, man."

Little Chandler took four or five sips from his glass.

"Tell me," he said, "is it true that Paris is so . . . immoral as they say?"

Ignatius Gallaher made a catholic gesture with his right arm.

"Every place is immoral," he said. "Of course you do find spicy bits in Paris. Go to one of the students' balls, for instance. That's lively, if you like, when the *cocottes* begin to let themselves loose. You know what they are, I suppose?"

"I've heard of them," said Little Chandler.

Ignatius Gallaher drank off his whisky and shook his head.

"Ah," he said, "you may say what you like. There's no woman like the Parisienne – for style, for go."

"Then it is an immoral city," said Little Chandler, with timid insistence – "I mean, compared with London or Dublin?"

"London!" said Ignatius Gallaher. "It's six of one and half-a-dozen of the other. You ask Hogan, my boy. I showed him a bit about London when he was over there. He'd open your eye. . . . I say, Tommy, don't make punch of that whisky: liquor up."

"No, really. . . . "

"Oh, come on, another one won't do you any harm. What is it? The same again, I suppose?"

"Well . . . all right."

"*François*, the same again. . . . Will you smoke, Tommy?"

Ignatius Gallaher produced his cigar-case. The two friends lit their cigars and puffed at them in silence until their drinks were served.

"I'll tell you my opinion," said Ignatius Gallaher, emerging after some time from the clouds of smoke in which he had taken refuge, "it's a rum world. Talk of immortality! I've heard of cases – what am I saying? – I've known them: cases of . . . immorality. . . . "

Ignatius Gallaher puffed thoughtfully at his cigar and then, in a calm historian's tone, he proceeded to sketch for his friend some pictures of the corruption which was rife abroad. He summarized the vices of many capitals and seemed inclined to award the palm to Berlin. Some things he could not vouch for (his friends had told him), but of others he had had personal experience. He spared neither rank nor caste. He revealed many of the secrets of religious houses on the Continent and described some of the practices which were fashionable in high society and ended by telling, with details, a story about an English duchess – a story which he knew to be true. Little Chandler was astonished.

"Ah, well," said Ignatius Gallaher, "here we are in old jog-along Dublin where nothing is known of such things."

"How dull you must find it," said Little Chandler, "after all the other places you've seen!"

"Well, said Ignatius Gallaher, "it's a relaxation to come over here, you know. And, after all, it's the old country, as they say, isn't it? You can't help having a certain feeling for it. That's human nature . . . But tell me something about yourself. Hogan told me you had . . . tasted the joys of connubial bliss. Two years ago, wasn't it?"

Little Chandler blushed and smiled.

"Yes," he said. "I was married last May twelve months."

"I hope it's not too late in the day to offer my best wishes," said Ignatius Gallaher. "I didn't know your address or I'd have done so at the time."

He extended his hand, which Little Chandler took.

"Well, Tommy," he said, "I wish you and yours every joy in life, old chap, and tons of money, and may you never die till I shoot you. And that's the wish of a sincere friend, and old friend. You know that?"

"I know that," said Little Chandler.

"Any youngsters?" said Ignatius Gallaher.

Little Chandler blushed again.

"We have one child," he said.

"Son or daughter?"

"A little boy."

Ignatius Gallaher slapped his friend sonorously on the back.

"Bravo," he said, "I wouldn't doubt you, Tommy."

Little Chandler smiled, looked confusedly at his glass and bit his lower lip with three childishly white front teeth.

"I hope you'll spend an evening with us," he said, "before you go back. My wife will be delighted to meet you. We can have a little music and – "

"Thanks awfully, old chap," said Ignatius Gallaher, "I'm sorry we didn't meet earlier. But I must leave tomorrow night."

"Tonight perhaps, . . . ?"

"I'm awfully sorry, old man. You see I'm over here with another fellow, clever young chap he is too, and we arranged to go to a little card-party. Only for that. . . . "

"O, in that case. . . . "

"But who knows?" said Ignatius Gallaher considerably. "Next year I may take a little skip over here now that I've broken the ice. It's only a pleasure deferred."

"Very well," said Little Chandler, "the next time you come we must have an evening together. That's agreed now, isn't it?"

"Yes, that's agreed," said Ignatius Gallaher. "Next year if I come, parole d'honneur."

"And to clinch the bargain," said Little Chandler, "we'll just have one more now."

Ignatius Gallaher took out a large gold watch and looked at it.

"Is it to be the last?" he said. "Because you know, I have an a.p."

"O, yes, positively," said Little Chandler.

"Very well, then," said Ignatius Gallaher, "let us have another one as a *deoc an dorius* – that's good vernacular for a small whisky I believe."

Little Chandler ordered the drinks. The blush which had risen to his face a few moments before was establishing itself. A trifle made him blush at any time: and now he felt warm and excited. Three small whiskies had gone to his head and Gallaher's strong cigar had confused his mind, for he was a delicate and abstinent person. The adventure of meeting Gallaher after eight years, of finding himself with Gallaher in Corless's surrounded by lights and noise, of listening to Gallaher's stories and of sharing for a brief space Gallaher's vagrant and triumphant life, upset the equipoise of his sensitive nature. He felt acutely the contrast between his own life and his friend's, and it seemed to him unjust. Gallaher was his inferior in birth and education. He was sure that he could do something better than his friend had ever done, or could ever do, something higher than mere tawdry journalism if he only got the chance. What was it that stood in his way? His unfortunate timidity! He wished to vindicate himself in some way, to assert his manhood. He saw behind Gallaher's refusal of his invitation. Gallaher was only patronizing him by his friendliness just as he was patronizing Ireland by his visit.

The barman brought their drinks. Little Chandler pushed one glass towards his friend and took up the other boldly.

"Who knows?" he said, as they lifted their glasses. "When you come next year I may have the pleasure of wishing long life and happiness to Mr. and Mrs. Ignatius Gallaher."

Ignatius Gallaher in the act of drinking closed one eye expressively over the rim of his glass. When he had drunk he smacked his lips decisively, set down his glass and said:

"No blooming fear of that, my boy. I'm going to have my fling first and see a bit of life and world before I put my head in the sack – if I ever do."

"Some day you will," said Little Chandler calmly.

Ignatius Gallaher turned his orange tie and slate-blue eyes full upon his friend.

"You think so?" he said.

"You'll put your head in the sack," repeated Little Chandler stoutly, "like everyone else if you can find the girl."

He had slightly emphasized his tone and he was aware that he had betrayed himself; but, though the colour had heightened in his cheek, he did not flinch from his friend's gaze. Ignatius Gallaher watched him for a few moments and then said:

"If ever it occurs, you may bet your bottom dollar there'll be no mooning and spooning about it. I mean to marry money. She'll have a good fat account at the bank or she won't do for me."

Little Chandler shook his head.

"Why, man alive," said Ignatius Gallaher, vehemently, "do you know what it is? I've only to say the word and tomorrow I can have the woman and the cash. You don't believe it? Well, I know it. There are hundreds – what am I saying? – thousands of rich Germans and Jews, rotten with money, that'd only be too glad. . . . You wait a while, my boy. See if I don't play my cards properly. When I go about a thing I mean business, I tell you. You just wait."

He tossed his glass to his mouth, finished his drink and laughed loudly. Then he looked thoughtfully before him and said in a calmer tone:

"But I'm in no hurry. They can wait. I don't fancy tying myself up to one woman, you know."

He imitated with his mouth the act of tasting and made a wry face.

"Must get a bit stale, I should think," he said.

Little Chandler sat in the room off the hall, holding a child in his arms. To save money they kept no servant but Annie's young sister Monica came for an hour or so in the morning and an hour or so in the evening to help. But Monica had gone home long ago. It was a quarter to nine. Little Chandler had come home late for tea and, moreover, he had forgotten to bring Annie home the parcel of coffee from Bewley's. Of course she was in a bad humour and gave him short answers. She said she would do without any tea but when it came near the time at which the shop at the corner closed she decided to go out herself for a quarter of a pound of tea and two pounds of sugar. She put the sleeping child deftly in his arms and said:

"Here. Don't waken him."

A little lamp with a white china shade stood upon the table and its light fell over a photograph which was enclosed in a frame of crumpled horn. It was Annie's photograph. Little Chandler looked at it, pausing at the thin tight lips. She wore the pale blue summer blouse which he had brought her home as a present one Saturday. It had cost him ten and elevenpence; but what an agony of nervousness it had cost him! How he had suffered that day, waiting at the shop door until the shop was empty, standing at the counter and trying to appear at his ease while the girl piled ladies' blouses before him, paying at the desk and forgetting to take up the odd penny of his change, being called back by the cashier, and finally, striving to hide his blushes as he left the shop by examining the parcel to see if it were securely tied. When he brought the blouse home Annie kissed him and said it was very pretty and stylish; but when she heard the price she threw the blouse on the table and said it was a regular swindle to charge ten and elevenpence for it. At first she wanted to take it back but when she tried it on she was delighted with it, especially with the make of the sleeves, and kissed him and said he was very good to think of her.

Hm! . . .

He looked coldly into the eyes of the photograph and they answered coldly. Certainly they were pretty and the face itself was pretty. But he found something mean in it. Why was it so unconscious and ladylike? The composure of the eyes irritated him. They repelled him and defied him: there was no passion in them, no rapture. He thought of what Gallaher had said about rich Jewesses. Those dark Oriental eyes, he thought, how full they are of passion, of voluptuous longing! . . . Why had he married the eyes in the photograph?

He caught himself up at the question and glanced nervously around the room. He found something mean in the pretty furniture which he had bought for his house on the hire system. Annie had chosen it herself and it reminded him of her. It too was prim and pretty. A dull resentment against his life awoke within him. Could he not escape from his little house? Was it too late for him to try to live bravely like Gallaher? Could he go to London? There was the furniture still to be paid for. If he could only write a book and get it published, that might open the way for him.

A volume of Byron's poems lay before him on the table. He opened it cautiously with his left hand lest he should waken the child and began to read the first poem in the book:

> Hushed are the winds and still the evening gloom,
> Not e'en a Zephyr wanders through the grove,
> Whilst I return to view my Margaret's tomb
> And scatter flowers on the dust I love.

He paused. He felt the rhythm of the verse about him in the room. How melancholy it was! Could he, too, write like that, express the melancholy of his soul in verse? There were so many things he wanted to describe: his sensation of a few hours before on Grattan Bridge, for example. If he could get back again into that mood. . . .

The child awoke and began to cry. He turned from the page and tried to hush it: but it would not be hushed. He began to rock it to and fro in his arms but its wailing cry grew keener. He rocked it faster while his eyes began to read the second stanza:

> Within this narrow cell reclines her clay,
> That clay where once . . .

It was useless. He couldn't read. He couldn't do anything. The wailing of the child pierced the drum of his ear. It was useless! He was a prisoner for life. His arms trembled with anger and suddenly bending to the child's face he shouted:

"Stop!"

The child stopped for an instant, had a spasm of fright and began to scream. He jumped up from his chair and walked hastily up and down the room with the child in his arms. It began to sob piteously, losing its breath for four or five seconds, and then bursting out anew. The thin walls of the room echoed the sound. He tried to soothe it but it sobbed more convulsively. He looked at the contracted and quivering face of the child and began to be alarmed. He counted seven sobs without a break between them and caught the child to his breast in fright. If it died! . . .

The door was burst open and a young woman ran in, panting.

"What is it? What is it?" she cried.

The child, hearing its mother's voice, broke out into a paroxysm of sobbing.

"It's nothing, Annie . . . it's nothing. . . . He began to cry . . . "

She flung her parcels on the floor and snatched the child from him.

"What have you done to him?" she cried, glaring into his face.

Little Chandler sustained for one moment the gaze of her eyes and his heart closed together as he met the hatred in them. He began to stammer:

"It's nothing. . . . He . . . began to cry. . . . I couldn't . . . I didn't do anything. . . . What?"

Giving no heed to him she began to walk up and down the room, clasping the child tightly in her arms and murmuring:

"My little man! My little mannie! Was 'ou frightened, love? . . . There now, love. There now! . . . Lambabaun! Mamma's little lamb of the world! . . . There now!"

Little Chandler felt his cheeks suffused with shame and he stood back out of the lamplight. He listened while the paroxysm of the child's sobbing grew less and less; and tears of remorse started to his eyes.

---

1. In "A Little Cloud," James Joyce makes extensive use of detailed physical description.

   a) Record in your notebook four or five specific details from descriptions of Little Chandler, Ignatius Gallaher, and the city of Dublin.

   b) Discuss with a classmate how each of the literal descriptions is also symbolic.

2. In a small group, explore the contrasts Joyce draws and discuss their significance in the story.

3. "Character is destiny." In a short literary essay, to be included in your writing folder, show how this aphorism applies or does not apply to Little Chandler.

4. "There was no doubt about it: if you wanted to succeed you had

to go away." In a small group, assess the validity of Little Chandler's observation, supporting your opinions with reference to Canadian society.

5. As Annie, write a letter to a friend telling her about your life with Little Chandler and your feelings and thoughts about the future.

6. In your notebook, explain in a concise paragraph the significance of the title of Joyce's story.

Read the introductory and concluding paragraphs as a preview of the following essay. In point form set forth the characteristics of the method you expect Huxley to use in developing his ideas.

IS WAR INEVITABLE?
Julian Huxley

*I*n order to answer the question whether the human species possesses a war instinct or not we must first define the two terms "war" and "instinct." This sounds irritatingly academic but is not really so: on the correct answer depends the answer to the further intensely practical question, whether or not it is worth our trying to prevent war. For if war is instinctive in man, the only way to prevent it would be generations of selective breeding devoted to reducing or abolishing or altering his war instinct, just as man by selection has altered the instinctive savagery of the wolf to the friendly loyalty of the dog, or modified the dog's hunting instinct toward pointing in pointers, retrieving in retrievers, coursing by sight in greyhounds, or hunting by scent in foxhounds.

Even if we could start at once on such large-scale eugenics, there would be ample chance for war to destroy civilization before the lengthy process of selection had had an effect on our war instinct. If we are endowed with the instinct to make war, then the best anti-war social or economic or political machinery could only somewhat reduce the frequency of war or perhaps alter its manifestations – never prevent it. But if there is no such thing as a war instinct, then there is hope that something effective could be done and that war might really be abolished, or at any rate that it might be reduced to the status of a rare curiosity or a local and essentially unimportant phenomenon.

First, then, war. We may begin by making clear what war is not. Fighting between individuals is not war, even if it involves bloodshed or death. This applies to man – a duel is not war, nor is a murder – and also to animals – half a dozen lions fighting over a carcass are not engaged in war, nor are two stags fighting for a harem of hinds. Competition between two different species is not war.

The introduced American grey squirrel has ousted the indigenous red squirrel over much of Britain: but that has not involved war. We speak of the war against disease germs or against pests: but that is only war in a metaphorical sense. Still less is it war when one kind of animal preys upon another. We speak of the lion as the natural enemy of the zebra, or owls as the enemies of mice; but that again is metaphorical: the word enemy is used in a different sense from that of the enemy in a human war.

War means only one thing – organized conflict between groups of the same (or closely related) species, aimed at the imposing of the will of one group on the other. Strictly speaking, it means organized physical conflict, and it is in this sense that I shall use the term, though it might be extended to cover other types of group conflict, such as economic war, trade war, or class war.

Under this definition there are only three kinds of animals that practise war. One is a mammal – man; the other two are certain kinds of social insects – some bees and some ants.

There are other animal activities that represent stages on the way toward war, namely, fighting over breeding or feeding territory. Such fighting occurs regularly among the males of most songbirds, among various lizards and a few fish, and a number of mammals. But it is not true war, for it does not involve fighting between groups organized for the purpose.

Where, however, as in some ants, there are battles between ants' nests which are too close to each other, so that they compete for the same food territory, then we may speak of war. Thus Forel writes: "Among ants . . . collective ownership is represented by a portion of a meadow, a tree or several trees, a wood or even a stretch of sand. A strong colony tries to enlarge its domain at its neighbour's expense. . . . This is the source of war." He adds that "if the two formicaries are approximately equal in strength, they exterminate each other without any definite result" – a moral lesson for man!

Fighting of this sort is still a primitive sort of warfare. It is essentially unorganized as compared with the more specialized kinds of animal warfare found in other ants. Organized slave-raiding wars have been waged by the "bloody ant," *Formica sanguinea*, against *Formica glebaria*, in which the *sanguinea* transported all the *glebaria* pupae to their own nest, where they were destined to grow up as unconscious slaves.

But the most remarkable ant wars occur between neighbouring nests of Harvester ants. Harvesters collect seeds from various wild grasses and store them in underground granaries in their nests. Sometimes a colony will sally forth to try to seize the grain belonging to another nest.

Battles between hive-bee colonies have also been recorded, the prize here being the stored honey.

Thus the most developed types of warfare among social insects concern property – slaves and food-stores.

For our purpose, however, the most important fact concerning the wars of social insects is that they have a truly instinctive basis. In wars between nests of the same species, the tactics will be identical on both sides, so that the issue is usually decided by mere weight of numbers. In wars between different species, however, the fighting methods and tactics will be instinctively different, and may give a real advantage to one type. Their natural selection can here step in to improve the instincts involved in war.

As regards the more important question of a specific war-making instinct (as opposed to those concerned in the waging of wars once begun) there are all gradations. At the bottom we have the "territorial instinct" to defend the nest or the food-domain. We then have the instinct to enlarge the food territory at the expense of neighbouring colonies of the same species, which is the beginning of truly aggressive warfare. And as a specialized brand, not found anywhere else in the animal world, we have the highly organized warfare of slave-making ants against other species.

The "territorial instinct" grows directly out of the instinct of pugnacious self-defence. This is widespread, but by no means universal. There are many animals like hares and rabbits, deer and antelopes which run away rather than fight, and either do not actively defend themselves, or do so only when actually cornered. And there are others which seek to escape detection by remaining immobile, or even "sham dead" in various ways, never resorting to violence.

However, though human beings will, of course, in certain circumstances seek safety by flight or by concealment, they certainly have a good dose of self-preservative pugnacity. Furthermore, this pugnacity can also readily be called into play on what in animals we generally call "territorial" grounds – defense of home, mate, family, or property. In human evolution, moreover, this territorial pugnacity seems to have played an important role for a long period. It must have been operative during the pre-human, semi-human, and early human periods. It was doubtless operative whenever the social units came into competition for food or other territorial needs.

In the more developed societies of the hunting phase this territorial pugnacity often became the basis of true warfare. The classical example is that of many American Indians.

What can be studied among the Indians holds good for all the more complex manifestations of war in the evolution from settled barbarism to industrial civilization. The only element which can possibly be called instinctive in war is man's propensity to fight, his innate pugnacity. But this is not an instinct in the strict or biological sense of the word. For one thing, it is not always elicited, and when elicited is not always a reaction to the same stimulus or set of circumstances; nor does it manifest itself in the same stereotyped way or within the same innately determined limits. Thus it is best called an impulse, urge or drive rather than an instinct. But we will not be pedantic, and will say that there does exist an instinctive basis on which war depends, in the shape of man's pugnacity.

However, whereas a true war instinct would make war inevitable, man's pugnacious impulses merely make it possible. In order that the possibility shall become realized in actual war, our pugnacious impulses must be disciplined, developed, rationalized, organized. Above all, they must be combined with all sorts of other impulses, motives, and complex emotions and dispositions, to form what McDougall calls a *sentiment* – an organized system or piece of mental structure – in this case focussed upon war.

Among the psychological elements which may thus be combined with the impulse of pugnacity to produce the complex war sentiment we may catalogue patriotism, love of power, love of glory, self-interest, fear, dislike of what is alien, the feeling of superiority, the sense of shame, belief in one's ideals and those of one's group, and many more. Such a sentiment or disposition cannot be inherited as such, but must be built up anew in every individual.

Furthermore, it will not be the same in every individual of a given society, nor will its different elements occur in the same proportions, or even always recur, in different societies or in the same society, at different times. The arrogant belief in Germanic superiority, which was combined with their leader's lust for power to bring the German people into the last war, were ingredients almost wholly lacking from the war sentiment of the British, in which self-preservation and the upholding of a particular way of life were prominent, or from that of the Americans, to which an idealization of the democratic free enterprise principle contributed, and also a certain missionary spirit.

The war sentiment may be deliberately cultivated as part of the very existence of the tribe or nation, as among the American Indians in old days or in Nazi Germany in its brief appalling career. Or it may be provoked by attack, as happened to Britain when Germany invaded Poland, or to America when the Japanese attacked Pearl Harbor, or to Russia in June, 1941.

Even after provocation, however, it requires cultivating and intensifying: we all know the orgy of propaganda and patriotic campaigns, both general and special, which were found necessary for the British and American and Russian war effort. Propaganda is indeed specially necessary in antimilitarist countries like the United States, which has always mistrusted the mere suspicion of a standing army; or Britain, where the soldier in peacetime has almost invariably been looked at askance.

But though the war sentiment always needs to be cultivated or stimulated in some way, if it is to develop to a stage which makes war possible, its development also demands a certain kind of environment. The conditions which permit the development of war sentiment and of actual warfare seem various enough, but in reality they all fall under one of two main heads.

The first main condition is that the human beings concerned shall be organized in separate compact societies, be they tribes or kingdoms, empires or modern nation-states. And the second is that there should be serious competition of some sort between those groups, whether for hunting-grounds or sources of oil, for living space or world markets.

Even if war is not the automatic product of a war instinct in man, but only an expression of a war sentiment which needs particular conditions for its development, yet, as Norman Cousins well puts it, "the expression of man's nature will continue to be warlike if the same conditions are continued that have provoked warlike expression in him in the past."

These conditions, we have seen, boil down to two essentials – organization in separate groups, and serious competition. So we should be able to reduce the incidence and possibility of war either by reducing the separateness of human organized groups (in other words, by promoting unitary world organization) or by reducing the intensity of competition between groups (in other words, by promoting all-round productivity) or preferably, of course, by doing both at once.

One of the factors which make war more possible is unrestricted national sovereignty. If we want to reduce war from the status of a likely to an unlikely phenomenon, we must not abolish nationhood by any means, but subordinate it to world sovereignty. National Governments must somehow become agencies within a single world government, just as local and regional authorities are agencies of government within nations.

But even with a single World Government, there would still be the possibility (though assuredly a reduced possibility) of war – in this case civil war or rebellion.

To minimize this risk, we must reduce to a minimum the competition between different groups or regions for the good things of the world. And this means, as indicated above, planning for a world of abundance. Furthermore, the abundance must not be too unevenly spread; or else, even if the thin-spread regions really have enough for health and comfort, the contrast with the heavy spreading of other regions may still promote jealousy and unrest and war. In particular, the United States must beware of concentrating solely or mainly on developing her own productivity and prosperity to unexampled heights. Apart from the envies and jealousies to which this will undoubtedly give rise, it is likely to lead to an imbalance in the world's economic structure, which will one day crash, bringing down rich and poor countries alike in its fall.

There is finally the task of finding and providing what William James called "a moral equivalent of war" – some outlet for frustration and repressed hate and aggressivity, some canalization of man's basic urges to pugnacity and self-assertion. Though the causes of the former may be removed by a proper economic and social system, the latter will always be with us, and need to be got rid of in some form of activity, preferably a sublimated one. This task cannot be adequately or fully tackled until the more urgent problems of providing the world with a unitary government and a high all-round standard of life have been coped with.

When the time comes, however, I do not see why it should not be successfully tackled. It will need a good deal of psychology to find out what kind of activities are most suitable and satisfying for what people; a good deal of organization, to see that the requisite jobs and leisure activities can actually be provided in the right proportions; and a good deal of education and propaganda in the right sense of the word, to make people realize that the jobs and activities are not only worthwhile, but will provide deep and full satisfactions.

To sum up very briefly, the biologist denies emphatically that there are human war instincts, either for the waging of war in a particular way, or to make war in general. But there does exist a human drive or impulse of pugnacity, which can be used as the foundation of a war sentiment; and this will continue to express itself in war as long as external conditions encourage or permit this expression of human nature. It is up to us to alter the conditions so as to prevent human pugnacity from expressing itself in war, and to encourage its use in other sentiments leading to activities and outlets of use or value. And to do this we need a unitary World Government, a general high level of productivity, and outlets and activities which will provide a moral equivalent of war.

---

1. a) In your notebook, construct an outline of headings and sub-headings for the essay to demonstrate how Huxley's conclusion is a logical outcome of his argument.
   b) Comparing your outline with that of a classmate, resolve any differences between your analyses.
   c) Together, examine any two transitional paragraphs to determine how Huxley links the stages of his argument.

2. Julian Huxley is defensive about seeming to be "irritatingly academic" and "pedantic" in his essay. Examine paragraphs one and eighteen and, with a classmate, discuss what he means by these criticisms and how he defends himself against them.

3. a) Formulate a list of specific recommendations for political and social changes that, according to Huxley, might reduce the chance of war.
b) Reread the second-to-last paragraph. In a small group, discuss the controversial implications of Huxley's proposal. Brainstorm for arguments one might use both to defend and to attack his proposal.
c) As an observer of world events today, write a short postscript to Huxley's article evaluating the likelihood of such political and social changes coming about.

Harry Bruce's essay is about organized sports in North America. In a small group, try to predict from the title what his attitude toward his subject will be, as well as some points you might expect him to make.

AND MAY THE BEST CHEATER WIN

Harry Bruce

Every youth knows he can get into deep trouble by stealing cameras, peddling dope, mugging winos, forging cheques, or copying someone else's answers during an exam. Those are examples of not playing by the rules. Cheating. But every youth also knows that in organized sports across North America, cheating is not only perfectly okay, it's *recommended*. "The structure of sport . . . actually promotes deviance," says U.S. sport sociologist D.S. Eitzen.

The downy-cheeked hockey player who refuses to play dirty may find himself fired off the team. The boy soccer player who refuses to rough up a superior striker to "throw him off his game" may find himself writhing under a coach's tongue-lashing. The basketball player who refuses to foul a goal-bound enemy star in the last seconds of a close game may find himself riding the bench next week. Thus, we have that cynical paradox, "the good foul," a phrase that makes about as much sense as "a beneficial outbreak of bubonic plague."

If organized sports offer benefits to youngsters, they also offer a massive program of moral corruption. The recruiting of college athletes in the United States, and the use of academic fraud to maintain their "eligibility," stunk so powerfully in 1980 that *Newsweek* decided "cheating has become the name of the game," and spoke of the fear on U.S. campuses of "an epidemic of corruption." But the epidemic had already arrived, and what really worried *Newsweek* was national acceptance of corruption as normal: "Many kids are admitting that they have tried to take the bribes and inducements on the sleazy terms with which they are offered. Their complaints are not so much that illegalities exist, but that they aren't getting their share of the goodies." Fans, alumni, coaches, college administrators, players, and their parents all believed nothing could ever be more important than winning (or more disgraceful than losing), and that cheating in victory's cause was therefore commendable.

"Candidates for big-time sport's Hall of Shame have seemed suddenly to break out all over like an ugly rash," William Oscar Johnson wrote last year in *Sports Illustrated*. He constructed a dismal catalogue of assaults on cops, drunken brawls, adventures in the cocaine trade, credit-card frauds, and other sordid activities by rich professional athletes who, in more naïve times, might have earned the adulation of small boys. Jim Finks, then Chicago Bears general manager, speculated that the trouble with the younger lawbreakers was that they had "been looked after all the way from junior high school. Some of them have had doctored grades. This plus the affluence (astronomical salaries) means there has never been any pressing need for them to work things out for themselves. They have no idea how to face reality."

No one in all their lives had taught them about fair play. "In the early days of playground and high-school leagues, one of the key issues was moral regulation," says Alan Ingham, a teacher at the University of Washington. "You got sports, and you got Judeo-Christian principles thrown in, too." Now, however, "the majority of things taught in sports are performance things." John Pooley of the School of Recreation, Physical and Health Education at Dalhousie University, Nova Scotia asked Calvin Hill, a former Dallas Cowboy, what percentage of all the football rookies he'd ever met had said that, as college players, they'd encountered no cheating. Hill's reply was short: "None."

So here we have the most powerful nation in the world, and it blithely corrupts children so they'll mature as athletic machines without an ounce of the moral sense that might prevent their sniffing cocaine or complicate their lust for victory. Pray for nuclear disarmament, fans.

Still, Canadians are little better. We all know who invented the game that inspired Paul Newman to star in *Slap Shot*, a black and bloody comedy about butchery on ice. We can't argue that it's only American coaches who teach peewees to draw tripping penalties rather than let an enemy player continue a break-away on your goal. Moreover, I happen to live in Halifax, where only last winter St. Mary's University was disgraced for allowing a ringer from Florida to play varsity basketball. The coach of a rival but inferior team ferreted out the truth about the player's ineligibility. In doing so, he imported one of the fine old traditions of amateur sports in the States: if you can't beat them, hire a private dick. Oh well, that's what universities are supposed to be all about: the pursuit of truth.

Pursuing another truth, Pooley of Dalhousie surveyed recent graduates of three down-east universities. The grads were both men and women, and they had all played intercollegiate field hockey, ice hockey, soccer, or basketball. "With one exception (a woman field-hockey player), all felt there was immense pressure to win," Pooley said. Typical responses: "Winning is everything in university sport. . . . The measure of success was not how well you played but the win-loss record. . . . There is incredible pressure to perform because there are always two or three guys on the bench ready to take your place."

Half said their coaches had urged "winning at any cost." One grad revealed, "Some coaches send their players 'out to get' a good player on the other team." Another described "goon coaches who stressed intimidation and rough play." Coaches had not only condoned tactical fouls, but had actually taught the arts of fouling during routine practice. A player who had competed against British and Bermudian teams said they played "intensely but fairly" while the Maritimers "sometimes used dirty tactics" or "blatantly tried to stop a player."

Pooley wondered if the grads, after years in intercollegiate sport, felt it had promoted fair play. Only the field-hockey players said yes. Answers from the others were shockers: "Everyone cheats and the best cheater wins. . . . Fair play and sportsmanship are *not* promoted. This is a joke. . . . You did whatever you could to win. . . . You are taught to gain an advantage, whatever it takes." Such cynicism, from people so young they've barely doffed their mortarboards, confirms the sad opinion of one Kalevi Heinila, who told a world scientific congress in 1980 that fair play was "ripe to be dumped in the waste basket of sport history."

The irony in all this – and it's both ludicrous and nauseating – is that universities defend their expensive programs for intercollegiate sports with lip service to the notion that keen teamwork in clean competition nurtures good citizens. Fair play in sports, don't you know, spawns fair players for the worlds of politics, the professions and business.

That's a crock. What intercollegiate sport really teaches is how to get away with murder, how to be crooked within the law. Just listen to one of the fresh-faced grads in Pooley's survey as he sets out to make his way in the world, his eyes shining with idealism: "University sport teaches you to play as close to the limits as possible; and this is the attitude that will get you ahead in the business world." Another acknowledged that his "concept of fair play decreased"; but, on the other hand, he had learned to "stretch the rules to my advantage." A young woman confided, "University sport has made me tough, less sensitive to other people's feelings." Still others stressed that college sport had prepared them for "the real world," for "real life," in which winning was all.

Cheating in amateur sport, Pooley says, "gives it a hollow feeling. Many coaches do not have integrity. I'm still sickened by that. It upsets me, at all levels." A tall, talkative, forceful man with a bony face and a thick brush of steely hair, Pooley has coached soccer in six countries, once played for professional teams in Britain, and now, at 53, cavorts on a team for men over 35. "I'm still playing league soccer," he wrote in a paper for the 1984 Olympic Scientific Congress in Eugene, Oregon, "because: a) I helped to organize and plan my own youth soccer experiences; b) coming second or being beaten was okay; c) I was always much more interested in playing well than playing to win; d) I never minded playing less well than I'd earlier played; and e) I always felt successful at the level played."

Those are highly un-American reasons for playing any sport, but Pooley is originally from northern England, the nation that invented "fair play" and knew that certain things just weren't cricket. That was in a time long before Americans institutionalized cheating even in soap box derbies, before athletes gobbled steroids, before universities invented courses in weight lifting and raquetball so quarterbacks could qualify as "students." Moreover, Pooley believes that the few adults who stick with team sports until middle age do so because, as youngsters, "They preferred the feel of the ball, the pass well made, the sweetness of the stroke or the power in the shot, rather than whether they won or lost the game." Such people don't need to cheat.

Some scholars believe that the sleaziness of organized sports simply reflects the sleaziness of our entire culture. Pooley points out, for instance, that one sociologist offers two reasons why cheating in sports shouldn't be "disproportionately reprimanded." The first is that it's "endemic in society," and the second is that even more cheating probably occurs in other fields. Pooley disagrees. He says this argument is like saying you should not disproportionately reprimand the clergy for being dishonest. Poor Pooley. He has such quaint ideas about sports. He actually believes they should not be immoral, and should be fun.

---

1. Bruce draws a distinction between British and North American attitudes toward playing sports. With a classmate, identify the distinction he makes and assess its validity, drawing on your own experience if possible.

2. Compare Harry Bruce's article with Lynda Hurst's column (p. 22) in terms of the two writers' language. Consider particularly

the purpose and effectiveness of words and images that are charged with emotion. Summarize your findings in a concise paragraph to be polished and kept in your writing folder.

3. Citing reliable sources is a valid way of supporting an argument. With a classmate, list Bruce's sources and evaluate their effectiveness.

4. In a group of four divided into opposing teams, prepare arguments for and then debate the resolution "The sleaziness of organized sports simply reflects the sleaziness of our entire culture." Use another group as an audience and ask them to present a critique of the arguments presented.

Appoint one or two members of your class to conduct a survey. Have them ask several students and teachers to respond to the following questions:

- What is your more regular source of news coverage, television or newspapers?
- Which do you find more believable, what you see on a television newscast or what you read in a newspaper?
- Which medium do you think is capable of providing more reliable coverage of the news, television or newspapers?

The pollsters should tabulate their results and present them to the class.

CAN TV TELL THE TRUTH?
Morris Wolfe

According to polls, people believe what they see on TV newscasts far more than what they read in the papers. That's an astonishing statistic. What it reveals is that the majority of people don't read much, certainly not much news. Because anyone who relies on both print *and* the electronic media for information can have little doubt about the very real limitations of TV news.

First, there are severe limitations of space. The entire text of *The National*, for example, which runs twenty-two minutes, fills only about half a page of *The Globe and Mail*. Individual items are rarely longer than two or three minutes or perhaps 300 to 400 words. Try to say something substantial on a subject you know something about in so little space. Usually, items are much shorter, particularly if it's a story – however important – that's not inherently visual. Anyone interested in the details of the Reichmann brothers' takeover of Gulf Canada wouldn't find them on TV. Television still hasn't learned how to do business and economic stories well. For most stories, TV provides little more than a headline service.

Then there are the structural limitations of the medium. Watching the news on TV is different from reading a newspaper. A good newspaper contains several hundred items. ("All the news that's fit to print," says *The New York Times*.) One can choose to read, skim, or ignore as many or as few items as one wishes. The same freedom isn't there on TV. The viewer is locked into the dozen or so items that have been selected by a lineup editor and the order he or she has chosen to put them in. The first story on almost all newscasts as I write in early August is the major league baseball strike. South Africa has temporarily been relegated to second place. There's no way the TV viewer can skip the baseball story as the newspaper reader can. Ultimately, we're told, television will offer viewers the same kind of freedom that newspaper readers have. We'll be able to plug into only the items we want, but that is still a long way off.

And there's another important structural difference between TV news stories and newspaper stories. A newspaper story is not only longer and contains more facts, it's also more untidy than a TV story and in that sense it's more true-to-life. A good newspaper story starts with the most important facts and observations and trails off into less important details. The assumption of the writer and the editor is that most people aren't going to read the whole piece. A TV news story, on the other hand, is a neat, dramatically structured package with a clear introduction, body, and conclusion, and few, if any, loose ends. If there's something a bit inconclusive about the typical newspaper story, there's something too certain about the TV news story.

It's important to realize, too, that there are far more people involved in putting together a TV news story. The system works something like this. (I'm using *The National* as my model.) An assignment editor and a reporter agree on a piece. The reporter and a cameraperson, occasionally a soundperson and sometimes a producer (or researcher) go out in the field and do the necessary interviewing and taping. The reporter writes a script and goes over it and its taped inserts with a story editor who decides, in consultation with the lineup editor, what the length of the finished item should be. The reporter then goes off and together with an editor produces the piece. Before it goes on air, the lineup editor and the program's producer will probably screen the item and may ask for changes. Given the number of people involved, the question of accountability on TV is obviously a tricky one. If a mistake is made is the reporter to blame? The producer? The editor? The researcher? All of them? American media critic Hodding Carter III contends that newspaper reporting is more rigorous than TV reporting because the reporter is more clearly accountable.

Because of brevity, structure, and the large number of people involved in putting a story together, TV news demands of us an even greater suspension of disbelief than do newspapers. The print story, as *Toronto Life* publisher and former CBC executive Peter Herrndorf suggests, "has a built-in b.s. detector." One can go back and reread portions of the text to make sure that a point has been clearly made. Unless one's using a videocassette player, it's impossible to do that with television. What it all comes down to on TV is the credibility of the reporter – we have to trust that he or she has *fairly* (after all, only objects can be objective) reduced a story to its essentials. The good TV reporter has to be able, as reporter and anchorman for *The Journal* Bill Cameron says, "to tell us quickly what the point is." And that, adds Herrndorf, makes the television reporter's job more difficult than that of the print reporter. It requires *more* expertise not less. Obviously we can't know what footage the TV reporter hasn't used any more than we can know what material the print journalist has chosen to omit. "*All* editing processes," argues *The National* anchorman Knowlton Nash, "are susceptible to manipulation."

But it's not just the editing process we have to worry about with TV. Part of the reason we trust television more than print is that we've been taught to believe that "the camera doesn't lie," that "one picture is worth a thousand words." There's no doubt that pictures *are* far more powerful and direct than words. "It's much easier," Herrndorf points out, "to make a six-hankie TV movie than it is to write a three-hankie magazine article." In that sense, TV is inherently more manipulative than print. Writer and broadcaster Warner Troyer has written that "Unless directed by an incompetent, a close-up lens is a truth machine." Knowlton Nash reminds me that TV destroyed Joseph McCarthy; it did what print couldn't do. At the same time, we know that we don't always see what we're told we're seeing on TV. In *Campus Giveaway*, an item dealing with the growing number of foreign students at the University of Toronto, CTV's *W5* misidentified Chinese-Canadian students as foreigners. (Chinese all look alike.) We know that in baseball on TV, different camera angles can show a player to be safe and out at the same time. We know that Robert Stanfield, who was universally described by reporters as an intelligent, decent and funny man, was a disaster on TV. We know that John Kennedy won his 1960 debate with Richard Nixon on television. But we forget that on radio, Nixon won.

Television can manipulate us in other ways. We know that events are stage managed by the various interest groups who compete with one another for snippets of air time. Governments stage press conferences for the camera; people demonstrate or riot for the camera. The IRA holds terrorist funerals – "all berets and gear," says *The Economist*, designed "to convey the impression of a legitimate army for a legitimate cause." No one can doubt the potential propaganda value of the visual image. Eisenstein taught us that.

The TV networks, of course, do their own staging of events. Last summer, NBC flew some hostage families to Frankfurt so they could be taped being reunited with loved ones who'd been on a hijacked TWA plane. ABC's *World News Tonight* once illuminated the entire front of a Viennese cathedral in order to provide a backdrop for a news item.

("Why not?" asked the program's executive producer. "It may not mean much in the book of life, but it made a pretty shot.") Unfortunately, pretty shots *are* of crucial importance. That fact, as reporter and anchorman Peter Trueman says in *Smoke & Mirrors*, "puts undue emphasis on the abnormal. Normal is dull, and unlike a newspaper, which is not intended to be read cover to cover, television cannot afford dull patches. Too many of those drive the viewer to change channels or shut the set off completely." Therefore, disasters – plane crashes, hurricanes and the like – still get a disproportionate amount of TV news time. They're relatively easy to cover and viewers lap them up. I suspect that part of the brain that's attracted to chaos is turned on by such footage.

TV news also manipulates us in the sense that it makes us feel that we know more than we do. Its certainty encourages ours. One of the results is that we've become infomaniacs because TV news is oddly reassuring. We're terrified of war, convinced that the world around us is out of control. And with good reason. Serious newspapers and magazines reinforce those fears. But TV news makes us feel we've got a handle on things. So like ravenous Pac-Men we consume more and more TV news and current affairs shows. They become addictive. And the amount of such material available is increasing. I know people who have CNN, the Cable News Network, on in the background all the time. It provides them with Newzak.

One of the programs most responsible for this phenomenon is *60 Minutes*. Each segment of the show is structured to provide us with the kind of "sweet resolution of anxiety," as a CBS executive puts it, that we get when our favourite team wins. *Time* magazine has suggested that *60 Minutes*, "has elements of high melodrama: most of its investigative pieces are playlets in which a Lone Ranger journalist corners a villain, not with a gun but with an interview." Audiences come to feel that if Mike Wallace or whoever is looking into a problem, everything's under control.

Sometimes, it's argued, television does things because it can rather than because it should. Is it telling the truth when cameras are stuck in front of a grieving mother's face? Or are we willing to sacrifice that bit of "truth" out of respect for her right to some privacy? (Canadian television appears prepared to make that sacrifice more often than does American television.) It's not that TV can't show restraint. It has learned to do so when it comes to streakers and drunks at sports events. But should exercising restraint extend to *not* giving terrorists the publicity they seek? That's what Henry Kissinger argues. Or are events such as the TWA hostage taking in Lebanon legitimate news stories that warrant coverage whatever the risks? That's the position of the American networks: in a democratic society the public has a right to know.

I have a neo-Marxist friend who believes that the TV networks consciously act as "gatekeepers," allowing some views to be heard and ignoring others. Pluralism extends only so far, he says. Terrorists, he argues, are people who believe their point of view *isn't* being presented, and who therefore create events in order to grab the media by the throat. (Film-maker Peter Watkins recently circulated a lengthy memorandum to various key people in television in which he states that the CBC acted as a gatekeeper at last year's "Shamrock" Summit between Ronald Reagan and Brian Mulroney. The corporation paid too much attention, he maintains, to government stage managing and too little to that by demonstrators.)

Unlike newspapers, television doesn't usually have the equivalent of a letters to the editor column in which one can point out mistakes and offer alternative points of view. The text of *The National* recently described Forbes Burnham, who had just died, as the president of the Caribbean nation of Guyana, In fact, Guyana isn't in the Caribbean; it's in South America. That's a small error, but small errors can undermine credibility too. The error was neither corrected nor acknowledged. John Owen, managing editor of CBC National Television News, regrets that the mistake wasn't caught on the newscast. But he feels that correcting it later would have drawn too much attention to it. It's different, he says, when the *Globe* apologizes for its mistakes on page two. In the context of an entire newspaper, it doesn't seem unreasonable to acknowledge a couple of errors. But to do so on a twenty-two minute newscast, he suggests, is different. He agrees, though, that a way must be found to deal with mistakes and complaints on air.

When the Chinese-Canadian community objected to *Campus Giveaway*, CTV stonewalled. It took seven months for the network to finally admit it had made a mistake and to issue an abject apology. In the meantime, CTV attempted to make a program researcher the scapegoat but backed off when she hired Clayton Ruby to represent her. Eventually, she was shifted out of *W5* and the program's editorial director was fired.

Does all the above mean that we shouldn't believe TV? Not at all. Only that we have to be realistic about what TV can and can't do. None of the media has a monopoly on truth. The "truth" comes to us in dribs and drabs from a variety of sources. We need to get whatever we can from as many sources as we can.

Certainly, it should be remembered that mistakes are made by the print media too. Investigative reporter Robert Reguly's reputation was damaged by what turned out to be false accusations in *The Toronto Sun* against former Liberal Cabinet minister John Munro. And it's not just "honest" mistakes. There are cases of deliberate fabrication. In 1981, *Washington Post* reporter Janet Cook won a Pulitzer Prize for a story she concocted about an 8-year-old heroin addict. She was forced to return the prize and resign. Less than a month later, Michael Daly of

The New York Daily News resigned when it was revealed that he had invented some of the details in a story about British soldiers in Northern Ireland.

There's no doubt that governments are afraid of the power television has to tell the truth. On a number of occasions in the past twenty years they have intervened to prevent material from being seen. In 1965, for instance, the Liberal Party stopped *Mr. Pearson, a cinéma vérité* documentary about the prime minister, from being shown on the CBC. Shots of Pearson with his feet up, watching the World Series on television during a crisis, embarrassed his advisors.

In October, 1970, before the War Measures Act was invoked, Gérard Pelletier, the secretary of state, phoned George Davidson, president of the CBC. Pelletier later said he called Davidson as an "individual" rather than as the minister to whom Davidson was responsible. Davidson, on the other hand, was sure Pelletier was acting as an official government spokesman. But he insisted Pelletier's call hadn't influenced him. Whatever the truth, it's clear that *after* their conversation the CBC began censoring itself in what became the most shameful episode in its history. Part of what made it shameful is that no CBC journalist resigned in protest. On October 15, a day *before* the War Measures Act was brought in, Peter Trueman, then executive producer of the CBC's national news, was called into his superior's office. In *Smoke & Mirrors*, Trueman recalls: "We were to avoid commentary and speculation of all kinds. We were not to use man-on-the-street interviews or shoot film of any public demonstration. We were to air no panel discussions on the October Crisis and were to avoid reporting speculation, particularly speculation about what the government was doing."

In 1983, the American government, following the example of Russia in Afghanistan, forbade direct press coverage of the American invasion of Grenada. In doing so, it echoed the sign the British censor had over his desk during World War II: "It's more important to win this war than to write about it." But it seems clear the ban was directed especially against television. The Reagan administration has reason to be afraid of TV. Television can, and has, told Americans the truth about the horrors of war. Vietnam demonstrated that an unpopular war will end more quickly if TV cameras are present. Indeed, one wonders what effect television would have had on a *popular* war. What would reaction to D-day have been if TV cameras had been there to record the slaughter?

The National, despite its limitations, is the best front page in English Canada. There is no better place to go for a fast overview of the day's news. It would be foolish not to go further – to newspapers, magazines and other radio and TV programs – and equally foolish not to be skeptical, but *The National* is a useful starting point. Print addict though I am, I wouldn't want to be without it. I want to be able to see the people in the news – Pieter Botha, for example; the visual component helps fill in the spaces around the words they speak.

At times, *The National* is superb. For instance, I've found most coverage of the civil war in Lebanon confusing; trying to keep all the sides straight without a score card is extraordinarily difficult. On TV, the soldiers, the vehicles, the guns, the shattered buildings of all the factions are virtually indistinguishable. I found those events confusing until Ann Medina put them in perspective in a way that nothing else I'd seen or read had done. Medina is a superb storyteller. She has a quality of mind that allows her to cut through the underbrush of a story as effectively as any journalist I can think of. Herrndorf compared her to René Lévesque on Radio-Canada in the 1950s. At its best, television can not only tell us the "truth," it can also mobilize us into action in a way that print can't. Brian Stewart's reports from drought-stricken Africa had that effect on the relief effort. And it wasn't just the emaciated bodies that touched us. One could see Brian Stewart himself being transformed by the story he was telling.

Obviously, one needs more than a front page. The best current affairs shows on television – programs such as *Canada AM* and *Question Period* on CTV, the *MacNeil/Lehrer Newshour* on PBS, and *Meet the Press* on NBC – help provide that something more. *The Journal*, which follows *The National* Monday to Friday, reminds us that most stories in the news are far more complicated than TV news alone can tell us. (If the news offers certainty, current affairs shows at their best offer ambiguity.) *The Journal* does so in two ways – through interviews with newsmakers and their critics, and through documentaries. Interviews rarely offer more than a couple of points of view – Union Carbide and the environmentalists, Michael Wilson and the opposition finance critics. That's their major limitation. But in the hands of the skilled interviewer (and there's none better than Ted Koppel of *Nightline*), our ability to see and pursue weakness in argument is developed in a way that print can't quite replicate. Thus the good TV interviewer, as Bill Cameron puts it, "becomes a kind of prosecuting attorney." We are the jury.

A documentary item, which is put together over a much longer period of time (the TV news interviewer, after all, has only a few hours to prepare) allows us to see and weigh a multiplicity of points of view. On *The Journal*, a documentary item can run as long as half an hour. On *the fifth estate*, a story can be explored in even more detail; it can run an hour, or occasionally ninety minutes as in the case of the award-winning *Just Another Missing Kid*. And television is slowly becoming better at handling ideas. David Suzuki's *A Planet for the Taking* is an eight-hour TV essay whose point is essentially nonvisual.

Television is a young medium; in Canada it's not yet thirty-five years old. *The National* still has many things wrong with it. It's far too short. It still doesn't have enough reporters in the field to make it sufficiently national or international. But it's improved enormously in the past decade. Ten years ago it was far less reflective, far more reactive. It responded to events rather than trying to put them in perspective.

Regional stories were frequently used as kickers – as a light touch at the end of a newscast. A lot of American film footage was used and was never identified. (That's still occasionally true of CTV.) Today, much of that's changed.

So, can TV tell the truth? Yes, but not the whole truth, and it takes sophisticated, vigilant viewers to ensure that it tells as much as it can. The informed citizen clearly needs as much information as possible from as many diverse sources as possible. Schools teach children a little – although not nearly enough – about how to deal with the credibility of print sources. It's time they began teaching about the content and structure of television.

--- ●●● ---

1. In your notebook, construct a chart to show the distinctions Wolfe draws between television and newspaper reporting. Compare your chart with a classmate's as a means of checking its accuracy and completeness. Add to your charts any new points that come from your sharing of ideas.

2. a) Form five or six small groups to conduct a class research project comparing coverage of news events in a week by *The National* and a major provincial or national newspaper available in your community. Each group should select a different day to do its critical viewing and reading, and each group's report should mention
   ● which events were covered by *The National*, and which significant news stories covered by the newspaper were omitted from the newscast;
   ● which medium provided the deepest and most thorough coverage of particular events.
   After the groups have reported, the class should work together to draw general conclusions from its research, comparing its assessment with Wolfe's.
   b) Make a concise summary of your comparison and conclusions and add it to your notebook.

3. Read the text of Margaret Atwood's "Amnesty International: An Address" (p. 101).
   a) With a classmate, discuss how certain points raised in Atwood's address might serve to explain the Canadian audience's preference for television coverage of the news.
   b) Write a letter to Wolfe on the subject of a journalist's responsibility to society. Ask a classmate to help you edit and revise your letter. Include the polished version in your writing folder.

THE GIRL NEXT DOOR
Norman Levine

In October 1976 I came back to Ottawa and rented three rooms in an old house on Cobourg Street just below Rideau. It wasn't anything – plain bare rooms with brightly coloured wallpaper – but the windows looked out over a small park. And that made all the difference.

For the first two days – apart from going out to buy some small cigars and groceries – I stayed in and looked at the park.

It's a lovely little park . . . made for the human scale . . . people look right when they are in it. The two Lombardy poplars. One, at the edge of the park, by the sidewalk, in front of the window. The other, towards the middle of the park but off centre, raised, where the earth formed a mound. And on top of the mound, on a small plateau, a gazebo. And beside the gazebo – with its open arches, its sloping brick coloured roof – this other, very tall, Lombardy poplar.

I could tell a wind's direction not only by the arrow on top of the gazebo but, from the near poplar's leaves showing their light green underside, I could also tell its strength. Elsewhere there were maple trees – young and old – their leaves, in autumn colours, some lying thick, underneath, on the grass.

I was quite happy to stay by a window. There was always something moving. A leaf from a **maple**, people walking, grey and black squirrels, boys throwing passes **or** kicking a rugby ball, others rolling from the gazebo down the slope. Pigeons, sparrows, and the occasional gull flying slowly over.

I watched until the park lights came on. Then it was too dark to see. That's when I switched on a small radio and listened to the news (the local, national, international), the sports, the time, the temperature, the weather forecast, and the commercials in between.

On the third day I woke up, drew back the curtain, and there was snow. It was the first snow I had seen in years. I made some coffee, lit up an Old Port cigarillo, and watched a man dressed in black with a black umbrella above his head walk through the all white park. The wind picked up some loose leaves and moved them swiftly on top of the snow. Fascinating to see fallen leaves lifted then carried by the wind across the snow. They look like small birds. They are small birds.

I decided to go out. I had no destination. I walked along Rideau to the Chateau Laurier. In the lobby I took off my coat and sat down in a leather chair, as if I was waiting for someone. There were others also sitting down and watching.

I left the lobby as the bell in the Peace Tower was ringing ten and walked across Confederation Square, down Elgin, to the National Gallery. And found this Monet.

There was a Renoir to the left, of a mother and child. And a Braque to the right, of the Port of Antwerp. And elsewhere in the room: a red landscape of Vlaminck, a red nude of Duchamp, a Derain, a Léger, an Epstein, some Cézannes, Pissarros, Sisleys, and Gauguins, several Degas, and a Van Gogh of some irises.

But it was this Monet, *Waterloo Bridge – The Sun in a Fog, 1903*, that I kept coming back to see.

When I was close to it it was just paint. But when I went back, about ten feet, the sun was round at the top coming faintly through the fog. The sun was orange on the water in the front and, further away, on the water through an arch of the bridge. While the darker shapes, of the bridge, the barges, came visibly through.

At the end of the second week Lynn moved into the apartment next door. I had pulled back the curtain and saw that the little park was almost hidden by fog. Only the gazebo – the arches filled with fog – and the near poplar and the near maples were visible. The rest was fog and the sun trying to come through. When a taxi drove up. A slim girl with long hair that almost hid her face came out. She was about five foot six or seven, dressed in jeans, a black sweater, and a black duffle coat. The taxi driver helped bring in her few things.

Next evening I knocked on her door.

"I saw you move in yesterday. I live in the next apartment."

"Come in," she said quietly.

The room was like mine. But she had put up art posters of Chagall and Picasso. And a Snoopy poster that said:

No problem is
So big that you
Can't run away
From it.

There were picture post-cards and a row of paperbacks by the wall. There was a small wooden table and two wooden chairs.

"I haven't had time to do this right. Would you like coffee? It won't take long."

She filled an electric kettle and plugged it in. I noticed that she was left-handed.

"How long have you been here?"

"Two weeks."

"Will you stay?"

"I don't know. How about you?"

"I've got to sort myself out," she said.

I saw Jung's *Modern Man in Search of a Soul*, Sylvia Plath's *The Bell Jar*, books on psychology, poetry, philosophy. And art books on Klee, Magritte, Kandinsky, Munch.

"I go to the National Gallery," I said. "They have a lovely Monet."

"I like Monet," she said.

"Where are you from?"

"From New Brunswick," she said, "near Fredericton, in the country."

"I've been to Fredericton," I said, "about ten or eleven years ago. I deliberately go to places – some I know some I don't – and isolate myself because I want to work. Why don't we go to my apartment. I have a bottle of wine and some records."

I put on Bix Beiderbecke and Sydney Bechet. And she took off her shoes and began to dance in heavy white woollen socks. She danced, for a while, by herself. Then she came over and stretched out her hands.

"Dance."

I got up and we danced. She was very firm, no fat at all.

After that we would see each other every day.

She had dark straight hair that she parted in the middle that almost hid her face. Now and then I caught a glimpse of her blue eyes, the longish straight nose, a small mouth and, occasionally, a shy smile. When she smiled she also seemed to look amused. I liked her from the start.

After I told her I was a writer she would turn up at the door with a piece of paper and say. "Do you know this?"

When Spring comes round
If I should be dead,
Flowers will bloom just the same,
And trees will be no less green than they were last Spring,
Reality doesn't need me.

She wouldn't read it aloud. But gave me the paper that she had written it on. It was through Lynn that I got to know the poetry of Pessoa and Osip Mandelstam. She also gave me several paperbacks of Hermann Hesse. I think he was her favourite. But I didn't get very far with Hesse. I didn't try. I don't read much when I'm writing. And I was working on a long story, a novella, and I was often thinking of that even when I wasn't writing.

She would come to see me in the morning, in bare feet, a Hudson Bay blanket draped around her shoulders.

"Walking in bare feet," I said, "that's the quickest way to get a cold."

"It's the way I grew up," she said.

She would light a cigarette and we would have coffee together and talk about writers, books, painters, movies, music, the weather . . .

After the coffee she would go out shopping. She always asked me if I wanted anything. About twice a week I would ask her to get some apples, grapes, tins of soup, salmon, coffee, rye bread (if she was passing Rideau Bakery), or nuts, if she was going near the mall. She always came back with a small white paper bag full of warm nuts from the Nut House. That's another thing we had in common. We both liked nuts.

She also went out every day for walks. And she would come back and tell me what she saw. She didn't tell me right away. There was this reserve – the silences – the shy smile – then she would say:

"I saw some gulls. Against the snow they looked dirty."

Or else I would have to guess what took place when she said,

"I went to the cafeteria at the National Gallery to have a cup of coffee and listened to the conversations around me. People talk a lot of nonsense – don't they?"

"Do you know anyone in Ottawa?"

"Only you," she said.

"Why did you come here, Lynn?"

"I had a quarrel with my boyfriend. He's white. But he works for a black revolutionary organization in Africa. We were together nearly a year. I let my heart rule my head. Because I was in love with him I became interested in politics. Then we had a quarrel. And he left."

"What did you do before?"

"I went to college for a while. Then to Art School. I was trying the wrong things. I left Art School after two years. They were all on an ego trip."

"Can't you go home?"

"There's only my father. We don't get on. He wanted boys. But he got three girls. I'm the eldest."

"How old are you?"

"Twenty-three."

"You're young," I said. "You still have your life ahead of you."

"I don't know," she said. "There are times when I don't see any point –"

I thought, if I was twenty years younger it would be different.

"I'm the wrong person for you," I said.

She didn't say anything. But she appeared at the door more often. And now I found that she began to stay too long. Her visits became more like interruptions. I would say.

"Yes, come in Lynn. But you can't stay too long. I have to do some work."

Finally I said. "I'm sorry Lynn – I'm busy."

She went away. But the next time I became annoyed.

"Lynn – I can't see you. I'm working."

"Work. Work. That's all you do. What's so important about work?"

"Without my work," I said, "I'm nothing."

She walked away, slamming the door.

I didn't see her next morning. But in the afternoon the phone rang.

"Hello."

Silence.

"Hello," I said. "Hello –"

I thought I heard a voice but far away.

"– is that you Lynn?"

Silence.

Then quickly she said. "I'm going to kill myself."

"Where are you?"

"In a phone box – by the Chateau Laurier."

"Stay there. I'll be right over."

I got a taxi on Rideau and saw Lynn inside the phone booth, leaning in a corner with her head down. Her hair hiding her face. I put my arm around her and brought her to the taxi.

"I'm sorry," she said when we were inside her apartment. "I'm all right now. I feel tired. I'll lie down. You can go now."

Next morning she came around for coffee – in her bare feet, the Hudson Bay blanket around her – and we talked as if nothing happened. She asked me if she could do any shopping. Was there anything I wanted mailed.

"No thanks," I said.

When she came back that afternoon from her walk she came back with a small present, a jar of honey, that she wrapped up very neatly in Snoopy wrapping paper.

She left me alone, but not for long. The following day she came around and wanted to talk. We did for a while. Then I had to say. "You'll have to go now. I must get back to work."

She went out. A few minutes later a piece of paper was pushed underneath the door. On it she had written. "I'm going – and I won't come back."

That afternoon I found myself going to the window, looking out to see if I could see her.

She did come back as the light in the park was fading.

"Where did you go?"

"To the Chateau Laurier," she said. "I sat in the lobby and watched people. I did that for an hour. Then I went to the National Gallery and looked at the Monet. Then I walked. I walked until I got cold. So I went into department stores to keep warm. What's wrong with me?"

"Nothing," I said. "Just wait. Time has to go by. Things have to happen."

"You're lucky," she said. "You are doing what you want to do. I don't know what I want to do. I like going out for walks. I like looking at things – paintings, reading books." Tears appeared in her eyes. "Isn't there a place for someone like me?"

I went over and kissed her.

"Yes," she said quietly. "There's always that."

For the next three days it went more or less all right. She still went out for her walks. But instead of telling me about them when she came back, she showed me sketches that she did. Of the market, and people in the market, of people crossing near the cenotaph, of the mall, the frozen Rideau River with the snow, the trees, and the white Minto bridges.

On Friday she came in, around noon, with her sketch-book and a pencil. She wrote something on the paper, tore the piece off, and gave it to me. It said.

"I can't talk."

"Of course you can," I replied.

"No," she wrote. "I woke this morning and I wanted to speak but I couldn't."

"It will come back," I said.

Silence.

"Has this ever happened before?"

"No," she wrote.

Silence.

"I had a letter from my boyfriend," she wrote. "He wants me to come to Toronto."

"Why don't you go."

"Do you think I should," she wrote.

"Yes," I said.

She must have packed before she came to see me for when I saw her again, a half-hour later, she was ready to leave.

"Thanks for talking to me," she said. "You don't know how much all those talks we had meant to me."

And I felt bad. All I could think of was how abrupt I was with her. How little I did give of myself.

I watched her go with her few belongings into a taxi.

A month later I walked to the National Gallery to see the Monet again. And as it was a particularly cold day I decided to go to the Lord Elgin, into Murray's, to have a cup of coffee. The large room was crowded with civil servants having their morning break. I found a seat by a table in a corner. It was pleasantly warm. The coffee was hot. I sat and smoked a small cigar and looked at the lights near the ceiling. They were set in round wooden circles, like wooden crowns. When I noticed a lively group of boys and girls come in. They were talking and joking together. They all looked excited, handsome. Lynn was one of them. Her hair was short. She wore a bright yellow sweater. A tall young man was beside her. And like the others she smiled and laughed a lot.

— • • • —

1. Discuss with a classmate why Levine might have chosen the cliché "the girl next door" for the title of his short story.

2. In a short piece of writing, speculate on why Monet's painting *Waterloo Bridge – The Sun in a Fog, 1903* is described so carefully within the narrative.

3. a) In a small group, draft a character sketch of the narrator, basing your judgments on his description of his interests and activities before Lynn's arrival.
   b) Discuss how the narrator's account of his relationship with Lynn confirms, or fails to confirm, the reader's first impressions of his character.

4. "On Friday she came in, around noon, with her sketch-book and a pencil." In Lynn's voice, write a diary entry for that Friday; describe the events of the day, along with your feelings and deliberations. Compose a second entry, written a month later, that records how your life has changed, your current state of mind, and your reflections on your time on Cobourg Street. Compare your entries with a classmate's. Talk about any discrepancies between them and about the assumptions you made before you assumed Lynn's persona. You may wish to keep the diary entries in your writing folder.

5. Imagine you are going to direct a short film of "The Girl Next Door." Write a synopsis of the plot and a description of the two main characters as you see them. Include your interpretation of the story's conclusion and explain the mood you wish to convey in the film. Present your director's file to your cast and crew (a few of your classmates) and answer any questions they have about your proposal.

from
"MAN AS A FALSE GENERIC"
Casey Miller and Kate Swift

"Development of the Uterus in Rats, Guinea Pigs, and Men"

*G*eneric terms, like *rats* and *guinea pigs* are equally applicable to a class or group and to its individual members. Terms used of a class or group that are not applicable to all its members are false generics. The reason the research-report title quoted above sounds incongruous is that *men* in that context is a false generic. This was not always so.

HISTORICAL BACKGROUND

Ercongota, the daughter of a seventh-century English king, is described in *The Anglo-Saxon Chronicle* as "a wonderful man." In Old English the word *man* meant "person" or "human being," and when used of an individual was equally applicable to either sex. It was parallel to the Latin *homo*, "a member of the human species," not *vir*, "an adult male of the species." English at the time of Ercongota had separate words to distinguish the sexes: *wer* (equivalent to the Latin *vir*) meant "adult male," and *wif* meant "adult female." The combined forms *waepman* and *wifman* meant, respectively, "adult male person" and "adult female person."

In the course of time *wifman* evolved into the modern word *woman*, and *wif* narrowed in meaning to become *wife* as we use that word today. *Man* eventually ceased to be used of individual women and replaced *wer* and *waepman* as a specific term distinguishing an adult male from an adult female. But *man* continued to be used in generalizations about both sexes. As long as most generalizations about people were made by men about men, the ambiguity nestling in this dual usage was either not noticed or thought not to matter.

By the eighteenth century the modern, narrow sense of *man* was firmly established as the predominant one. When Edmund Burke, writing of the French Revolution, used *men* in the old inclusive way, he took pains to spell out his meaning: "Such a deplorable havoc is made in the minds of men (both sexes) in France . . . " Thomas Jefferson did not make the same distinction in declaring that "all men are created equal" and "governments are instituted among men, deriving their just powers from the consent of the governed." In a time when women, having no vote, could neither give nor withhold consent Jefferson had to be using the word *men* in its principal sense of "males," and it probably never occurred to him that anyone would think otherwise.

Current dictionaries still define *man* in both its narrow and broad senses. The Shorter Oxford English Dictionary includes among its definitions: "A human being. Now surviving in general or indefinite applications in the sense 'person' . . . The human creature regarded abstractly" and also "An adult male person." In the New College Edition of the American Heritage Dictionary (1978), the definition is "1. An adult male human being, as distinguished from a female. 2. Any human being, regardless of sex or age; a member of the human race; a person. 3. The human race; mankind . . . " The point at issue, therefore, is whether parts 2 and 3 of that definition are still fully operative or whether the first and exclusive meaning has, in effect, become the only valid one.

Recent studies of college students and school children indicate that the broad definitions of *man* and *men*, although still taught, have to a significant degree become inoperative at a subliminal level. Phrases like *thinking men, men of letters, economic man* and *political man*, or statements like "An Englishman's home is his castle," "Man domesticated animals" and "Man is a dreamer," it turns out, tend to call up images of male people only, not female people or females and males together.

Lexicographers appear to agree. Although they do not label the supposedly generic meaning of *man* obsolete, they write some definitions as though we all know it is. For example, Webster's New Collegiate Dictionary (1979) defines a man-about-town as "a worldly and socially active man." But if *man* sometimes means "any human being," should not the definition of *man-about-town* read "a worldly and socially active person of the male sex"? How can the definers be sure we will know without being told that a man-about-town is never a woman?

Lexicographers are aware, of course, that ever since English lost a specifically male-gender counterpart to *woman*, *man* has been shifting away from generality towards specificity. They also know that the limited meaning of *man* is the only one native speakers of English internalize as applying to an individual. Thus when Diana Nyad swam from Bimini to the Florida coast the news media did not report that

> Marathon swimmer Diana Nyad became the first man to swim the 60 miles from the Bahamas to Florida.

They said, with incidental variations,

> "Marathon swimmer Diana Nyad became the first person to swim . . . "

What lexicographers and grammarians are less attuned to, however, is the extent to which this narrowing is felt. Because gender in modern English corresponds to sex or its absence, native speakers of the language increasingly sense the same contradiction in calling women "men" that they would feel in calling girls "boys" or daughters "sons." In reporting the remark of a member of Congress,

> " 'Every man on this subcommittee is for public works'."

the *Wall Street Journal* appended a comment:

> "There are two women on the subcommittee, and they are for public works, too."

Writers who persist in using *man* in its old sense often slip unconsciously from the general meaning to the limited one. The switch, unfortunately, is rarely discernible to their readers, who have no way of telling that generalizations about human beings have become generalizations about males. Yet we know it does happen – if not how often – because every once in a while an author's unconscious lapse shows through, as in this example from a book review:

> "[T]he book can be read with interest by people who . . . wonder about strange facts: why men speak and animals don't, why man feels so sad in the 20th century, why war is man's greatest pleasure."

Readers who assume that "men speak" and "man feels so sad" refer to all of us are brought up short by the final phrase. Whether war is the greatest pleasure of most men is debatable, but would anyone assert that it is the greatest pleasure of women?

Other lapses are even more revealing. One author, ostensibly generalizing about all human beings, wrote:

> "As for man, he is no different from the rest. His back aches, he ruptures easily, his women have difficulties in childbirth . . . "

If *man* and *he* were truly generic, the parallel phrase would have been

> he has difficulties in childbirth.

And in a magazine article on aggression, where the context also indicated *man* was supposed to include women, readers were startled to come upon the statement

> "[M]an can do several things which the animal cannot do. . . . Eventually, his vital interests are not only life, food, access to females, etc., but also values, symbols, institutions . . . "

In each case the present meaning of *man* had asserted itself, leading the writer to equate the species with its male members.

An article on unemployment difficulties for Catholic workers in Northern Ireland was headlined

"Where one man's religion is another's passport to a job."

Should readers assume that *women* seeking employment in Northern Ireland are not subject to sectarian prejudice?

As we know from modern psychology, man overlooks what he does not want to see – and so does woman. But males may have a greater vested interest in preserving the way things were than in acknowledging the way they are. If the word *man* were not so emotionally charged and politically useful, its ambiguity would have led long ago to its disuse in any but the limited sense it immediately brings to mind. So the question for writers and speakers becomes, how can we get along without *man* in the old sense, that archaic crutch we no longer need but to which we have become habituated?

ALTERNATIVES TO "GENERIC" MAN

" . . . it is now thought that a million years ago and more, earth was populated with more or less man-like creatures, descended not from apes but from some forefather of both apes and men."

"The personal commitment of a man to his skill, the intellectual commitment and the emotional commitment working together as one, has made the Ascent of Man."

"Man has learned a lot. He has invented ever so many things. Someday you may even be able to go and visit the other planets."

Because scientists have traditionally "translated" the Latin term *homo sapiens* as "man" rather than "human being," resistance to giving up this once-generic term is particularly strong in the scientific community. Those who write about anthropology and the biological sciences, including the authors of children's books on these subjects, are frequently addicted to using *man* in contexts like the above. From *near-man* through *early man* to *true man* and *modern man*, accounts of human evolution are couched in terms of *mankind* and *forefathers*, with frequent references to "his" cultural artifacts, the effect of erect posture in enabling "him" to see further, "his" animals, crops, pottery, villages and so on.

For initial broadcasting in 1981 the BBC announced a major new series called "The Making of Mankind" (sic). A Sunday newspaper called it:

> "A grand anthropological sweep, tracing man's origins. . . . The controversy concerns the date and manner of man's emergence from the apes."

Then, ironically, comes this revelation:

> "Central to [the] dispute is 'Lucy' . . . [about 3.5 million years old and with] both ape-like qualities and some human-like features . . . she was the best evidence that man had evolved 'recently'."

Had the writer of this piece been absolutely comfortable with "man" as a generic term then it is unlikely he would have needed to switch to "human-like" when looking directly at Lucy. But then why not use *human* throughout? Or one of the other choices below:

> "The Making of Humanity" *or* "The Beginning of Human Life" *or* "Our First Ancestors";

then

> A grand anthropological sweep, tracing the origins of human

beings . . . the controversy concerns the date and manner of our human ancestors' (*or* human beings') emergence from the apes.

An image entirely different from that elicited by the Sunday newspaper is projected in a story headlined "New Clues to Ancient Life" published in the newsletter *Indian Affairs*. Reporting on archaeological findings at the Koster site in Illinois, the writer, instead of relying on *man*, used terms like "people" and "ancient people," "residents of the ancient village," "the site's inhabitants," and "these early human populations." The newsletter is a model of non-biased writing, and its commitment is evidently shared by the leader of the Koster exploration, archaeologist Stuart Struever, who is quoted in the article:

> "If we are to measure 'cultural success' in part by the ability of a human population to establish an equilibrium with its environment that can be sustained over the long haul, then these Koster residents were successful people, indeed."

Used in broad, sweeping generalizations, *man* frequently – perhaps usually – conveys misinformation.

> "When ancient man developed agriculture . . ."

rejects, as far as a listener or reader has any way of knowing, the extensive evidence now available indicating that women were the earliest cultivators of plants.

> "Men have always hoped to conquer disease."

not only appears to disregard women's interest in ending illness but also to ignore the important advances toward that goal made by women – from the anonymous healers and discoverers of curative plants to Nobel laureates. Authenticity is better served by phrases like

When our ancestors (*or* people *or* human beings *or* our forebears) first developed agriculture . . .

Human societies (*or* Men and women *or* Women and men) have always hoped to conquer disease.

Sometimes the best solution is to rephrase a thought completely:

The conquest of disease has always been a goal of human societies.

The statement

"It is not man as an animal with sexual and aggressive drives who appears in the [Lacanian] theory, but man as the language user"

could be rephrased

It is not as animals with sexual and aggressive drives that we appear in the [Lacanian] theory, but as language users.

Writing of Tasmanian aboriginals of mixed descent, a journalist warned us:

"Their whole human status is at stake because they are treated as invisible men, as ghosts, who have through some inexplicable inadvertence slipped over the rim of the globe."

How much less visible are the women, a situation which could have been retrieved by the simple substitution of *people* for *men*.

The historian Mary Beard pointed out many years ago that most historians use *man* in ways that obscure women's contributions to civilization; unfortunately they, and others, continue to do so. The list of books with titles like *The Condition of Man, The Identity of Man, Man's*

Unconquerable Mind, The Family of Man, Man and the Universe, The Tree Where Man Was Born, and *Mars and the Mind of Man* appears to be endless. The popular writer Peter Farb, an anthropologist and linguist who once wrote a book called *Man's Rise to Civilization as Shown by the Indians of North America,* has apparently had second thoughts about what such titles imply. He called a later book *Humankind.*

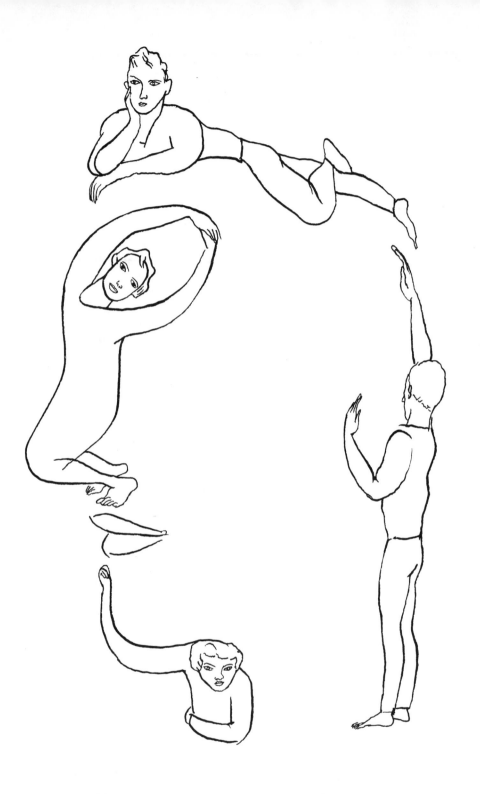

THE WEB OF OUR LIFE

The phrase "The web of our life," although it was written by Shakespeare *(All's Well That Ends Well),* has a modern ring to it. On the one hand, the image suggests the innumerable and tangled strands of each person's experiences. On the other, it corresponds to the contemporary view of society as a vast system or network in which people are connected to one another in a myriad of ways – as family, friends, consumers, workers, and as national and global citizens. The selections here include a whimsical description of a community on holiday, a poignant story of conflict within a family, a tale of cross-cultural identification, and a carefully reasoned argument about the responsibility of the writer in today's world. We hope that these pieces, and the others, will give you an impression of the variety of the roles and relationships in the web of our life, an impression you are encouraged to supplement with incidents from your own experience.

"I bend but do not break." – *Jean de la Fontaine*

With a classmate, brainstorm for and record the names of characters from literature who are distinguished by their refusal to bend. Hagar, of *The Stone Angel*, and King Lear are two names to start with. State what effects their determination has on their lives and the lives of those around them.

A WEST COAST WOMAN
Jan Hopaklyissumqwa Gould

ou will not bury him at Saqwiss. He lost the right." My Grandfather was shouting, his face was twisted up, he was that mad. "He lost it all."

"But you're his Grandfather," shrieked Sadie. "I'm his sister. Did you forget?"

"I tell you he lost it all. When he went to work for that Jensen Logging, he lost it all. Take him away. Throw him in the Pass. Let the seals get a bite. That's what he's worth."

And then they both started shouting. All their words got mixed up together. Yes, Sadie, little Sadie, she was in some white boat that guy at Tahsis let her have to carry the coffin down the Inlet. Yes, they were shouting so loud that even the ravens took off.

I never saw Sadie like that before. No, she was like that pool – the sacred pool, the one our Grandfather went to before he was old . . . when he took his thoughts to the Maker. Yes, that pool was where my Great Uncle Joe got his spirit power. You had to clean yourself real good, had to rub the fir and cedar boughs up and down your bones and then you got into that cold, cold pool.

We went up there once when I was twelve, all my brothers and Sadie. We went with my Grandfather. It was some ride. We went in his fishboat, the Twin Sisters, yes. Right down the Inlet and to the Point, past Tahanees Rock and into Cook Bay and through the woods. Then we had to go up that mountain. I was so tired. Oh, I was tired. And I was so thirsty. There was yuk╵╌ṛa, yes, that's what you white people call salal. That was there, lots of berries so I ate those. But my legs hurt. It was so far. And we went up and up and up. Then we came to this wood with the stream running through it and then hit big pool. It was so big – but I was little and I could have dived right into it because I was so tired. It was beautiful. Like a huge mirror. And we sat around it and my Grandfather talked a lot about the old ways. I looked down into it and I thought I would see myself there. Only what I saw was Sadie. Yes, little Sadie, it was her eyes looking back at me. She was like the pool – still, always at peace.

Yes, Sadie, she was like the pool. Always like that. Not Mark, he was real steamed up, like that little hotsprings near Cook Cove. Sure – only he didn't let it last long. Like that time he was deckhand with that Norwegian guy and they got into some fight at a party and sliced each other up a bit. The RCMP came, they went to court but the magistrate, he just shook his head. They told him they didn't know why they were fighting. They didn't remember and they were good friends. That magistrate, he shook his head a lot and then he fined them both.

Mark was smart. He went to the University for a year. People wanted him to become a lawyer or maybe to work at the Museum. Only he got back fishing, then he went logging and he said he liked it where he was, thank you all. But he got busy and made some of those big logging companies clean up the streams, made them pay damages to us sometimes. And he went over to Jensen Logging to talk about all this and Jensen hired him. Hired a lot of Indians. And he had a good camp with Tee-Vees and a cook came from some place like Paris and they had mobile homes. My brother Simon, he went there, too. But then the Government Project got going and it was all Indian. My other brothers, they went there and Simon's wife kept making noises so he quit Jensen's and went to the Government Project. And suddenly there was all this fighting. Some of the Reserve people said everyone should leave Jensen Logging and work for the Government Project because it was all Indian. Mark, he refused. He said Jensen was fair and good. And he said the Government Project wasn't going to last long. And it didn't have no good mechanic like Jensen did – they had Johnny Amos.

So there we were . . . divided. Half of the people wanted everyone working for the Government Project and half for Jensen Logging. Then people got mad and we had fights a lot. Some of the men working for Jensen were married into families who were working for the Government Project and things got real bad. The Government Camp had this accident. Stephen Smith got killed. It was the last log being loaded onto one of the trucks and it came down and crushed him. He was sixteen. They buried him in a new suit and some special fancy shirt with lace. And it got worse on the Reserve with no mahmuckmee – none of you white people – coming here. Oh the priest did, but not those guys from Tahsis not even Peter Buckington who's married to the Chief's daughter.

There was just Mark and Damien Callicum working for Jensen when Mark got killed in some rockslide when he was falling with one of Jensen's sons. Oh that was bad. Real bad. They said you couldn't recognize the Jensen boy he was just bits and pieces in the rock but Mark they knew, by his hair. And they had this real big funeral at Zeballos. I went, my great-aunt came from Queen's Cove, my great-uncle came from Alberni. And all my cousins came from Ahousat but my Grandfather, no he wouldn't come. My brothers didn't come. Sadie, she gave this real good speech about Mark. She said he always wanted what was right for everyone. Mr. Jensen, he tried to talk, but he was too sad. But they took that Jensen boy's coffin some place before they all went to some coffee party. Sadie she kept Mark's coffin in that hall we used. She said she would stay with it all night in case her Grandfather came over. Only, I know he would not. He was too mad because Mark worked for Jensen.

It was the next day Sadie came to the Reserve.

"I want his camera," she said, "to put on the grave."

Mark used to take pictures of our Elders, he had two books full of them in my Grandfather's house.

"You don't need his camera. He's not Indian any more – he's nothing. He shoulda worked for the Project," stormed my Grandfather and suddenly his voice softened. "Sadie . . . little Sadie, just get on your way."

Sadie sat down then in the prow of the boat. Her voice was like those little waves that pat the beach before the big wash from some freighter comes in. "I will bury him where he belongs. He never stopped being Indian. He was proud of it."

And then my Grandfather started shouting and so did she so I ran between the boat and my Grandfather, standing on the dock while all the kids came running out. I told them about the spawning stream that got all choked up with wood chips and how the trees near that stream acted. It was the story my Grandfather told us when we were real young. The trees that bent to that flood, they lived and grew strong. The ones that didn't bend at all, they were broke off and carried away.

"Stop fighting, Mark cannot hear you now," I said. And for a minute, my Grandfather looked upset. He walked away. I told Sadie to bury Mark at Zeballos for the time being. That later, everything would quieten down.

"Later?" she said. "Later, Martha? We are his sisters. It must be done now . . . ." And she left.

I walked over to where my Grandfather stood, bent a little, his bad leg bothering him some, his scarred old fisherman's hands curled up like hooks. He stared at Magic Island where the old stands of yellow cedar are and didn't speak. I could see the white boat getting smaller and smaller. Then it was real quiet and it was cold on the Reserve. Like when the fog comes in and say someone's sick and the planes can't get in or out, that's how it was, like a bad, bad fog covering the Reserve.

It was real fog we had the next day so my Grandfather and Norma Amos put off going to Saqwiss. They talked of keeping Sadie out, making sure that she didn't take Mark there. And the fog rolled in. I wondered where Sadie was. I thought of her as she sat in the boat, like a Nootka Princess, calm at first. Real pretty, too. Sure, she was wearing jeans and boots, yes, and one of those thick shirts. She's a West Coast woman. Who's going to wear high heels and those Department Store dresses up here when you're going over docks and log booms? There's no roads here on the Reserves, no Tee-Vee. Sadie's not gonna wear high heels or sit in some fancy car.

The fog lifted a bit and some of our men came in from the Project in the tribal boat. They heard that Mark's coffin was still in the white boat someplace and that Sadie had found the old rifle, the hunting gun my Grandfather gave Mark. And they said Sadie was sitting in some coffee shop talking and crying a lot with some of the guys who worked for Jensen.

It was a real light night with the full moon and I heard later that Sadie and two guys from Jensen's camp went over to Saqwiss before more fog rolled in. Sadie told them she wanted to stay one night, that it was the Indian way so they left her there, then they had to wait a full day to go get her and they couldn't find her so they came over here and Simon went with them.

They found Mark's coffin which had been carved by the men over at the Jensen camp and they said it was really something. They had carved out a whaling canoe on the lid. And the old hunting gun wasn't there but there were some pieces of red cedar bark which Mark used when he was dancing at Potlatches and his watch, that was on the coffin. Yes, that's our way. My Grandmother, when she was buried there, we put her sewing machine on the grave.

Simon tracked through the long grass into the woods and he found Sadie, little Sadie, by one of the cedars with the gun by her side. She must have made some deal with someone because there were three new bullets left in the pocket of her flannel shirt. She had had to do it two times. Yes, two times. And Simon carried her into the tribal boat and brought her here and I cleaned her up. We had the funeral right here with one of the priests who used to come and play crib with my Grandfather, only my Grandfather didn't come. He took off to the woods. For two days. He came back stiff with a real bad cold, too.

But all those people came to that funeral and we had all the boats, fishing boats, the tribal boat, the little boats, all of them made a procession when we took Sadie to Saqwiss.

And even Jensen came and his wife and some men from that boat came. And Jensen cried and cried, yes, he's got his big belly and no hair and he's a tough guy – but he cried.

My Grandfather, he went to bed when he came out of those woods. He's there a lot. He doesn't play crib with the priest and he doesn't talk much. Simon says he has lost his power and some of his brains. And the Indian Project ended when the Government ran out of money so all our men were sitting on the Reserve all day, getting bored.

The last time I took the kids over to Saqwiss they asked me why it all happened. I told them the old story about the stream being jammed and the flood and then the trees bending and some not bending and dying. That Grandfather and Sadie were like those trees that didn't bend. The kids thought about this but then Josie, that's my big girl, she saw this otter floating on its back so all the kids forgot about the graves. They went running and running through that tall grass and right down to the sea.

---

1. a) With a classmate, examine the narrative method employed by Gould, with particular attention to point of view, voice, and the narrator's audience.
   b) The time-frame of Gould's story is complicated, especially given the brevity of the tale. In point form, outline the progress of the narrative as it moves from time to time. Compare your outline with those of two other classmates, discuss any differences, and reconcile them in a polished outline, upon which you all agree.
   c) In a short expository piece, explain the purpose of the story-within-a-story of Martha's trip to the mountain pool. Your explanation should suggest how the episode relates to the rest of the story.

2. In a small group, analyse the conflict between Sadie and her grandfather, determining the reasons for its tragic outcome.

3. a) In a piece of personal writing, respond to the final paragraph of the story.
   b) Compare your reaction with that of a classmate and, together, assess in particular the effect of the final image.

4. a) In the voice of Mr. Jensen, write a letter to Grandfather expressing your feelings about the deaths of Mark and Sadie and attempting to console him.
   b) Exchange letters with a classmate and edit one another's work. Underline, in particular, any clichéd expressions of condolence.

Together, rewrite the expressions in more original language. Put both drafts of your letter in your writing folder.

5. If you have read Sophocles' *Antigone*, write an introductory paragraph for a comparative essay on the similarities between that Greek tragedy and "A West Coast Woman." Make an outline to show how you would develop your comparison and organize the essay.

gei•sha *n.* [Japan.], a Japanese professional
singing and dancing girl – *Webster's New
World Dictionary*

In a small group, jot down everything you
know about the geisha – their dress, their
roles, their training, and so on. Speculate, as
well, on how a girl might become a geisha,
and on what the course of her life might be
like. Compare your ideas with Lafcadio
Hearn's description of the geisha's life in
turn-of-the-century Japan.

OF A DANCING-GIRL
Lafcadio Hearn

Nothing is more silent than the beginning of a Japanese banquet;
and no one, except a native, who observes the opening scene
could possibly imagine the tumultuous ending.

The robed guests take their places, quite noiselessly and without
speech, upon the kneeling-cushions. The lacquered services are laid
upon the matting before them by maidens whose bare feet make no
sound. For a while there are only smiling and flitting, as in dreams.
You are not likely to hear any voices from without, as a banqueting-
house is usually secluded from the street by spacious gardens. At last
the master of ceremonies, host or provider, breaks the hush with the
consecrated formula, *"O-somatsu degozarimasu ga! – dōzo o-hashi!"* where-
at all present bow silently, take up their *hashi* (chopsticks), and fall to.
But hashi, deftly used, cannot be heard at all. The maidens pour warm
saké into the cup of each guest without making the least sound; and it
is not until several dishes have been emptied, and several cups of saké
absorbed, that tongues are loosened.

Then, all at once, with a little burst of laughter, a number of young
girls enter, make the customary prostration of greeting, glide into the
open space between the ranks of the guests, and begin to serve the
wine with a grace and dexterity of which no common maid is capable.

They are pretty; they are clad in very costly robes of silk; they are girdled like queens; and the beautifully dressed hair of each is decked with fresh flowers, with wonderful combs and pins, and with curious ornaments of gold. They greet the stranger as if they had always known him; they jest, laugh, and utter funny little cries. These are the *geisha*, or dancing-girls, hired for the banquet.

Samisen – guitars of three strings – tinkle. The dancers withdraw to a clear space at the farther end of the banqueting-hall, always vast enough to admit of many more guests than ever assemble upon common occasions. Some form the orchestra, under the direction of a woman of uncertain age; there are several samisen, and a tiny drum played by a child. Others, singly or in pairs, perform the dance. It may be swift and merry, consisting wholly of gracious posturing, and girls dancing together with such coincidence of step and gesture as only years of training could render possible. But more frequently it is rather like acting than like what we Occidentals call dancing, – acting accompanied with extraordinary waving of sleeves and fans, and with a play of eyes and features, sweet, subtle, subdued, wholly Oriental.

There are more voluptuous dances known to geisha, but upon ordinary occasions and before refined audiences they portray beautiful old Japanese traditions, like the legend of the fisher Urashima, beloved by the Sea God's daughter; and at intervals they sing ancient Chinese poems, expressing a natural emotion with delicious vividness by a few exquisite words. And always they pour the wine, – that warm, pale yellow, sleepy wine which fills the veins with soft contentment, making a faint sense of ecstasy, through which, as through some poppied sleep, the commonplace becomes wondrous and blissful, and the geisha Maids of Paradise and the world much sweeter than, in the natural order of things, it could ever possibly be.

The banquet, at first so silent, slowly changes to a merry tumult. The company break ranks, form groups; and from group to group the girls pass, laughing, prattling, – still pouring saké into the cups which are being exchanged and emptied with low bows. Men begin to sing old samurai songs, old Chinese poems. One or two even dance. A geisha tucks her robe well up to her knees; and the samisen strike up the quick melody, "*Kompira funé-funé.*" As the music plays, she begins to run lightly and swiftly in a figure of 8, and a young man, carrying a saké bottle and cup, also runs in the same figure of 8. If the two meet on a line, the one through whose error the meeting happens must drink a cup of saké. The music becomes quicker and quicker, and the runners run faster and faster, for they must keep time to the melody: and the geisha wins. In another part of the room, guests and geisha are playing *ken*. They sing as they play, facing each other, and clap their hands, and fling out their fingers at intervals with little cries; and the samisen keep time.

Now, to play ken with a geisha requires a perfectly cool head, a quick eye, and much practice. Having been trained from childhood to play all kinds of ken, – and there are many, – she generally loses only for politeness, when she loses at all. The signs of the most common ken are a Man, a Fox, and a Gun. If the geisha makes the sign of the Gun, you must instantly, and in exact time to the music, make the sign of the Fox, who cannot use the Gun. For if you make the sign of the Man, then she will answer with the sign of the Fox, who can bewitch the Man, and you lose. And if she makes the sign of the Fox first, then you should make the sign of the Gun, by which the Fox can be killed. But all the while you must watch her bright eyes and supple hands. These are pretty: and if you suffer yourself, just for one fraction of a second, to think how pretty they are, you are bewitched and vanquished.

Notwithstanding all this apparent comradeship, a certain rigid decorum between guest and geisha is invariably preserved at a Japanese banquet. However flushed with wine a guest may have become, you will never see him attempt to caress a girl; he never forgets that she appears at the festivities only as a human flower, to be looked at, not to be touched. The familiarity which foreign tourists in Japan frequently permit themselves with geisha or with waiter-girls, though endured with smiling patience, is considered by native observers an evidence of extreme vulgarity.

For a time the merriment grows; but as midnight draws near, the guests begin to slip away, one by one, unnoticed. Then the din gradually dies down, the music stops; and at last the geisha, having escorted the latest of the feasters to the door, with laughing cries of *Sayōnara*, can sit down alone to break their long fast in the deserted hall.

Such is the geisha's role. But what is the mystery of her? What are her thoughts, her emotions, her secret self? What is her veritable existence beyond the night circle of the banquet lights, far from the illusion formed around her by the mist of wine? Is she always as mischievous as she seems while her voice ripples out with mocking sweetness the words of an ancient song?

Always in the dwelling which a band of geisha occupy, there is a strange image placed in the alcove. Sometimes it is of clay, rarely of gold, most commonly of porcelain. It is reverenced: offerings are made to it, sweetmeats and rice-bread and wine; incense smoulders in front of it, and a lamp is burned before it. It is the image of a kitten erect, one paw outstretched as if inviting, – whence its name, "the Beckoning Kitten." It is the *genius loci*: it brings good fortune, the patronage of the rich, the favour of banquet-givers. Now, they who know the soul of the geisha aver that the semblance of the image is the semblance of herself, – playful and pretty, soft and young, lithe and caressing, and cruel as a devouring fire.

Worse, also, than this they have said of her: that in her shadow treads the God of Poverty, and that the Fox-Women are her sisters;

that she is the ruin of youth, the waster of fortunes, the destroyer of families; that she knows love only as the source of the follies which are her gain, and grows rich upon the substance of men whose graves she has made; that she is the most consummate of pretty hypocrites, the most dangerous of schemers, the most insatiable of mercenaries, the most pitiless of mistresses. This cannot all be true. Yet thus much is true, – that, like the kitten, the geisha is by profession a creature of prey.

The geisha is only what she has been made in answer to foolish human desire for the illusion of love mixed with youth and grace, but without regrets or responsibilities: wherefore she has been taught, besides ken, to play at hearts. Now, the eternal law is that people may play with impunity at any game in this unhappy world except three, which are called Life, Love, and Death. Those the gods have reserved to themselves, because nobody else can learn to play them without doing mischief. Therefore, to play with a geisha any game much more serious than ken, or at least *go*, is displeasing to the gods.

The girl begins her career as a slave, a pretty child bought from miserably poor parents under a contract, according to which her services may be claimed by the purchasers for eighteen, twenty, or even twenty-five years. She is fed, clothed, and trained in a house occupied only by geisha; and she passes the rest of her childhood under severe discipline. She is taught etiquette, grace, polite speech; she has daily lessons in dancing; and she is obliged to learn by heart a multitude of songs with their airs. Also she must learn games, the service of banquets and weddings, the art of dressing and looking beautiful. Whatever physical gifts she may have are carefully cultivated. Afterwards she is taught to handle musical instruments: first, the little drum (*tsudzumi*), which cannot be sounded at all without considerable practice; then she learns to play the samisen a little, with a plectrum of tortoiseshell or ivory. At eight or nine years of age she attends banquets, chiefly as a drum-player. She is then the most charming little creature imaginable, and already knows how to fill your wine-cup exactly full, with a single toss of the bottle and without spilling a drop, between two taps of her drum.

Thereafter her discipline becomes more cruel. Her voice may be flexible enough, but lacks the requisite strength. In the iciest hours of winter nights, she must ascend to the roof of her dwelling-house, and there sing and play till the blood oozes from her fingers and the voice dies in her throat. The desired result is an atrocious cold. After a period of hoarse whispering, her voice changes its tone and strengthens. She is ready to become a public singer and dancer.

In this capacity she usually makes her first appearance at the age of twelve or thirteen. If pretty and skillful, her services will be much in demand, and her time paid for at the rate of twenty to twenty-five *sen* per hour. Then only do her purchasers begin to reimburse themselves for the time, expense, and trouble of her training; and they are not apt to be generous. For many years more all that she earns must pass into their hands. She can own nothing, not even her clothes.

At seventeen or eighteen she has made her artistic reputation. She has been at many hundreds of entertainments, and knows by sight all the important personages of her city, the character of each, the history of all. Her life has been chiefly a night life; rarely has she seen the sun rise since she became a dancer. She has learned to drink wine without ever losing her head, and to fast for seven or eight hours without ever feeling the worse. She has had many lovers. To a certain extent she is free to smile upon whom she pleases; but she has been well taught, above all else, to use her power of charm for her own advantage. She hopes to find somebody able and willing to buy her freedom.

At this point of her career we may leave the geisha: thereafter her story is apt to prove unpleasant, unless she dies young. Should that happen, she will have the obsequies of her class, and her memory will be preserved by divers curious rites.

Some time, perhaps, while wandering through Japanese streets at night, you hear sounds of music, a tinkling of samisen floating through the great gateway of a Buddhist temple, together with shrill voices of singing girls; which may seem to you a strange happening. And the deep court is thronged with people looking and listening. Then, making your way through the press to the temple steps, you see two geisha seated upon the matting within, playing and singing, and a third dancing before a little table. Upon the table is an *ihai*, or mortuary tablet; in front of the tablet burns a little lamp, and incense in a cup of bronze; a small repast has been placed there, fruits and dainties, – such a repast as, upon festival occasions, it is the custom to offer to the dead. You learn that the *kaimyō* upon the tablet is that of a geisha; and that the comrades of the dead girl assemble in the temple on certain days to gladden her spirit with songs and dances. Then whosoever pleases may attend the ceremony free of charge.

———————————————◆•◆•◆◀———————————————

1. a) With a classmate, share your impressions of the geisha's life as Hearn describes it. Together, create a list of five words that best represent your impressions. Exchange lists with another pair, discussing any differences in your responses.
   b) You have been asked to communicate the gist of Hearn's essay to a class of younger students. Condense the piece into a version you could read aloud in one or two minutes. Ask a classmate to listen to your version as you read it and to evaluate whether you have communicated the most important aspects of Hearn's essay in an appropriate manner.

2. For your writing folder, write a poem on the geisha, using the kitten as its central image.

3. Hearn's essay is divided into three sections. In your notebook, suggest a suitable subtitle or heading for each and, in one sentence per section, comment on the smoothness of the transitions between sections. Compare your analysis with a classmate's and speculate together on the logic behind the structure of the essay.

4. Do some research to find out how the traditions and life of the geisha have changed between Hearn's time (he wrote the article in 1899) and our own.
OR
Investigate the life of Lafcadio Hearn.
In either case, present the information you collect in the form of a brief afterword to "Of a Dancing-Girl," which could be written on a single page or ditto master to be duplicated and shared with your classmates.

"Travel, in the younger sort, is a part of education . . . " – *Francis Bacon*

With a few of your classmates, discuss the ways in which travel may provide learning experiences different from those you encounter in school. If you have any anecdotes about things you have learned while travelling, share them with your group.

JUST A LITTLE JAPANESE
Eric Patrick

My knees were aching as I leaned forward in the lotus position and fumbled with my chopsticks to pick up a slice of raw horse meat. The Japanese call it sashimi; I call it disgusting. The cold, fleshy taste remained in my mouth long after I downed a shot glass of warm sake. I swallowed hard and dug into some squid. The rubber-like meat slipped through my chopsticks and fell into the boiling miso soup. Scalding hot broth spattered all over my kimono.

I looked around the sushi shop which was to be my home for the next six weeks. The contrasts struck me repeatedly. Across the low burl table sat my host mother in her traditional silk kimono taking hamburgers out of the Panasonic microwave. In the corner of the room my host sister, wearing a Mickey Mouse T-shirt, was praying to the family shrine. My host brother, in the meantime, was watching Saturday Night Sumo Wrestling on a large-screen t.v. I cringed every time the giants collided; bone meeting bone, muscle to muscle, fat to fat.

I lay back on the tatami floor, stretched my legs out painfully, and shut my eyelids tight, trying to assimilate all the exotic new sights, sounds, and smells. "Am I actually here?" I wondered. Only twenty-four hours before I had been eating normal food on a normal table in a normal room. But this was normal, for the Japanese. "How extraordinary!" I thought, "What an opportunity, this exchange." I wondered how many people could say that they had ever been to Japan, let alone lived with Japanese families.

I remembered my visions of an ancient, feudal Japan; the romantic misconceptions held by most of the starry-eyed students who had flown with me to Tokyo. "Beep. Beep." I glanced at my Seiko digital watch. The Japan of kimono-clad geishas and armour-clad samurai faded into an industrial reality.

Toyota and Toshiba. Casio and Canon. Mitsubishi and Minolta. The world of *Shogun* could never be realized; it had long since disappeared, existing now only in western imagination. I looked back up. My "brother," Anike, was motioning for me to stand up. Time to go to bed. I would sleep upstairs tonight.

The following morning my "sister" informed me that I was to watch an Obon festival in Aizu-Wakamats, a nearby town. Obon is the season of the dead, a week in early August when everyone in Japan is supposed to return to their family shrine in order to pay homage to their ancestors. "Terrific!" I thought, "I'm certainly glad I am getting a chance to see a few of the older traditions." We set out for the Aizu-Wakamats Grand Hotel, a quaint old place which, as it turned out, fell rather short of its ostentatious title.

The lobby was filled with parade participants putting finishing touches on each other's white painted faces. My "mother" walked straight to the reception desk where she obtained a neatly folded kimono after a brief exchange with the clerk. She motioned for me to come to the desk. The clerk, a small, pretty girl, leaned forward and then suddenly blurted out in broken English, "Please remove your clothes." I looked at her, dismayed, and then turned to my "mother," who nodded her head and tapped an impatient finger on her watch. "What?" I exclaimed. "There is no way you are getting me to take my clothes off!" My mother took the kimono, unfolded it carefully, and held it up against me. "Ah! Walkarooh – I understand." I sighed. It barely reached below my waist. "I wonder why they want me to change?" I thought. The clerk tapped me on the shoulder and pointed toward the washrooms.

I slowly undid the buttons of my short-sleeved shirt, stepped out of my running shoes, and slid off my jeans.

I took the kimono in hand, running the rough, heavy material between my thumb and forefinger. I swung the kimono over my shoulders and slipped my arms through the large, hanging sleeves. I shook my shoulders. I felt strange in these clothes. And yet there was something almost familiar about this kimono. "Really rather striking," I thought, admiring myself in the mirror. "It suits me very well."

I tied the thin blue obe around my waist in an irregular knot and strutted out the door. My "mother" looked me up and down with a critical eye, retied the obe around my hips, pulled the kimono tighter together, and then after an approving nod motioned for me to follow her. We left the hotel and walked along the central street, passing various groups of dancers preparing for the festivities. She pointed out a group of men who were dressed in short blue kimonos similar to mine, and sporting thin red headbands. I followed them along the street to a narrow dirt path which led up to an old wooden temple. A thin, bearded priest wearing black flowing robes and a purple, cardinal-like headpiece was standing on the steps of the temple. A glade of tall maples stood like silent sentinels around the temple perimeter.

The priest yelled a call, turned, and ascended the steps, followed by the sixteen men in kimonos. He slid open the large, highly-decorated doors and disappeared along with the men into the temple. Soon he reappeared at the head of four, thick, evenly-spaced bamboo poles, each supported by two of the men. As the men marched out of the darkness and down the top of the steps, the large wooden shrine they were bearing came into sight. It was ornately carved, covered with purple and gold decorative plates, and capped by a black lacquered cupola. Finally, the last eight polebearers emerged. The shrine was carried down the steps and placed on the dew-covered grass at the foot of the temple. The priest stepped forward, and all the men bowed, their hands placed together in front of their faces, as he blessed them in an ancient ritual. I looked on in silence, completely absorbed in a ceremony which had been performed for centuries, embodying the very essence of Japan's rich cultural heritage.

When the ceremony was completed the men took their respective places around the poles. One man, at the front far-left pole, beckoned me over. He stepped forward, flashed a childish grin, and slowly undid his red headband. I raised an eyebrow. He handed me the piece of cloth, which I accepted, quite unsure of what to do. He then reached out and patted the vacated portion of the pole. I pointed to myself, with a questioning look. He nodded and smiled. I laughed excitedly. "Me? I'm going to be in the festival?" I couldn't believe what was happening. "Wow!" I exclaimed, "This is just too incredible. I am getting a chance to see the festival from the inside out!"

I pulled back my hair and tied the headband neatly 'round my brow. I took my position under the front of the pole, bending my 198-cm frame almost double while the others had only to bend their knees. With one tremendous effort we lifted the shrine on our shoulders and started on our way, kicking up a fine cloud of dust as we shuffled along the winding dirt path in our getas chanting a traditional Japanese festival song. The man to my right would yell "Watashee!", which all the others then echoed in unison. My colleagues were singing with enthusiasm, with emotion, with a real heart-felt gusto. The spirit and soul of Japan, I discovered, normally veiled by a neatly-tailored three-piece business suit, was beginning to reveal itself.

We reached the end of the path and moved around a parked Toyota Corolla onto the central street. We lifted the shrine off our shoulders and lowered it slowly onto two movable wooden supports which another man always carried along behind.

I straightened myself up and then rubbed my shoulder, quite sore by now. We stood around in a group, waiting for the rest of the parade to reach us. Those who knew any English practised it out on me. "Me standard, you giant!" one man exclaimed, laughingly.

"Oh no. In Japan me giant, but in Canada, me baby!" I replied with mock seriousness. "My friends . . . " I looked up and around. This ignited a veritable hurricane of unintelligible Japanese. Our "conversation," however, was soon interrupted by the approach of various groups of dancers. Women wearing brightly coloured and patterned kimonos, their hair done up in traditional styles, did graceful and complicated movements to the beat of the giant kodo drums. Presently we wrestled the shrine up onto our shoulders and joined in the parade.

We danced our way along the crowded streets, swinging back and forth sideways as much as ahead. The townspeople, some of them wearing "Superman" or "I love California" T-shirts, and others in their traditional garb, lined the sidewalks, often spilling out into the street. Little children stopped, pointed, and shouted excitedly before turning and clinging to the familiar and reassuring folds of their mothers' kimonos as I passed them by. Everyone, in fact, looked on in utter disbelief, glancing around to confirm what they saw before laughing and then shouting encouragement. I stared back in equal disbelief, looking around to confirm what I saw. "Here I am," I thought, "dancing through the streets of a tiny town in northern Japan, parading a gilded shrine with fifteen other kimono-clad men in an ancient festival which I know nothing about!" And yet I did know something about it. But not in an academic sense. Rather, in a spiritual sense. I was beginning to understand the timeless values and beliefs enshrined in this celebration; was taking a privileged look behind the industrial façade at the Japan which had developed since prehistory, and which no amount of modernization could ever destroy, as it lives on in the hearts of the people who perpetuate such traditions.

By now I was becoming exhausted. The extra weight which I was bearing because of my height was beginning to take its toll. A man ahead of us was walking backwards, swinging a gigantic red fan by its two-metre bamboo pole to the beat of the kodo drums. With each and every step I felt as though I could not take another, and yet with every resuscitating breath of fan-forced air I managed to coax my body forward once again. Finally, we were able to put the shrine down. We then turned around, and grabbing the poles underhand, hurled the shrine up into the air with one tremendous heave. With that the crowd broke, rushing out onto the street and practically mobbing us. Men, women, and children offered us cups of warm sake, which I accepted eagerly in order to dull the sharp pain in my shoulder. As I was the centre of attention, nearly everyone flocked around me, and before long the pain in my shoulder was very well dulled indeed.

We heaved the shrine up onto our shoulders for the last stretch of the parade. We were all exhausted as we stumbled along, sweat beading on our brows to be absorbed by our often-wrung headbands, kimonos hanging open, expending every last ounce of energy just to keep one foot ahead of the other. The blood-red sun hung heavily over the distant horizon as our rag-tag entourage struggled uphill towards the temple which was to be our final destination. By now the crowds had disappeared and I cast a tired glance at the empty sidewalk and shuttered shops which lined our path.

Fatigue overcame a number of men, and only thirteen of us were left to bear the extra load. I was suffering from sporadic cramps in my legs, and the pain in my shoulder was such that I knew I could not continue on much longer. "Watashee!" I yelled hoarsely, resurrecting the chant which we had first set out singing. The rest of the men echoed my cry as we staggered forward, driven on by sheer force of will, by the oneness we felt as a group, and by the burden of responsibility we had accepted in bearing the shrine and all the traditions it embodied. We had only a few more steps until we reached the temple. "Watashee!" I screamed. "Watashee! Watashee! Watashee!" we chanted together before collapsing at the foot of the temple.

The sun was now completely eclipsed by the undulating lines of the horizon. We stretched out all over the temple steps, laughing and joking and downing more sake. I looked at my shoulder. It was covered in dry, sticky blood. I didn't care.

My "mother" was waiting for me in the lobby of the hotel. She looked me up and down, winced, and then commented to the clerk. I wandered into the bathroom and took a good look at myself in the mirror. My hair was hanging over my headband and my kimono was hanging open. My face was flushed, and a trickle of dried blood ran down my left arm. I looked as though I had been thrown in the ring with a couple of sumo wrestlers and told to keep them apart. I slowly undid my obe, folded it, and placed it on the counter. I withdrew first my left and then my right arm from the long, hanging sleeves of my kimono. I carefully swung it off my shoulders and placed in on the counter in front of me.

I looked in the mirror.
I then put on the change of clothes;
jeans and a short-sleeved shirt.
I looked in the mirror again.
These clothes felt uncomfortable. They didn't seem to fit.
They could have been a stranger's.
They were no longer mine.

1. "Just a Little Japanese," an award-winning essay by a Vancouver student, begins with a description of a Japanese meal.
   a) With a classmate, discuss the tone of the description. Decide whether it complements the tone of the rest of the essay. Support your argument with examples from the text.
   b) In "Of a Dancing-Girl" (p. 84), Hearn also introduced his topic peripherally, with a description of dining. Read his essay and then examine with your classmate the similarities and differences between Hearn's and Patrick's introductions. In your notebook, write a brief evaluation of the effectiveness of both introductions.

2. In the final paragraphs of the story, the author suggests a transformation in the protagonist in two ways. In one or two analytical paragraphs, identify the two ways and state exactly what they signal to the reader.

3. Make an outline for a personal essay, similar to Patrick's, about a guest from another country who comes to your home. Specify a typically Canadian ritual in which your guest might participate, and suggest how he or she might perceive it.

4. In a small group, discuss the implicit thesis of the essay and express it in a one-sentence statement. Compare your statement with those of other groups.

"Wit has truth in it; wisecracking is simply calisthenics with words." – *Dorothy Parker*

Discuss the above aphorism with a classmate to ensure that you understand the distinction Dorothy Parker is making. When both of you are certain of her meaning, read her account of a formal dinner party, and judge for yourself whether wit or wisecracking predominates.

BUT THE ONE ON THE RIGHT
Dorothy Parker

I knew it. I knew if I came to this dinner, I'd draw something like this baby on my left. They've been saving him up for me for weeks. Now, we've simply got to have him – his sister was so sweet to us in London; we can stick him next to Mrs. Parker – she talks enough for two. Oh, I should never have come, never. I'm here against my better judgment, to a decision. That would be a good thing for them to cut on my tombstone: Wherever she went, including here, it was against her better judgment. This is a fine time of the evening to be thinking about tombstones. That's the effect he's had on me, already, and the soup hardly cold yet. I should have stayed at home for dinner. I could have had something on a tray. The head of John the Baptist, or something. Oh, I should not have come.

Well, the soup's over, anyway. I'm that much nearer to my Eternal Home. Now the soup belongs to the ages, and I have said precisely four words to the gentleman on my left. I said, "Isn't this soup delicious?"; that's four words. And he said, "Yes, isn't it?"; that's three. He's one up on me.

At any rate, we're in perfect accord. We agree like lambs. We've been all through the soup together, and never a cross word between us. It seems rather a pity to let the subject drop, now we've found something on which we harmonize so admirably. I believe I'll bring it up again; I'll ask him if that wasn't delicious soup. He says, "Yes, wasn't it?" Look at that, will you; perfect command of his tenses.

Here comes the fish. Goody, goody, goody, we got fish. I wonder if he likes fish. Yes, he does; he says he likes fish. Ah, that's nice. I love that in a man. Look, he's talking! He's chattering away like a veritable magpie. He's asking me if I like fish. Now does he really want to know, or is it only a line? I'd better play it cagey. I'll tell him, "Oh pretty well." Oh, I like fish pretty well; there's a fascinating bit of autobiography for him to study over. Maybe he would rather wrestle with it alone. I'd better steal softly away, and leave him to his thoughts.

I might try my luck with what's on my right. No, not a chance there. The woman on his other side has him cold. All I can see is his shoulder. It's a nice shoulder, too; oh, it's a nice, *nice* shoulder. All my life, I've been a fool for a nice shoulder. Very well, lady; you saw him first. Keep your Greek god, and I'll go back to my Trojan horse.

Let's see, where were we? Oh, we'd got to where he had confessed his liking for fish. I wonder what else he likes. Does he like cucumbers? Yes, he does; he likes cucumbers. And potatoes? Yes, he likes potatoes, too. Why, he's a regular old Nature-lover, that's what he is. I would have to come out to dinner, and sit next to the Boy Thoreau. Wait, he's saying something! Words are simply pouring out of him. He's asking me if I'm fond of potatoes. No, I don't like potatoes. There, I've done it! I've differed from him. It's our first quarrel. He's fallen into a moody silence. Silly boy, have I pricked your bubble? Do you think I am nothing but a painted doll with sawdust for a heart? Ah, don't take it like that. Look, I have something to tell you that will bring back your faith. I do like cucumbers. Why, he's better already. He speaks again. He says, yes, he likes them, too. Now we've got that all straightened out, thank heaven. We both like cucumbers. Only he likes them twice.

I'd better let him alone now, so he can get some food. He ought to try to get his strength back. He's talked himself groggy.

I wish I had something to do. I hate to be a mere drone. People ought to let you know when they're going to sit you next to a thing like this, so you could bring along some means of occupation. Dear Mrs. Parker, do come to us for dinner on Friday next, and don't forget your drawn-work. I could have brought my top bureau drawer and tidied it up, here on my lap. I could have made great strides towards getting those photographs of the groups on the beach pasted up in the album. I wonder if my hostess would think it strange if I asked for a pack of cards. I wonder if there are any old copies of *St. Nicholas* lying about. I wonder if they wouldn't like a little help out in the kitchen. I wonder if anybody would want me to run up to the corner and get a late paper.

I could do a little drinking, of course, all by myself. There's always that. Oh, dear, oh, dear, oh, dear, there's always that. But I don't want to drink. I'll get *vin triste*. I'm melancholy before I even start. I wonder what this stiff on my left would say, if I told him I was in a fair way to get *vin triste*. Oh, look at him, hoeing into his fish! What does he care whether I get *vin triste* or not? His soul can't rise above food. Purely physical, that's all he is. Digging his grave with his teeth, that's what he's doing. Yah, yah, ya-ah! Digging your grave with your tee-eeth! Making a god of your stommick! Yah, yah, ya-ah!

He doesn't care if I get *vin triste*. Nobody cares. Nobody gives a damn. And me so nice. All right, you baskets, I'll drink myself to death, right in front of your eyes, and see how you'll feel. Here I go. . . . Oh, my God, it's Chablis. And of a year when the grapes failed, and they used Summer squash, instead. Fifteen dollars for all you can carry home on your shoulder. Oh, now, listen, where I come from, we feed this to the pigs. I think I'll ask old Chatterbox on my left if this isn't rotten wine. That ought to open up a new school of dialectics for us. Oh, he says he really wouldn't know – he never touches wine. Well, that fairly well ends that. I wonder how he'd like to step to hell, anyway. Yah, yah, ya-ah! Never touches wi-yine! Don't know what you're miss-sing! Yah, yah, ya-ah!

I'm not going to talk to him any more. I'm not going to spend the best years of my life thinking up pearls to scatter before him. I'm going to stick to my Chablis, rotten though it be. From now on, he can go his way, and I'll go mine. I'm better than anybody at this table. Ah, but am I really? Have I, after all, half of what they have? Here I am lonely, unwanted, silent, and me with all my new clothes on. Oh, what would Louiseboulanger say if she saw her gold lamé going unnoticed like this? It's life, I suppose. Poor little things, we dress, and we plan, and we hope – and for what? What is life, anyway? A death sentence. The longest distance between two points. The bunch of hay that's tied to the nose of the tired mule. The –

Well, well, well, here we are at the *entrecôte*. Button up your *entrecôte*, when the wind is free – no, I guess not. Now I'll be damned if I ask old Loquacity if he likes meat. In the first place, his likes and dislikes are nothing to me, and in the second – well, look at him go after it! He must have been playing hard all afternoon; he's Mother's Hungry Boy, tonight. All right, let him worry it all he wants. As for me, I'm on a higher plane. I do not stoop to him. He's less than the dust beneath my chariot wheel. Yah, yah, ya-ah! Less than the du-ust! Before I'd be that way. Yah, yah, ya-ah!

I'm glad there's red wine now. Even if it isn't good, I'm glad. Red wine gives me courage. The Red Badge of Courage. I need courage. I'm in a thin way, here. Nobody knows what a filthy time I'm having. My precious evening, that can never come again, ruined, ruined, ruined, and all because of this Somewhat Different Monologist on my left. But he can't lick me. The night is not yet dead, no, nor dying. You know, this really isn't bad wine.

Now what do you suppose is going on with the Greek God on my right? Ah, no use. There's still only the shoulder – the nice, nice shoulder. I wonder what the woman's like, that's got him. I can't see her at all. I wonder if she's beautiful. I wonder if she's Greek, too. When Greek meets immovable body – you might be able to do something with that, if you only had the time. I'm not going to be spineless any longer. Don't think for a minute, lady, that I've given up. He's still using his knife and fork. While there's hands above the table, there's hope.

Really, I suppose out of obligation to my hostess, I ought to do something about saying a few words to this macaw on my left. What shall I try? Have you been reading anything good lately, do you go much to the play, have you ever been to the Riviera? I wonder if he would like to hear about my Summer on the Riviera; hell, no, that's no good without lantern slides. I bet, though, if I started telling him about That One Night, he'd listen. I won't tell him – it's too good for him. Anybody that never touches wine can't hear that. But the one on the right – he'd like that. He touches wine. Touches it, indeed! He just threw it for a formidable loss.

Oh, look, old Silver Tongue is off again! Why, he's mad with his own perfume! He's rattling away like lightning. He's asking me if I like salad. Yes, I do; what does he want to make of that? He's telling me about salad through the ages. He says it's so good for people. So help me God, if he gives me a talk on roughage, I'll slap his face. Isn't that my life, to sit here, all dressed up in my best, and listen to this thing talk about romaine? And all the time, right on my right –

Well, I thought you were never going to turn around. . . . You haven't. . . . You have? Oh, Lord, I've been having an awful time, too. . . . Was she? . . . Well, you should have seen what I drew. . . . Oh, I don't see how we could. . . . Well. . . . Well, yes, that's true. . . . Look, right after dinner, I'll say I have this horrible headache, and you say you're going to take me home in your car, and –

---

1. a) Reread "But the One on the Right," jotting down notes on the kind of character Parker portrays. Using your notes as a guide, describe to a classmate the sort of person the narrator is, speaking as if you had met her yourself.
   b) This story is an interior monologue. In your notebook, list the characteristics of the interior monologue and the advantages and disadvantages it offers the writer.

2. Assume the persona of the taciturn guest on the narrator's left and write an interior monologue describing your reactions to the evening's events. You may wish to put this piece of writing in your folder.

3. With a classmate, assume the roles of the narrator and the man on her left and dramatize the interaction between them. Use the dialogue provided in the story as your script, developing appropriate tone, pace, expression, and body language to enliven it.

4. "But the One on the Right" depicts a familiar stereotype: "Here I am," the narrator laments, "lonely, unwanted, silent, and me with all my new clothes on. Oh what would Louiseboulanger say if she saw her gold lamé going unnoticed like this? It's life, I suppose. Poor little things, we dress, and we plan, and we hope – and for what?" In a small group that includes both sexes discuss the extent to which the narrator is a stereotype.

Amnesty International is an organization dedicated to helping the victims of oppressive political states. Its means are peaceful: publicity and lobbying. The following is the text of an address delivered by Margaret Atwood during a world meeting of Amnesty International in Toronto late in 1981. Before you read it, consider with a couple of classmates how you would answer the central question she poses: "What is the writer's responsibility, if any, to the society in which he or she lives?"

AMNESTY INTERNATIONAL:

AN ADDRESS
Margaret Atwood

he subject we have come together to address is one which increases in importance as the giants of this world move closer and closer to violent and fatal confrontation. Broadly put, it is: what is the writer's responsibility, if any, to the society in which he or she lives? The question is not a new one; it's been with us at least since the time of Plato; but more and more the answers of the world's governments have taken the form of amputation: of the tongue, of the soul, of the head.

We in Canada are ill-equipped to come to grips even with the problem, let alone the solution. We live in a society in which the main consensus seems to be that the artist's duty is to entertain and divert, nothing more. Occasionally our critics get a little heavy and start talking about the human condition, but on the whole the audience prefers art not to be a mirror held up to life but a Disneyland of the soul, containing Romanceland, Spyland, Pornoland, and all the other Escapelands which are so much more agreeable than the complex truth. When we take an author seriously, we prefer to believe that her vision derives from her individual and subjective and neurotic tortured soul – we like artists to have tortured souls – not from the world she is looking at. Sometimes our artists believe this version too, and the ego takes over. *I, me* and *mine* are our favourite pronouns; *we, us* and *ours* are low on the list. The artist is not seen as a lens for focussing the world but as a solipsism. We are good at measuring an author's production in terms of his craft. We are not good at analysing it in terms of his politics, and by and large we do not do so.

By "politics" I do not mean how you voted in the last election, although that is included. I mean who is entitled to do what to whom, with impunity; who profits by it; and who therefore eats what. Such material enters a writer's work not because the writer is or is not consciously political but because a writer is an observer, a witness, and such observations are the air he breathes. They are the air all of us breathe; the only difference is that the author looks, and then writes down what he sees. What he sees will depend on how closely he looks and at what, but look he must.

In some countries, an author is censored not only for what he says but for how he says it, and an unconventional style is therefore a declaration of artistic freedom. Here we are eclectic; we don't mind experimental styles, in fact we devote learned journals to their analysis; but our critics sneer somewhat at anything they consider "heavy social commentary" or – a worse word – "message." Stylistic heavy guns are dandy, as long as they aren't pointed anywhere in particular. We like the human condition as long as it is seen as personal and individual. Placing politics and poetics in two watertight compartments is a luxury, just as specialization of any kind is a luxury, and it is possible only in a society where luxuries abound. Most countries in the world cannot afford such luxuries, and this North American way of thinking is alien to them. It was even alien in North America, not long ago. We've already forgotten that in the 1950s many artists, both in the United States and here, were persecuted solely on the grounds of their presumed politics. Which leads us to another mistaken Canadian belief: the belief that it can't happen here.

It has happened here, many times. Although our country is one of the most peaceful and prosperous on earth, although we do not shoot artists here, although we do not execute political opponents, and although this is one of the few remaining countries in which we can have a gathering like this without expecting to be arrested or blown up, we should not overlook the fact that Canada's record on civil rights issues is less than pristine. Our treatment of our native peoples has been shameful. This is the country in which citizens of Japanese origin were interned during the Second World War and had their property stolen (when a government steals property it is called "confiscation"); it is also the country in which thousands of citizens were arrested, jailed and held without warrant or explanation, during the time of the War Measures Act, a scant eleven years ago. There was no general outcry in either case. Worse things have not happened not because we are genetically exempt but because we lead pampered lives.

Our methods of controlling artists are not violent, but they do exist. We control through the marketplace and through critical opinion. We are also controlled by the economics of culture, which in Canada still happen to be those of a colonial branch-plant. In 1960 the number of Canadian books published here was minute, and the numbers sold pathetic. Things have changed very much in twenty years, but Canadian books still account for a mere 25 percent of the overall book trade and paperback books for under 5 percent. Talking about this situation is still considered nationalistic chauvinism. Nevertheless, looked at in the context of the wider picture, I suppose we are lucky to have any percent at all; they haven't yet sent in the Marines and if they do it won't be over books, but over oil.

We in this country should use our privileged position not as a shelter from the world's realities but as a platform from which to speak. Many are denied their voices; we are not. A voice is a gift; it should be cherished and used, to utter fully human speech if possible. Powerlessness and silence go together; one of the first efforts made in any totalitarian takeover is to suppress the writers, the singers, the journalists, those who are the collective voice. Get rid of the union leaders and pervert the legal system and what you are left with is a reign of terror.

As we read the newspapers, we learn we are existing right now in a state of war. The individual wars may not be large and they are being fought far from here, but there is really only one war, that between those who would like the future to be, in the words of George Orwell, a boot grinding forever into a human face, and those who would like it to be a state of something we still dream of as freedom. The battle shifts according to the ground occupied by the enemy. Greek myth tells of a man called Procrustes, who was a great equalizer. He had a system for making all human beings the same size: if they were too small he stretched them, if they were too tall he cut off their feet or their heads. The Procrustes today are international operators, not confined to any one ideology or religion. The world is full of perversions of the notion of equality, just as it is full of perversions of the notion of freedom. True freedom is not being able to do whatever you like to whomever you want to do it to. Freedom that exists as a result of the servitude of others is not true freedom.

The most lethal weapon in the world's arsenals is not the neutron bomb or chemical warfare; but the human mind that devises such things and puts them to use. But it is the human mind also that can summon up the power to resist, that can imagine a better world than the one before it, that can retain memory and courage in the face of unspeakable suffering. Oppression involves a failure of the imagination: the failure to imagine the full humanity of other human beings.

If the imagination were a negligible thing and the act of writing a mere frill, as many in this society would like to believe, regimes all over the world would not be at such pains to exterminate them. The ultimate desire of Procrustes is a population of lobotomized zombies. The writer, unless he is a mere word processor, retains three attributes that power-mad regimes cannot tolerate: a human imagination, in the many forms it may take; the power to communicate; and hope. It may seem odd for me to speak of hope in the midst of what many of my fellow Canadians will call a bleak vision, but as the American writer Flannery O'Connor once said, people without hope do not write novels.

————————————————————————————▶ •●• ◀————————————————————————————

1. a) As a journalist covering Amnesty International's meeting in Toronto, write a succinct account of the substance of Atwood's address. Before writing your report, identify the audience for whom it is intended: for example, readers of a daily newspaper, of a tabloid, of a weekly newsmagazine, or of a literary journal. Begin your article with a suitable headline.
   b) Compare your report of Atwood's address with a report aimed at another audience. With the classmate who wrote the other report, examine differences in language, selection of detail, presentation of content, and assess how each of the reports is suitable for its particular readership.

2. Select two students from the class each to prepare a polished oral delivery of the final three paragraphs of the address. After listening to the two interpretations, the class should break up into small groups to identify and evaluate
   • the techniques Atwood uses to appeal to her audience;
   • the methods of oratory used by the two student speakers.

3. Atwood's address is polemic. In your notebook, itemize the controversial points in the speech. Compare your list with a classmate's and explain the thinking behind your choices.

4. In a small group, examine Atwood's contention that Canadians generally prefer art "not to be a mirror held up to life but a Disneyland of the soul." Prepare a list of literary works (some of them Canadian) that you think *do* hold a mirror up to life. For each item, provide a synopsis and a statement of its relevance. Share your guide with another group. You may wish to select a class editor to compile a master list from those prepared in the small groups, creating a reading guide for Canadian senior students.

NURSES' NEW ROLE: PATIENTS' ADVOCATE

Arthur Schafer

here has been a quiet revolution in nursing ethics, and some members of the medical profession are beginning to look anxiously over their shoulders.

An Ontario woman recently won a medical malpractice suit against her anesthetist. The case attracted a good deal of media attention, partly because it was revealed that the anesthetist had worked on a crossword puzzle during the operation and partly because the Supreme Court of Ontario awarded the victim damages and compensation of more than $1 million – the largest award against a physician in Ontario.

However, one feature of this case has not been widely noted: the crucial role played at the trial by a nurse. One of the operating room nurses, Jackie Coathup, saw the anesthetist working on a crossword puzzle during the operation and saw him tear the puzzle into pieces and crumple it after things went wrong. Her testimony at the trial was of decisive importance. The patient was left severely brain-damaged and physically handicapped after what should have been a routine operation. Nevertheless, the patient might not have won her case if none of those who witnessed the operation had been willing to testify.

Nurse Coathup's action should not be seen as an isolated event. Increasingly, over the past two decades, the nursing profession has come to see its role as including patient advocacy, even when this means "blowing the whistle" on doctors or hospitals or other members of the health-care team.

"With loyalty will I endeavour to aid the physician in his work." These words of the Nightingale Pledge encapsulate the essence of traditional nursing ethics. In the war against disease, the doctor was viewed as the captain of the health-care team; nurses were taught to view themselves as loyal foot-soldiers. As Isabel Robb declared, in Nursing Ethics (1901), "implicit, unquestioning obedience is one of the first lessons a probationer (nurse) must learn, for this is a quality that will be expected from her in her professional capacity for all future times."

By contrast, the newly promulgated Code of Ethics of the Canadian Nurses Association makes no mention of loyalty to doctors, or unquestioning obedience. The model of nurse as obedient foot-soldier has been replaced by the model of nurse as patient advocate. The pledge of loyalty to physicians has been replaced by the obligation "to take steps to ensure that the client receives competent and ethical care."

The journey from the Nightingale Pledge to the CNA's new Code of Ethics has been long and interesting. Two legal cases stand out as landmarks.

In 1921, nurse Lorenza Somera was convicted of manslaughter and sentenced to prison. Her crime: she failed to question the orders of a physician. The attending doctor instructed Nurse Somera to administer cocaine to a tonsillectomy patient, when he meant to order procaine. When the patient died as a result of this mistake, both physician and nurse were accused of manslaughter. The doctor was acquitted. The nurse was convicted.

Although Nurse Somera was later pardoned, her case aroused worldwide indignation among nurses. Paradoxically, although the conviction was unjust, it represented an important advance for the status of nurses. By holding Nurse Somera independently responsible and accountable for her actions, the court in effect was affirming that nurses were genuine professionals, required to exercise their autonomy and their professional judgment, and accountable when they failed to do so.

Without at least some degree of legally recognized autonomy, nursing would be merely an occupation, not a profession.

A more recent U.S. legal case has once again brought into focus the difficult ethical issues involved. In Tuma versus Board of Nursing (1979), nurse Jolene Tuma lost her job and had her nursing licence suspended because she discussed treatment alternatives with a dying leukemia patient. The doctor had strongly recommended chemotherapy, but the patient had doubts and wished to discuss alternatives with Nurse Tuma.

The nurse was aware of the risks, but felt her obligation to the patient required that she answer the patient's questions. She was charged with interfering unethically with the physician-patient relationship. Nurse Tuma challenged the suspension of her licence and won reinstatement after an appeal to the state's supreme court.

Nurse Tuma probably would have been found innocent of any breach of ethics had she been tried under the CNA's new Code of Ethics. For the code affirms that "nurses should respond freely to their clients' requests for information and explanation when in possession of the knowledge required to respond accurately."

Should the general public welcome these dramatic changes in nursing ethics? Is the patient better served by a nursing profession committed to the old virtues of loyalty and obedience (to the doctor) or to the new role of patient advocate?

To answer properly, one must first explore the rationale for the old virtues. The primary moral commitment of the nurse (like that of the physician) is to the health of the patient. It is widely accepted that the patient's confidence in the doctor and in the treatment prescribed by the doctor is an essential part of good therapy. Thus, it would seem to follow that the nurse's loyalty to the patient is best expressed by protecting the patient's faith in the doctor.

This argument is plausible, but it has obvious limitations. In an ideal world, loyalty to patients and loyalty to doctors would always coincide. But doctors are sometimes incompetent or unethical, so conflicts of obligation are inescapable.

Moreover, nurses generally spend far more time with the patient than do physicians. Their opportunities to know the patient, to empathize with the patient, and to understand the patient's attitudes and needs usually exceed those of the physician. Thus, many nurses believe it is proper to serve as patient advocate and, when necessary, to challenge a physician's orders.

"Obey and grieve." This used to be, and to some extent still is, the motto governing the nurse-doctor relationship. But nurses' challenges to medical authority are likely to increase. While previously a nurse might indirectly question a doctor's authority by asking whether he really meant to order such-and-such, today's nurse might directly challenge him if the indirect approach failed to produce results. A case in point is the willingness of three nurses at Mount Sinai Hospital in Toronto in 1976 to face suspension rather than accept what they considered an unsafe patient load on their unit.

Every recent opinion survey of physicians and nurses shows a marked change of attitudes and values in both professions. There seems little doubt that Canadian nurses have been deeply influenced by the feminist movement, by a growing sense of professional autonomy, and by the growth of a consumers' rights perspective among patients.

But if we focus exclusively on potential conflict and controversy between doctors and nurses, we run the danger of neglecting their common commitment to patient welfare. As the nursing Code of Ethics acknowledges, "relationships in the health-care team should not be disrupted unnecessarily." Conflict between doctor and nurse could harm patients. The relationship toward which the medical and nursing professions should be working is mutual respect and co-operation. Each profession must acknowledge its limitations and recognize the special skills and competence of the other. Some conflict is inevitable, but the shared goal of patient benefit provides the context within which all such conflicts must be resolved.

---

1. Schafer states in his article that the "journey from the Nightingale Pledge to the CNA's new Code of Ethics has been long and interesting." Prepare a brief outline which might be used for study purposes summarizing the significant stages of this revolutionary journey.

2. Working with a classmate, prepare arguments for both sides of a debate on the resolution "A patient is better served by a nursing profession committed to the old virtues of loyalty and obedience to the doctor." Use your own arguments as well as arguments from Schafer's article.

3. Through an examination of the language, assess the extent to which Schafer
   ● conveys factual information;
   ● attempts to persuade the reader of a point of view.
   Compare your findings with another classmate's.

4. Imagine that Schafer's article is to be printed in a medical journal and that you, as a doctor, have been asked to write an accompanying editorial recommending acceptance of the new role of nurses to your colleagues. Write the editorial and include it in your writing folder.

Now as I was young and easy under the apple
boughs
About the lilting house and happy as the grass
was green,
The night above the dingle starry,
Time let me hail and climb
Golden in the heydays of his eyes,
And honoured among wagons I was prince of
the apple towns
And once below a time I lordly had the trees
and leaves
Trail with daisies and barley
Down the rivers of the windfall light.
Dylan Thomas, from "Fern Hill"

In a small group, study the first stanza of
"Fern Hill," comparing your impressions. (You
may wish to read and study the whole poem.)
Jot down notes on the images and turns of
phrase Thomas uses and on the themes in the
poem.

from "HOLIDAY MEMORY"
Dylan Thomas

ugust Bank Holiday. A tune on an ice-cream cornet. A slap of
sea and a tickle of sand. A fanfare of sunshades opening.
A wince and whinny of bathers dancing into deceptive water.
A tuck of dresses. A rolling of trousers. A compromise of paddlers. A
sunburn of girls and a lark of boys. A silent hullabaloo of balloons.

I remember the sea telling lies in a shell held to my ear for a whole
harmonious, hollow minute by a small, wet girl in an enormous
bathing-suit marked "Corporation Property."

I remember sharing the last of my moist buns with a boy and a lion.
Tawny and savage, with cruel nails and capacious mouth, the little boy
tore and devoured. Wild as seed-cake, ferocious as a hearth-rug, the
depressed and verminous lion nibbled like a mouse at his half a bun,
and hiccupped in the sad dusk of his cage.

I remember a man like an alderman or a bailiff, bowlered and collarless, with a bag of monkey-nuts in his hand, crying "Ride 'em, cowboy!" time and again as he whirled in his chairoplane giddily above the upturned laughing faces of the town girls bold as brass and the boys with padded shoulders and shoes sharp as knives; and the monkey-nuts flew through the air like salty hail.

Children all day capered or squealed by the glazed or bashing sea, and the steam-organ wheezed its waltzes in the threadbare playground and the waste lot, where the dodgems dodged, behind the pickle factory.

And mothers loudly warned their proud pink daughters or sons to put that jellyfish down; and fathers spread newspapers over their faces; and sand-fleas hopped on the picnic lettuce; and someone had forgotten the salt.

In those always radiant, rainless, lazily rowdy and sky-blue summers departed, I remember August Monday from the rising of the sun over the stained and royal town to the husky hushing of the roundabout music and the dowsing of the naptha jets in the seaside fair: from bubble-and-squeak to the last of the sandy sandwiches.

There was no need, that holiday morning, for the sluggardly boys to be shouted down to breakfast; out of their jumbled beds they tumbled, scrambled into their rumpled clothes; quickly at the bath-room basin they catlicked their hands and faces, but never forgot to run the water loud and long as though they washed like colliers; in front of the cracked looking-glass bordered with cigarette-cards, in their treasure-trove bedrooms, they whisked a gap-tooth comb through their surly hair; and with shining cheeks and noses and tide-marked necks, they took the stairs three at a time.

But for all their scramble and scamper, clamour on the landing, catlick and toothbrush flick, hair-whisk and stair-jump, their sisters were always there before them. Up with the lady lark, they had prinked and frizzed and hot-ironed; and smug in their blossoming dresses, ribboned for the sun, in gym-shoes white as the blanco'd snow, neat and silly with doilies and tomatoes they helped in the higgledy kitchen. They were calm; they were virtuous; they had washed their necks; they did not romp, or fidget; and only the smallest sister put out her tongue at the noisy boys.

And the woman who lived next door came into the kitchen and said that her mother, an ancient uncertain body who wore a hat with cherries, was having "one of her days" and had insisted, that very holiday morning, in carrying all the way to the tram-stop a photograph album and the cut-glass fruit-bowl from the front room.

This was the morning when father, mending one hole in the thermos-flask, made three; when the sun declared war on the butter, and the butter ran; when dogs, with all the sweet-binned backyards to wag and sniff and bicker in, chased their tails in the jostling kitchen, worried sandshoes, snapped at flies, writhed between legs, scratched among towels, sat smiling on hampers.

And if you could have listened at some of the open doors of some of the houses in the street you might have heard:

"Uncle Owen says he can't find the bottle-opener . . . "

"Has he looked under the hallstand?"

"Willy's cut his finger . . . "

"Got your spade?"

"If somebody doesn't kill that dog . . . "

"Uncle Owen says why should the bottle-opener be under the hallstand?"

"Never again, never again . . . "

"I know I put the pepper somewhere . . . "

"Willy's bleeding . . . "

"Look, there's a bootlace in my bucket . . . "

"Oh come *on*, come on . . . "

"Let's have a look at the bootlace in your bucket . . . "

"If I lay my hands on that dog . . . "

"Uncle Owen's found the bottle-opener . . . "

"Willy's bleeding over the cheese . . . "

And the trams that hissed like ganders took us all to the beautiful beach.

There was cricket on the sand, and sand in the sponge cake, sand-flies in the watercress, and foolish, mulish, religious donkeys on the unwilling trot. Girls undressed in slipping tents of propriety; under invisible umbrellas, stout ladies dressed for the male and immoral sea. Little naked navvies dug canals; children with spades and no ambiition built fleeting castles; wispy young men, outside the bathing-huts, whistled at substantial young women and dogs who desired thrown stones more than the bones of elephants. Recalcitrant uncles huddled over luke ale in the tiger-striped marquees. Mothers in black, like wobbling mountains, gasped under the discarded dresses of daughters who shrilly braved the goblin waves. And fathers, in the once-a-year sun, took fifty winks. Oh, think of all the fifty winks along the paper-bagged sand.

Liquorice allsorts, and Welsh hearts, were melting, and the sticks of rock, that we all sucked, were like barbers' poles made of rhubarb.

In the distance, surrounded by disappointed theoreticians and an ironmonger with a drum, a cross man on an orange-box shouted that holidays were wrong.

And the waves rolled in, with rubber ducks and clerks upon them.

I remember the patient, laborious, and enamouring hobby, or profession, of burying relatives in sand.

I remember the princely pastime of pouring sand, from cupped hands or buckets, down collars and tops of dresses; the shriek, the shake, the slap.

I can remember the boy by himself, the beachcombing lone-wolf, hungrily waiting at the edge of family cricket; the friendless fielder, the boy uninvited to bat or to tea.

I remember the smell of sea and seaweed, wet flesh, wet hair, wet bathing-dresses, the warm smell as of a rabbity field after rain, the smell of pop and splashed sunshades and toffee, the stable-and-straw smell of hot, tossed, tumbled, dug, and trodden sand, the swill-and-gaslamp smell of Saturday night, though the sun shone strong, from the bellying beer-tents, the smell of the vinegar on shelled cockles, winkle-smell, shrimp-smell, the dripping-oily backstreet winter-smell of chips in newspapers, the smell of ships from the sun-dazed docks round the corner of the sand-hills, the smell of the known and paddled-in sea moving, full of the drowned and herrings, out and away and beyond and further still towards the antipodes that hung their koala-bears and Maoris, kangaroos, and boomerangs, upside down over the backs of the stars.

And the noise of pummelling Punch, and Judy falling, and a clock tolling or telling no time in the tenantless town; now and again a bell from a lost tower or a train on the lines behind us clearing its throat, and always the hopeless, ravenous swearing and pleading of the gulls, donkey-bray and hawker-cry, harmonicas and toy trumpets, shouting and laughing and singing, hooting of tugs and tramps, the clip of the chair-attendant's puncher, the motor-boat coughing in the bay, and the same hymn and washing of the sea that was heard in the Bible.

"If it could only just, if it could only just?" your lips said again and again as you scooped, in the hob-hot sand, dungeons, garages, torture-chambers, train tunnels, arsenals, hangars for zeppelins, witches' kitchens, vampires' parlours, smugglers' cellars, trolls' grog-shops, sewers, under a ponderous and cracking castle, "If it could only just be like this for ever and ever amen." August Monday all over the earth, from Mumbles where the aunties grew like ladies on a seaside tree to brown, bear-hugging Henty-land and the turtled Ballantyne Islands.

"Could donkeys go on the ice?"

"Only if they got snowshoes."

We snowshoed a meek, complaining donkey and galloped him off in the wake of the ten-foot-tall and Atlas-muscled Mounties, rifled and pemmicanned, who always, in the white Gold Rush wastes, got their black-oathed-and-bearded Man.

"Are there donkeys on desert islands?"

"Only sort-of donkeys."

"What d'you mean, sort-of donkeys?"

"Native donkeys. They hunt things on them!"

"Sort-of walruses and seals and things?"

"Donkeys can't swim!"

"These donkeys can. They swim like whales, they swim like any-thing, they swim like – "

"Liar."

"Liar yourself."

And two small boys fought fiercely and silently in the sand, rolling together in a ball of legs and bottoms.

Then they went and saw the pierrots, or bought vanilla ices.

Lolling or larriking that unsoiled, boiling beauty of a common day, great gods with their braces over their vests sang, spat pips, puffed smoke at wasps, gulped and ogled, forgot the rent, embraced, posed for the dickybird, were coarse, had rainbow-coloured armpits, winked, belched, blamed the radishes, looked at Ilfracombe, played hymns on paper-and-comb, peeled bananas, scratched, found seaweed in their panamas, blew up paper-bags and banged them, wished for nothing.

But over all the beautiful beach I remember most the children playing, boys and girls tumbling, moving jewels, who might never be happy again. And "happy as a sandboy" is true as the heat of the sun.

Dusk came down; or grew up out of the sands and the sea; or curled around us from the calling docks and the bloodily smoking sun. The day was done, the sands brushed and ruffled suddenly with a seabroom of cold wind.

And we gathered together all the spades and buckets and towels, empty hampers and bottles, umbrellas and fish-frails, bats and balls and knitting, and went – oh, listen, Dad! – to the fair in the dusk on the bald seaside field.

---

1. In a small group, prepare an oral reading of the excerpt from "Holiday Memory." Perform your reading for another group of classmates. Ask them to listen carefully to the changes in rhythm and tempo. Together, discuss how the writer achieves the various effects. Discuss also whether shifts in style complement developments in content.

2. a) Thomas delights in using words in unexpected or unusual ways. With a classmate, choose four or five phrases or sentences that you find interesting. Identify in your examples the figures of speech and poetic devices that Thomas employs. In your notebook, annotate each example by providing an interpretation, with an accompanying explanation of how you arrived at it.
   b) Write a prose appreciation of the excerpt from "Holiday Memory." (You may need to consult with your teacher about the characteristics of prose appreciations.) Consider particularly Thomas's use of various figures of speech and of the sound qualities of the words.

3. Make a list in your notebook of any unfamiliar details or references in the excerpt, and prepare (using dictionaries and an encyclopedia) brief annotations that other readers could use to help them

understand the memoir. You may wish to write your notes in the form of footnotes or end notes and to make them available to your classmates.

4. Modelling your prose style on that of the excerpt from "Holiday Memory," write three paragraphs of personal reminiscence on one of the following:
   - a day of your holidays;
   - an annual family celebration, such as Christmas, Hanukkah, or Chinese New Year;
   - a typical school day.

   Ask a classmate to read your reminiscence and to make editorial suggestions and comments on it. Your revised and polished draft might then be submitted to your school yearbook or newspaper for possible publication.

Imagine that you are sitting on a very crowded bus. The large and aggressive-seeming person next to you keeps demanding in an obnoxious way that you move over to make more room. You can't move over and there is nowhere else to sit or stand in the bus. Write the dialogue that might take place in those circumstances. Ask a classmate to read the other role while you read your own part.

WE HAVE TO SIT OPPOSITE
Ethel Wilson

ven in the confusion of entering the carriage at Salzburg, Mrs. Montrose and her cousin Mrs. Forrester noticed the man with the blue tooth. He occupied a corner beside the window. His wife sat next to him. Next to her sat their daughter of perhaps seventeen. People poured into the train. A look passed between Mrs. Montrose and Mrs. Forrester. The look said, "These people seem to have filled up the carriage pretty well, but we'd better take these seats while we can as the train is so full. At least we can have seats together." The porter, in his porter's tyrannical way, piled their suitcases onto the empty rack above the heads of the man with the blue tooth, and his wife, and his daughter, and departed. The opposite rack was full of baskets, bags, and miscellaneous parcels. The train started. Here they were. Mrs. Montrose and Mrs. Forrester smiled at each other as they settled down below the rack which was filled with miscellaneous articles. Clinging vines that they were, they felt adventurous and successful. They had travelled alone from Vienna to Salzburg, leaving in Vienna their doctor husbands to continue attending the clinics of Dr. Bauer and Dr. Hirsch. And now, after a week in Salzburg, they were happily on their way to rejoin their husbands, who had flown to Munich.

Both Mrs. Montrose and Mrs. Forrester were tall, slight, and fair.

They were dressed with dark elegance. They knew that their small hats were smart, suitable and becoming, and they rejoiced in the simplicity and distinction of their new costumes. The selection of these and other costumes, and of these and other hats in Vienna had, they regretted, taken from the study of art, music, and history a great deal of valuable time. Mrs. Montrose and Mrs. Forrester were sincerely fond of art, music, and history and longed almost passionately to spend their days in the Albertina Gallery and the Kunsthistorische Museum. But the modest shops and shop windows of the craftsmen of Vienna had rather diverted the two young women from the study of art and history, and it was easy to lay the blame for this on the museums and art galleries which, in truth, closed their doors at very odd times. After each day's enchanting pursuits and disappointments, Mrs. Montrose and Mrs. Forrester hastened in a fatigued state to the cafe where they had arranged to meet their husbands who by this time had finished their daily sessions with Dr. Bauer and Dr. Hirsch.

This was perhaps the best part of the day, to sit together happily in the sunshine, toying with the good Viennese coffee or a glass of wine, gazing and being gazed upon, and giving their senses to the music that flowed under the chestnut trees. (Ah Vienna, they thought, Vienna, Vienna.)

No, perhaps the evenings had been the best time when after their frugal pension dinner they hastened out to hear opera or symphony or wild atavistic gypsy music. All was past now. They had been very happy. They were fortunate. Were they too fortunate?

Mrs. Montrose and Mrs. Forrester were in benevolent good spirits as they looked round the railway carriage and prepared to take their seats and settle down for the journey to Munich to meet their husbands. In their window corner, opposite the man with the blue tooth, was a large hamper. *"Do* you mind?" asked Mrs. Montrose, smiling sweetly at the man, his wife, and his daughter. She prepared to lift the hamper on which the charming view from the carriage window was of course wasted, intending to move it along the seat, and take its place. The man, his wife, and his daughter had never taken their eyes off Mrs. Montrose and Mrs. Forrester since they had entered the carriage.

"*If* you please," said the man loudly and slowly in German English, "*if* you please, that place belongs to my wife or to my daughter. For the moment they sit beside me, but I keep that place for my wife or my daughter. That seat is therefore reserved. It is our seat. You may of course use the two remaining seats."

"I'm sorry," said Mrs. Montrose, feeling snubbed, and she and Mrs. Forrester sat down side by side on the two remaining seats opposite the German family. Beside them the hamper looked out of the window at the charming view. Their gaiety and self-esteem evaporated. The train rocked along.

The three continued to stare at the two young women. Suddenly the mother leaned toward her daughter. She put up her hand to her mouth and whispered behind her hand, her eyes remaining fixed on Mrs. Montrose. The daughter nodded. She also stared at Mrs. Montrose. Mrs. Montrose flushed. The mother sat upright again, still looking at Mrs. Montrose, who felt very uncomfortable, and very much annoyed at blushing.

The man ceased staring at the two young women. He looked up at the rack above him, which contained their suitcases.

"Those are your suitcases," he asked, or rather announced.

"Yes," said Mrs. Montrose and Mrs. Forrester without smiles.

"They are large," said the man in a didactic manner, "they are too large. They are too large to be put on racks. A little motion, a very little motion, and they might fall. If they fall they will injure myself, my wife, or my daughter. It is better," he continued instructively, "that if they fall, they should fall upon your heads, not upon our heads. That is logical. They are not my suitcases. They are your suitcases. You admit it. Please to move your suitcases to the opposite rack, where, if they fall, they will fall upon your own heads." And he continued to sit there motionless. So did his wife. So did his daughter.

Mrs. Montrose and Mrs. Forrester looked at the suitcases in dismay. "Oh," said Mrs. Forrester, "they are so heavy to move. If you feel like that, please won't you sit on this side of the carriage, and we will move across, under our own suitcases, though I can assure you they will not fall. Or perhaps you would help us?"

"We prefer this side of the carriage," said the man with the blue tooth. "We have sat here because we prefer this side of the carriage. It is logical that you should move your suitcases. It is not logical that my wife, my daughter, and I should give up our seats in this carriage, or remove your suitcases."

Mrs. Montrose and Mrs. Forrester looked at each other with rage in their hearts. All their self-satisfaction was gone. They got up and tugged as the train rocked along. They leaned resentfully across the erectly sitting man, and his wife and his daughter. They experienced with exasperation the realization that they had better make the best of it. The train, they knew, was crowded. They had to remain in this carriage with this disagreeable family. With much pulling and straining they hauled down the heavy suitcases. Violently they removed the parcels of the German family and lifted their own suitcases onto the rack above their heads, disposing them clumsily on the rack. Panting a little (they disliked panting), they settled down again side by side with high colour and loosened wisps of hair. They controlled their features so as to appear serene and unaware of the existence of anyone else in the railway carriage, but their hearts were full of black hate.

The family exchanged whispered remarks, and then resumed their scrutiny of the two young women, whose elegance had by this time a sort of tipsy quality. The girl leaned toward her mother. She whispered behind her hand to her mother, who nodded. Both of them stared at Mrs. Forrester. Then they laughed.

"Heavens!" thought the affronted Mrs. Forrester, "this is outrageous! Why can't Alice and I whisper behind our hands to each other about these people and make them feel simply awful! But they wouldn't feel awful. Well, we can't, just because we've been properly brought up, and it would be too childish. And perhaps they don't even know they're rude. They're just being natural." She breathed hard in frustration, and composed herself again.

Suddenly the man with the blue tooth spoke. "Are you English?" he said loudly.

"Yes – well – no," said Mrs. Forrester.

"No – well – yes," said Mrs. Montrose, simultaneously.

A derisive look came over the man's face. "You must know what you are," he said, "either you are English or you are not English. Are you, or are you not?"

"No," said Mrs. Montrose and Mrs. Forrester, speaking primly. Their chins were high, their eyes flashed, and they were ready for discreet battle.

"Then you are Americans?" said the man in the same bullying manner.

"No," said Mrs. Montrose and Mrs. Forrester.

"You can't deceive *me*, you know," said the man with the blue tooth, "I know well the English language. You *say* you are not English. You *say* you are not American. What, then, may I ask, are you? You must be something."

"We are Canadians," said Mrs. Forrester, furious at this catechism.

"*Canadians*," said the man.

"Yes, Canadians," said Mrs. Montrose.

"This," murmured Mrs. Forrester to Mrs. Montrose, "is more than I can bear!"

"What did you say?" said the man, leaning forward quickly, his hands on his knees.

"I spoke to my friend," said Mrs. Forrester coldly, "I spoke about my bear."

"Yes," said Mrs. Montrose, "she spoke about her bear."

"Your bear? Have you a bear? But you cannot have a bear!" said the man with some surprise.

"In Canada I have a bear. I have two bears," said Mrs. Forrester conceitedly.

"That is true," said Mrs. Montrose nodding, "she has two bears. I myself have five bears. My father has seven bears. That is nothing. It is the custom."

"What do you do with your bears?" asked the man.

"We eat them," said Mrs. Forrester.

"Yes," said Mrs. Montrose, "we eat them. It is the custom."

The man turned and spoke briefly to his wife and daughter, whose eyes opened wider than ever.

Mrs. Montrose and Mrs. Forrester felt pleased. This was better.

The man with the blue tooth became really interested. "Are you married?" he asked Mrs. Forrester.

"Yes," she replied. (We'll see what he'll say next, then we'll see what we can do.)

"And you?" he enquired of Mrs. Montrose. Mrs. Montrose seemed uncertain. "Well, yes, in a way, I suppose," she said.

The man with the blue tooth scrutinized Mrs. Montrose for a moment. "*Then,*" he said, as though he had at last found her out, "If you are married, where is your husband?"

Mrs. Montrose took out her pocket handkerchief. She buried her face in her hands, covering her eyes with her handkerchief. She shook. Evidently she sobbed.

"Now you see what you've done!" said Mrs. Forrester. "You shouldn't ask questions like that. Just look at what you've done."

The three gazed fascinated on Mrs. Montrose. "Is he dead or what is he?" asked the man of Mrs. Forrester, making the words almost quietly with his mouth.

"Sh!!" said Mrs. Forrester very loudly indeed. The three jumped a little. So did Mrs. Montrose.

There was silence while Mrs. Montrose wiped her eyes. She looked over the heads opposite. The wife leaned toward her husband and addressed him timidly behind her hand. He nooded, and spoke to Mrs. Forrester.

"Well," he said, "at least you admit that *you* have a husband. If you have a husband then, where is he?"

"Oh, I don't know," said Mrs Forrester lightly.

"No, she doesn't know," said Mrs. Montrose.

The three on the opposite seat went into a conference. Mrs. Montrose and Mrs. Forrester did not dare to look at each other. They were enjoying themselves. Their self-esteem had returned. They had impressed. Unfavourably, it is true. But still they had impressed.

The man with the blue tooth pulled himself together. He reasserted himself. Across his waistcoat hung a watch chain. He took his watch out of his pocket and looked at the time. Then to the surprise of Mrs. Montrose and Mrs. Forrester he took another watch out of his pocket at the other end of the chain. "You see," he said proudly, "I have two watches."

Mrs. Montrose and Mrs. Forrester were surprised, but they had themselves well in hand.

Mrs. Montrose looked at the watches disparagingly. "My husband has six watches," she said.

"Yes, that is true," nodded Mrs. Forrester, "her husband *has* got six watches, but my husband, like you, unfortunately has only two watches."

The man put his watches back. Decidedly the battle was going in favour of the two young women. How horrid of us, he was so pleased with his watches, thought Mrs. Montrose. Isn't it true that horridness just breeds horridness. We're getting horrider every minute She regarded the man, his wife, and his daughter with distaste but with pity.

"You *say*," said the man, who always spoke as though their statements were open to doubt, which of course they were, "that you come from Canada. Do you come from Winnipeg? I know about Winnipeg."

"No," said Mrs. Montrose, and she spoke this time quite truthfully, "I come from Vancouver." Mrs. Forrester remained silent.

"And you, where do you come from?" persisted the man in a hectoring tone, addressing Mrs. Forrester. Mrs. Forrester remained silent, she had almost decided to answer no more questions.

"Oh, do not tell, please do not tell," begged Mrs. Montrose in an anguished way.

"No," said Mrs. Forrester importantly, "I shall not tell. Rest assured. I shall not tell."

"Why will she not tell?" demanded the man. He was tortured by curiosity. So was his wife. So was his daughter.

"Sh!!" said Mrs. Montrose very loudly.

The man seemed ill at ease. By this time nothing existed in the world for him, or for his wife, or for his daughter but these two Canadian women who ate bears.

"How is it," asked the man, "that you no longer buy my trousers?"

"I beg your pardon?" faltered Mrs. Montrose. For a moment she lost ground.

"I said," replied the man, "why is it that you no longer buy my trousers?"

The ladies did not answer. They could not think of a good answer to that one.

"I," said the man, "am a manufacturer of trousers. I make the most beautiful trousers in Germany. Indeed in the world." (You do not so, thought Mrs. Forrester, picturing her husband's good London legs.) "For three years I receive orders from Winnipeg for my trousers. And now, since two years, yes, since 1929, I receive no more orders for my trousers. Why is that?" he asked, like a belligerent.

"Shall we tell him?" asked Mrs. Forrester, looking at Mrs. Montrose. Neither of them knew why he had received no more orders for his trousers, but they did not wish to say so. "Shall we tell him?" asked Mrs. Forrester.

"You tell him," said Mrs. Montrose.

"No, *you* tell him," said Mrs. Forrester.

"I do not like to tell him," said Mrs. Montrose, "I'd rather you told him."

The man with the blue tooth looked from one to the other.

"Very well. I shall tell him," said Mrs. Forrester. "The fact is," she said, looking downward, "that in Canada men no longer wear trousers."

"What are you saying? That is not true, never can that be true!" said the man in some confusion.

"Yes," said Mrs. Montrose, corroborating sombrely. "Yes, indeed it is true. When they go abroad they wear trousers, but in Canada, no. It is a new custom."

"It is the climate," said Mrs. Forrester.

"Yes, that is the reason, it is the climate." agreed Mrs. Montrose.

"But in Canada," argued the man with the blue tooth, "your climate is cold. Everyone knows your climate is cold."

"In the Arctic regions, yes, it is really intensely cold, we all find it so. But not in Winnipeg. Winnipeg is very salubrious." (That's a good one, thought Mrs. Montrose.)

The man turned and spoke rapidly to his wife. She also turned, and looked askance at her daughter. The expressions of the man, his wife, and his daughter were a blend of pleasure and shock. The two liars were delighted.

At last the man could not help asking, "But they *must* wear something! It is not logical."

"Oh, it's logical, all right!" said Mrs. Forrester.

"But what *do* they wear?" persisted the man.

"I never looked to see," said Mrs. Montrose.

"*I* did, I looked," said Mrs. Forrester.

"Well?" asked the man.

"Oh, they just wear kilts," said Mrs. Forrester.

"Kilts? What are kilts? I do not know kilts," said the man.

"I would rather not tell you," said Mrs. Forrester primly.

"Oh," said the man.

Mrs. Montrose took out her vanity case, and inspected herself, powder puff in hand.

"I do not allow my wife and daughter to paint their faces so," said the man with the blue tooth.

"No?" said Mrs. Montrose.

"It is not good that women should paint their faces so. Good women do not do that. It is a pity."

(Oh, Alice, thought Mrs. Forrester in a fury, he shall not dare!) "It is a pity," she hissed, "that in your country there are no good dentists!"

"Be careful, be careful," whispered Mrs. Montrose.

"What do you mean?" demanded the man with the blue tooth.

(She will go too far, I know she will, thought Mrs. Montrose, alarmed, putting out her hand.)

"In our country," said the rash Mrs. Forrester, "anyone needing attention is taken straight to the State Dentist by the Police. This is done for aesthetic reasons. It is logical."

"I am going to sleep," said Mrs. Montrose very loudly, and she shut her eyes tight.

"So am I," said Mrs. Forrester, in a great hurry, and she shut her eyes too. This had been hard work but good fun for Mrs. Montrose and Mrs. Forrester. They felt, though, that they had gone a little bit too far. It might be as well if they slept, or pretended to sleep, until they reached Munich. They felt that outside their closed eyes was something frightening. The voice of the man with the blue tooth was saying, "I wish to tell you, I wish to tell you . . . " but Mrs. Montrose was in a deep sleep, and so was Mrs. Forrester. They sat with their eyes tightly closed, beside the hamper which still occupied the seat with the view by the darkening window. Mrs. Montrose had the inside corner, and so by reason of nestling down in the corner, and by reason of having an even and sensible temperament, she really and truly fell asleep at last.

Not so Mrs. Forrester. Her eyes were tightly closed, but her mind was greatly disturbed. Why had they permitted themselves to be baited? She pondered on the collective mentality that occupied the seat near to them (knees almost touching), and its results which now filled the atmosphere of the carriage so unpleasantly. She had met this mentality before, but had not been closely confined with it, as now. What of a world in which this mentality might ever become dominant? Then one would be confined with it without appeal or relief. The thought was shocking. She felt unreasonably agitated. She felt rather a fool, too, with her eyes shut tightly. But, if she opened them, she would have to look somewhere, presumably at the family, so it seemed safer to keep them closed. The train sped on. After what seemed to her a very long time, she peeped. The wife and daughter were busy. The husband sat back, hands on his knees, chin raised, expectant, eyes closed. His wife respectfully undid his tie, his collar, and his top shirt button. By this time the daughter had opened the hamper, and had taken from it a bottle and a clean napkin. These she handed to her mother. The wife moistened the napkin from the bottle and proceeded to wash her husband, his face, his ears, round the back of his neck, and inside his shirt collar, with great care. "Like a cat," thought Mrs. Forrester, who had forgotten to shut her eyes.

The man with the blue tooth lowered his raised chin and caught her. "You see," he said loudly, "you see, wives should look properly after their husbands, instead of travelling alone and . . . " But Mrs. Forrester was fast asleep again. The whole absurd encounter had begun to hold an element of terror. They had been tempted into folly. She knew – as she screwed up her closed eyes – that they were implicated in fear and folly.

The two young women took care to sleep until the train reached Munich. Then they both woke up.

Many people slept until they reached Munich. Then they all began to wake up.

1. Reread the first four paragraphs of the story. In your notebook, explain, in two to three sentences for each, how the paragraphs contribute to
   - the characterization of Mrs. Montrose and Mrs. Forrester;
   - the creation of atmosphere;
   - the establishment of the writer's tone (her attitude towards her audience).

2. a) Look up the word *surrealism* and, in your notebook, define it in your own words.
   b) Make a note of four or five surrealistic elements in "We Have to Sit Opposite." Compare your notes with a classmate's and discuss how the elements you identified affect the reader.
   c) Experiment with a surrealistic style. In a piece of personal writing, describe one of your own dreams, nightmares, daydreams, or even an incident from your life that had some aspect of the surreal. You may wish to make it public, rather than private, writing.

3. a) Munich was a seed-bed of Naziism prior to the outbreak of World War II. In a small group, discuss how the author uses that fact in her story.
   b) At the end of the story, Mrs. Forrester realizes that both she and her friend were "implicated in fear and folly." Explain in a concise paragraph the basis of Mrs. Forrester's insight.

4. In the story there are certain stereotypes of Canada and Canadians. Working with two or three classmates, identify the stereotypes and suggest why the author introduced them.

5. In a small group, prepare and perform a dramatization of the story.

NOTES ON PUNCTUATION
Lewis Thomas

here are no precise rules about punctuation (Fowler lays out some general advice (as best he can under the complex circumstances of English prose (he points out, for example, that we possess only four stops (the comma, the semicolon, the colon and the period (the question mark and exclamation point are not, strictly speaking, stops; they are indicators of tone (oddly enough, the Greeks employed the semicolon for their question mark (it produces a strange sensation to read a Greek sentence which is a straightforward question: Why weepest thou; (instead of Why weepest thou? (and, of course, there are parentheses (which are surely a kind of punctuation making this whole matter much more complicated by having to count up the left-handed parentheses in order to be sure of closing with the right number (but if the parentheses were left out, with nothing to work with but the stops, we would have considerably more flexibility in the deploying of layers of meaning than if we tried to separate all the clauses by physical barriers (and in the latter case, while we might have more precision and exactitude for our meaning, we would lose the essential flavour of language, which is its wonderful ambiguity)))))))))))).

The commas are the most useful and usable of all the stops. It is highly important to put them in place as you go along. If you try to come back after doing a paragraph and stick them in the various spots that tempt you you will discover that they tend to swarm like minnows into all sorts of crevices whose existence you hadn't realized and before you know it the whole long sentence becomes immobilized and lashed up squirming in commas. Better to use them sparingly, and with affection, precisely when the need for each one arises, nicely, by itself.

I have grown fond of semicolons in recent years. The semicolon tells you that there is still some question about the preceding full sentence; something needs to be added; it reminds you sometimes of the Greek usage. It is almost always a greater pleasure to come across a semicolon than a period. The period tells you that that is that; if you didn't get all the meaning you wanted or expected, anyway you got all the writer intended to parcel out and now you have to move along. But with a semicolon there you get a pleasant little feeling of expectancy; there is more to come; read on; it will get clearer.

Colons are a lot less attractive, for several reasons: firstly, they give you the feeling of being rather ordered around, or at least having your nose pointed in a direction you might not be inclined to take if left to yourself, and, secondly, you suspect you're in for one of those sentences that will be labelling the points to be made: firstly, secondly and so forth, with the implication that you haven't sense enough to keep track of a sequence of notions without having them numbered. Also, many writers use this system loosely and incompletely, starting out with number one and number two as though counting off on their fingers but then going on and on without the succession of labels you've been led to expect, leaving you floundering about searching for the ninethly or seventeenthly that ought to be there but isn't.

Exclamation points are the most irritating of all. Look! they say, look at what I just said! How amazing is my thought! It is like being forced to watch someone else's small child jumping up and down crazily in the centre of the living room shouting to attract attention. If a sentence really has something of importance to say, something quite remarkable, it doesn't need a mark to point it out. And if it is really, after all, a banal sentence needing more zing, the exclamation point simply emphasizes its banality!

Quotation marks should be used honestly and sparingly, when there is a genuine quotation at hand, and it is necessary to be very rigorous about the words enclosed by the marks. If something is to be quoted, the *exact* words must be used. If part of it must be left out because of space limitations, it is good manners to insert three dots to indicate the omission, but it is unethical to do this if it means connecting two thoughts which the original author did not intend to have tied together. Above all, quotation marks should not be used for ideas that you'd like to disown, things in the air so to speak. Nor should they be put in place around clichés; if you want to use a cliché you must take full responsibility for it yourself and not try to fob it off on anon., or on society. The most objectionable misuse of quotation marks, but one which illustrates the dangers of misuse in ordinary prose, is seen in advertising, especially in advertisements for small restaurants, for example "just around the corner," or "a good place to eat." No single, identifiable, citable person ever really said, for the record, "just around the corner," much less "a good place to eat," least likely of all for restaurants of the type that use this type of prose.

The dash is a handy device, informal and essentially playful, telling you that you're about to take off on a different tack but still in some way connected with the present course – only you have to remember that the dash is there, and either put a second dash at the end of the notion to let the reader know that he's back on course, or else end the sentence, as here, with a period.

The greatest danger in punctuation is for poetry. Here it is necessary to be as economical and parsimonious with commas and periods as with the words themselves, and any marks that seem to carry their own subtle meanings, like dashes and little rows of periods, even semicolons and question marks, should be left out altogether rather than inserted to clog up the thing with ambiguity. A single exclamation point in a poem, no matter what else the poem has to say, is enough to destroy the whole work.

The things I like best in T.S. Eliot's poetry, especially in the *Four Quartets*, are the semicolons. You cannot hear them, but they are there, laying out the connections between the images and the ideas. Sometimes you get a glimpse of a semicolon coming, a few lines farther on, and it is like climbing a steep path through woods and seeing a wooden bench just at a bend in the road ahead, a place where you can expect to sit for a moment, catching your breath.

Commas can't do this sort of thing; they can only tell you how the different parts of a complicated thought are to be fitted together, but you can't sit, not even take a breath, just because of a comma,

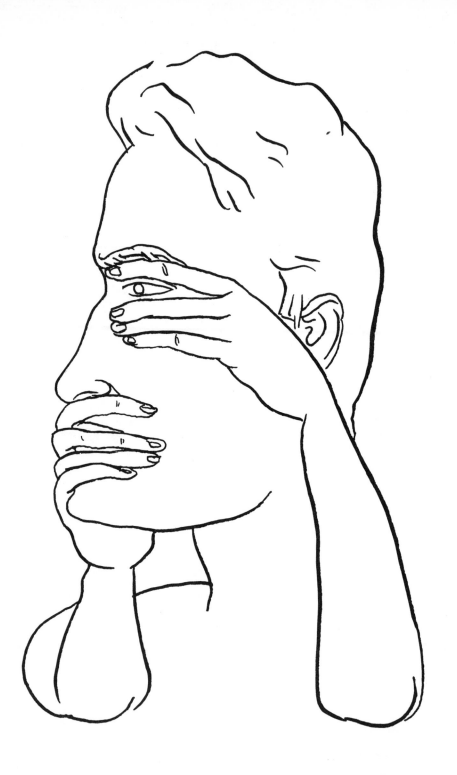

ERIPETEIA

peripeteia *n.* [Gr., literally "falling around"], a sudden change of fortune or reverse of circumstances (in a tragedy, etc., or, by extension, in the actual course of affairs).
The Oxford English Dictionary

Peripeteia can be described as the reversal that follows a moment of discovery. Aristotle, in his *Poetics*, argues that discovery and *peripeteia* are key stages in the development of a character in a tragedy, like Œdipus. These terms, understood in a broader sense, can be applied to other kinds of composition: the short stories and essays in this unit, for example. Discovery may occur when a growing pool of evidence can no longer be ignored or denied, or it may take the form of a sudden illumination. *Peripeteia* may involve a dramatic alteration in the course of a character's life, or a change in attitude, either subtle or radical. As you read the selections that follow, you are likely to find yourself caught up in the process of discovery and reversal, sometimes by identifying with a character, sometimes by responding to the arguments of a skilful essayist. That sort of participation of the reader with the author and the text is the heart of the reading process.

from "THE CREATURE FROM THE MARSH"

Loren Eiseley

he greatest prize of all," once confessed the British plant explorer F. Kingdon Ward, "is the skull of primitive man." Ward forgot one thing: there are other clues to primitive men than those confined to skulls. The bones of fossil men are few because the earth tolerated them in scant numbers. We call them missing links on the road to ourselves. A little less tooth here, a little more brain there, and you can see them changing toward ourselves in that long historyless time when the great continental ice sheets ebbed and flowed across the northern continents. Like all the students of that age, I wanted to find a missing link in human history. That is what this record is about, for I stumbled on the track of one.

Some men would maintain that a vague thing called atmosphere accounts for such an episode as I am about to relate, that there are houses that demand a murder and wait patiently until the murderer and his victim arrive, that there are great cliffs that draw the potential suicide from afar or mountains of so austere a nature that they write their message on the face of a man who looks up at them. This all may be. I do not deny it. But when I encountered the footprint in the mud of that remote place I think the thing that terrified me most was the fact that I knew to whom it belonged and yet I did not want to know him. He was a stranger to me and remains so to this day. Because of a certain knowledge I had, however, he succeeded in impressing himself upon me in a most insidious manner. I have never been the same since the event took place and often at night I start up sweating and think uncannily that the creature is there with me in the dark. If the sense of his presence grows, I switch on the light, but I never look into the mirror. This is a matter of old habit with me.

First off, though, we must get straight what we mean by a missing link.

A missing link is a day in the life of a species that is changing its form and habits, just as, on a smaller scale, one's appearance and behaviour at the age of five are a link in one's development to an adult man or woman. The individual person may have changed and grown but still the boy or girl of many years ago is linked to the present by a long series of steps. And if one is really alive and not already a living fossil, one will go on changing till the end of one's life and perhaps be the better for it. The term "missing link" was coined because some of the physical links in the history of man as a species are lost, and those people who, like myself, are curious about the past look for them.

My album is the earth, and the pictures in it are faded and badly torn and have to be pieced together by detective work. If one thinks of oneself at five years of age, one may get a thin wisp of disconnected memory pictures. By contrast, the past of a living species is without memory except as that past has written its physical record in vestigial organs like the appendix or a certain pattern on our molar teeth. To eke out what those physical stigmata tell us, we have to go grubbing about in caves and gravel for the bones of very ancient men. If one can conceive of the trouble an archaeologist might have in locating one's remains a half-million years from now, supposing they still existed, one will get an idea of the difficulties involved in finding traces of man before his bones were crowded together in cities and cemeteries.

I was wandering inland along a sunken shore when the thing happened – the thing I had dreamed of so long. In other words, I got a clue to man. The beaches on that coast I had come to visit are treacherous and sandy and the tides are always shifting things about among the mangrove roots. It is not a place to which I would willingly return and you will get no bearings from me. Anyway, what it was I found there could be discovered on any man's coast if he looked sharp for it. I had come to that place with other things in mind, and a notion of being alone. I was tired. I wanted to lie in the sun or clamber about like an animal in the swamps and the forest. To secure such rest from the turmoil of a modern city is the most difficult thing in the world to accomplish and I have only achieved it twice: once in one of the most absolute deserts in the world and again in this tropical marsh.

By day and night strange forms of life scuttled and gurgled underfoot or oozed wetly along outthrust branches; luminous tropical insects blundered by in the dark like the lamps of hesitant burglars. Overhead, on higher ground, another life shrieked distantly or was expectantly still in the treetops. Somehow, alone as I was, I got to listening as if all that world were listening, waiting for something to happen. The trees drooped a little lower listening, the tide lurked and hesitated on the beach, and even a tree snake dropped a loop and hung with his face behind a spider web, immobile in the still air.

A world like that is not really natural, or (the thought strikes one later) perhaps it really is, only more so. Parts of it are neither land nor sea and so everything is moving from one element to another, wearing uneasily the queer transitional bodies that life adopts in such places. Fish, some of them, come out and breathe air and sit about watching you. Plants take to eating insects, mammals go back to the water and grow elongate like fish, crabs climb trees. Nothing stays put where it began because everything is constantly climbing in, or climbing out, of its unstable environment.

Along drowned coasts of this variety you only see, in a sort of speeded-up way, what is true of the whole world and everything upon it: the Darwinian world of passage, of missing links, of beetles with soldered, flightless wings, of snakes with vestigial feet dragging slowly through the underbrush. Everything is marred and maimed and slightly out of focus – everything in the world. As for man, he is no different from the rest. His back aches, he ruptures easily, his women have difficulties in childbirth – all because he has struggled up upon his hind legs without having achieved a perfect adjustment to his new posture.

On this particular afternoon, I came upon a swamp full of huge waterlilies where I had once before ventured. The wind had begun to rise and rain was falling at intervals. As far as I could see, giant green leaves velvetly impervious to water were rolling and twisting in the wind. It was a species of lily in which part of the leaves projected on stalks for a short distance above the water, and as they rolled and tossed the whole swamp flashed and quivered from the innumerable water drops that were rolling around and around like quicksilver in the great cupped leaves. Everything seemed flickering and changing as if in some gigantic illusion, but so soft was the green light and so delicate the brushing of the leaves against each other that the whole effect was quite restful, as though one could be assured that nothing was actually tangible or real and no one in his senses would want it to be, as long as he could sway and nod and roll reflecting water drops about over the surface of his brain.

Just as I finally turned away to climb a little ridge I found the first footprint. It was just a patch of damp, exposed mud and was pointed away from the water as though the creature had emerged directly out of the swamp and was heading up the shore toward the interior. I had thought I was alone, and in that place it was wise to know one's neighbours. Worst of all, as I stood studying the footprint, and then another, still heading up the little rise, it struck me that though undoubtedly human the prints were different in some indefinable way. I will tell you once more that this happened on the coast of another country in a place where form itself is an illusion and no shape of man or beast is totally impossible. I crouched anxiously in the mud while all about the great leaves continued to rotate on their stems and to flash their endlessly rolling jewels.

But there were these footprints. They did not disappear. As I fixed the lowermost footprint with every iota of scientific attention I could muster, it became increasingly apparent that I was dealing with some transitional form of man. The arch, as revealed in the soft mud, was low and flat and implied to the skilled eye an inadequate adjustment to the upright posture. This, in its turn, suggested certain things about the spine and the nature of the skull. It was only then, I think, that the full import of my discovery came to me.

Good Lord, I thought consciously for the first time, the thing is alive. I had spent so many years analysing the bones of past ages or brooding over lizard tracks turned to stone in remote epochs that I had never contemplated this possibility before. The thing was alive and it was human. I looked uneasily about before settling down into the mud once more. One could make out that the prints were big but what drew my fascinated eye from the first was the nature of the second toe. It was longer than the big toe, and as I crawled excitedly back and forth between the two wet prints in the open mud, I saw that there was a remaining hint of prehensile flexibility about them.

Most decidedly, as a means of ground locomotion this foot was transitional and imperfect. Its loose, splayed aspect suggested inadequate protection against sprains. That second toe was unnecessarily long for life on the ground, although the little toe was already approximating the rudimentary condition so characteristic of modern man. Could it be that I was dealing with an unreported living fossil, an archaic ancestral survival? What else could be walking the mangrove jungle with a foot that betrayed clearly the marks of ancient intimacy with the arboreal attic, an intimacy so long continued that now, after hundreds of thousands of years of ground life, the creature had squiggled his unnecessarily long toes about in the mud as though an opportunity to clutch at something had delighted his secret soul.

I crouched by the footprint and thought. I remembered that comparisons with the living fauna, whenever available, are good scientific procedure and a great aid to precise taxonomy. I sat down and took off my shoes.

I have never had much occasion to look critically at my own feet before. In modern man they are generally encased in shoes – something that still suggests a slight imperfection in our adaptations. After all, we don't normally find it necessary to go about with our hands constantly enclosed in gloves. As I sat contemplating and comparing my feet with the footprints, a faintly disturbing memory floated hazily across my mind. It had involved a swimming party many years before at the home of one of the most distinguished comparative anatomists in the world. As we had sat on the bench alongside his pool, I had glanced up suddenly and caught him staring with what had seemed unnecessary fascination at my feet. I remembered now that he had blushed a deep pink under his white hair and had diverted my inquiring glance deftly to the scenery about us.

Why I should have remembered the incident at all was unclear to me. I thought of the possibility of getting plaster casts of a footprint and I also debated whether I should attempt to trail the creature farther up the slope toward which he appeared to have been headed. It was no moment for hesitation. Still, I did hesitate. The uneasy memory grew stronger, and a thought finally struck me. A little sheepishly and with a glance around to see that I was not observed, I lowered my own muddy foot into the footprint. It fitted.

I stood there contemplatively clutching, but this time consciously, the mud in my naked toes. I was the dark being on that island shore whose body carried the marks of its strange passage. I was my own dogging Man Friday, the beast from the past who had come with weapons through the marsh. The wind had died and the great green leaves with their rolling jewels were still. The mistake I had made was the mistake of all of us.

The story of man was not all there behind us in the caves of remote epochs. Even our physical bodies gave evidence that the change was not completed. As for our minds, they were still odd compounds of beast and saint. But it was not by turning back toward the marsh out of which we had come that the truly human kingdom was to be possessed and entered – that kingdom dreamed of in many religions and spoken of in many barbarous tongues. A philosopher once said in my presence, "The universe is a series of leaping sparks – everything else is interpretation." But what, I hesitated, was man's interpretation to be?

I drew a foot out of the little steaming swamp that sucked at it. The air hung heavily about me. I listened as the first beast might have listened who came from the water up the shore and did not return again to his old element. Everything about me listened in turn and seemed to be waiting for some decision on my part. I swayed a moment on my unstable footing.

Then, warily, I stepped higher up the shore and let the water and the silt fill in that footprint to make it, a hundred million years away, a fossil sign of an unknown creature slipping from the shadows of a marsh toward something else that awaited him. I had found the missing link. He walked on misshapen feet. The stones hurt him and his belly sagged. There were dreams like Christmas ornaments in his head, intermingled with an ancient malevolent viciousness. I knew because I was the missing link, but for the first time I sensed where I was going.

I have said I never look into the mirror. It is a matter of old habit now. If that other presence grows too oppressive I light the light and read.

---

1. The essay opens and closes with the writer's admission of fear, but he leaves it to the reader to formulate what has frightened him and why.
   a) In a written interior monologue, explore the reactions of the narrator when he discovers that the footprint is his own. Share your monologue with a classmate.
   b) Together, speculate on the reasons why the narrator will not look in a mirror, and on the thoughts that he attempts to banish by reading at night. Jot down your ideas and compare them with those of other classmates.
   c) Review the statement you wrote before you read "The Creature from the Marsh." Write the response you think the narrator would make.

2. a) Identify the sections of the essay that are narrative and those that are exposition.
   b) Assess as a group how the combination of modes affects the readability of the piece and the clarity and impact of its thesis.

3. Write a memoir of a moment of discovery that changed your perception of yourself, of others, or of the world around you. Select and indicate the audience for whom you are writing. (You may wish to read "Just a Little Japanese," p. 90, to see how another student handled the theme.)

4. With a classmate, evaluate Eiseley's use of pathetic fallacy and anthropomorphism to describe the natural environment.

5. "As for man, he is no different from the rest. His back aches, he ruptures easily, his women have difficulties in childbirth. . . ." Miller and Swift, in "*Man* as a False Generic" (p. 67), use the above quotation from "The Creature from the Marsh" in their argument. Read their article. In your own words, explain what they object to in the quotation. Compare your explanation with those of two or three of your classmates. Together, rewrite part or all of "The Creature from the Marsh" without using *man* as a generic.

"The world seeks balance; extremism begets extremism." In "Saturday Climbing," a father learns the meaning and the power of the above insight. In a small group, discuss what the statement is saying and whether events in the world today confirm or refute its thesis. You may wish to clip newspaper and magazine articles that support your group's assessment of the statement's validity.

SATURDAY CLIMBING
W.D. Valgardson

ixty feet up the cliff, the toe of his climbing boot resting on a ledge no wider than a dime, two fingers curled around a nubbin of rock, Barry was suddenly afraid that he would fall. "Rope," he called.

At the foot of the cliff, his daughter let out the golden line of rope that joined them. As Barry felt the rope go slack, he raised his right knee and pressed his toe into a shallow depression. Grunting with the strain, he stood up on his right leg, then paused, uncertain of his next move.

The cliff had proven to be deceptive. The conglomerate, with its rough, gravel-like surface, had looked easy. Close to the base, there were large handholds, so that at first the climbing was little more difficult than walking up stairs. Then, unexpectedly, the surfaces smoothed; the places where he could get a secure hold were spread farther and farther apart. At the same time, the numerous cracks dwindled until there was no place to set any protection. Unable to go back because of his pride, he had continued on until he now found himself dangerously far above his last piton. If he fell, he would drop twenty-five feet to the piton, then twenty-five feet past it before his rope came taut and held him. There was, because of the elasticity of the rope, a chance that he would ground out.

The thought flitted through his mind that it would be like falling from the top of a six-storey building. Tensing his fingers, he straightened his elbow and leaned back from the rock so that he could search for his next hold. Above him, there was a half-inch ledge. He reached up, got a good grip, then lifted his left leg higher than he had ever imagined he could and set his foot on a rough patch that would provide the necessary friction to hold his weight.

He had been scared many times but never like this. Never before had he been this close to paralysis, to a sensation of letting go so that the tension and the fear would be over. The way he felt, he imagined, was the way a wounded animal felt when it finally gave up fleeing and allowed itself to be killed.

Six inches from his left hand there was a vertical crack that seemed hardly wider than a fingernail. Cautiously, he explored it with his fingers. Just within his reach it widened slightly. He ran his hand over his rack and unsnapped the smallest chock nut. He forced the aluminum wedge deep into the crack. From the wedge there hung a wire loop and from that a carabiner. Catching hold of the rope tied to his harness, he lifted it up, forced open the spring-loaded gate of the carabiner and fitted the rope into the aluminum oval.

Once the gate snapped shut, he sighed with relief. The chock nut, the wire loop, the carabiner, the rope, fragile as they looked, would hold ten times his weight. If he wanted to, he could let go and simply hang in space.

"You all right?" his daughter called. "Yeah," he lied. "Just resting."

His voice sounded faint and breathy. He was glad she could not see his momentary weakness. He could not control the trembling of his legs. The muscle of his right arm jerked spasmodically. Ever since his wife had left him, he had tried to compensate by providing unhesitating leadership for his daughter. He did his best to keep life simple and uncomplicated. It was, he thought, the way to provide security.

He glanced down. Among the scattered grey boulders, Moira's red hair gleamed like a burnished cap.

"You're doing fine," she hollered. The crosscurrents of air that played over the cliff face blurred her voice, making it seem farther away than it really was. To hear what she said, he had to strain toward the sound. "You've got another twenty feet to a big ledge. You can do it easy."

He was grateful for her confidence. Before they had started climbing, there had crept into his daughter's voice a constant note of disparagement and disappointment. The times he had managed to overcome his own insecurity and had asked her what was the matter, she had turned her back on him, answering, "Nothing," with a tightly controlled voice.

Bewildered, he had sought the advice of women at work who had teenage daughters. They had been no help. Behind their competent, efficient professional selves, they too, he realized, were just as confused as he was. In desperation, he had gone so far as to pose the question of the relationship of fathers and daughters to his class. He had not been prepared for the reaction he got. From every corner of the room came cries of bitter disappointment and resentment.

As he had left the classroom, one student had called to him. He had stopped to wait for her. She had frizzy dark hair, wore long dresses that might have come from a western movie set, a rainbow assortment of beads, and a nose ring. She always talked as if she was thinking in some exotic language and was translating it badly. She was the only student he'd ever had who insisted on analysing *War and Peace* by consulting the *I Ching*.

"The caged bird proves nothing but the power of the captor," she had intoned.

For a moment, he suffered vertigo, and the cliff seemed to sway as if in an earthquake. He pressed his forehead to the cool stone and shut his eyes. Inside his flesh, his bones trembled.

Taking up rock-climbing had been an act of desperation. All the past activities Moira and he had done together – going to foreign films, visiting Seattle, beachcombing – she dismissed with a contemptuous shrug of her shoulders. At one time, they had played chess nearly every day. Lately, she pretended she had never seen the game. When he had noticed an advertisement for rock-climbing, he remembered that she had spoken admiringly of classmates who had hiked the West Coast Trail. He had registered them and paid their fees. Then he informed her.

He hoped she would be pleased. Instead, she was incensed that he had committed her to something without her consent. He knew she was right to be angry but he was too frantic to care. Over the previous month, she had come home late a number of times. Each time, the sweet-sour smell of marijuana clung to her, and her pupils seemed unnaturally large. He had not dared to accuse her of smoking dope. If he was wrong, she would never forgive him for being unjust. Being right frightened him even more. If she said, "That's right, I'm smoking dope, six joints a day, and sniffing coke and participating in orgies," he didn't know what he would do. Ranting and raving had ceased to work. Reasoning with her had no effect. He felt utterly helpless.

By emphasizing that the money was spent and there was no refund, he won the argument over rock-climbing. However, he took the car to the first class while she took her bike. She went prepared to sneer at everything, but once she saw her classmates, her attitude changed. Instead of Moira being isolated by her youth, Barry was isolated because of his age. Of the fifteen members, eleven were under twenty. The instructor still didn't need to shave more than once a week.

By the time the three hours were over and he realized that rock-climbing wasn't going to be rough hiking, it was too late to back out. There were only three girls in the class. In return for the attention of one-third of the young men, Moira was prepared to scale the Himalayas.

Barry began with an attitude that was typical of someone raised on the Prairies. Anything over three feet was a substantial elevation. During the second class, he was expected to climb vertical cliffs. He gave some thought to dropping out of the class but realized that, after the fuss he had made about the fees, he would look like a dreadful hypocrite.

Gradually, as a dozen Saturdays passed, what had seemed impossible was reduced to the merely difficult. Cliffs that had looked flat and smooth as polished marble became a series of problems and solutions. The names of the unfamiliar equipment became a part of his vocabulary. Young men in climbing boots frequented his backyard and kitchen. To his relief, Moira accepted him enough to spend an occasional hour practising knot-tying with him.

This weekend there had been no class. In an attempt to heal a rift caused by an argument over her going away to college – she was two years ahead of herself in school and, therefore, in spite of being in grade 12 was only 16 – he had offered to go climbing with her. To his surprise, she'd accepted.

"Climbing," he called.

"Climb on," Moira answered.

He stepped up, away from the safety of his perch. His life, he realized, was in her hands. If he fell, she was his protection.

The thought of giving her so much responsibility was like the prick of a thorn. In all other things, he had been trying to keep her from rushing headlong into taking on too much responsibility at once. The result had been a long series of disagreements. She did not have the decency to let one dispute finish before she began another. Sometimes three or four overlapped.

On Fridays, when he went to the faculty club, he ordered double brandies and brooded over whether he shouldn't have insisted on Sunday school in a good fundamentalist church all the past years. His colleagues, the majority of whom were the epitome of liberal tolerance about most things, when they talked about their teenage children reverted to wistful fantasies about convents and boarding schools in inaccessible locations.

The weekend past, Moira had wanted to go to an all-night party with a boy he just vaguely recognized as having drifted through the house two or three times. Barry was dumbfounded. At the same age, he'd had to have his girlfriends in before midnight. If he had kept a girl out all night, her father would have met them with a shotgun.

"Good girls," he said, quoting something he'd heard in adolescence, "don't stay out all night."

"Good fathers," she shot back, "don't think the worst of their daughters."

That afternoon was filled with slamming doors, weeping and raised voices. He found himself fighting so hard against her staying out all night that he compromised on three o'clock and afterward, when he had calmed down, wondered how it had happened. He had been determined to start with a deadline of midnight and let himself be persuaded to accept one o'clock. Although Moira claimed not to remember the chess moves, he had the distinct feeling that he'd been checkmated.

The final blow had been her insistence on going away to college. They had the money, he admitted. It just wasn't sensible, at sixteen, to travel 2,000 miles to attend a school when the local university was every bit as good, even if it did have him on the faculty. He suspected the choice had more to do with her all-night-party boy than with academic excellence.

Now, as he worked his way up toward the large ledge where he was to set up a belay station, it was as if Barry were in danger of being pulled backward by the sheer weight of his memories. It was with a sense of relief that he heaved himself onto the ledge. He paused to catch his breath, then anchored himself to a boulder.

"On belay," he shouted down, giving Moira the signal that he was ready.

His daughter, eighty feet below, seemed so small that Barry felt he could lift her into his arms. She looked no larger than she had been when, at three, she had eaten a bottle of aspirin. He had scooped her up and run with her four blocks to the hospital. After that desperate race and the struggle to hold her down – it had taken both him and a nurse to control her flailing limbs while the doctor had pumped her stomach – he was acutely aware of how tenuous her life was, of how much he would suffer if he lost her. For a long time afterward, he thought of her as being intricately constructed of fragile paper.

"Climbing," Moira answered.

"Climb on," he shouted.

From time to time, she paused to pull loose the chock nuts and pitons her father had left behind. These, since they would be needed later, she clipped to a sling that hung over her shoulder. Once, when she deviated from the route her father had taken, she became stuck at an overhang. Not having dealt with the obstacle himself, Barry could not help and had to leave her to find her own solution.

The climb seemed agonizingly slow, as if it would never be completed. Then, when it was over, and his daughter, grinning, breathless, was climbing over the edge, it was as if hardly any time had passed.

They sat side by side, sipping orange juice, their feet dangling in space.

"I thought you were in trouble," Moira said.

"I thought you were too," he replied, matching his weakness with hers. Then, ashamed, he admitted, "I gripped."

Moira twisted about. Her red hair was snugged at the back with a rubber band. Being outside had sprinkled her nose with light freckles.

She studied the cliff face. It rose another hundred feet. There was a crack that ran more than halfway, then a small series of outcrops. He tried to see the route they should take, but the last ten or fifteen feet seemed impossible.

"I'd come home for Christmas," she said in a rush, "and classes are out in April. It's not as if it was such a long time to be away."

She had caught him unawares, and none of his carefully prepared arguments were at hand.

"It's just so unexpected," was all that he could manage.

"I've got to leave sometime."

The house will be so empty, he wanted to say. How will I get used to being alone? It is as if you lost your first tooth only last year. As if I took you to kindergarten six months ago. You're barely rid of your braces.

She lifted her index finger and rubbed the side of her nose. She had done it as long as he could remember. It was her signal that she was going to impart a confidence or confess a wrongdoing – that she liked some boy in her class, that she had got a detention or spent all her allowance before the end of the week and needed more money.

"I'm not innocent, you know."

He wondered what she meant by that but was afraid to ask.

"I mean," she continued, "Vic Hi's a big school. You hear a lot. Everybody's on the Pill. The dope's there if you want it. There's lots of opportunity."

He was tempted to let loose his anxiety in a lecture, but the memory of the frizzy-haired student in his class stopped him. She had stood on one foot all the time they were talking, the sole of her left sandal pressed to her right knee. She had passed her hand before his face in an affected arc. He'd heard her father was a prominent lawyer in the East but found it hard to believe.

She had talked in aphorisms and riddles, then a silence had fallen between them. He'd wondered why she had bothered to call after him, what she had really wanted to say. He had left her but, after a few steps, glanced back. She had given up her storklike stance and was standing with feet together, shoulders slumped, her face slack beneath her gaudy makeup. For the first time, he had seen how much younger she was than he had thought. If he had not known better, he'd have said she was a lost child.

Just then, she had seen him watching her. Immediately, she had drawn up her shoulders, flung back her head, given an exaggerated sway of her hips and pranced away. That had been the last time he'd seen her. She had never come back to his class, and one day a yellow drop-slip with her name on it had appeared in his mailbox.

"I want to lead this pitch," Moira said.

Barry was startled. She had never led. Always before she'd been second or third on a rope.

"I was thinking of rappelling down," he answered. "I can't see a clear route up."

"There," she said. "There and there and there." She jabbed her fingertip at a series of holds.

"But where would you set your protection?"

Her hand wove a series of stitches in the air. "There. Up there. To the side. Back across. Up about six feet."

His fear for her was not without reason. The climbing, after seeming so dangerous at first, had begun to lose its aura of hazard. They all fell from time to time, but their ropes kept them from suffering more than bruised knees and elbows. Then, one of the climbers who was leading had ignored instructions and, overconfident, had put in only one piece of protection. He placed it improperly, and when he slipped and fell, his weight jerked it loose. For a moment, no one had been able to move, then those who were not belaying or climbing had run toward the boy who lay sprawled on his back. Bright red blood seeped from his nose and ear.

"Jackets," Barry had demanded. Red Cross training that he'd not thought about in years came back with an intense clarity. "Every piece of clothing you can spare. We mustn't let him get cold."

They all had moved automatically, clumsily, unable to think. Having done as he instructed, they all stood stupefied. Their faces were shocked white beneath their tans.

He sent two of the students racing down the hill for help.

For an hour, they huddled in a ragged circle around the boy whose hair was paler than the sun-drenched grass and whose skin might have been moulded from wax. He slipped in and out of consciousness. Each time his eyes shut, they all tensed, afraid that he had died. But then, he would groan or let out his breath harshly, and the moment would pass. Someone, Barry had not noticed who, had started collecting gear. One, and then another, began to pack. They moved slowly, silently, as if any noise would disturb the delicate balance between life and death.

Grounded out. That was what they called it. Because his safety had not been properly set, he had grounded out. Barry remembered that the air force had been like that too. Pilots never failed. They washed out. They never died. They bought it. *Grounded out.* The semantics covered up the fear.

Now, for a moment, it was as if, once again, he could hear the sharp startled cry; see the backward arc, the body, falling without grace or beauty, the rope writhing and twisting, the red-shirted boy settling in a cloud of unexpected dust.

"Ron," Barry protested, surprising himself at remembering the boy's name.

"Do you think I'd be so careless?"

It was asked in a tone that allowed no argument.

Stiffly, he stood up and tested his belay.

Don't climb, he thought, *it's too dangerous. Let us go back the way we came and find somewhere that'll always be safe.* But even as he thought it, he knew that it was impossible.

Once again, it was as if he were standing before the frizzy-haired girl, watching her long green nails sweep slowly before his face. At the time, he had not wanted to understand. "The world seeks balance," she'd said. "Extremism begets extremism."

"On belay," he said.

"Climbing," Moira replied.

His daughter, easily, with the supreme confidence of youth, grasped a handhold and pulled herself onto a flake. Smoothly, she worked her way up one side of the crack, straddled it and crossed over.

Below her, her father, ever watchful, full of fear, smoothly payed out the rope, determined to give her all the slack she needed while, at the same time, keeping his hands tensed, ready to lock shut, ready to absorb the shock of any fall.

---

1. In a piece of personal writing, describe and account for the feelings that this story evoked in you.
OR
Explore your feelings about the interdependence of parents and children.

2. a) In a small group, speculate on Valgardson's purpose for writing the story, and on whether it is aimed at a particular audience. Ensure that your opinions are substantiated by the story.
b) In a few paragraphs, and with specific reference to the story, suggest why the author chose to make Barry and Moira rock climbers.

3. Writing as Moira, confide in your diary your feelings at the end of the day's climb.
OR
Writing as Moira, compose some of the diary entries you would have made in the months preceding the Saturday climb. The entries should record the changes in your relationship with your father, and your emotional reactions to the fluctuating situation.

4. Write an article entitled "The Delicate Art of Compromise: Living in a Family." Identify the type of magazine for which you are writing and direct your article to that publication's audience. Ask a classmate to help you revise and then proofread the draft of your article. You may wish to send the final version to the publication you identified and to keep a copy in your writing folder.

5. a) "The semantics covered up the fear." People employ euphemisms to mask painful or frightening truths. In a small group, brainstorm a list of common euphemisms.
   b) Imagine that you are a public figure – an athlete or a politician, for instance – who has been caught in an embarrassing situation. Issue a statement to the press, using as many euphemisms as possible to save your dignity. Give your statement to another group; it is their task to "translate" the euphemisms to discover what might really have happened. Your group should do a similar translation of the other group's press statement.

THE LAST WIFE
Marian Engel

at was up on a ladder shoving plaster into the hole in Nick's ceiling when the telephone rang. She had been putting off the job for the longest time, had indeed had an estimate from a plasterer, then decided that six small holes left from the rewiring were something she could handle herself. She was, in fact, enjoying pushing the squishy stuff into the crevices when the telephone summoned her. She felt as if she were back in school, getting the little ones to work off their tensions by manipulating clay. She had procrastinated only to discover plastering was very satisfying: good.

The telephone rang. She got down off the ladder automatically. It might be a job for Chris and goodness knew he needed it. Too late she realized she was leaving three doorknobs and a newel post smeared with white.

She picked up the phone, half amused; glanced at the calendar beside it. "It's twenty years today since I met Marina," she thought. Because it was her birthday.

Twenty years. My God. She felt exactly the same as she had at seven and now she was old enough to have known someone for twenty years.

"Hello?"

It was Marina, of course. Marina, to wish her a happy birthday, if not to acknowledge that it was twenty years since they met at the College of Art. "Pat, happy birthday, how are you, the most terrible thing . . ." Marina, all in a rush, without punctuation even by breath.

"Marina, I'm plastering."

"Plastering, what the hell for, can't you afford a plasterer?"

"Cash flow, dear."

"You get into such ugly words when you go into the same business as your husband. Why don't you go back to painting?"

"Marina, it's drying on the phone."

"Listen, I've got to talk to you, can I phone you back?"

"Half an hour, eh? That's what it'll take me to finish and clean up."

She got a rag in the kitchen and retraced her chipping progress, enjoying the texture of the flaking plaster as she went. They had made so many small changes in this house as they went along that it was half made of Polyfilla. Kids grow up, she thought, you reshape your living quarters. And yourself.

She got up on the ladder again and daubed, scraped, patted. Thought more about Marina, who lived in a fluster, in a rush. From crisis to crisis. Was she always upset because she was an artist, because her life had to contain chaos so she could reshape it in order? In twenty years she had bounced like a tennis ball from style to style, form to form, husband to husband, a rushing torrent. And produced. Her work was perhaps not first-rate but it had energy, colour: it caught and held interest. You could forgive a person who produced good work a lot.

But Marina always made her feel guilty. Here she was peaceful, domestic, still with Chris. Still at home. Other mums went out and worked but she found that if she did, Chris missed half his phone calls, the kids missed their home-made food, and she lacked the energy to juggle so many worlds. Funny, she thought, to feel guilty at leading a life that so obviously contained the Christian virtues that she had been brought up to fulfil. She loved Chris, liked to help him, got on well with him. Was sometimes annoyed at the boys, did too much for them, manipulated their moods. Sometimes she thought the four of them were the last happy family.

Dangerous, that, with what was in the air these days: never be smug. She got down off the ladder, collected her implements, washed them, phoned Marina.

Marina had rushed off.

She loved working with her hands. She chipped the drying plaster off the plastic pail very slowly, thinking, Marina, Marina how you have rushed through life as if you were a bit of glass in a kaleidoscope, and how I have stood still. Is it Michael in jail for cocaine this time, or Jerry making a row over David's visiting arrangements, or your dealer shafting you? Has your crazy sister in Halifax made another impossible demand?

Twenty years. She looked at herself in the mirror. There was a definite sag under her chin. They had once both been girls in plaid skirts and saddle shoes, filling in forms at the College of Art. "Hey, that's my birthday." Then she, the plain stolid one, had flown into Marina's vortex, double-dating, lending pencils, sharing an apartment, moving out because of the lovers.

I wasn't so plain, she thought. I had something. I still have Chris.

She did not, she thought, have Marina's energy. She was not passive, no, there was something stubbornly active still inside her; but she was not fit for the hurly-burly aggressive artist's world. She had settled for a stool in a drawing office, drawing exquisite forms to order. She was not a real artist, not an independent.

Marina phoned again as Pat was putting the dinner in the oven. Michael was in jail; her dealer was ripping her off; her sister in Halifax was in bed with a broken ankle and she was going to leave her there, it was time she learned if you were going to have six kids you found help closer than Toronto. But Jerry was cool, he was speaking to her again, which helped David; in fact he had even bought a picture at her show. And wasn't it soooooo-per that they had known each other twenty years now and would she come out and celebrate?

"I'm sorry, Marina, but I think Chris and the boys have something planned for tonight."

"Pat, you're so square!"

"Well, it's too late to change now. Do you want to come over for a while?" From your rainbow to my plateau? Marina didn't. She needed her whirl.

Chris and the boys had pink wine and pink roses for her. Chris looked wiped out, too tired. Times are getting tough, she thought. I'm glad the house is paid off. I'm glad I can do my part. He's so hopeless with his hands.

Afterwards, she sanded the plaster in Nick's room while she and Chris told each other their day: the old ritual. "Marina called when I was up on the ladder and I left plaster all over the house," was her sole adventure.

"What's up with Marina?"

"I can't even remember. She's like an eggbeater, isn't she? I don't know how she does her work."

"Her strength is as the strength of ten because her heart is pure. Who's she with now?"

"She's alone. Mike's in jail. She'll stay clear of him when he comes out."

"I don't understand a woman like Marina, bouncing like that from man to man."

"Her psychiatrist told her she wasn't monogamous."

"Jerry could have told her that."

"Well, he wasn't exactly, either. Do you know, we've known each other twenty years now?"

"I've always thought she was a strange friend for you."

"Ying and yang, I guess so – oh, I don't mean sex, Chris." Because he had flinched. "We complement each other."

"She hasn't your stillness, your peace. You're like a pillow. I rest on you."

She looked down and smiled at him, then. "I need her turmoil, I think. She lives my borrowed life. Sometimes she makes me feel ashamed of my stodginess, but I love to hear about the way she lives: she gets hurt, but she's so . . . alive."

"So are you."

"She says I should go back to painting."

"Do you want to?" He was flinching again.

So often in a marriage, she thought, you have to decide whether to be good or to be honest.

"I don't think so," she said. "When I feel creative I work on the house. People say it's a cop-out to give up your art. I think, if you can give it up, it wasn't art."

Chris looked disapproving. "You were very good."

"Oh, precise; but I never took off. I hadn't the energy, I think. Anyway, you and the kids need me, and I like to be needed."

They went to bed early, after showering the flakes of plaster out of their hair. In the morning a new job came in and Chris was pleased and excited. He leapt off, leaving her a list of things to do.

She didn't do them. She read the paper slowly, and sat down to think about her life. Marina had lit some kind of fire. What was she doing with herself but aging slowly, in the service of other people, and was that right? What if Chris, who was edgy these days, took off with someone less like a pillow? What if the business failed utterly in some kind of depression?

Maybe I'll start drawing again, take a course somewhere, try the Open Studio.

The fact was, she decided, that hers wasn't a marketable talent. It had been a very small one, and without nurturing, it would not have grown. What she liked to do with it now was arrange anchovies perfectly on a salad.

Chris came home unexpectedly, found her moping. "What are you doing, doing nothing?"

"Thinking."

"Where's the lens for the Nikon?"

"On the sideboard."

"Oh, yes; thanks."

He dashed out again. When he was happy his face filled out; his thinness did not show. Though he ate like a horse. She loved him the way she loved her house; they were both seemly and beautiful.

She sighed and made his phone calls. At least, in case something happened, she had a half-interest in the house. "Why am I thinking like that?" she wondered.

Later, Marina called again, as she had every day for years. Pat was impatient with her.

"Why are you snarky?"

"You know me too well."

"Well, give over, why?"

"Oh, I think about your life and about mine and I like my life but I don't like to feel square."

"Then find a lover. It would tone you up, do you good."

"Heavens, I wouldn't know how."

"Listen, is there something wrong between you and Chris?"

"There's something wrong between me and the world. I'm the last wife."

"Good for you. I couldn't stand it the twice I tried, but it's nothing against you. As long as you're doing what you want."

"Oh, I am; but I'm beginning to feel that I oughtn't to want what I want."

"Watch that number, Pat; it's a bummer. I've been everywhere. I ought to know."

A house, children, a garden; enough to do. Chris, who was sometimes her father, sometimes her friend, sometimes her youngest child. It was like the bland, perfect pictures she had drawn when she was out working, before she entered Chris's world. It frightened her: the whole world was upset and she was happy. She cut herself grating the carrots.

Marina called that night when they were in bed. Her sister had died. How could anybody die of a broken ankle? She was more irritable than heart-broken. Her sister had been limp, the brother-in-law was limp, none of the family could cope, she was the only one who had any money . . .

"I pray for that girl," Pat said as she hung up.

"You what?" Chris asked, suddenly awake.

"I pray for that girl."

"Do you still say prayers?"

"Not formal ones. But I do when I feel like it."

"I thought we agreed we didn't believe in God."

"Did we? I don't remember."

"Good heavens, woman. You're going back to the old, primitive things."

"It does no harm," she said defensively.

"I hate to see you falling back into superstition."

She lay back with her elbows behind her head and thought awhile. "Religion is private," she said. "I don't think you should tell me what to feel."

"You're bringing up my children. What have you taught them?"

"Nothing, except that if they feel like praying, it might help."

"Honestly, Pat. I thought you were a good rationalist."

She was half amused. He might be accusing her of having an affair. "Look, Chris, anything that can help you keep your still centre is good. You get drunk, sometimes, and spew out all your bad feelings. Do I object? Then why shouldn't I have little pleading conversations with the corner of the Lord I can't disbelieve in?"

He got up and paced around the bedroom. He ranted and raved. She had not realized that his rationalism was still so important to him. She was almost amused. She let him go on, and found herself saying she disagreed.

"Oh well," he said sulkily. "please yourself. Only don't go dragging the boys to church."

"Heavens, I couldn't."

"I'm astonished at you. All this time you've had a kind of secret life."

"Haven't you? How can anyone know everything about another person?"

"I mean you expect Marina to go around casting hexagrams and chanting and taking up every new religion that comes along, but not you."

Suddenly she felt him fall into sleep. She lay in the dark for a long time, warm beside him, and immensely more content. The reason her drawings had not been good was that they were too easy, too perfect; they did not reach out, or strive. Her life had a flaw in it now, and she felt better.

---

1. a) Work in a group of three. One of you should take the role of Pat, one the role of Chris, and the third the role of Marina. Imagine how your character would describe the other two to someone who didn't know them, and then role-play the descriptions for your group.

   b) Discuss the descriptions and, as a group, assess whether they were true to Engel's characters, considering diction as well as content.

   c) Talk about whether it is possible to create an objective character sketch. Describe in a paragraph one of the characters as objectively as possible.

2. a) Marian Engel has chosen to tell her story in the third person

from the point of view of one character, Pat. With a classmate, discuss and evaluate the effect upon the reader of the third-person limited point of view.

b) Write a diary as Pat to relate one of the events or conversations in the story.

3. "Pat is stronger and more independent than Marina." Reread the story and come to your own conclusion about Pat. With specific references to the story, write a paragraph defending or attacking the statement above.

4. In a piece of personal writing for your writing folder, examine the attitudes to religion that are revealed during the last argument between Pat and Chris. State what the two positions are and then explore your own reactions to both positions.

5. Read "How Do You Know It's Good?" by Marya Mannes (p. 4), and compare what she says about the relationship between craft and purpose with what you and a classmate decided in response to the pre-reading suggestion for "The Last Wife." You may wish to make revisions to your original response.

During an idyllic trip to the beach, a party of
family and friends is reminded that "in the
midst of life we are in death." Share with a
classmate a personal experience or an
experience from your reading, viewing, or
conversing that confirms the statement.

INLAND BEACH
Margaret Creal

Nora and Monica, with Nora's mother and Monica's children – Jean and Ben – and two friends of Jean's, arrived at the beach around midday. Another family party was leaving, laden with snorkels and swim-fins and a sleeping baby in a basket. The young father, stepping aside to make room for the new arrivals on the path down the dunes, said, "It's all yours," and gestured at the deserted cove beneath the dunes and the long white sandspit that ran out into the bay. Not even a boat in the bay, nothing but sky and sea and sand and, far off, the dunes across the water.

They had come to this inland beach to gather the shells for which it was noted and to have a change from surf swimming. Nora and Monica were delighted by the privacy and tranquility; the children were not.

"Dullsville," one of Jean's friends said, not quite *sotto voce*.

Ben read the sign beside the path. *"Danger. Strong Tides."* He looked disdainfully at the blue water, still as glass. "There aren't any waves. Not even a little old ripple."

Nora, for long a summer resident on Nantucket and an experienced sailor, said, "You can't judge the pull of the tide by the height of the waves, Ben. Away out there" – she pointed – "the bay empties through a narrow neck into the ocean. When the tide runs out, the suction is tremendous. You know what happens when you pull the plug out of the bathtub?''

Ben disregarded the simplification. "You'd get swept out to sea?''

"No, dummy. In a bathtub, you'd be swept down the drain," Jean said.

This reminded Ben of an incident in *Stuart Little,* and he told them about it over their picnic lunch. "So if I got swept out to sea," he finished, biting into a peach, "I'd just give three sharp tugs on my little string and you could haul me in again.''

"Fat chance," Jean said, in the disparaging voice she was using these days with her nine-year-old brother, and helping themselves to fruit and cookies she and her friends skipped off on some private exploration.

Nora's mother and Ben constructed a drip-castle, with moats and towers and shell battlements. Nora and Monica lolled, lazily talking; the girls came back; they all went swimming.

The children, untiring, were still swimming when Nora and Monica settled down to shell gathering. The floor of the bay was like a mosaic, so richly encrusted was it with shells of all sorts coruscating under the limpid water. Kneeling, the two women chose with care the special shells they wanted, their companionable silence broken by the shrieks and splashes of the children who were playing an underwater hide-and-seek game that they called Marco Polo.

Monica, one hand full of translucent orange shells, looked up and across the sandspit, where towels and blankets and beach-wraps made a bright hump on the sands. Ben was on the other side, all by himself, happily porpoising around. She waited for him to surface, then called to him. "Swim with the others, Ben! Come back on this side. Please.'' Turning to Nora, she said, "I know how bored he is with my saying that. And how bored I am saying it. Do you realize that for over twenty years I've been standing on beaches, bellowing, 'Stay with the other swimmers!'''

Nora – whose children, like Monica's older ones, were in college – said, "How lucky you are still to have someone to say it to.'' She was dabbling in the water with a graceful hand. In the other hand she held a mesh bag half full of shells. "I can't think what we're going to do with all these, can you? Shall we make sailor's valentines?''

"Or plaques saying *God Bless Our Home,* to surprise people with at Christmas. Your mother's putting hers in apothecary jars. She has about a hundred of them.''

"So that's where they got to. I've been looking all over the house for those jars.''

"I'm sure she could spare you a couple of dozen.'' Monica sat back on her heels, fondly looking at Nora's mother who with a book in hand was walking towards the dunes. The purple of her long full skirt, the pink of the silk shirt she had borrowed from Nora, the orange of her conical straw hat – these colours blazed against the scintillating sand. "If I could look like her when I'm eighty I wouldn't mind being old." She glanced across the sandspit, said, "Damn," and got up abruptly, leaving Nora immersed in her shell collecting. She ran across the spit, the sand burning her feet. I'm tired of bossing people around, she thought. I'll be glad when he's grown up.

To him she said shortly, "Ben, you're too old to forget rules. Come back with the others, and come at once." It vexed her to have to nag. He was just a few yards away, and only waist-deep, but rules were rules.

The water around him was indigo, though closer in it was colourless. Every pebble could be seen and schools of minnow darting zigzag. Miniature fern-fronds moved gently in their sunlit world. How beautiful it all was, the water and the light and the enamelled sky. Perhaps as lovely a summer day as she would ever see. She watched Ben indulgently, not wanting to destroy her pleasure in the day with a battle of wills. After all, he wasn't doing anything, he wasn't ignoring her or disappearing from sight, as he had liked to do all week long in the tumultuous ocean surf. He was just paddling with his hands and doing a kind of on-the-spot marching.

"Come on, Benjamin," she said cajolingly. He said something in reply, and she frowned, reacting to his words without quite hearing them. "What? What did you say?"

"I said, I'm trying to come in, and I can't." He was smiling as if he were perplexed, but amused.

"Don't be silly," Monica said. "Of course you can come in."

"I can't. I can't get in."

Fear pricked at her heart, but only momentarily. He was so close to her – a few strides, and she could reach him. He was in no danger, and perhaps it was good for him to have some experience of the sea's strength. She waded into the water and said, "Now. Just swim, or walk, to me."

"I'm trying."

Hearing a note of alarm beneath the cheerfulness, she began to move towards him. She was still holding the shells in her hand, and waist-deep, thought, What shall I do with them? And answered herself, I'll hang on to them. Holding the shells made it clear that there was nothing seriously wrong. "Good, strong strokes," she said, wanting him to take care of this by himself.

He began swimming, his brown arms stretching well ahead of him, his feet kicking rhythmically. But he was not getting any closer to her. All at once, with a shudder of cold and surprise, Monica was up to her neck. The firm, sandy bottom had disappeared, and Ben was several yards from her. It's serious, she thought, it's a terrific current. She let the shells go and began to swim. With a few strokes, she was beside him. She put an encouraging hand on his back and, turning, saw that the shore was much farther away than it should have been. They were drifting fast.

"We'll take it easy," she told him confidently, while inwardly cursing her folly. All that talk about drains and currents and rules, and she had let this happen. Ben nodded, looking into her eyes with a trust and confidence that smote her heart. Together, they swam. Ben had to work much too hard. Why don't they teach the breast stroke nowadays? she wondered, and remembered her father teaching her, long before she had learned Ben's kind of fast, fancy crawl. It was fine for racing down a swimming pool, but it left him with no staying power.

"Take it easy," she said, "It's not the Olympics."

The beach was deserted. No sign of the others. She began to realize the current was pulling them not only out, but down towards the end of the long spit of beach, beyond any reach of shore. This side of the bay was scalloped with coves, and with the tide running out from all of them – "I'm tired," Ben said, and Monica grabbed his right arm, pulling him towards her. "Rest. Don't talk." Wavelets of dark water ran over them, around them. But it was warm water, the sun was warm, they could keep going for some time. "You be the cart," she said. "I'm the horse."

He did not smile. He sputtered along, his head thrown rigidly back. She dared not look towards the shore, to measure their progress. She knew they should drift with the current, but if they did, could they make it back to shore? And what shore?

She stopped thinking. Ben was thrashing wildly. "You're – trying – to – drown – me! Let go!" Stupid, she thought, letting him go, of course he can't swim with one arm. At once he was upon her, his hands on her neck, clutching. She drew her feet up to her chest, made a heavy ball of herself, and went down, down. Lights sparked in front of her eyes. But he had released her.

Surfacing, she seized his arms, pushed him up so that his head was well out of the water. "Tread water," she ordered. "We're all right. Hear? We're getting back, but we have to be strong." She let him down again, still holding him by the arms, feeling by his lightness that he was obeying her. Her heart thundered as if it would burst out of her chest. His panic had scared her. And cost them dearly – the shore was farther away than ever. Behind Ben there was nothing but blue, endless, endless, until blue sky fell into blue water. But Ben was calm. His eyes, which had been full of terror, were brave and believing again.

"Ready?" she asked, and side by side they swam. If only she could tell him to float when he needed a rest! But there was no use; he was one of those people who couldn't float. Something to do with his centre of gravity or the way he breathed? She couldn't remember. She stole a look towards shore, and there, praise be, was Nora, up to her knees in water, her coronet of hair gleaming in the sun. How strong she looked, how reassuring, standing there firm as a rock.

"Don't – come!" Monica's voice rasped out, as if from the back of her head. Nora must stay there, out of the current, and *will* them back in.

"You're not far out," Nora shouted. "Can you touch bottom?"

Brilliant idea. Monica said to Ben, "You swim. I'll walk along beside you."

"OK." He was desperate with bravery.

But when she tried to stand, there was no bottom, and the current yanked her legs right out from under her. It was a nasty shock, after a moment of hope. But at least she knew what they had to do. They had to stay on the surface, swimming with the little waves that were running in to shore. No more treading water, no more reaching for the bottom.

Swimming along, very close to Ben, she tried to make plans. When he tires, she thought, I'll get him on his back, pull him along. But now, while they could, they must swim. She said – was it really her voice, so strained and gulping? – "I'll get behind and push your feet. Take four big strokes, and I'll push again."

It worked. The shore seemed closer. But Nora – Nora was ignoring them. She was kneeling in the sand, her back turned. She thinks we're all right, she's sorting her god-damn shells, Monica thought, and for a part of a second was bewildered, caught somewhere between incredulity and anger at such callousness. "Again," she said to Ben, and once more she said, and again, "Again." Her chest was burning. There was a fire where once her heart had been thundering.

Then Ben gave up. "Can't!" He gasped, swallowing salt water, choking. She grabbed him, tried to slam him on the back. "Tired . . . ahhh" – on a long wail – "I'm drowning. We're going . . . out to sea." Panic-possessed, pitiful, he turned on her, arms flailing.

She held him off, thinking, I'll have to hit him. How? Her breath came hard from somewhere along her backbone, as if her lungs, like her heart, had ceased to exist. She squeezed out, "You're all right. Ben!" But they were not all right. For the first time, Monica knew that she too was terrified.

"No! Oh – help me!" He flung back his head, eyes shut, face waxen, and as he struck out at her, sending up an iridescent spray, Monica saw his hand with the missing middle finger sheared off by the hoof of a horse that, rearing, had thrown him. The strong, broken little hand seemed to be saying something important about the nature of life, about its frailty and finitude.

Struggling with Ben, struggling for breath, her mind confused and strength spent, stricken with sorrow for her child whose choked laments, as they rocked together, crashed with sea sounds in her ears, Monica thought, It isn't worth it. She had used up her heart and lungs, steel bands were clamping around her shoulders and arms and her thighs. Why fight so bitterly, just to get back? And then, blessedly, peacefully, she knew that it would not be terrible to drown in the sun-struck blue.

At the same time, she was astonished to think that on this lovely summer's afternoon she was going to die. She thought, fleetingly, of her husband and her other children, of life and its bright joys, all vanished. But Ben – it must not be terrible for him. She must comfort him, teach him how to die. But first, quiet his shouting. It was unbearable.

It was not Ben shouting. It was Nora. Her voice came at them, ugly, strident, a rumble of harshness. "Cut out that crying . . . silly little fool . . . swim, stop bawling . . . swim."

The words, the sense of them, flayed Monica's spirit. How could she be so cruel to Ben, now? With an effort, she raised her head, wanting to protest, and through the water-splashed air saw Nora at the very end of the beach, swinging some kind of cumbersome rope. And she remembered, suddenly, that Nora's father and brother – the mother's husband and son – had been drowned in a sailing accident. What anguish this must be, for them!

So, with a great, death-defying resolution, she croaked at Ben, "Swim!" She shoved his feet and began it all again, shoving and swimming, shoving and swimming, her breath clattering out of her.

Then there was nothing to shove. Gone, she thought, indifferent. But she heard a great cry, and lifting her head from the tumble of water, she saw Ben sailing away from her, hanging on to a rope. Nora was laughing. Her white teeth shone.

Monica had a sensation of extreme joy: it was like some other mo-ment of earthshaking happiness, she could not bother to remember where, or when. This was enough. Moments later, she was on the shore.

"Saved by a clothesline," Nora said exuberantly, and Monica dropped the dripping tangle of jerseys and shirts and fell into Nora's arms. She had not thought a woman's embrace would be so comforting, so strengthening. It flashed in her mind: We are the same, we are one. We know what birth and death are.

Nora was speaking to her. Monica tried to move but could not; she was heavy as stone. Jean was there too, and her friends behind her, silent and with shocked faces.

"Mother, Mother," cried Jean, "what's happened to you? Your face is all twisted!"

Nora said, "Darling, your mother has had a terribly hard swim. Let her rest."

Monica tried to put out an arm to Jean, but it fell limply down Nora's back.

"Are you all right?" Jean asked fearfully.

Monica nodded. "My face'll untwist soon." Her words sounded twisted too, as if she had been heavily drugged or had had a stroke, and she still had not the energy to move away from Nora who must be tired of holding her up, but kept saying, "Everything's all right. Ben's all right, you're all right." Her abundant golden hair had fallen from its coils and lay in wet strands over her shoulders, streaking Monica's face.

"How long were we out there?" Monica asked, stupidly, as if it mattered.

"About ten years."

"Am I laughing or crying? . . . Your mother. I suddenly remembered about – and I thought how awful if — "

"She didn't see a thing. She's down there in the cove, no doubt reading her study book on Zen. I just happened to look up, and at first I thought you and Ben were having a cozy little swim. And the girls didn't have an inkling. Just as well, I guess. One lost head and I'd have lost mine, gone plunging into the current after you or, more likely, have raced off to town to buy a life preserver. And you know how long it would have taken me to find a parking place." Nora's lightness was tonic, exactly what Monica needed. "Now the girls are finding out what happened. They're giving Ben the third degree."

Smiling, Monica was aware that her face felt less grotesque. Through the blanket Nora had wrapped around her she could feel Nora's hand massaging deep into her back, her shoulders. Warmth and well-being began to flood through her, and more than that, a great elation. So short a time ago she had thought with tranquility of death; now she was jubilant to be alive. How little it takes to satisfy us, she thought, life itself is enough. This chain of moments is what we have. The bad ones, of disappointment, failure, frustration, grief, terror. And the good ones, like this one, when all was splendid – sky and sea and grass-speared dunes, her daughter racing past, hair flying, brown legs shining.

"I'm taking Ben some cookies. He's ravenously hungry." Jean slowed down, stopped. "Are you all right, Mother? Your face is normal again."

Love, the greatest good, Monica thought, and waggled a hand at Jean. Love, friendship, physical strength. Drawing apart from her friend, she kissed her on the cheek. "Thank you, Nora."

"Oh, my dear. . . ." Saying that, Nora's voice was unsteady. Recovering she said, "Ben, I thought you were a whole regiment of Arabs coming across the sand."

He was swathed in striped towels, trailing another that had been hitched around his waist. His eyes, caught in full sunlight, were like lapis lazuli.

A thread of memory unwound: Monica was one of a row of schoolgirls, teeth banded in wire, pigtails banded in elastic, messy tunics, ties askew, *Aeneids* dutifully open on their desks, listening with apathetic faces to the Latin mistress, shy, scholarly, English, describing to them the colour and texture of lapis lazuli. But Monica had not been bored. For that alone, for lapis lazuli, she had thought, the *Aeneid* is worth reading.

In Siena, years later, she had wandered into an antique shop on San Pietro and had found a tiny bowl carved from the blue, gold-flecked stone and immediately had smelled the chalky smell of the schoolroom, seen the bushes weighted with purple lilac outside the window, heard the precise light voice of the teacher and, from a distance, the *kthwop* of tennis ball on backboard.

Now, seeing the colour, gold-dusted by the sun, in her young son's eyes, she was startled with pleasure and put out her hand to gently touch his face. His fair hair had dried in stiff wisps around his ears; beneath the skin's summer brown there was a touch of pallor.

He looked at her, taking her hand, twisting with his fingers the rings she wore on hers, and said gravely, "I'm sorry, Mother."

"Sorry!" She was incredulous, because for her there was only rejoicing. Bending to hug him she felt sudden hot tears on her cold cheeks, salt mingling with salt, pain with joy, and was swept back to that other moment when, tears of happiness spilling from her eyes and running over her sweaty face and into her damp and tangled hair, she had first looked at this child, scarlet and wrinkled, angrily mewing, still tied to her by the primal lifeline. What purity of bliss that had been. The rocking, explosive moment of birth, then all at once a liquid soft rippling – she herself a sand carving slipping heavily, languorously through deep sunlit waters. For an instant, piercing in its sweetness, she relived that moment when the universe had stood still, suspended in joy that had at its centre her newborn son and herself.

"Mother?" Worried by the tears that prickled his face, brushing them off, he drew away to look at her.

And she was recalled to this moment, and to her duty. She could not burden him with gratitude for the joy his birth had given her. She whispered, "We're a fine team, you and I," and released him.

With the unstudied courtliness that was part of his affectionate nature, he dropped a quick kiss on her hand and was off, careering across the hard sand, tossing away the towels as he ran, with arms outstretched like the wings of the white gull that, above him, slowly stroked on the wind blowing off the sea.

---

1. "Inland Beach" is narrated in the third person from Monica's point of view. The story consists of a series of discoveries culminating in a reprise of "that moment when the universe stood still."
   a) Reread the story, taking note of all the important moments.
   b) Discuss with a classmate the significance of Monica's insights during those moments and speculate on how they might affect her life.

2. Explain in your notebook the role or function of the following, writing a few sentences for each:

- lapis lazuli;
- Dullsville;
- clothesline;
- sand castles;
- strong, broken little hand.

In a small group, examine each other's explanations.

3. In a short essay, drawing upon personal experience, this story, and any other materials in this unit, argue, in writing, for or against one of the following:
   - "How little it takes to satisfy us . . . life itself is enough."
   - "The old cannot burden the young with gratitude for the joy they give."
   - "The careless moment is followed by an eternity of regret."

4. Work in a group of five. Each group member should assume the persona of one of these characters: Nora, Monica, Jean, Ben, Nora's mother. In a dramatic monologue, recount your perception of and reactions to the events of the day.

Much has been written of the impact on
children of mass media, with their excesses of
violence and sex and their distortion of reality.
Bergen Evans suggests in this ironic little
piece that the trouble may start at the parents'
knee with indoctrination through nursery
rhymes. In a small group, make a list of
rhymes and stories that you remember and
discuss their unpleasant overtones. (For
example, did you ever think of the "four and
twenty blackbirds" being baked alive?)

NURSERY CRIMES
Bergen Evans

hat the older generation is what it is surprises no one with any
knowledge of psychology who has examined the pabulum upon
which its members were nourished in their most impressionable
years. In fact, it redounds to our credit that we are not more abandoned
than we are when we consider that at a formative age we were taught
to admire such things as Jack's murderous requital of the giant's hos-
pitality, little Goldilocks's atrocious greediness, and the unscrupulous
mendacity of little Hans! Who could estimate, for instance, the effect
upon our infantile morality of such tales as that of Grimm's of the
soldier who, by merely striking upon his tinder box, could have his
dog, with eyes as big as saucers, convey to his bedroom whatsoever
young lady pleased him and who, when finally detected by a sagacious
counselor, thwarted justice by forcibly subverting the machinery of
civic order?

These tales, however, do not generally reach us before the age of
three or four. It is to the nursery rhymes, the very bases of our mental
fabric and social attitudes, which are taught us much earlier, that we
must look for the more dangerous influences. "Let me write a nation's
songs," a sage observed, "and I care not who writes its laws." And

certainly the forces which dictated the baneful ballads of our bassinets were sinister!

What objectionable practices, for instance, are condoned in "Higgledy-piggledy, my son John" and "Little Polly Flinders"! Surely the amused toleration of sleeping in one's trousers and sitting among the cinders could not be without a deleterious effect upon the child's later attitudes toward public sanitation and social hygiene! And in the latter there is a noticeable trace of that sadism which is all too common in these little poems. It is found again, for example, combined with hysteria, in "Three Blind Mice," where a foolish farmer's wife, after yielding to an absurd phobia, seeks satisfaction in mutilating the former objects of her terror. This inculcation of harmful fears is also observable in "Little Miss Muffet."

In so far, of course, as the attitudes and complexes engendered affect only the individual, they are the concern of the psychologist and the psychoanalyst, but there can be little doubt that in the subliminal depths of our nurseries forces are deliberately at work to condition the child's social attitudes. And these forces are directed and controlled by those to whose advantage it is to maintain the status quo and to continue the old system of capitalistic and bourgeois oppression of the masses. The evidence lies plainly before us in the nursery rhymes.

Is it merely the exigency of rhyme, think you, that compels Higgledy-piggledy, my black hen, to lay eggs but for *gentlemen?* Or is there not a direct implication that the proletariat is not entitled to a substantial breakfast?

And does not Simple Simon (simple indeed!) symbolically set forth the luckless unemployed? That the pieman, the capitalist, should be pictured as en route to a merrymaking at the very moment of his callous refusal is indicative of the coarse frankness with which the possessing classes avow their selfishness.

And what shall we say to the underhand manner in which the incompetence of the worker, and hence his lack of right to a share of this world's goods, are suggested in such verses as "Jack and Jill," "Little Boy Blue," and "Little Bo-Peep"?

2

Perhaps it is as well to treat the subject in a purely scientific manner by quoting some of these rhymes, once in every child's mouth, and appending a brief note in which the underlying force and the psychological effect are considered.

The following are typical: –

> Goosie, goosie, gander, whither shall I wander?
> Upstairs and downstairs and in my lady's chamber.
> There I met an old man who wouldn't say his prayers –

I took him by the left leg and threw him downstairs.

Here we see, held up for the delectation of the young, a representation of someone, apparently a member of the leisured classes, wandering about a house in a state of dangerous aimlessness and indolence, boldly disregarding all privacy. In the course of this peregrination he chances upon an elderly man upon whom he attempts to force his own religious practices and, not meeting with immediate and slavish acquiescence, proceeds to employ brutal violence.

Surely this is the nurture of fanaticism!

> Little Jack Horner sat in a corner
> Eating his Christmas pie.
> He put in his thumb and pulled out a plum,
> And said, "What a good boy am I!"

Obviously a picture of a sullen and inhibited child, who, conscious of his own greediness and execrable table manners, soothes himself with dangerous self-laudation. Students of the subject are undecided, but it is not likely that there is a sinister political suggestion in the approval expressed at the obtaining of the plum in a manner which openly defies convention.

That corruption in office is regarded with complacency by the majority of our citizens need no longer astonish us.

> Sing a song of sixpence, a pocket full of rye,
> Four and twenty blackbirds baked in a pie.
> When the pie was opened the birds began to sing,
> And wasn't that a dainty dish to set before a king?
>
> The king was in his counting-house, counting out his money.
> The queen was in the parlour, eating bread and honey.
> The maid was in the garden, hanging out the clothes,
> When by came a blackbird and pecked off her nose!

Passing over the vulgar ostentation of the first few lines and the intimation of the atrocious cuisine which would leave the birds so underdone, we find put forth for the amusement of the young an account of avarice and gluttony in high places. In neither king nor queen is there any suggestion of social responsibility, and the phrase "*his* money" is deliberately misleading. While the monarch gloats over extorted pelf, no doubt wrung from horny-handed peasants, and his degenerate consort pampers herself in greedy sloth, the worker, upon whose efforts their cleanliness and health depend, is foully mutilated by what was most probably an escaped victim of their bizarre appetites and barbaric cookery. And yet they manifest no concern!

Such literature is the food of young Harrimans and Romanoffs!

> Hey diddle diddle, the cat and the fiddle,
> The cow jumped over the moon.
> The little dog laughed to see such fun,
> And the dish ran away with the spoon.

This famous old rhyme belongs to a group which, though apparently innocuous, is really the most dangerous of all. Verses in this group, such as "The Man in the Moon came down too soon" and "Pease porridge hot," are composed of colossal masses of absurdity and are intended to destroy the last vestiges of the child's truth sense so that he may easily be led to regard the stock exchange as a safe road to wealth and the present state of society as in every way desirable.

Closely allied are other poems which encourage the young to indulge in those irrational hopes upon which the predatory members of society subsist. Here we would place "If wishes were horses" and "Bobbie Shaftoe." The latter is particularly illustrative in the confident manner in which it predicts that Shaftoe, despite the fact that common experience ascribes to seafaring men a course of conduct diametrically opposite, will fulfill his matrimonial obligations.

> There was an old woman who lived in a shoe;
> She had so many children she didn't know what to do.
> She gave them some gruel without any bread
> And whipped them all soundly and sent them to bed.

Here we see the crowded and unsanitary living conditions of the proletariat, their prolificity and their meagre diet, treated with a hardhearted levity. That the old woman did not know what to do about her excessive fecundity would only earn her the scorn of the inmates of any modern nursery. The suggestion of sadism, so often an accompaniment of the overstrained nerves and enfeebled constitutions of the poor, gives a macabre touch to the grim picture.

When this is the stuff of risibility for bourgeois juveniles we need not wonder at revolutions!

> Georgie Porgie, pudding and pie,
> Kissed the girls and made them cry.
> When the boys came out to play,
> Georgie Porgie ran away.

An interesting illustration of the state of affairs all too prevalent under the bourgeois sex morality. Here, instead of innocent and natural love play, we see the attitude engendered by the parental teaching of shame.

Georgie, though from his cognomen we may assume him to be some-what heavy and phlegmatic, is possessed of normal instincts and emotions. When, however, he proceeds to allow their natural expression, the girls, warped by a perverse morality, pretend pain instead of pleasure. This, of course, has its effect upon Georgie, who, finding his natural feelings inhibited, becomes introverted and shuns the society of his playmates.

There is little doubt that we have here the root of much of the need for the expensive system of asylums and mental hospitals which our decadent society must support.

> See-saw, Margery Daw,
> Jenny shall have a new master.
> She shall have but a penny a day,
> Because she won't work any faster!

It is dreadful to think that this instance of the mistreatment of a worker is taught to babes as a merry song! Jenny's wages are to be cut below the level of subsistence because of her effort to maintain a rate of production that would ensure continued employment. There is much uncertainty regarding Margery Daw, but as "see-saw" carries an un-mistakable suggestion of the fluctuations of dividends it is generally assumed that she was an irate stockholder whose greed initiated the oppressive measures.

> "Orange and lemons," say the bells of St. Clements;
> "I owe you five farthings," say the bells of St. Martins;
> "When will you pay me?" ask the bells of Old Bailey.
> "I don't know," says the big bell of Bow.

Or

> "When I get rich," say the bells of Shoreditch.

This attempt to suggest the sound of money in all things, even in the harmless ringing of the bells, may well account for the mercenary attitude so characteristic of the bourgeois. The inexorable demand for so trifling a sum is exceeded in baseness only by the flat refusal of the one version and the despicable evasion of the other.

That national obligations were repudiated and the gold standard abandoned by adults whose infancy had been thus conditioned should surprise no one who has made a study of psychology.

> Curlylocks, Curlylocks, wilt thou be mine?
> Thou shalt not wash dishes, nor yet feed the swine,

But sit on a cushion and sew a fine seam,
And feed upon strawberries, sugar and cream.

What a complete illustration of the unenlightened attitude toward women! The wooer, after tickling the young lady's vanity by an allusion to her coiffure, attempts to induce her to become his chattel by assuring her that, denied any share in their common labour and reduced to enervating indolence, she shall waste her time and ruin her eyesight on worthless needlework while she is pampered with a dangerous diet of fruit, sugar, and fat which will serve only to obviate in time the need for the cushion.

A dark picture indeed! And one that would deny all hope of emancipation were it not that the indomitable spirit of man has injected a ray of truth even into the profoundest depths of tyranny. "Old Mother Hubbard," for instance, infuses a salutary touch of economic realism into the nursery, which has done much to counteract some of the pernicious doctrines alluded to above, while the bold application of Communism by the Knave of Hearts has, as many mothers can testify, stirred the more vigorous of the young to emulation. Even Tom the Piper's son, though his lack of technical proficiency is to be deplored, shows a splendid disregard of vested interests, and Little Tommy Tittlemouse, who, we are told, caught fishes in other men's ditches, deserves to be ranked among the village Hampdens for his brave struggle against feudal privilege. In these and a few others we see the beginnings of that glorious counterpropaganda which in our neonurseries is sweeping all before it.

---

1. a) In your notebook, list up to ten words that are new to you and, using a dictionary, define them. Make an effort to incorporate the new vocabulary into your writing.
   b) Evans's use of sophisticated vocabulary and syntax helps to create the ironic tone of the essay. Select four examples and write a close analysis of their effect.

2. In "Nursery Crimes," Evans parodies the psychologist, the sociologist, and the politician, among others. Select a nursery rhyme and, in a paragraph, analyse it as Evans does, parodying the tone, diction, and attitudes of a "voice," either one that Evans mocks, or one of your own choosing (e.g., high school teacher). Read your piece to a classmate and together evaluate the accuracy of your presentation of the selected voice.

3. a) Evans employs a wide range of literary and rhetorical devices

to increase the impact of his parody. Find examples of the following in his essay:

- appeal to authority – quotations from and references to people of renown;
- hyperbole;
- inflated language;
- rhetorical questions;
- false deductions and/or misleading parallels;
- *reductio ad absurdum;*
- stereotyping.

b) In a group look for and analyse these techniques (and others) in advertisements, essays, editorials, letters to the editor, and other types of persuasive writing. (You may wish to inspect some of the selections in this book.) Present your findings to the class. If you like, compile a handbook of rhetoric, using your clippings as illustrations of the various techniques.

It is often asserted that great literature, Shakespeare's drama for example, is universal. In a small group, discuss how one of Shakespeare's plays that you have read (*Hamlet*, preferably) might be considered relevant for all times and places. At the end of your discussion, read the following amusing memoir, in which the author tests the wisdom of her theory that *Hamlet* is "universally intelligible."

SHAKESPEARE IN THE BUSH
Laura Bohannan

ust before I left Oxford for the Tiv in West Africa, conversation turned to the season at Stratford. "You Americans," said a friend, "often have difficulty with Shakespeare. He was, after all, a very English poet, and one can easily misinterpret the universal by misunderstanding the particular."

I protested that human nature is pretty much the same the whole world over; at least the general plot and motivation of the greater tragedies would always be clear – everywhere – although some details of custom might have to be explained and difficulties of translation might produce other slight changes. To end an argument we could not conclude, my friend gave me a copy of *Hamlet* to study in the African bush: it would, he hoped, lift my mind above its primitive surroundings, and possibly I might, by prolonged meditation, achieve the grace of correct interpretation.

It was my second field trip to that African tribe, and I thought myself ready to live in one of its remote sections – an area difficult to cross even on foot. I eventually settled on the hillock of a very knowledgeable old man, the head of a homestead of some hundred and forty people, all of whom were either his close relatives or their wives and children.

Like the other elders in the vicinity, the old man spent most of his time performing ceremonies seldom seen these days in the more accessible parts of the tribe. I was delighted. Soon there would be three months of enforced isolation and leisure, between the harvest that takes place just before the rising of the swamps and the clearing of new farms when the water goes down. Then, I thought, they would have even more time to perform ceremonies and explain them to me.

I was quite mistaken. Most of the ceremonies demanded the presence of elders from several homesteads. As the swamps rose, the old men found it too difficult to walk from one homestead to the next, and the ceremonies gradually ceased. As the swamps rose even higher, all activities but one came to an end. The women brewed beer from maize and millet. Men, women, and children sat on their hillocks and drank it.

People began to drink at dawn. By midmorning the whole homestead was singing, dancing, and drumming. When it rained, people had to sit inside their huts: there they drank and sang or they drank and told stories. In any case, by noon or before, I either had to join the party or retire to my own hut and my books. "One does not discuss serious matters when there is beer. Come, drink with us." Since I lacked their capacity for the thick native beer, I spent more and more time with *Hamlet*. Before the end of the second month, grace descended on me. I was quite sure that *Hamlet* had only one possible interpretation, and that one universally obvious.

Early every morning, in the hope of having some serious talk before the beer party, I used to call on the old man at his reception hut – a circle of posts supporting a thatched roof above a low mud wall to keep out wind and rain. One day I crawled through the low doorway and found most of the men of the homestead sitting huddled in their ragged cloths on stools, low plank beds, and reclining chairs, warming themselves against the chill of the rain around a smoky fire. In the centre were three pots of beer. The party had started.

The old man greeted me cordially. "Sit down and drink." I accepted a large calabash full of beer, poured some into a small drinking gourd, and tossed it down. Then I poured some more into the same gourd for the man second in seniority to my host before I handed my calabash over to a young man for further distribution. Important people shouldn't ladle beer themselves.

"It is better like this," the old man said, looking at me approvingly and plucking at the thatch that had caught in my hair. "You should sit and drink with us more often. Your servants tell me that when you are not with us, you sit inside your hut looking at a paper."

The old man was acquainted with four kinds of "papers": tax receipts, bride price receipts, court fee receipts, and letters. The messenger who brought him letters from the chief used them mainly as a badge of office, for he always knew what was in them and told the old man. Personal letters for the few who had relatives in the government or mission stations were kept until someone went to a large market where there was a letter writer and reader. Since my arrival, letters were brought to me to be read. A few men also brought me bride price receipts, privately, with requests to change the figures to a higher sum. I found moral arguments were of no avail, since in-laws are fair game, and the technical hazards of forgery difficult to explain to an illiterate people. I did not wish them to think me silly enough to look at any such papers for days on end, and I hastily explained that my "paper" was one of the "things of long ago" of my country.

"Ah," said the old man. "Tell us."

I protested that I was not a storyteller. Storytelling is a skilled art among them; their standards are high, and the audiences critical – and vocal in their criticism. I protested in vain. This morning they wanted to hear a story while they drank. They threatened to tell me no more stories until I told them one of mine. Finally, the old man promised that no one would criticize my style "for we know you are struggling with our language." "But," put in one of the elders, "you must explain what we do not understand, as we do when we tell you our stories." Realizing that here was my chance to prove *Hamlet* universally intelligible, I agreed.

The old man handed me some more beer to help me on with my storytelling. Men filled their long wooden pipes and knocked coals from the fire to place in the pipe bowls; then, puffing contentedly, they sat back to listen. I began in the proper style, "Not yesterday, not yesterday, but long ago, a thing occurred. One night three men were keeping watch outside the homestead of the great chief, when suddenly they saw the former chief approach them."

"Why was he no longer their chief?"

"He was dead," I explained. "That is why they were troubled and afraid when they saw him."

"Impossible," began one of the elders, handing his pipe on to his neighbour, who interrupted, "Of course it wasn't the dead chief. It was an omen sent by a witch. Go on."

Slightly shaken, I continued. "One of these three was a man who knew things" – the closest translation for scholar, but unfortunately it also meant witch. The second elder looked triumphantly at the first. "So he spoke to the dead chief saying, 'Tell us what we must do so you may rest in your grave,' but the dead chief did not answer. He vanished, and they could see him no more. Then the man who knew things – his name was Horatio – said this event was the affair of the dead chief's son, Hamlet."

There was a general shaking of heads round the circle. "Had the dead chief no living brothers? Or was this son the chief?"

No," I replied. "That is, he had one living brother who became the chief when the elder brother died."

The old men muttered: such omens were matters for chiefs and elders, not for youngsters; no good could come of going behind a chief's back; clearly Horatio was not a man who knew things.

"Yes, he was," I insisted, shooing a chicken away from my beer. "In our country the son is next to the father. The dead chief's younger brother had become the great chief. He had also married his elder brother's widow only about a month after the funeral."

"He did well," the old man beamed and announced to the others, "I told you that if we knew more about Europeans, we would find they really were very like us. In our country also," he added to me, "the younger brother marries the elder brother's widow and becomes the father of his children. Now, if your uncle, who married your widowed mother, is your father's full brother, then he will be a real father to you. Did Hamlet's father and uncle have one mother?"

His question barely penetrated my mind; I was too upset and thrown too far off balance by having one of the most important elements of *Hamlet* knocked straight out of the picture. Rather uncertainly I said that I thought they had the same mother, but I wasn't sure – the story didn't say. The old man told me severely that these genealogical details made all the difference and that when I got home I must ask the elders about it. He shouted out the door to one of his younger wives to bring his goatskin bag.

Determined to save what I could of the other motif, I took a deep breath and began again. "The son Hamlet was very sad because his mother had married again so quickly. There was no need for her to do so, and it is our custom for a widow not to go to her next husband until she has mourned for two years."

"Two years is too long," objected the wife, who had appeared with the old man's battered goatskin bag. "Who will hoe your farms for you while you have no husband?"

"Hamlet," I retorted without thinking, "was old enough to hoe his mother's farms himself. There was no need for her to remarry." No one looked convinced. I gave up. "His mother and the great chief told Hamlet not to be sad, for the great chief himself would be a father to Hamlet. Furthermore, Hamlet would be the next chief: therefore he must stay to learn the things of a chief. Hamlet agreed to remain, and all the rest went off to drink beer."

While I paused, perplexed at how to render Hamlet's disgusted soliloquy to an audience convinced that Claudius and Gertrude had behaved in the best possible manner, one of the younger men asked me who had married the other wives of the dead chief.

"He had no other wives," I told him.

"But a chief must have many wives! How else can he brew beer and prepare food for all his guests?"

I said firmly that in our country even chiefs had only one wife, that they had servants to do their work, and that they paid them from tax money.

It was better, they returned, for a chief to have many wives and sons who would help him hoe his farms and feed his people; then everyone loved the chief who gave much and took nothing – taxes were a bad thing.

I agreed with the last comment, but for the rest fell back on their favourite way of fobbing off my questions: "That is the way it is done, so that is how we do it."

I decided to skip the soliloquy. Even if Claudius was here thought quite right to marry his brother's widow, there remained the poison motif, and I knew they would disapprove of fratricide. More hopefully I resumed, "That night Hamlet kept watch with the three who had seen his dead father. The dead chief again appeared, and although the others were afraid, Hamlet followed his dead father off to one side. When they were alone, Hamlet's dead father spoke."

"Omens can't talk!" The old man was emphatic.

"Hamlet's dead father wasn't an omen. Seeing him might have been an omen, but he was not." My audience looked as confused as I sounded. "It *was* Hamlet's dead father. It was a thing we call a 'ghost'." I had to use the English word, for unlike many of the neighbouring tribes, these people didn't believe in the survival after death of any individuating part of the personality.

"What is a 'ghost'? An omen?"

"No, a 'ghost' is someone who is dead but who walks around and can talk, and people can hear him and see him but not touch him."

They objected. "One can touch zombis."

"No, no! It was not a dead body the witches had animated to sacrifice and eat. No one else made Hamlet's dead father walk. He did it himself."

"Dead men can't walk," protested my audience as one man.

I was quite willing to compromise. "A 'ghost' is the dead man's shadow."

But again they objected. "Dead men cast no shadows."

"They do in my country," I snapped.

The old man quelled the babble of disbelief that arose immediately and told me with that insincere, but courteous, agreement one extends to the fancies of the young, ignorant, and superstitious, "No doubt in your country the dead can also walk without being zombis." From the depths of his bag he produced a withered fragment of kola nut, bit off one end to show it wasn't poisoned, and handed me the rest as a peace offering.

"Anyhow," I resumed, "Hamlet's dead father said that his own brother, the one who became chief, had poisoned him. He wanted Hamlet to avenge him. Hamlet believed this in his heart, for he did not like his father's brother." I took another swallow of beer. "In the country of the great chief, living in the same homestead, for it was a very large one, was an important elder who was often with the chief to advise and help him. His name was Polonius. Hamlet was courting his daughter, but her father and her brother . . . [I cast hastily about for some tribal analogy] warned her not to let Hamlet visit her when she was alone on the farm, for he would be a great chief and so could not marry her."

"Why not?" asked the wife, who had settled down on the edge of the old man's chair. He frowned at her for asking stupid questions and growled, "They lived in the same homestead."

"That was not the reason," I informed them. "Polonius was a stranger who lived in the homestead because he helped the chief, not because he was a relative."

"Then why couldn't Hamlet marry her?"

"He could have," I explained, "but Polonius didn't think he would. After all, Hamlet was a man of great importance who ought to marry a chief's daughter, for in his country a man could have only one wife. Polonius was afraid that if Hamlet made love to his daughter, then no one else would give a high price for her."

"That might be true," remarked one of the shrewder elders, "but a chief's son would give his mistress's father enough presents and patronage to more than make up the difference. Polonius sounds like a fool to me."

"Many people think he was," I agreed. "Meanwhile Polonius sent his son Laertes off to Paris to learn the things of that country, for it was the homestead of a very great chief indeed. Because he was afraid that Laertes might waste a lot of money on beer and women and gambling, or get into trouble by fighting, he sent one of his servants to Paris secretly, to spy out what Laertes was doing. One day Hamlet came upon Polonius's daughter Ophelia. He behaved so oddly that he frightened her. Indeed" – I was fumbling for words to express the dubious quality of Hamlet's madness – "the chief and many others had also noticed that when Hamlet talked one could understand the words but not what they meant. Many people thought that he had become mad." My audience suddenly became much more attentive. "The great chief wanted to know what was wrong with Hamlet, so he sent for two of Hamlet's age mates [school friends would have taken long explanation] to talk to Hamlet and find out what troubled his heart. Hamlet, seeing that they had been bribed by the chief to betray him, told them nothing. Polonius, however, insisted that Hamlet was mad because he had been forbidden to see Ophelia, whom he loved."

"Why," inquired a bewildered voice, "should anyone bewitch Hamlet on that account?"

"Bewitch him?"

"Yes, only witchcraft can make anyone mad, unless, of course, one sees the beings that lurk in the forest."

I stopped being a storyteller, took out my notebook and demanded to be told more about these two causes of madness. Even while they spoke and I jotted notes, I tried to calculate the effect of this new factor on the plot. Hamlet had not been exposed to the beings that lurk in the forests. Only his relatives in the male line could bewitch him. Barring relatives not mentioned by Shakespeare, it had to be Claudius who was attempting to harm him. And, of course, it was.

For the moment I staved off questions by saying that the great chief also refused to believe that Hamlet was mad for the love of Ophelia and nothing else. "He was sure that something much more important was troubling Hamlet's heart."

"Now Hamlet's age mates," I continued, "had brought with them a famous storyteller. Hamlet decided to have this man tell the chief and all his homestead a story about a man who had poisoned his brother because he desired his brother's wife and wished to be chief himself. Hamlet was sure the great chief could not hear the story without making a sign if he was indeed guilty, and then he would discover whether his dead father had told him the truth."

The old man interrupted, with deep cunning, "Why should a father lie to his son?" he asked.

I hedged: "Hamlet wasn't sure that it really was his dead father." It was impossible to say anything, in that language, about devil-inspired visions.

"You mean," he said, "it actually was an omen, and he knew witches sometimes send false ones. Hamlet was a fool not to go to one skilled in reading omens and divining the truth in the first place. A man-who-sees-the-truth could have told him how his father died, if he really had been poisoned, and if there was witchcraft in it; then Hamlet could have called the elders to settle the matter."

The shrewd elder ventured to disagree. "Because his father's brother was a great chief, one-who-sees-the-truth might therefore have been afraid to tell it. I think it was for that reason that a friend of Hamlet's father – a witch and an elder – sent an omen so his friend's son would know. Was the omen true?"

"Yes," I said, abandoning ghosts and the devil; a witch-sent omen it would have to be. "It was true, for when the storyteller was telling his tale before all the homestead, the great chief rose in fear. Afraid that Hamlet knew his secret he planned to have him killed."

The stage set of the next bit presented some difficulties of translation. I began cautiously. "The great chief told Hamlet's mother to find out from her son what he knew. But because a woman's children are always first in her heart, he had the important elder Polonius hide behind a cloth that hung against the wall of Hamlet's mother's sleeping hut. Hamlet started to scold his mother for what she had done."

There was a shocked murmur from everyone. A man should never scold his mother.

"She called out in fear, and Polonius moved behind the cloth. Shouting, 'A rat!' Hamlet took his machete and slashed through the cloth." I paused for dramatic effect. "He had killed Polonius!"

The old men looked at each other in supreme disgust. "That Polonius truly was a fool and a man who knew nothing! What child would not know enough to shout, 'It's me!'" With a pang, I remembered that these people are ardent hunters, always armed with bow, arrow, and machete; at the first rustle in the grass an arrow is aimed and ready, and the hunter shouts "Game!" If no human voice answers immediately, the arrow speeds on its way. Like a good hunter Hamlet had shouted, "A rat!"

I rushed in to save Polonius's reputation. "Polonius did speak. Hamlet heard him. But he thought it was the chief and wished to kill him to avenge his father. He had meant to kill him earlier that evening. . . ." I broke down, unable to describe to these pagans, who had no belief in individual afterlife, the difference between dying at one's prayers and dying "unhousell'd, disappointed, unaneled."

This time I had shocked my audience seriously. "For a man to raise his hand against his father's brother and the one who has become his father – that is a terrible thing. The elders ought to let such a man be bewitched."

I nibbled at my kola nut in some perplexity, then pointed out that after all the man had killed Hamlet's father.

"No," pronounced the old man, speaking less to me than to the young men sitting behind the elders. "If your father's brother has killed your father, you must appeal to your father's age mates; *they* may avenge him. No man may use violence against his senior relatives." Another thought struck him. "But if his father's brother had indeed been wicked enough to bewitch Hamlet and make him mad that would be a good story indeed, for it would be his fault that Hamlet, being mad, no longer had any sense and thus was ready to kill his father's brother."

There was a murmur of applause. *Hamlet* was again a good story to them, but it no longer seemed quite the same story to me. As I thought over the coming complications of plot and motive, I lost courage and decided to skim over dangerous ground quickly.

"The great chief," I went on, "was not sorry that Hamlet had killed Polonius. It gave him a reason to send Hamlet away, with his two treacherous age mates, with letters to a chief of a far country, saying that Hamlet should be killed. But Hamlet changed the writing on their papers, so that the chief killed his age mates instead." I encountered a reproachful glare from one of the men whom I had told undetectable forgery was not merely immoral but beyond human skill. I looked the other way.

"Before Hamlet could return, Laertes came back for his father's funeral. The great chief told him Hamlet had killed Polonius. Laertes swore to kill Hamlet because of this, and because his sister Ophelia, hearing her father had been killed by the man she loved, went mad and drowned in the river."

"Have you already forgotten what we told you?" The old man was reproachful. "One cannot take vengeance on a madman; Hamlet killed Polonius in his madness. As for the girl, she not only went mad, she was drowned. Only witches can make people drown. Water itself can't hurt anything. It is merely something one drinks and bathes in."

I began to get cross. "If you don't like the story, I'll stop."

The old man made soothing noises and himself poured me some more beer. "You tell the story well, and we are listening. But it is clear that the elders of your country have never told you what the story really means. No, don't interrupt! We believe you when you say your marriage customs are different, or your clothes and weapons. But people are the same everywhere; therefore, there are always witches and it is we, the elders, who know how witches work. We told you it was the great chief who wished to kill Hamlet, and now your own words have proved us right. Who were Ophelia's male relatives?"

"There were only her father and her brother." Hamlet was clearly out of my hands.

"There must have been many more; this also you must ask of your elders when you get back to your country. From what you tell us, since Polonius was dead, it must have been Laertes who killed Ophelia, although I do not see the reason for it."

We had emptied one pot of beer, and the old men argued the point with slightly tipsy interest. Finally one of them demanded of me, "What did the servant of Polonius say on his return?"

With difficulty I recollected Reynaldo and his mission. "I don't think he did return before Polonius was killed."

"Listen," said the elder, "and I will tell you how it was and how your story will go, then you may tell me if I am right. Polonius knew his son would get into trouble, and so he did. He had many fines to pay for fighting, and debts from gambling. But he had only two ways of getting money quickly. One was to marry off his sister at once, but it is difficult to find a man who will marry a woman desired by the son of a chief. For if the chief's heir commits adultery with your wife, what can you do? Only a fool calls a case against a man who will someday be his judge. Therefore Laertes had to take the second way: he killed his sister by witchcraft, drowning her so he could secretly sell her body to the witches."

I raised an objection. "They found her body and buried it. Indeed Laertes jumped into the grave to see his sister once more – so, you see, the body was truly there. Hamlet, who had just come back, jumped in after him."

"What did I tell you?" The elder appealed to the others. "Laertes was up to no good with his sister's body. Hamlet prevented him, because the chief's heir, like the chief, does not wish any other man to grow rich and powerful. Laertes would be angry, because he would have killed his sister without benefit to himself. In our country he would try to kill Hamlet for that reason. Is this not what happened?"

"More or less," I admitted. "When the great chief found Hamlet was still alive, he encouraged Laertes to try to kill Hamlet and arranged a fight with machetes between them. In the fight both the young men were wounded to death. Hamlet's mother drank the poisoned beer that the chief meant for Hamlet in case he won the fight. When he saw his mother die of poison, Hamlet, dying, managed to kill his father's brother with his machete."

"You see, I was right!" exclaimed the elder.

"That was a very good story," added the old man, "and you told it with very few mistakes. There was just one more error, at the very end. The poison Hamlet's mother drank was obviously meant for the survivor of the fight, whichever it was. If Laertes had won, the great chief would have poisoned him, for no one would know that he arranged Hamlet's death. Then, too, he need not fear Laertes' witchcraft; it takes a strong heart to kill one's only sister by witchcraft.

"Sometime," concluded the old man, gathering his ragged toga about him, "you must tell us some more stories of your country. We, who are elders, will instruct you in their true meaning, so that when you return to your own land your elders will see that you have not been sitting in the bush, but among those who know things and who have taught you wisdom."

---

1. In the voice of the narrator, write a letter to the friend who gave you *Hamlet*. Recount your experiences in the bush and your eventual opinion of Shakespeare's universality.
   OR
   Script and/or dramatize a conversation between Bohannan and her friend when they meet after her return to Oxford.

2. Working in a group, dramatize a section of "Shakespeare in the Bush." Present your dramatization for the class or a larger group.

3. Bohannan shows how "one can easily misinterpret the universal by misunderstanding the particular." Pattern a narrative on "Shakespeare in the Bush," using a setting and literary work of your choice. The audience's misunderstanding of the story must be central to your narrative. James Thurber's "The *Macbeth* Murder Mystery" could serve as another pattern for your narrative.

4. For a magazine, write a light-hearted article arguing the truth of the saying *"Plus ça change, plus c'est la même chose."* Draw some of your arguments from Bohannan's memoir and some from your personal experience. Give your article a suitable title.

"Poetry is the spontaneous overflow of powerful feelings; it takes its origin from emotion recollected in tranquillity."
– *William Wordsworth*, Lyrical Ballads

Wordsworth's definition of poetry also describes Alistair MacLeod's recollections of his father, although they are expressed in the form of a short story. Take a few moments to relax and recollect an important and moving event in your own life. Try to remember not only the circumstances, but also your feelings at the time. Write a brief memoir of the event that includes both physical and psychological description.

THE BOAT
Alistair MacLeod

There are times even now, when I awake at four o'clock in the morning with the terrible fear that I have overslept; when I imagine that my father is waiting for me in the room below the darkened stairs or that the shorebound men are tossing pebbles against my window while blowing their hands and stomping their feet impatiently on the frozen steadfast earth. There are times when I am half out of bed and fumbling for socks and mumbling for words before I realize that I am foolishly alone, that no one waits at the base of the stairs and no boat rides restlessly in the waters by the pier.

At such times only the grey corpses on the overflowing ashtray beside my bed bear witness to the extinction of the latest spark and silently await the crushing out of the most recent of their fellows. And then because I am afraid to be alone with death, I dress rapidly, make a great to-do about clearing my throat, turn on both faucets in the sink and proceed to make loud splashing ineffectual noises. Later I go out and walk the mile to the all-night restaurant.

In the winter it is a very cold walk and there are often tears in my eyes when I arrive. The waitress usually gives a sympathetic little shiver and says, "Boy, it must be really cold out there; you got tears in your eyes."

"Yes," I say, "it sure is; it really is."

And then the three or four of us who are always in such places at such times make uninteresting little protective chit-chat until the dawn reluctantly arrives. Then I swallow the coffee which is always bitter and leave with a great busy rush because by that time I have to worry about being late and whether I have a clean shirt and whether my car will start and about all the other countless things one must worry about when he teaches at a great Midwestern university. And I know then that that day will go by as have all the days of the past ten years, for the call and the voices and the shapes and the boat were not really there in the early morning's darkness and I have all kinds of comforting reality to prove it. They are only shadows and echoes, the animals a child's hands make on the wall by lamplight, and the voices from the rain barrel; the cuttings from an old movie made in the black and white of long ago.

I first became conscious of the boat in the same way and at almost the same time that I became aware of the people it supported. My earliest recollection of my father is a view from the floor of gigantic rubber boots and then of being suddenly elevated and having my face pressed against the stubble of his cheek, and of how it tasted of salt and of how he smelled of salt from his red-soled rubber boots to the shaggy whiteness of his hair.

When I was very small, he took me for my first ride in the boat. I rode the half-mile from our house to the wharf on his shoulders and I remember the sound of his rubber boots galumphing along the gravel beach, the tune of the indecent little song he used to sing, and the odour of the salt.

The floor of the boat was permeated with the same odour and in its constancy I was not aware of change. In the harbour we made our little circle and returned. He tied the boat by its painter, fastened the stern to its permanent anchor and lifted me high over his head to the solidity of the wharf. Then he climbed up the little iron ladder that led to the wharf's cap, placed me once more upon his shoulders and galumphed off again.

When we returned to the house everyone made a great fuss over my precocious excursion and asked, "How did you like the boat?" "Were you afraid in the boat?" "Did you cry in the boat?" They repeated "the boat" at the end of all their questions and I knew it must be very important to everyone.

My earliest recollection of my mother is of being alone with her in the mornings while my father was away in the boat. She seemed to be always repairing clothes that were "torn in the boat," preparing food "to be eaten in the boat" or looking for "the boat" through our kitchen window which faced upon the sea. When my father returned about noon, she would ask, "Well, how did things go in the boat today?" It was the first question I remember asking: "Well, how did things go in the boat today?" "Well, how did things go in the boat today?"

The boat in our lives was registered at Port Hawkesbury. She was what Nova Scotians called a Cape Island boat and was designed for the small inshore fishermen who sought the lobsters of the spring and the mackerel of summer and later the cod and haddock and hake. She was thirty-two feet long and nine wide, and was powered by an engine from a Chevrolet truck. She had a marine clutch and a high speed reverse gear and was painted light green with the name *Jenny Lynn* stencilled in black letters on her bow and painted on an oblong plate across her stern. Jenny Lynn had been my mother's maiden name and the boat was called after her as another link in the chain of tradition. Most of the boats that berthed at the wharf bore the names of some female member of their owner's household.

I say this now as if I knew it all then. All at once, all about boat dimensions and engines, and as if on the day of my first childish voyage I noticed the difference between a stencilled name and a painted name. But of course it was not that way at all, for I learned it all very slowly and there was not time enough.

I learned first about our house which was one of about fifty which marched around the horseshoe of our harbour and the wharf which was its heart. Some of them were so close to the water that during a storm the sea spray splashed against their windows while others were built farther along the beach as was the case with ours. The houses and their people, like those of the neighbouring towns and villages, were the result of Ireland's discontent and Scotland's Highland Clearances and America's War of Independence. Impulsive emotional Catholic Celts who could not bear to live with England and shrewd determined Protestant Puritans who, in the years after 1776, could not bear to live without.

The most important room in our house was one of those oblong old-fashioned kitchens heated by a wood- and coal-burning stove. Behind the stove was a box of kindlings and beside it a coal scuttle. A heavy wooden table with leaves that expanded or reduced its dimensions stood in the middle of the floor. There were five wooden home-made chairs which had been chipped and hacked by a variety of knives. Against the east wall, opposite the stove, there was a couch which sagged in the middle and had a cushion for a pillow, and above it a shelf which contained matches, tobacco, pencils, odd fish-hooks, bits of twine, and a tin can filled with bills and receipts. The south wall was dominated by a window which faced the sea and on the north there was a five-foot board which bore a variety of clothes hooks and the burdens of each. Beneath the board there was a jumble of odd footwear, mostly of rubber. There was also, on this wall, a barometer, a map of the marine area and a shelf which held a tiny radio. The kitchen was shared by all of us and was a buffer zone between the immaculate order of ten other rooms and the disruptive chaos of the single room that was my father's.

My mother ran her house as her brothers ran their boats. Everything was clean and spotless and in order. She was tall and dark and powerfully energetic. In later years she reminded me of the women of Thomas Hardy, particularly Eustacia Vye, in a physical way. She fed and clothed a family of seven children, making all of the meals and most of the clothes. She grew miraculous gardens and magnificent flowers and raised broods of hens and ducks. She would walk miles on berry-picking expeditions and hoist her skirts to dig for clams when the tide was low. She was fourteen years younger than my father, whom she had married when she was twenty-six and had been a local beauty for a period of ten years. My mother was of the sea as were all of her people, and her horizons were the very literal ones she scanned with her dark and fearless eyes.

Between the kitchen clothes rack and barometer, a door opened into my father's bedroom. It was a room of disorder and disarray. It was as if the wind which so often clamoured about the house succeeded in entering this single room and after whipping it into turmoil stole quietly away to renew its knowing laughter from without.

My father's bed was against the south wall. It always looked rumpled and unmade because he lay on top of it more than he slept within any folds it might have had. Beside it, there was a little brown table. An archaic goose-necked reading light, a battered table radio, a mound of wooden matches, one or two packages of tobacco, a deck of cigarette papers and an overflowing ashtray cluttered its surface. The brown larvae of tobacco shreds and the grey flecks of ash covered both the table and the floor beneath it. The once-varnished surface of the table was disfigured by numerous black scars and gashes inflicted by the neglected burning cigarettes of many years. They had tumbled from the ashtray unnoticed and branded their statements permanently and quietly into the wood until the odour of their burning caused the snuffing out of their lives. At the bed's foot there was a single window which looked upon the sea.

Against the adjacent wall there was a battered bureau and beside it there was a closet which held his single ill-fitting serge suit, the two or three white shirts that strangled him and the square black shoes that pinched. When he took off his more friendly clothes, the heavy woollen sweaters, mitts and socks which my mother knitted for him and the woollen and doeskin shirts, he dumped them unceremoniously on a single chair. If a visitor entered the room while he was lying on the bed, he would be told to throw the clothes on the floor and take their place upon the chair.

Magazines and books covered the bureau and competed with the clothes for domination of the chair. They further overburdened the heroic little table and lay on top of the radio. They filled a baffling and unknowable cave beneath the bed, and in the corner by the bureau they spilled from the walls and grew up from the floor.

The magazines were the most conventional: *Time, Newsweek, Life, Maclean's, Family Herald, Reader's Digest*. They were the result of various cut-rate subscriptions or of the gift subscriptions associated with Christmas, "the two whole years for only $3.50."

The books were more varied. There were a few hard-cover magnificents and bygone Book-of-the-Month wonders and some were Christmas or birthday gifts. The majority of them, however, were used paperbacks which came from those second-hand bookstores which advertise in the backs of magazines: "Miscellaneous Used Paperbacks 10¢ Each." At first he sent for them himself, although my mother resented the expense, but in later years they came more and more often from my sisters who had moved to the cities. Especially at first they were very weird and varied. Mickey Spillane and Ernest Haycox vied with Dostoyevsky and Faulkner, and the Penguin Poets edition of Gerard Manley Hopkins arrived in the same box as a little book on sex technique called *Getting the Most Out of Love*. The former had been assiduously annotated by a very fine hand using a very blue-inked fountain pen while the latter had been studied by someone with very large thumbs, the prints of which were still visible in the margins. At the slightest provocation it would open almost automatically to particularly graphic and well-smudged pages.

When he was not in the boat, my father spent most of his time lying on the bed in his socks, the top two buttons of his trousers undone, his discarded shirt on the ever-ready chair and the sleeves of the woollen Stanfield underwear, which he wore both summer and winter, drawn half way up to his elbows. The pillows propped up the whiteness of his head and the goose-necked lamp illuminated the pages in his hands. The cigarettes smoked and smouldered on the ashtray and on the table and the radio played constantly, sometimes low and sometimes loud. At midnight and at one, two, three and four, one could sometimes hear the radio, his occasional cough, the rustling thud of a completed book being tossed to the corner heap, or the movement necessitated by his sitting on the edge of the bed to roll the thousandth cigarette. He seemed never to sleep, only to doze, and the light shone constantly from his window to the sea.

My mother despised the room and all it stood for and she had stopped sleeping in it after I was born. She despised disorder in rooms and in houses and in hours and in lives, and she had not read a book since high school. There she had read *Ivanhoe* and considered it a colossal waste of time. Still the room remained, like a solid rock of opposition in the sparkling waters of a clear deep harbour, opening off the kitchen where we really lived our lives, with its door always open and its contents visible to all.

The daughters of the room and of the house were very beautiful.

They were tall and willowy like my mother and had her fine facial features set off by the reddish copper-coloured hair that had apparently once been my father's before it turned to white. All of them were very clever in school and helped my mother a great deal about the house. When they were young they sang and were very happy and very nice to me because I was the youngest and the family's only boy.

My father never approved of their playing about the wharf like the other children, and they went there only when my mother sent them on an errand. At such times they almost always overstayed, playing screaming games of tag or hide-and-seek in and about the fishing shanties, the piled traps and the tubs of trawl, shouting down to the perch that swam languidly about the wharf's algae-covered piles, or jumping in and out of the boats that tugged gently at their lines. My mother was never uneasy about them at such times, and when her husband criticized her she would say, "Nothing will happen to them there," or "They could be doing worse things in worse places."

By about the ninth or tenth grade my sisters one by one discovered my father's bedroom and then the change would begin. Each would go into the room one morning when he was out. She would go with the ideal hope of imposing order or with the more practical objective of emptying the ashtray, and later she would be found spellbound by the volume in her hand. My mother's reaction was always abrupt, bordering on the angry. "Take your nose out of that trash and come and do your work," she would say, and once I saw her slap my youngest sister so hard that the print of her hand was scarletly emblazoned upon her daughter's cheek while the broken-spined paperback fluttered uselessly to the floor.

Thereafter my mother would launch a campaign against what she had discovered but could not understand. At times although she was not overly religious she would bring in God to bolster her arguments, saying, "In the next world God will see to those who waste their lives reading useless books when they should be about their work." Or without theological aid, "I would like to know how books help anyone to live a life." If my father were in, she would repeat the remarks louder than necessary, and her voice would carry into his room where he lay upon his bed. His usual reaction was to turn up the volume of the radio, although that action in itself betrayed the success of the initial thrust.

Shortly after my sisters began to read the books, they grew restless and lost interest in darning socks and baking bread, and all of them eventually went to work as summer waitresses in the Sea Food Restaurant. The restaurant was run by a big American concern from Boston and catered to the tourists that flooded the area during July and August. My mother despised the whole operation. She said the restaurant was not run by "our people," and "our people" did not eat there, and that it was run by outsiders for outsiders.

"Who are these people anyway?" she would ask, tossing back her dark hair, "and what do they, though they go about with their cameras for a hundred years, know about the way it is here, and what do they care about me and mine, and why should I care about them?"

She was angry that my sisters should even conceive of working in such a place and more angry when my father made no move to prevent it, and she was worried about herself and about her family and about her life. Sometimes she would say softly to her sisters, "I don't know what's the matter with my girls. It seems none of them are interested in any of the right things." And sometimes there would be bitter savage arguments. One afternoon I was coming in with three mackerel I'd been given at the wharf when I heard her say, "Well I hope you'll be satisfied when they come home knocked up and you'll have had your way."

It was the most savage thing I'd ever heard my mother say. Not just the words but the way she said them, and I stood there in the porch afraid to breathe for what seemed like the years from ten to fifteen, feeling the damp moist mackerel with their silver glassy eyes growing clammy against my leg.

Through the angle in the screen door I saw my father who had been walking into his room wheel around on one of his rubber-booted heels and look at her with his blue eyes flashing like clearest ice beneath the snow that was his hair. His usually ruddy face was drawn and grey, reflecting the exhaustion of a man of sixty-five who had been working in those rubber boots for eleven hours on an August day, and for a fleeting moment I wondered what I would do if he killed my mother while I stood there in the porch with those three foolish mackerel in my hand. Then he turned and went into his room and the radio blared forth the next day's weather forecast and I retreated under the noise and returned again, stamping my feet and slamming the door too loudly to signal my approach. My mother was busy at the stove when I came in, and did not raise her head when I threw the mackerel in a pan. As I looked into my father's room, I said, "Well, how did things go in the boat today?" and he replied, "Oh not too badly, all things considered." He was lying on his back and lighting the first cigarette and the radio was talking about the Virginia coast.

All of my sisters made good money on tips. They bought my father an electric razor which he tried to use for a while and they took out even more magazine subscriptions. They bought my mother a great many clothes of the type she was very fond of, the wide-brimmed hats and the brocaded dresses, but she locked them all in trunks and refused to wear any of them.

On one August day my sisters prevailed upon my father to take some of their restaurant customers for an afternoon ride in the boat. The tourists with their expensive clothes and cameras and sun glasses awkwardly backed down the iron ladder at the wharf's side to where my father waited below, holding the rocking *Jenny Lynn* in snug against the wharf with one hand on the iron ladder and steadying his descending passengers with the other. They tried to look both prim and windblown like the girls in the Pepsi-Cola ads and did the best they could, sitting on the thwarts where the newspapers were spread to cover the splattered blood and fish entrails, crowding to one side so that they were in danger of capsizing the boat, taking the inevitable pictures or merely trailing their fingers through the water of their dreams.

All of them liked my father very much and, after he'd brought them back from their circles in the harbour, they invited him to their rented cabins which were located high on a hill overlooking the village to which they were so alien. He proceeded to get very drunk up there with the beautiful view and the strange company and the abundant liquor, and late in the afternoon he began to sing.

I was just approaching the wharf to deliver my mother's summons when he began, and the familiar yet unfamiliar voice that rolled down from the cabins made me feel as I had never felt before in my young life or perhaps as I had always felt without really knowing it, and I was ashamed yet proud, young yet old, and saved yet forever lost, and there was nothing I could do to control my legs which trembled nor my eyes which wept for what they could not tell.

The tourists were equipped with tape recorders and my father sang for more than three hours. His voice boomed down the hill and bounced off the surface of the harbour, which was an unearthly blue on that hot August day, and was then reflected to the wharf and the fishing shanties where it was absorbed amidst the men who were baiting their lines for the next day's haul.

He sang all the old sea chanties which had come across from the old world and by which men like him had pulled ropes for generations, and he sang the East Coast sea songs which celebrated the sealing vessels of Northumberland Strait and the long liners of the Grand Banks, and of Anticosti, Sable Island, Grand Manan, Boston Harbor, Nantucket and Block Island. Gradually he shifted to the seemingly unending Gaelic drinking songs with their twenty or more verses and inevitable refrains, and the men in the shanties smiled at the coarseness of some of the verses and at the thought that the singer's immediate audience did not know what they were applauding nor recording to take back to staid old Boston. Later as the sun was setting he switched to the laments and the wild and haunting Gaelic war songs of those spattered Highland ancestors he had never seen, and when his voice ceased, the savage melancholy of three hundred years seemed to hang over the peaceful harbour and the quiet boats and the men leaning in the doorways of their shanties with their cigarettes glowing in the dusk and the women looking to the sea from their open windows with their children in their arms.

When he came home he threw the money he had earned on the

kitchen table as he did with all his earnings but my mother refused to touch it and the next day he went with the rest of the men to bait his trawl in the shanties. The tourists came to the door that evening and my mother met them there and told them that her husband was not in although he was lying on the bed only a few feet away with the radio playing and the cigarette upon his lips. She stood in the doorway until they reluctantly went away.

In the winter they sent him a picture which had been taken on the day of the singing. On the back it said, "To Our Ernest Hemingway" and the "Our" was underlined. There was also an accompanying letter telling how much they had enjoyed themselves, how popular the tape was proving and explaining who Ernest Hemingway was. In a way it almost did look like one of those unshaven, taken-in-Cuba pictures of Hemingway. He looked both massive and incongruous in the setting. His bulky fisherman's clothes were too big for the green and white lawn chair in which he sat, and his rubber boots seemed to take up all of the well-clipped grass square. The beach umbrella jarred with his sunburned face and because he had already been singing for some time, his lips which chapped in the winds of spring and burned in the water glare of summer had already cracked in several places, producing tiny flecks of blood at their corners and on the whiteness of his teeth. The bracelets of brass chain which he wore to protect his wrists from chafing seemed abnormally large and his broad leather belt had been slackened and his heavy shirt and underwear were open at the throat revealing an uncultivated wilderness of white chest hair bordering on the semi-controlled stubble of his neck and chin. His blue eyes had looked directly into the camera and his hair was whiter than the two tiny clouds which hung over his left shoulder. The sea was behind him and its immense blue flatness stretched out to touch the arching blueness of the sky. It seemed very far away from him or else he was so much in the foreground that he seemed too big for it.

Each year another of my sisters would read the books and work in the restaurant. Sometimes they would stay out quite late on the hot summer nights and when they came up the stairs my mother would ask them many long and involved questions which they resented and tried to avoid. Before ascending the stairs they would go into my father's room and those of us who waited above could hear them throwing his clothes off the chair before sitting on it or the squeak of the bed as they sat on its edge. Sometimes they would talk to him a long time, the murmur of their voices blending with the music of the radio into a mysterious vapour-like sound which floated softly up the stairs.

I say this again as if it all happened at once and as if all of my sisters were of identical ages and like so many lemmings going into another sea and, again, it was of course not that way at all. Yet go they did, to Boston, to Montreal, to New York with the young men they met during the summers and later married in those far-away cities. The young men were very articulate and handsome and wore fine clothes and drove expensive cars and my sisters, as I said, were very tall and beautiful with their copper-coloured hair and were tired of darning socks and baking bread.

One by one they went. My mother had each of her daughters for fifteen years, then lost them for two and finally forever. None married a fisherman. My mother never accepted any of the young men, for in her eyes they seemed always a combination of the lazy, the effeminate, the dishonest and the unknown. They never seemed to do any physical work and she could not comprehend their luxurious vacations and she did not know whence they came nor who they were. And in the end she did not really care, for they were not of her people and they were not of her sea.

I say this now with a sense of wonder at my own stupidity in thinking I was somehow free and would go on doing well in school and playing and helping in the boat and passing into my early teens while streaks of grey began to appear in my mother's dark hair and my father's rubber boots dragged sometimes on the pebbles of the beach as he trudged home from the wharf. And there were but three of us in the house that had at one time been so loud.

Then during the winter that I was fifteen he seemed to grow old and ill at once. Most of January he lay upon the bed, smoking and reading and listening to the radio while the wind howled about the house and the needle-like snow blistered off the ice-covered harbour and the doors flew out of people's hands if they did not cling to them like death.

In February when the men began overhauling their lobster traps he still did not move, and my mother and I began to knot lobster trap headings in the evenings. The twine was as always very sharp and harsh, and blisters formed upon our thumbs and little paths of blood snaked quietly down between our fingers while the seals that had drifted down from distant Labrador wept and moaned like human children on the ice-floes of the Gulf.

In the daytime my mother's brother who had been my father's partner as long as I could remember also came to work upon the gear. He was a year older than my mother and was tall and dark and the father of twelve children.

By March we were very far behind and although I began to work very hard in the evenings I knew it was not hard enough and that there were but eight weeks left before the opening of the season on May first. And I knew that my mother worried and my uncle was uneasy and that all of our very lives depended on the boat being ready with her gear and two men, by the date of May the first. And I knew then that *David Copperfield* and *The Tempest* and all of those friends I had dearly come to love must really go forever. So I bade them all good-bye.

The night after my first full day at home and after my mother had gone upstairs he called me into his room where I sat upon the chair beside his bed. "You will go back tomorrow," he said simply.

I refused then, saying I had made my decision and was satisfied.

"That is no way to make a decision," he said, "and if you are satisfied I am not. It is best that you go back." I was almost angry then and told him as all children do that I wished he would leave me alone and stop telling me what to do.

He looked at me a long time then, lying there on the same bed on which he had fathered me those sixteen years before, fathered me his only son, out of who knew what emotions when he was already fifty-six and his hair had turned to snow. Then he swung his legs over the edge of the squeaking bed and sat facing me and looked into my own dark eyes with his of crystal blue and placed his hand upon my knee. "I am not telling you to do anything," he said softly, "only asking you."

The next morning I returned to school. As I left, my mother followed me to the porch and said, "I never thought a son of mine would choose useless books over the parents that gave him life."

In the weeks that followed he got up rather miraculously and the gear was ready and the *Jenny Lynn* was freshly painted by the last two weeks of April when the ice began to break up and the lonely screaming gulls returned to haunt the silver herring as they flashed within the sea.

On the first day of May the boats raced out as they had always done, laden down almost to the gunwales with their heavy cargoes of traps. They were almost like living things as they plunged through the waters of the spring and manoeuvred between the still floating icebergs of crystal white and emerald green on their way to the traditional grounds that they sought out every May. And those of us who sat that day in the high school on the hill, discussing the water imagery of Tennyson, watched them as they passed back and forth beneath us until by afternoon the piles of traps which had been stacked upon the wharf were no longer visible but were spread about the bottoms of the sea. And the *Jenny Lynn* went too, all day, with my uncle tall and dark, like a latter-day Tashtego standing at the tiller with his legs wide apart and guiding her deftly between the floating pans of ice and my father in the stern standing in the same way with his hands upon the ropes that lashed the cargo to the deck. And at night my mother asked, "Well, how did things go in the boat today?"

And the spring wore on and the summer came and school ended in the third week of June and the lobster season on July first and I wished that the two things I loved so dearly did not exclude each other in a manner that was so blunt and too clear.

At the conclusion of the lobster season my uncle said he had been offered a berth on a deep sea dragger and had decided to accept. We all knew that he was leaving the *Jenny Lynn* forever and that before the next lobster season he would buy a boat of his own. He was expecting another child and would be supporting fifteen people by the next spring and could not chance my father against the family that he loved.

I joined my father then for the trawling season, and he made no protest and my mother was quite happy. Through the summer we baited the tubs of trawl in the afternoon and set them at sunset and revisited them in the darkness of the early morning. The men would come tramping by our house at four A.M. and we would join them and walk with them to the wharf and be on our way before the sun rose out of the ocean where it seemed to spend the night. If I was not up they would toss pebbles to my window and I would be very embarrassed and tumble downstairs to where my father lay fully clothed atop his bed, reading his book and listening to his radio and smoking his cigarette. When I appeared he would swing off his bed and put on his boots and be instantly ready and then we would take the lunches my mother had prepared the night before and walk off toward the sea. He would make no attempt to wake me himself.

It was in many ways a good summer. There were few storms and we were out almost every day and we lost a minimum of gear and seemed to land a maximum of fish and I tanned dark and brown after the manner of my uncles.

My father did not tan – he never tanned – because of his reddish complexion, and the salt water irritated his skin as it had for sixty years. He burned and reburned over and over again and his lips still cracked so that they bled when he smiled, and his arms, especially the left, still broke out into the oozing salt-water boils as they had ever since as a child I had first watched him soaking and bathing them in a variety of ineffectual solutions. The chafe-preventing bracelets of brass linked chain that all the men wore about their wrists in early spring were his the full season and he shaved but painfully and only once a week.

And I saw then, that summer, many things that I had seen all my life as if for the first time and I thought that perhaps my father had never been intended for a fisherman either physically or mentally. At least not in the manner of my uncles; he had never really loved it. And I remembered that, one evening in his room when we were talking about *David Copperfield*, he had said that he had always wanted to go to the university and I had dismissed it then in the way one dismisses his father's saying he would like to be a tight-rope walker, and we had gone on to talk about the Peggotys and how they loved the sea.

And I thought then to myself that there were many things wrong with all of us and all our lives and I wondered why my father, who was himself an only son, had not married before he was forty and then

I wondered why he had. I even thought that perhaps he had had to marry my mother and checked the dates on the flyleaf of the Bible where I learned that my oldest sister had been born a prosaic eleven months after the marriage, and I felt myself then very dirty and debased for my lack of faith and for what I had thought and done.

And then there came into my heart a very great love for my father and I thought it was very much braver to spend a life doing what you really do not want rather than selfishly following forever your own dreams and inclinations. And I knew then that I could never leave him alone to suffer the iron-tipped harpoons which my mother would forever hurl into his soul because he was a failure as a husband and a father who had retained none of his own. And I felt that I had been very small in a little secret place within me and that even the completion of high school was for me a silly shallow selfish dream.

So I told him one night very resolutely and very powerfully that I would remain with him as long as he lived and we would fish the sea together. And he made no protest but only smiled through the cigarette smoke that wreathed his bed and replied, "I hope you will remember what you've said."

The room was now so filled with books as to be almost Dickensian, but he would not allow my mother to move or change them and he continued to read them, sometimes two or three a night. They came with great regularity now, and there were more hard covers, sent by my sisters who had gone so long ago and now seemed so distant and so prosperous, and sent also pictures of small red-haired grandchildren with baseball bats and dolls which he placed upon his bureau and which my mother gazed at wistfully when she thought no one would see. Red-haired grandchildren with baseball bats and dolls who would never know the sea in hatred or in love.

And so we fished through the heat of August and into the cooler days of September when the water was so clear we could almost see the bottom and the white mists rose like delicate ghosts in the early morning dawn. And one day my mother said to me, "You have given added years to his life."

And we fished on into October when it began to roughen and we could no longer risk night sets but took our gear out each morning and returned at the first sign of the squalls; and on into November when we lost three tubs of trawl and the clear blue water turned to a sullen grey and the trochoidal waves rolled rough and high and washed across our bows and decks as we ran within their troughs. We wore heavy sweaters now and the awkward rubber slickers and the heavy woollen mitts which soaked and froze into masses of ice that hung from our wrists like the limbs of gigantic monsters until we thawed them against the exhaust pipe's heat. And almost every day we would leave for home before noon, driven by the blasts of the northwest wind, coating our eyebrows with ice and freezing our eyelids closed as we leaned into a visibility that was hardly there, charting our course from the compass and the sea, running with the waves and between them but never confronting their towering might.

And I stood at the tiller now, on these homeward lunges, stood in the place and in the manner of my uncle, turning to look at my father and to the stern, drenched and dripping with the snow and the salt and the spray and his bushy eyebrows caked in ice. But on November twenty-first, when it seemed we might be making the final run of the season, I turned and he was not there and I knew even in that instant that he would never be again.

On November twenty-first the waves of the grey Atlantic are very very high and the waters are very cold and there are no signposts on the surface of the sea. You cannot tell where you have been five minutes before and in the squalls of snow you cannot see. And it takes longer than you would believe to check a boat that has been running before a gale and turn her ever so carefully in a wide and stupid circle, with timbers creaking and straining, back into the face of the storm. And you know that it is useless and that your voice does not carry the length of the boat and that even if you knew the original spot, the relentless waves would carry such a burden perhaps a mile or so by the time you could return. And you know also, the final irony, that your father like your uncles and all the men that form your past, cannot swim a stroke.

The lobster beds off the Cape Breton coast are still very rich and now, from May to July, their offerings are packed in crates of ice, and thundered by the gigantic transport trucks, day and night, through New Glasgow, Amherst, Saint John and Bangor and Portland and into Boston where they are tossed still living into boiling pots of water, their final home.

And though the prices are higher and the competition tighter, the grounds to which the *Jenny Lynn* once went remain untouched and unfished as they have for the last ten years. For if there are no signposts on the sea in storm there are certain ones in calm and the lobster bottoms were distributed in calm before any of us can remember and the grounds my father fished were those his father fished before him and there were others before and before and before. Twice the big boats have come from forty and fifty miles, lured by the promise of the grounds, and strewn the bottom with their traps and twice they have returned to find their buoys cut adrift and their gear lost and destroyed. Twice the Fisheries Officer and the Mounted Police have come and asked many long and involved questions and twice they have received no answers from the men leaning in the doors of their shanties and the women standing at their windows with their children in their arms. Twice they have gone away saying: "There are no legal boundaries in the Marine area"; "No one can own the sea"; "Those grounds don't wait for anyone."

But the men and the women, with my mother dark among them, do not care for what they say, for to them the grounds are sacred and they think they wait for me.

It is not an easy thing to know that your mother lives alone on an inadequate insurance policy and that she is too proud to accept any other aid. And that she looks through her lonely window onto the ice of winter and the hot flat calm of summer and the rolling waves of fall. And that she lies awake in the early morning's darkness when the rubber boots of the men scrunch upon the gravel as they pass beside her house on their way down to the wharf. And she knows that the footsteps never stop, because no man goes from her house, and she alone of all the Lynns has neither son nor son-in-law that walks toward the boat that will take him to the sea. And it is not an easy thing to know that your mother looks upon the sea with love and on you with bitterness because the one has been so constant and the other so untrue.

But neither is it easy to know that your father was found on November twenty-eighth, ten miles to the north and wedged between two boulders at the base of the rock-strewn cliffs where he had been hurled and slammed so many many times. His hands were shredded ribbons as were his feet which had lost their boots to the suction of the sea, and his shoulders came apart in our hands when we tried to move him from the rocks. And the fish had eaten his testicles and the gulls had pecked out his eyes and the white-green stubble of his whiskers had continued to grow in death, like the grass on graves, upon the purple, bloated mass that was his face. There was not much left of my father, physically, as he lay there with the brass chains on his wrists and the seaweed in his hair.

---

1. For each row of the chart below, role-playing the characters in the left-hand column, describe your feelings about the setting in the right-hand column and the significance it holds for you. Assume different roles as you work through the settings.

Roles	Settings
mother, father, son	father's room
father, mother, son	the other rooms in the house
daughter, mother	Sea Food Restaurant
father, son, mother	the boat
father, mother, son, daughter	the sea

2. When the son grows up, he realizes that his "father had never been intended for a fisherman." Note the incidents that lead the son to that conclusion and write a detailed character sketch of

the father. Compare your sketch with a classmate's and produce your own polished version.

3. a) In a sentence or two for each, state the attitudes of the other characters in the story to the mother and her attitude to them.
b) The mother is an enigmatic character, torn between love and narrow-minded selfishness. In a small group, discuss and compare your personal reactions to the mother.

4. a) With a classmate, analyse the narrative techniques used by the writer and determine their effectiveness. Consider
   • first person narration and the memoir form;
   • unifying elements: (for example, the boat, the brass chains);
   • the framework of the story;
   • one other technique you discover in your reading.
b) Present your findings in a written critique of the story. Make sure that your attitude to the story is clearly stated. Ask another classmate to read your critique and to make editorial comments and suggestions. Revise as necessary and put the final draft in your writing folder.

5. Write a short story in which the central character is a child who gains a new insight into a parent or guardian, or in which an adult and child arrive at a mutual understanding and acceptance. (You may wish to read "Saturday Climbing," p. 136, for another model.)
OR
Write a poem that features some aspect – the themes, characters, images, or events – of "The Boat."

6. Working in a group, present a debate on one of these resolutions. "Opposites do not attract." "Know the parent, know the child."

A MADNESS OF NATURE
Franklin Russell

eyond the northern beach, a grey swell rolls in from Greenland and runs softly along the shore. The horizon is lost in a world of grey, and gulls glide, spectral in the livid air. Watching, I am enveloped in the sullen waiting time and feel the silence, drawn out long and thin. I wait for the sea to reveal a part of itself.

A capelin is perhaps the best-hunted creature on earth. It is not more than five inches long, about the size of a young herring, and undistinguished in appearance, except that when it is freshly caught, it is the colour of mercury. As the capelin dies, its silvery scales tarnish and the glitter goes out like a light, ending a small allegory about nature, a spectacle of victims, victors, and an imperative of existence. Its death illuminates a dark process of biology in which there are shadows of other, more complex lives.

The capelin are born to be eaten. They transform oceanic plankton into flesh which is then hunted greedily by almost every sea creature that swims or flies. Their only protection is fecundity. One capelin survives to adulthood from every ten thousand eggs laid, and yet a single school may stir square miles of sea.

In mid-June, the capelin gather offshore. They can be seen everywhere and at all times in history, symbols of summer and fertility, of

Providence and danger. I see them along the shores of Greenland, Iceland, Norway, and near Spitsbergen. I follow them across the northern coast of Russia. Chill air, grey seas, the northern silence are the capelin's world in Alaska, in the Aleutians, around Hudson Bay, and along the northeastern shores of North America. But the capelin of the Newfoundland coast are the most visible. Here, they spawn on the beaches rather than in deep water offshore, and I have come to see their rush for eternity.

They gather a thousand feet offshore, coalescing into groups of a hundred thousand to break the water's surface with bright chuckling sounds. They gather, and grow. Soon they are in the millions, with other millions swimming up from the offshore deeps. They gather, now in the billions, so densely packed together in places that the sea shimmers silver for miles and flows, serpentine, with the swelling body of a single, composite creature.

The fish do, in fact, possess a common sense of purpose. Nothing can redirect their imperative to breed. I once swam among them and saw them parting reluctantly ahead of me, felt their bodies flicking against my hands. Looking back, I saw them closing in, filling up the space created by my passage. The passive fish tolerated me, in their anticipation of what they were about to do.

At this time of the year they are so engrossed that they barely react when a host of creatures advances to kill them. Beneath and beyond them, codfish pour up out of the deep. They overtake the capelin, eat them, plunge their sleek, dark bodies recklessly into shallow water. Some have swum so rapidly from such depths that their swim bladders are distended by the sudden drop in water pressure. The cod are gigantic by comparison with the capelin. Many weigh one hundred pounds or more, and will not be sated until they have eaten scores of capelin each. The water writhes with movement and foam where cod, headlong in pursuit, drive themselves clear out of the sea and fall back with staccato slaps.

The attack of the codfish is a brutal opening to a ritual, and a contradiction in their character. Normally, they are sedentary feeders on the sea floor. Now, however, they are possessed. Their jaws rip and tear; the water darkens with capelin blood: the shredded pieces of flesh hang suspended or rise to the surface.

Now a group of seabirds, the parrotlike puffins, clumsy in flight, turn over the capelin, their grotesque, axe-like beaks probing from side to side as they watch the upper layers of the massacre. They are joined by new formations of birds until several thousand puffins are circling. They are silent, and there is no way of knowing how they were summoned from their nesting burrows on an island that is out of sight. They glide down to the water – stub-winged cargo planes – land awkwardly, taxi with fluttering wings and stamping paddle feet, then dive.

At the same time, the sea view moves with new invasions of seabirds. Each bird pumps forward with an urgency that suggests it has received the same stimulus as the cod. The gulls that breed on cliffs along a southern bay come first, gracefully light of wing, with raucous voice as they cry out their anticipation. Beneath them, flying flat, direct, silent, come murres, black-bodied, short-tailed, close relatives of the puffins. The murres land and dive without ceremony. Well offshore, as though waiting confirmation of the feast, shearwaters from Tristan da Cunha turn long, pointed wings across the troughs of waves and cackle like poultry.

The birds converge, and lose their identity in the mass thickening on the water. Small gulls – the kittiwakes, delicate in flight – screech and drop and rise and screech and drop like snowflakes on the sea. They fall among even smaller birds, lighter than they, which dangle their feet and hover at the water's surface, almost walking on water as they seek tiny pieces of shredded flesh. These are the ocean-flying petrels, the Mother Carey's chickens of mariners' legends, which rarely come within sight of land. All order is lost in the shrieking tumult of the hundreds of thousands of birds.

Underwater, the hunters meet among their prey. The puffins and murres dive below the capelin and attack, driving for the surface. The cod attack at mid-depth. The gulls smother the surface and press the capelin back among the submarine hunters. The murres and puffins fly underwater, their beating wings turning them rapidly back and forth. They meet the cod, flail wings in desperate haste, are caught, crushed, and swallowed. Now seabirds as well as capelin become the hunted. Puffin and murre tangle wings. Silver walls of capelin flicker, part, re-form. Some seabirds surface abruptly, broken wings dangling. Others, with a leg or legs torn off, fly frantically, crash, skitter in shock across the water.

I see the capelin hunters spread across the sea, but also remember them in time. Each year the hunters are different because many of them depend on a fortuitous meeting with their prey. A group of small whales collides with the capelin, and in a flurry of movement they eat several tons of them. Salmon throw themselves among the capelin with the same abandon as the codfish, and in the melee become easy victims for a score of seals that kill dozens of them, then turn to the capelin and gorge themselves nearly stuporous. They rise, well beyond the tumult of the seabirds, their black heads jutting like rocks from the swell, to lie with distended bellies and doze away their feast. Capelin boil up around them for a moment but now the animals ignore them.

The capelin are hosts in a ceremony so ancient that a multitude of species have adapted to seeking a separate share of the host's bounty. The riotous collision of cod, seal, whale, and seabird obscures the smaller guests at the feast. Near the shore wait small brown fish – the cunner – one of the most voracious species. Soon they will be fighting among themselves for pieces of flesh as the capelin begin their run for the beach, or when the survivors of the spawning reel back into deep water, with the dead and dying falling to the bottom. If the water is calm and the sun bright, the cunner can be seen in two fathoms, ripping capelin corpses to pieces and scattering translucent scales like silver leaves in a wind of the sea.

Closer inshore, at the wave line, the flounder wait. They know the capelin are coming and their role is also predetermined. They cruise rapidly under the purling water in uncharacteristic excitement. They are not interested in capelin flesh. They want capelin eggs, and they will gorge as soon as spawning starts.

Now, the most voracious of all the hunters appear. Fishing vessels come up over the horizon. They brought the Portuguese of the fifteenth century, who anchored offshore, dropped their boats, and rowed ashore to take the capelin with handnets, on beaches never before walked by white men. They brought Spaniards and Dutchmen, Englishmen and Irish, from the sixteenth to the twentieth centuries. Americans, Nova Scotians, Gloucestermen, schoonermen, bankermen, longliner captains have participated in the ritual. All of them knew that fresh capelin is the finest bait when it is skillfully used, and can attract a fortune in codfish flesh, hooked on the submarine banks to the south.

But presently, these hunters are Newfoundlanders. They bring their schooners flying inshore like great brown-and-white birds, a hundred, two hundred, three hundred sail. They heel through the screaming seabirds, luff, anchor, and drop their dories with the same precision of movement of the other figures in the ritual. In an hour, three thousand men are at work from the boats. They work as the codfish work, with a frenzy that knots forearms and sends nets spilling over the sterns to encircle the capelin. They lift a thousand tons of capelin out of the sea, yet they do not measurably diminish the number of fish.

Meanwhile, landbound hunters wait for the fish to come within range of their lead-weighted handnets. Women, children, and old people crowd the beach with the able-bodied men. The old people have ancestral memories of capelin bounty. In the seventeenth and eighteenth centuries, when food was often short, only the big capelin harvest stood between them and starvation during the winter.

Many of the shore people are farmers who use the capelin for fertilizer as well as for food. Capelin corpses, spread to rot over thin northern soils, draw obedient crops of potatoes and cabbages out of the ground, and these, mixed with salted capelin flesh, become winter meals.

The children, who remember dried capelin as their candy, share the excitement of waiting. They chase one another up and down the beach and play with their own nets and fishing rods. Some are already asleep because they awoke before dawn to rouse the village, as they do every capelin morning, with the cry: "They've a-come, they've a-come!"

At the top of the beach, old women lie asleep or sit watching the seabirds squabbling and the dorymen rowing. They are Aunt Sadie and Little Nell and Bessie Blue and Mother Taunton, old ladies from several centuries. They know the capelin can save children in hard winters when the inshore cod fishery fails. They get up at two o'clock in the morning when the capelin are running, to walk miles to the nearest capelin beach. They net a barrel of fish, then roll the barrel, which weighs perhaps a hundred pounds, back home. They have finished spreading the fish on their gardens, or salting them, before the first of their grandchildren awakes.

They have clear memories of catching capelin in winter, when the sea freezes close inshore and the tide cracks the ice in places. Then millions of capelin, resting out the winter, rise in the cracks. An old woman with a good net can take tons of passive fish out of the water for as long as her strength lasts and for as far as her net reaches.

A cry rises from the beach: "Here they come!"

The ritual must be played out, according to habit. The dorymen and the seabirds, the rampaging cod and cunner cannot touch or turn the purpose of the capelin. At a moment, its genesis unknown, they start for the shore. From the top of some nearby cliffs I watch and marvel at the precision of their behaviour. The capelin cease to be a great, formless mass offshore. They split into groups that the Newfoundlanders call *wads* – rippling grey lines, five to fifty feet wide – and run for the shore like advancing infantry lines. One by one, they peel away from their surviving comrades and advance, thirty to forty wads at a time.

Each wad has its discipline. The fish prepares to mate. Each male capelin seeks a female, darting from one fish to another. When he finds one, he presses against her side. Another male, perhaps two males, press against her other side. The males urge the female on toward the beach. Some are struck down by diving seabirds but others take their places. Cod dash among them and smash their sexual formations; they re-form immediately. Cunner rise and rip at them; flounder dart beneath them toward the beach.

The first wad runs into beach wavelets, and a hundred nets hit the water together; a silver avalanche of fish spills out on the beach. In each breaking wavelet the capelin maintain their formations, two or three males pressed tightly against their female until they are all flung up on the beach. There, to the whispering sound of tiny fins and tails vibrating, the female convulsively digs into the sand, which is still moving in the wake of the retreating wave. As she goes down, she extrudes up to fifty thousand eggs, and the males expel their milt.

The children shout; their bare feet fly over the spawning fish; the nets soar; sea boots grind down; the fish spill out; gulls run in the shallows under the children's feet; the flounder gorge. A codfish, two feet long, leaps out of the shallows and hits the beach. An old man scoops it up. The wads keep coming. The air is filled with birds. The dorymen shout and laugh.

The flood of eggs becomes visible. The sand glistens, then is greasy with eggs. They pile in driftlines that writhe back and forth in each wave. The female capelin wriggle into masses of eggs. The shallows are permeated with eggs. The capelin breathe eggs. Their mouths fill with eggs. Their stomachs are choked with eggs. The wads keep pouring onward, feeding the disaster on the beach.

Down come the boots and the nets, and the capelin die, mouths open and oozing eggs. The spawning is a fiasco. The tide has turned. Instead of spawning on the shore with the assurance of rising water behind them, each wad strikes ashore in retreating water. Millions are stranded but the wads keep coming.

In the background, diminished by the quantity of fish, other players gasp and pant at their nets. Barrels stack high on the beach. Horses whinny, driven hard up the bank at the back of the beach. Carts laden with barrels weave away. Carts bringing empty barrels bounce and roar down. The wads are still coming. Men use shovels to lift dead and dying fish from driftlines that are now two and three feet high. The easterly wind is freshening. The wavelets become waves. The capelin are flung up on the beach without a chance to spawn. They bounce and twist and the water flees beneath them.

It is twilight, then dark; torches now spot the beach, the offshore dories, and the schooners. The waves grow solidly and pile the capelin higher. The men shovel the heaps into pyramids, then reluctantly leave the beach. Heavy rain blots out beach and sea.

I remain to watch the blow piling up the sea. At the lowest point of the tide, it is driving waves high up on the beach, roiling the sand, digging up the partially buried eggs, and carrying them out to sea. By dawn most of the eggs are gone. The capelin have disappeared. The sea-birds, the schooners, the cod, flounder, cunner, seals, whales have gone. Nothing remains except the marks of human feet, the cart tracks on the high part of the beach, the odd pyramid of dead fish. The feast is done.

The empty arena of the beach suggests a riddle. If the capelin were so perfectly adapted to spawn on a rising tide, to master the task of burying eggs in running sand between waves, to *know* when the tide was rising, why did they continue spawning after the tide turned? Was that, by the ancient rules of the ritual, intentional? If it was, then it indicated a lethal error of adaptation that did not jibe with the great numbers of capelin.

I wonder, then, if the weak died and the strong survived, but dismiss the notion after recalling the indiscriminate nature of all capelin deaths. There was no Darwinian selection for death of the stupid or the inexperienced. Men slaughtered billions, this year and last year and for three hundred years before, but the capelin never felt this pin-pricking on their colossal corporate bodies. Their spawning was a disaster for reasons well beyond the influence of men.

A nineteenth-century observer, after seeing a capelin-spawning, recorded his amazement at "the astonishing *prosperity* of these creatures, cast so wilfully away. . . ." It was in the end, and indeed throughout the entire ritual, the sheer numbers of capelin that scored the memory. The *prosperity* of the capelin preceded the disaster but then, it seemed, created it. Prosperity was not beneficial or an assurance of survival. The meaning of the ritual was slowly growing into sense. Prosperity unhinges the capelin. Prosperity, abundance, success, drive them on. They become transformed and throw themselves forward blindly. . . .

I turn from the beach, warm and secure, and take a blind step forward.

---

1. Select from the essay and list in your notebook words and phrases that demonstrate the writer's keen observation and his descriptive power. Look up any terms that you do not understand and define them in your own words.

2. With a classmate, paraphrase each of the following statements and explain their significance in the development of Russell's ideas:
   • "As the capelin dies, its silvery scales tarnish and the glitter goes out like a light, ending a small allegory about nature, a spectacle of victims, victors, and an imperative of existence." (paragraph #2)
   • "The capelin are hosts in a ceremony so ancient that a multitude of species have adapted to seeking a separate share of the host's bounty." (paragraph #14)
   • "The *prosperity* of the capelin preceded the disaster but then, it seemed, created it. . . . Prosperity unhinges the capelin." (second-to-last paragraph)

3. A magazine editor refuses to publish "A Madness of Nature" because it is "a boring essay about a bunch of stupid fish." In a small group, prepare a defence of Russell's essay, pointing to specific passages to support your contentions.

4. Write a prose appreciation of three to four paragraphs evaluating "A Madness of Nature." Pay particular attention to sentence structure and length; description; and unity, coherence, and emphasis. Exchange your appreciation with a classmate's for the purpose of reading and responding to each other's analysis.

Give your classmate specific feedback on the

- perceptiveness of judgments;
- soundness of presentation;
- clarity of presentation.

Revise your own piece for your writing folder.

JOURNALESE AS A SECOND TONGUE
John Leo

As a cub reporter, Columnist Richard Cohen of the Washington *Post* rushed out one day to interview a lawyer described in many newspaper reports as "ruddy-faced." The man was woozily abusive and lurched about with such abandon that young Cohen instantly realized that the real meaning of ruddy-faced is drunk. This was his introduction to journalese, the fascinating second tongue acquired by most reporters as effortlessly as an Iranian toddler learns Farsi or a Marin County child learns psychobabble.

Fluency in journalese means knowing all about "the right stuff," "gender gap," "life in the fast lane," and the vexing dilemma of being caught "between a rock and a hard place," the current Scylla-Charybdis image. The Middle East is "strife-torn," except during those inexplicable moments when peace breaks out. Then it is always "much troubled." Kuwait is located just east of the adjective "oil-rich," and the Irish Republican Army always lurks right behind the word "outlawed." The hyphenated modifier is the meat and potatoes of journalese. Who can forget "the break-away province of Biafra," "the mop-top quartet" (the mandatory second reference to the Beatles) and the "ill-fated Korean jetliner," not to be confused with the "ill-fitting red wig" of Watergate fame. Murderers on death row are often saved by "eleventh-hour" reprieves, which would be somewhere between 10 and 11 p.m. in English but shortly before midnight in journalese.

Much of the difficulty in mastering journalese comes from its slight overlap with English. "Imposing," for instance, when used to describe a male, retains its customary English meaning, but when used in reference to a female, it always means battle-axe. "Feisty" refers to a person whom the journalist deems too short and too easily enraged, though many in the journalese-speaking fraternity believe it is simply the adjective of choice for any male under 5 ft. 6 in. who is not legally dead. This usage reflects the continual surprise among tall journalists that short people have any energy at all. Women are not often feisty, though they are usually short enough to qualify. No journalist in America has ever referred to a 6-ft. male as feisty. At that height, men are simply "outspoken" (*i.e.*, abusive).

In general, adjectives in journalese are as misleading as olive sizes. Most news consumers know enough to translate "developing nations" and "disadvantaged nations" back into English, but far smaller numbers know that "militant" means fanatic, and "steadfast" means pigheaded. "Controversial" introduces someone or something the writer finds appalling, as in "the controversial Miss Fonda," and "prestigious" heralds the imminent arrival of a noun nobody cares about, as in "the prestigious Jean Hersholt Humanitarian Award."

Television anchorpersons add interest to their monologues by accenting a few syllables chosen at random. Since print journalists cannot do this, except when reading aloud to spouse and children, they strive for a similar effect by using words like crisis and revolution. Crisis means any kind of trouble at all, and revolution means any kind of change at all, as in "the revolution in meat packing." "Street value" lends excitement to any drug-bust story, without bearing any financial relationship to the actual value of drugs being busted. Many meaningless adjectives, preferably hyphenated for proper rhythm, are permanently welded to certain nouns: blue-ribbon panel, fact-finding mission, devout Catholic, and rock-ribbed Republican. In journalese there are no devout Protestants or Jews, and no Democrats with strong or stony ribs.

Historians of journalese will agree that the first flowering of the language occurred in the sexist descriptions of women by splashy tabloids during the '30s and '40s. In contrast to Pentagonese, which favors oxymorons (Peacekeeper missiles, build-down), the tabloids relied on synecdoche (leggy brunette, bosomy blonde, full-figured redhead). Full-figured, of course, meant fat, and "well-endowed" did not refer to Ford Foundation funding. "Statuesque" (too large, mooselike) and "petite" (too small, mouselike) were adjectives of last resort, meaning that the woman under discussion had no bodily parts that interested the writer. A plain, short woman was invariably "pert." For years, masters of this prose cast about for a nonlibelous euphemism for "mistress." The winning entry, "great and good friend," used to describe Marion Davies's relationship to William Randolph Hearst, was pioneered, as it happens, by a non-Hearst publication, TIME magazine. "Constant companion" evolved later, and gave way to such clunking modernisms as "roommate" and "live-in lover." Nowadays, the only sexuality about which journalese is coy tends to be homosexuality, and that is adequately covered by "he has no close female friends" or "he is not about to settle down."

In political campaigns, underdogs fight uphill battles and hope for shifts of momentum and coattail effects, all leading to rising tides that will enable the favorite to snatch defeat from the jaws of victory. A politician who has no idea about what is going on can be described as one who prefers "to leave details to subordinates." A gangster who runs a foreign country will be referred to as "strongman" until his death, and dictator thereafter. Strongman, like many terms in journalese, has no true correlative. "Nicaraguan Strongman Somoza" is not balanced with "Cambodian Weakman Prince Sihanouk."

What to say about a public figure who is clearly bonkers? Since it is unsporting and possibly libelous to write: "Representative Forbush, the well-known raving psychopath," journalese has evolved the code words difficult, intense and driven. If an article says, "Like many of us, Forbush has his ups and downs," the writer is wigwagging a manic-depressive.

Political journalese, of course, requires a knowledge of sources. An unnamed analyst or observer can often be presumed to be the writer of the article. The popular plural "observers," or "analysts," refers to the writer and his cronies. Insiders, unlike observer-analysts, sometimes exist in the real world outside the newsroom. This, however, is never true of quotable chestnut vendors in Paris, Greenwich Village bartenders and other colourful folk conjured up on deadline to lend dash to a story.

Almost all sources, like most trial balloonists, live in or around Washington. In order of ascending rectitude, they are: informants, usually reliable sources, informed sources, authoritative sources, sources in high places and unimpeachable sources. Informants are low-level operatives, whose beans are normally spilled to police rather than to reporters. Informed sources, because of their informed nature, are consulted most often by savvy journalists. An unimpeachable source is almost always the President, with the obvious exception of Richard Nixon, who was not unimpeachable.

Journalese is controversial but prestigious, and observers are steadfast in averring that it has the right stuff.

HEROES AND IDEALISTS

I say to you in all sadness of conviction, that to think great thoughts you must be heroes as well as idealists.
Oliver Wendell Holmes Jr.

Holmes suggests that idealism necessitates action, that the great thinker is bound to be a champion of one sort or another. In this unit you will encounter people who not only "think great thoughts," but who also test their ideals in action. Some are presented in the context of a public life, some in situations that demand perseverance in the face of social inequity, and some in the sphere of everyday living, where idealism exists in no less valid a form. There are those who learn that their goals cannot be obtained and those who regret what they attempted. As you read these selections, keep Holmes's contention in mind, and speculate on the implications of his phrase "in all sadness of conviction."

In this mini-biography, Virginia Woolf highlights some aspects of the life of the writer of *Vindication of the Rights of Women*. It is almost 200 years since Mary Wollstonecraft's death, and the rights of women are not yet fully established. In a group, draw up a list of five basic rights for women and men. Compare your lists with another group's and agree on a mutually acceptable final set. As you read, note whether your concerns mirror Wollstonecraft's.

MARY WOLLSTONECRAFT
Virginia Woolf

*G*reat wars are strangely intermittent in their effects. The French Revolution took some people and tore them asunder; others it passed over without disturbing a hair of their heads. Jane Austen, it is said, never mentioned it; Charles Lamb ignored it; Beau Brummell never gave the matter a thought. But to Wordsworth and to Godwin it was the dawn; unmistakably they saw

> France standing on the top of golden hours,
> And human nature seeming born again.

Thus it would be easy for a picturesque historian to lay side by side the most glaring contrasts – here in Chesterfield Street was Beau Brummell letting his chin fall carefully upon his cravat and discussing in a tone studiously free from vulgar emphasis the proper cut of the lapel of a coat; and here in Somers Town was a party of ill-dressed, excited young men, one with a head too big for his body and a nose too long for his face, holding forth day by day over the tea-cups upon human perfectibility, ideal unity, and the rights of man. There was also a woman present with very bright eyes and a very eager tongue, and the young men, who had middle-class names, like Barlow and Holcroft and Godwin, called her simply "Wollstonecraft," as if it did not matter whether she were married or unmarried, as if she were a young man like themselves.

Such glaring discords among intelligent people – for Charles Lamb and Godwin, Jane Austen and Mary Wollstonecraft were all highly intelligent – suggest how much influence circumstances have upon opinions. If Godwin had been brought up in the precincts of the Temple and had drunk deep of antiquity and old letters at Christ's Hospital, he might never have cared a straw for the future of man and his rights in general. If Jane Austen had lain as a child on the landing to prevent her father from thrashing her mother, her soul might have burnt with such a passion against tyranny that all her novels might have been consumed in one cry for justice.

Such had been Mary Wollstonecraft's first experience of the joys of married life. And then her sister Everina had been married miserably and had bitten her wedding ring to pieces in the coach. Her brother had been a burden on her; her father's farm had failed, and in order to start that disreputable man with the red face and the violent temper and the dirty hair in life again she had gone into bondage among the aristocracy as a governess – in short, she had never known what happiness was, and, in its default, had fabricated a creed fitted to meet the sordid misery of real human life. The staple of her doctrine was that nothing mattered save independence. "Every obligation we receive from our fellow-creatures is a new shackle, takes from our native freedom, and debases the mind." Independence was the first necessity for a woman; not grace or charm, but energy and courage and the power to put her will into effect were her necessary qualities. It was her highest boast to be able to say, "I never yet resolved to do anything of consequence that I did not adhere readily to it." Certainly Mary could say this with truth. When she was a little more than thirty she could look back upon a series of actions which she had carried out in the teeth of opposition. She had taken a house by prodigious efforts for her friend Fanny, only to find that Fanny's mind was changed and she did not want a house after all. She had started a school. She had persuaded Fanny into marrying Mr. Skeys. She had thrown up her school and gone to Lisbon alone to nurse Fanny when she died. On the voyage back she had forced the captain of the ship to rescue a wrecked French vessel by threatening to expose him if he refused. And when, overcome by a passion for Fuseli, she declared her wish to live with him and was refused flatly by his wife, she had put her principle of decisive action instantly into effect, and had gone to Paris determined to make her living by her pen.

The Revolution thus was not merely an event that had happened outside her; it was an active agent in her own blood. She had been in revolt all her life – against tyranny, against law, against convention. The reformer's love of humanity, which has so much of hatred in it as well as love, fermented within her. The outbreak of revolution in France expressed some of her deepest theories and convictions, and she dashed off in the heat of that extraordinary moment those two eloquent and daring books – the *Reply to Burke* and the *Vindication of the Rights of Women,* which are so true that they seem now to contain nothing new in them – their originality has become our commonplace. But when she was in Paris lodging by herself in a great house, and saw with her own eyes the King whom she despised driving past surrounded by National Guards and holding himself with greater dignity than she expected, then, "I can scarcely tell you why," the tears came to her eyes. "I am going to bed," the letter ended, "and, for the first time in my life, I cannot put out the candle." Things were not so simple after all. She could not understand even her own feelings. She saw the most cherished of her convictions put into practice – and her eyes filled with tears. She had won fame and independence and the right to live her own life – and she wanted something different. "I do not wish to be loved like a goddess," she wrote, "but I wish to be necessary to you." For Imlay, the fascinating American to whom her letter was addressed, had been very good to her. Indeed, she had fallen passionately in love with him. But it was one of her theories that love should be free – "that mutual affection was marriage and that the marriage tie should not bind after the death of love, if love should die." And yet at the same time that she wanted freedom she wanted certainty. "I like the word affection," she wrote, "because it signifies something habitual."

The conflict of all these contradictions shows itself in her face, at once so resolute and so dreamy, so sensual and so intelligent, and beautiful into the bargain with its great coils of hair and the large bright eyes that Southey thought the most expressive he had ever seen. The life of such a woman was bound to be tempestuous. Every day she made theories by which life should be lived; and every day she came smack against the rock of other people's prejudices. Every day too – for she was no pedant, no cold-blooded theorist – something was born in her that thrust aside her theories and forced her to model them afresh. She acted upon her theory that she had no legal claim upon Imlay; she refused to marry him; but when he left her alone week after week with the child she had borne him her agony was unendurable.

Thus distracted, thus puzzling even to herself, the plausible and treacherous Imlay cannot be altogether blamed for failing to follow the rapidity of her changes and the alternate reason and unreason of her moods. Even friends whose liking was impartial were disturbed by her discrepancies. Mary had a passionate, an exuberant, love of Nature, and yet one night when the colours in the sky were so exquisite that Madeleine Schweizer could not help saying to her, "Come, Mary – come, nature lover – and enjoy this wonderful spectacle – this constant transition from colour to colour," Mary never took her eyes off the Baron de Wolzogen. "I must confess," wrote Madame Schweizer, "that this erotic absorption made such a disagreeable impression on me, that all my pleasure vanished." But if the sentimental Swiss was disconcerted by Mary's sensuality, Imlay, the shrewd man of business, was exasperated by her intelligence. Whenever he saw her he yielded to her charm, but then her quickness, her penetration, her uncompromising idealism harassed him. She saw through his excuses; she met all his reasons; she was even capable of managing his business. There was no peace with her – he must be off again. And then her letters followed him, torturing him with their sincerity and their insight. They were so outspoken; they pleaded so passionately to be told the truth; they showed such a contempt for soap and alum and wealth and comfort; they repeated, as he suspected, so truthfully that he had only to say the word, "and you shall never hear of me more," that he could not endure it. Tickling minnows he had hooked a dolphin, and the creature rushed him through the waters till he was dizzy and only wanted to escape. After all, though he had played at theory-making too, he was a business man, he depended upon soap and alum; "the secondary pleasures of life are very necessary to my comfort." And among them was one that for ever evaded Mary's jealous scrutiny. Was it business, was it politics, was it a woman that perpetually took him away from her? He shillied and shallied; he was very charming when they met; then he disappeared again. Exasperated at last, and half insane with suspicion, she forced the truth from the cook. A little actress in a strolling company was his mistress, she learnt. True to her own creed of decisive action, Mary at once soaked her skirts so that she might sink unfailingly, and threw herself from Putney Bridge. But she was rescued; after unspeakable agony she recovered, and then her "unconquerable greatness of mind," her girlish creed of independence, asserted itself again, and she determined to make another bid for happiness and to earn her living without taking a penny from Imlay for herself or their child.

It was in this crisis that she again saw Godwin, the little man with the big head, whom she had met when the French Revolution was making the young men in Somers Town think that a new world was being born. She met him – but that is a euphemism, for in fact Mary Wollstonecraft actually visited him in his own house. Was it the effect of the French Revolution? Was it the blood she had seen spilt on the pavement and the cries of the furious crowd that had run in her ears that made it seem a matter of no importance whether she put on her cloak and went to visit Godwin in Somers Town, or waited in Judd Street West for Godwin to come to her? And what strange upheaval of human life was it that inspired that curious man, who was so queer a mixture of meanness and magnanimity, of coldness and deep feeling – for the memoir of his wife could not have been written without unusual depth of heart – to hold the view that she did right – that he respected Mary for trampling upon the idiotic convention by which women's lives were tied down? He held the most extraordinary views on many subjects, and upon the relations of the sexes in particular. He thought that reason should influence even the love between men and women. He thought that there was something spiritual in their relationship. He had written that "marriage is a law, and the worst of all laws . . . marriage is an affair of property, and the worst of all properties." He held the belief that if two people of the opposite sex like each other, they should live together without any ceremony, or, for living together is apt to blunt love, twenty doors off, say, in the same street. And he went further; he said that if another man liked your wife "this will create no difficulty. We may all enjoy her conversation, and we shall all be wise enough to consider the sensual intercourse a very trivial object." True, when he wrote those words he had never been in love; now for the first time he was to experience that sensation. It came very quietly and naturally, working "with equal advances in the mind of each" from those talks in Somers Town, from those discussions upon everything under the sun which they held so improperly alone in his rooms. "It was friendship melting into love . . ." he wrote. "When, in the course of things, the disclosure came, there was nothing in a manner for either party to disclose to the other." Certainly they were in agreement upon the most essential points; they were both of opinion, for instance, that marriage was unnecessary. They would continue to live apart. Only when Nature again intervened, and Mary found herself with child, was it worth while to lose valued friends, she asked, for the sake of a theory? She thought not, and they were married. And then that other theory – that it is best for husband and wife to live apart – was not that also incompatible with other feelings that were coming to birth in her? "A husband is a convenient part of the furniture of the house," she wrote. Indeed, she discovered that she was passionately domestic. Why not, then, revise that theory too, and share the same roof? Godwin should have a room some doors off to work in; and they should dine out separately if they liked – their work, their friends, should be separate. Thus they settled it, and the plan worked admirably. The arrangement combined "the novelty and lively sensation of a visit with the more delicious and heartfelt pleasures of domestic life." Mary admitted that she was happy; Godwin confessed that, after all one's philosophy, it was "extremely gratifying" to find that "there is some one who takes an interest in one's happiness." All sorts of powers and emotions were liberated in Mary by her new satisfaction. Trifles gave her an exquisite pleasure – the sight of Godwin and Imlay's child playing together; the thought of their own child who was to be born; a day's jaunt into the country. One day, meeting Imlay in the New Road, she greeted him without bitterness. But, as Godwin wrote, "Ours is not an idle happiness, a paradise of selfish and transitory pleasures." No, it too was an experiment, as Mary's life had been an experiment from the start, an attempt to make human conventions conform more closely to human needs. And their marriage was only a beginning; all sorts of things were to follow after. Mary was going to have a child. She was going to write a book to be called *The Wrongs of Women*. She was going to reform education. She was going to come down to dinner the day after her child was born. She was going to employ a midwife and not a doctor at her confinement – but that experiment was her last. She died in child-birth. She whose sense of her own existence was so intense, who had cried out even in her misery, "I cannot bear to think of being no more – of losing myself – nay, it appears to me impossible that I should cease to exist," died at the age of thirty-six. But she has her revenge. Many millions have died and been forgotten in the hundred and thirty years that have passed since she was buried; and yet as we read her letters and listen to her arguments and consider her experiments, above all that most fruitful experiment, her relation with Godwin, and realize the high-handed and hot-blooded manner in which she cut her way to the quick of life, one form of immortality is hers undoubtedly: she is alive and active, she argues and experiments, we hear her voice and trace her influence even now among the living.

———————————— •••◄————————————

1. Although many years have elapsed since her death, some of Wollstonecraft's ideas are still revolutionary. Select one of her ideas with which you agree or disagree. In a personal essay, argue your point of view; exchange essays with a number of classmates and discuss the merits of each other's arguments.

2. Investigate one of the people mentioned in the essay and, in a short oral presentation to the class, describe the most intriguing aspects of that person's life.
   OR
   Do some background research and write a capsule biography of Virginia Woolf that highlights her achievements as a writer.

3. a) Reread the selection carefully and determine Woolf's attitude to Wollstonecraft, noting the words and phrases that reveal it.
   b) Rewrite an incident from Wollstonecraft's life as it might have been written by a biographer with a different attitude.

4. It could be argued that Wollstonecraft was a woman born out of step with her time.
   a) In a group, discuss the ways in which she anticipated changes in the relationships between men and women.
   b) Drawing upon newspapers, magazines, and so on, create a bulletin board, pamphlet, or other visual presentation to show that Wollstonecraft's vision of the world was prophetic.

In "The Blood of the Martyrs," Benét examines the impact of totalitarianism upon the individual and upon truth itself. With a few classmates, share your knowledge of the presentation of totalitarianism in literature you have read, e.g., Orwell's *1984*. Discuss the respective demands of state and conscience upon the individual in society. Under what circumstances would you disobey the laws of the nation?

THE BLOOD OF THE MARTYRS

Stephen Vincent Benét

*T*he man who expected to be shot lay with his eyes open, staring at the upper left-hand corner of his cell. He was fairly well over his last beating, and they might come for him any time now. There was a yellow stain in the cell corner near the ceiling; he had liked it at first, then disliked it; now he was coming back to liking it again.

He could see it more clearly with his glasses on, but he only put on his glasses for special occasions now – the first thing in the morning, and when they brought the food in, and for interviews with the General. The lenses of the glasses had been cracked in a beating some months before, and it strained his eyes to wear them too long. Fortunately, in his present life he had very few occasions demanding clear vision. But, nevertheless, the accident to his glasses worried him, as it worries all near-sighted people. You put your glasses on the first thing in the morning and the world leaps into proportion; if it does not do so, something is wrong with the world.

The man did not believe greatly in symbols, but his chief nightmare, nowadays, was an endless one in which, suddenly and without warning, a large piece of glass would drop out of one of the lenses and he would grope around the cell, trying to find it. He would grope very carefully and gingerly, for hours of darkness, but the end was always the same – the small, unmistakable crunch of irreplaceable glass beneath his heel or his knee. Then he would wake up sweating, with his hands cold. This dream alternated with the one of being shot, but he found no great benefit in the change.

As he lay there, you could see that he had an intellectual head – the head of a thinker or a scholar, old and bald, with the big, domed brow. It was, as a matter of fact, a well-known head; it had often appeared in the columns of newspapers and journals, sometimes when the surrounding text was in a language Professor Malzius could not read. The body, though stooped and worn, was still a strong peasant body and capable of surviving a good deal of ill-treatment, as his captors had found out. He had fewer teeth than when he came to prison, and both the ribs and the knee had been badly set, but these were minor matters. It also occurred to him that his blood count was probably poor. However, if he could ever get out and to a first-class hospital, he was probably good for at least ten years more of work. But, of course, he would not get out. They would shoot him before that, and it would be over.

Sometimes he wished passionately that it would be over – tonight – this moment; at other times he was shaken by the mere blind fear of death. The latter he tried to treat as he would have treated an attack of malaria, knowing that it was an attack, but not always with success. He should have been able to face it better than most – he was Gregor Malzius, the scientist – but that did not always help. The fear of death persisted, even when one had noted and classified it as a purely physical reaction. When he was out of here, he would be able to write a very instructive little paper on the fear of death. He could even do it here, if he had writing materials, but there was no use asking for those. Once they had been given him and he had spent two days quite happily. But they had torn up the work and spat upon it in front of his face. It was a childish thing to do, but it discouraged a man from working.

It seemed odd that he had never seen anybody shot, but he never had. During the war, his reputation and his bad eyesight had exempted him from active service. He had been bombed a couple of times when his reserve battalion was guarding the railway bridge, but that was quite different. You were not tied to a stake, and the airplanes were not trying to kill you as an individual. He knew the place where it was done here, of course. But prisoners did not see the executions, they merely heard, if the wind was from the right quarter.

He had tried again and again to visualize how it would be, but it always kept mixing with an old steel engraving he had seen in boyhood – the execution of William Walker, the American filibuster, in Honduras. William Walker was a small man with a white semi-Napoleonic face. He was standing, very correctly dressed, in front of an open grave, and before him a ragged line of picturesque natives were raising their muskets. When he was shot he would instantly and tidily fall into the grave, like a man dropping through a trap door; as a boy, the extreme neatness of the arrangement had greatly impressed Gregor Malzius. Behind the wall there were palm trees, and, somewhere off to the right, blue and warm, the Caribbean Sea. It would not be like that at all, for his own execution; and yet, whenever he thought of it, he thought of it as being like that.

Well, it was his own fault. He could have accepted the new regime; some respectable people had done that. He could have fled the country; many honourable people had. A scientist should be concerned with the eternal, not with transient political phenomena; and a scientist should be able to live anywhere. But thirty years at the university were thirty years, and, after all, he was Malzius, one of the first biochemists in the world. To the last, he had not believed that they would touch him. Well, he had been wrong about that.

The truth, of course, was the truth. One taught it or one did not teach it. If one did not teach it, it hardly mattered what one did. But he had no quarrel with any established government; he was willing to run up a flag every Tuesday, as long as they let him alone. Most people were fools, and one government was as good as another for them – it had taken them twenty years to accept his theory of cell mutation. Now, if he'd been like his friend Bonnard – a fellow who signed protests, attended meetings for the cause of world peace, and generally played the fool in public – they'd have had some reason to complain. An excellent man in his field, Bonnard – none better – but, outside of it, how deplorably like an actor, with his short grey beard, his pink cheeks and his impulsive enthusiasms! Any government could put a fellow like Bonnard in prison – though it would be an injury to science and, therefore, wrong. For that matter, he thought grimly, Bonnard would enjoy being a martyr. He'd walk gracefully to the execution post with a begged cigarette in his mouth, and some theatrical last quip. But Bonnard was safe in his own land – doubtless writing heated and generous articles on The Case of Professor Malzius – and he Malzius was the man who was going to be shot. He would like a cigarette, too, on his way to execution; he had not smoked in five months. But he certainly didn't intend to ask for one, and they wouldn't think of offering him any. That was the difference between him and Bonnard.

His mind went back with longing to the stuffy laboratory and stuffier lecture hall at the university; his feet yearned for the worn steps he had climbed ten thousand times, and his eyes for the long steady look through the truthful lens into worlds too tiny for the unaided eye. They had called him "The Bear" and "Old Prickly," but they had fought to work under him, the best of the young men. They said he would explain the Last Judgment in terms of cellular phenomena, but they had crowded to his lectures. It was Williams, the Englishman, who had made up the legend that he carried a chocolate éclair and a set of improper post cards in his battered brief case. Quite untrue, of course – chocolate always made him ill, and he had never looked at an improper post card in his life. And Williams would never know that he knew the legend, too; for Williams had been killed long ago in the war. For a moment, Professor Malzius felt blind hate at the thought of an excellent scientific machine like Williams being smashed in a war. But blind hate was an improper emotion for a scientist, and he put it aside.

He smiled grimly again; they hadn't been able to break up his classes – lucky he was The Bear! He'd seen one colleague hooted from his desk by a band of determined young hoodlums – too bad, but if a man couldn't keep order in his own classroom, he'd better get out. They'd wrecked his own laboratory, but not while he was there.

It was so senseless, so silly. "In Heaven's name," he said reasonably, to no one, "what sort of conspirator do you think I would make? A man of my age and habits! I am interested in cellular phenomena!" And yet they were beating him because he would not tell about the boys. As if he had even paid attention to half the nonsense! There were certain passwords and greetings – a bar of music you whistled, entering a restaurant; the address of a firm that specialized, ostensibly, in vacuum cleaners. But they were not his own property. They belonged to the young men who had trusted The Bear. He did not know what half of them meant, and the one time he had gone to a meeting, he had felt like a fool. For they were fools and childish – playing the childish games of conspiracy that people like Bonnard enjoyed. Could they even make a better world than the present? He doubted it extremely. And yet, he could not betray them; they had come to him, looking over their shoulders, with darkness in their eyes.

A horrible, an appalling thing – to be trusted. He had no wish to be a guide and counselor of young men. He wanted to do his work. Suppose they were poor and ragged and oppressed; he had been a peasant himself, he had eaten black bread. It was by his own efforts that he was Professor Malzius. He did not wish the confidences of boys like Gregopolous and the others – for, after all, what was Gregopolous? An excellent and untiring laboratory assistant – and a laboratory assistant he would remain to the end of his days. He had pattered about the laboratory like a fox terrier, with a fox terrier's quick bright eyes. Like a devoted dog, he had made a god of Professor Malzius. "I don't want your problems, man. I don't want to know what you are doing outside the laboratory." But Gregopolous had brought his problems and his terrible trust none the less, humbly and proudly, like a fox terrier with a bone. After all –well, what was a man to do?

He hoped they would get it over with, and quickly. The world should be like a chemical formula, full of reason and logic. Instead, there were all these young men, and their eyes. They conspired, hopelessly and childishly, for what they called freedom against the new regime. They wore no overcoats in winter and were often hunted and killed. Even if they did not conspire, they had miserable little love affairs and ate the wrong food – yes, even before, at the university, they had been the same. Why the devil would they not accept? Then they could do their work. Of course, a great many of them would not be allowed to accept – they had the wrong ideas or the wrong politics – but then they could run away. If Malzius, at twenty, had had to run from his country, he would still have been a scientist. To talk of a free world was a delusion; men were not free in the world. Those who wished got a space of time to get their work done. That was all. And yet, he had not accepted – he did not know why.

Now he heard the sound of steps along the corridor. His body began to quiver and the places where he had been beaten hurt him. He noted it as an interesting reflex. Sometimes they merely flashed the light in the cell and passed by. On the other hand, it might be death. It was a hard question to decide.

The lock creaked, the door opened. "Get up, Malzius!" said the hard, bright voice of the guard. Gregor Malzius got up, a little stiffly, but quickly.

"Put on your glasses, you old fool!" said the guard, with a laugh. "You are going to the General."

Professor Malzius found the stone floors of the corridor uneven, though he knew them well enough. Once or twice the guard struck him, lightly and without malice, as one strikes an old horse with a whip. The blows were familiar and did not register on Professor Malzius's consciousness; he merely felt proud of not stumbling. He was apt to stumble; once he had hurt his knee.

He noticed, it seemed to him, an unusual tenseness and officiousness about his guard. Once, even, in a brightly lighted corridor the guard moved to strike him, but refrained. However, that, too, happened occasionally, with one guard or another, and Professor Malzius merely noted the fact. It was a small fact, but an important one in the economy in which he lived.

But there could be no doubt that something unusual was going on in the castle. There were more guards than usual, many of them strangers. He tried to think, carefully, as he walked, if it could be one of the new national holidays. It was hard to keep track of them all. The General might be in a good humour. Then they would merely have a cat-and-mouse conversation for half an hour and nothing really bad would happen. Once, even, there had been a cigar. Professor Malzius, the scientist, licked his lips at the thought.

Now he was being turned over to a squad of other guards, with salutings. This was really unusual; Professor Malzius bit his mouth, inconspicuously. He had the poignant distrust of a monk or an old prisoner at any break in routine. Old prisoners are your true conservatives; they only demand that the order around them remains exactly the same.

It alarmed him as well that the new guards did not laugh at him. New guards almost always laughed when they saw him for the first time. He was used to the laughter and missed it – his throat felt dry. He would have liked, just once, to eat at the university restaurant before he died. It was bad food, ill cooked and starchy, food good enough for poor students and professors, but he would have liked to be there, in the big smoky room that smelt of copper boilers and cabbage, with a small cup of bitter coffee before him and a cheap cigarette. He did not ask for his dog or his notebooks, the old photographs in his bedroom, his incomplete experiments or his freedom. Just to lunch once more at the university restaurant and have people point out The Bear. It seemed a small thing to ask, but of course it was quite impossible.

"Halt!" said a voice, and he halted. There were, for the third time, salutings. Then the door of the General's office opened and he was told to go in.

He stood, just inside the door, in the posture of attention, as he had been taught. The crack in the left lens of his glasses made a crack across the room, and his eyes were paining him already, but he paid no attention to that. There was the familiar figure of the General, with his air of a well-fed and extremely healthy tomcat, and there was another man, seated at the General's desk. He could not see the other man very well – the crack made him bulge and waver – but he did not like his being there.

"Well, professor," said the General, in an easy, purring voice.

Malzius's entire body jerked. He had made a fearful, an unpardonable omission. He must remedy it at once. "Long live the state," he shouted in a loud thick voice, and saluted. He knew, bitterly, that this salute was ridiculous and that he looked ridiculous, making it. But perhaps the General would laugh – he had done so before. Then everything would be all right, for it was not quite as easy to beat a man after you had laughed at him.

The General did not laugh. He made a half turn instead, toward the man at the desk. The gesture said, "You see, he is well trained." It was the gesture of a man of the world, accustomed to deal with unruly peasants and animals – the gesture of a man fitted to be General.

The man at the desk paid no attention to the General's gesture. He lifted his head, and Malzius saw him more clearly and with complete unbelief. It was not a man but a picture come alive. Professor Malzius had seen the picture a hundred times; they had made him salute and take off his hat in front of it, when he had had a hat. Indeed, the picture had presided over his beatings. The man himself was a little smaller, but the picture was a good picture. There were many dictators in the world, and this was one type. The face was white, beaky and semi-Napoleonic; the lean, military body sat squarely in its chair. The eyes dominated the face, and the mouth was rigid. I remember also a hypnotist, and a woman Charcot showed me, at his clinic in Paris, thought Professor Malzius. But there is also, obviously, an endocrine unbalance. Then his thoughts stopped.

"Tell the man to come closer," said the man at the desk. "Can he hear me? Is he deaf?"

"No, Your Excellency," said the General, with enormous, purring respect. "But he is a little old, though perfectly healthy. . . . Are you not, Professor Malzius?"

"Yes, I am perfectly healthy. I am very well treated here," said Professor Malzius, in his loud thick voice. They were not going to catch him with traps like that, not even by dressing up somebody as the Dictator. He fixed his eyes on the big old-fashioned inkwell on the General's desk – that, at least, was perfectly sane.

"Come closer," said the man at the desk to Professor Malzius, and the latter advanced till he could almost touch the inkwell with his fingers. Then he stopped with a jerk, hoping he had done right. The movement removed the man at the desk from the crack in his lenses, and Professor Malzius knew suddenly that it was true. This was, indeed, the Dictator, this man with the rigid mouth. He began to talk.

"I have been very well treated here and the General has acted with the greatest consideration," he said. "But I am Professor Gregor Malzius – professor of biochemistry. For thirty years I have lectured at the university; I am a fellow of the Royal Society, a corresponding member of the Academy of Sciences at Berlin, at Rome, at Boston, at Paris and Stockholm. I have received the Nottingham Medal, the Lamarck Medal, the Order of St. John of Portugal and the Nobel Prize. I think my blood count is low, but I have received a great many degrees and my experiments on the migratory cells are not finished. I do not wish to complain of my treatment, but I must continue my experiments."

He stopped, like a clock that has run down, surprised to hear the sound of his own voice. He noted, in one part of his mind, that the General had made a move to silence him, but had himself been silenced by the Dictator.

"Yes, Professor Malzius," said the man at the desk, in a harsh, toneless voice. "There has been a regrettable error." The rigid face stared at Professor Malzius. Professor Malzius stared back. He did not say anything.

"In these days," said the Dictator, his voice rising, "the nation demands the submission of every citizen. Encircled by jealous foes, our reborn land yet steps forward toward her magnificent destiny." The words continued for some time, the voice rose and fell. Professor Malzius listened respectfully; he had heard the words many times before and they had ceased to have meaning to him. He was thinking of certain cells of the body that rebel against the intricate processes of

Nature and set up their own bellicose state. Doubtless they, too, have a destiny, he thought, but in medicine it is called cancer.

"Jealous and spiteful tongues in other countries have declared that it is our purpose to wipe out learning and science," concluded the Dictator. "That is not our purpose. After the cleansing, the rebirth. We mean to move forward to the greatest science in the world – our own science, based on the enduring principles of our nationhood." He ceased abruptly, his eyes fell into their dream. Very like the girl Charcot showed me in my young days, thought Professor Malzius; there was first the ebullition, then the calm.

"I was part of the cleansing? You did not mean to hurt me?" he said timidly.

"Yes, Professor Malzius," said the General, smiling, "you were part of the cleansing. Now that is over. His Excellency has spoken."

"I do not understand," said Professor Malzius, gazing at the fixed face of the man behind the desk.

"It is very simple," said the General. He spoke in a slow careful voice, as one speaks to a deaf man or a child. "You are a distinguished man of science – you have received the Nobel Prize. That was a service to the state. You became, however, infected by the wrong political ideas. That was treachery to the state. You had, therefore, as decreed by His Excellency, to pass through a certain period for probation and rehabilitation. But that, we believe, is finished."

"You do not wish to know the names of the young men any more?" said Professor Malzius. "You do not want the addresses?"

"That is no longer of importance," said the General patiently. "There is no longer opposition. The leaders were caught and executed three weeks ago."

"There is no longer opposition," repeated Professor Malzius.

"At the trial, you were not even involved."

"I was not even involved," said Professor Malzius. "Yes."

"Now," said the General, with a look at the Dictator, "we come to the future. I will be frank – the new state is frank with its citizens."

"It is so," said the Dictator, his eyes still sunk in his dream.

"There has been – let us say – a certain agitation in foreign countries regarding Professor Malzius," said the General, his eyes still fixed on the Dictator. "That means nothing, of course. Nevertheless, your acquaintance, Professor Bonnard, and others have meddled in matters that do not concern them."

"They asked after me?" said Professor Malzius, with surprise. "It is true, my experiments were reaching a point that – "

"No foreign influence could turn us from our firm purpose," said the Dictator. "But it is our firm purpose to show our nation first in science and culture as we have already shown her first in manliness and statehood. For that reason, you are here, Professor Malzius." He smiled.

Professor Malzius stared. His cheeks began to tremble.

"I do not understand," said Professor Malzius. "You will give me my laboratory back?"

"Yes," said the Dictator, and the General nodded as one nods to a stupid child.

Professor Malzius passed a hand across his brow.

"My post at the university?" he said. "My experiments?"

"It is the purpose of our regime to offer the fullest encouragement to our loyal sons of science," said the Dictator.

"First of all," said Professor Malzius, "I must go to a hospital. My blood count is poor. But that will not take long." His voice had become impatient and his eyes glowed. "Then – my notebooks were burned, I suppose. That was silly, but we can start in again. I have a very good memory, an excellent memory. The theories are in my head, you know," and he tapped it. "I must have assistants, of course; little Gregopolous was my best one – "

"The man Gregopolous has been executed," said the General, in a stern voice. "You had best forget him."

"Oh," said Professor Malzius. "Well, then, I must have someone else. You see, these are important experiments. There must be some young men – clever ones – they cannot all be dead. I will know them." He laughed a little, nervously. "The Bear always got the pick of the crop," he said. "They used to call me The Bear, you know." He stopped and looked at them for a moment with ghastly eyes. "You are not fooling me?" he said. He burst into tears.

When he recovered he was alone in the room with the General. The General was looking at him as he himself had looked once at strange forms of life under the microscope, with neither disgust nor attraction, but with great interest.

"His Excellency forgives your unworthy suggestion," he said. "He knows you are overwrought."

"Yes," said Professor Malzius. He sobbed once and dried his glasses.

"Come, come," said the General, with a certain bluff heartiness. "We mustn't have our new president of the National Academy crying. It would look badly in the photographs."

"President of the Academy?" said Professor Malzius quickly. "Oh, no; I mustn't be that. They make speeches; they have administrative work. But I am a scientist, a teacher."

"I'm afraid you can't very well avoid it," said the General, still heartily, though he looked at Professor Malzius. "Your induction will be quite a ceremony. His Excellency himself will preside. And you will speak on the new glories of our science. It will be a magnificent answer to the petty and jealous criticisms of our neighbours. Oh, you needn't worry about the speech," he added quickly. "It will be prepared; you will only have to read it. His Excellency thinks of everything."

"Very well," said Professor Malzius; "and then may I go back to my work?"

"Oh, don't worry about that," said the General, smiling. "I'm only a simple soldier; I don't know about those things. But you'll have plenty of work."

"The more the better," said Malzius eagerly. "I still have ten good years."

He opened his mouth to smile, and a shade of dismay crossed the General's face.

"Yes," he said, as if to himself. "The teeth must be attended to. At once. And a rest, undoubtedly, before the photographs are taken. Milk. You are feeling sufficiently well, Professor Malzius?"

"I am very happy," said Professor Malzius. "I have been very well treated and I come of peasant stock."

"Good," said the General. He paused for a moment, and spoke in a more official voice.

"Of course, it is understood, Professor Malzius – " he said.

"Yes?" said Professor Malzius. "I beg your pardon. I was thinking of something else."

"It is understood, Professor Malzius," repeated the General, "that your – er – rehabilitation in the service of the state is a permanent matter. Naturally, you will be under observation, but, even so, there must be no mistake."

"I am a scientist," said Professor Malzius impatiently. "What have I to do with politics? If you wish me to take oaths of loyalty, I will take as many as you wish."

"I am glad you take that attitude," said the General, though he looked at Professor Malzius curiously. "I may say that I regret the unpleasant side of our interviews. I trust you bear no ill will."

"Why should I be angry?" said Professor Malzius. "You were told to do one thing. Now you are told to do another. That is all."

"It is not quite so simple as that," said the General rather stiffly. He looked at Professor Malzius for a third time. "And I'd have sworn you were one of the stiff-necked ones," he said. "Well, well, every man has his breaking point, I suppose. In a few moments you will receive the final commands of His Excellency. Tonight you will go to the capitol and speak over the radio. You will have no difficulty there – the speech is written. But it will put a quietus on the activities of our friend Bonnard and the question that has been raised in the British Parliament. Then a few weeks of rest by the sea and the dental work, and then, my dear president of the National Academy, you will be ready to undertake your new duties. I congratulate you and hope we shall meet often under pleasant auspices." He bowed from the waist to Malzius, the bow of a man of the world, though there was still something feline in his mustaches. Then he stood to attention, and Malzius, too, for the Dictator had come into the room.

"It is settled?" said the Dictator. "Good. Gregor Malzius, I welcome you to the service of the new state. You have cast your errors aside and are part of our destiny."

"Yes," said Professor Malzius, "I will be able to do my work now."
The Dictator frowned a little.

"You will not only be able to continue your invaluable researches," he said, "but you will also be able – and it will be part of your duty – to further our national ideals. Our reborn nation must rule the world for the world's good. There is a fire within us that is not in other stocks. Our civilization must be extended everywhere. The future wills it. It will furnish the subject of your first discourse as president of the Academy."

"But," said Professor Malzius, in a low voice, "I am not a soldier. I am a biochemist. I have no experience in these matters you speak of."

The Dictator nodded. "You are a distinguished man of science," he said. "You will prove that our women must bear soldiers, our men abandon this nonsense of republics and democracies for trust in those born to rule them. You will prove by scientific law that certain races – our race in particular – are destined to rule the world. You will prove they are destined to rule by the virtues of war, and that war is part of our heritage."

"But," said Professor Malzius, "it is not like that. I mean," he said, "one looks and watches in the laboratory. One waits for a long time. It is a long process, very long. And then, if the theory is not proved, one discards the theory. That is the way it is done. I probably do not explain it well. But I am a biochemist; I do not know how to look for the virtues of one race against another, and I can prove nothing about war, except that it kills. If I said anything else, the whole world would laugh at me."

"Not one in this nation would laugh at you," said the Dictator.

"But if they do not laugh at me when I am wrong, there is no science," said Professor Malzius, knotting his brows. He paused. "Do not misunderstand me," he said earnestly. "I have ten years of good work left; I want to get to my laboratory. But, you see, there are the young men – if I am to teach the young men."

He paused again, seeing their faces before him. There were many. There was Williams, the Englishman, who had died in the war, and little Gregopolous with the fox-terrier eyes. There were all who had passed through his classrooms, from the stupidest to the best. They had shot little Gregopolous for treason, but that did not alter the case. From all over the world they had come – he remembered the Indian student and the Chinese. They wore cheap overcoats, they were hungry for knowledge, they ate the bad, starchy food of the poor restaurants, they had miserable little love affairs and played childish games of politics, instead of doing their work. Nevertheless, a few were promising – all must be given the truth. It did not matter if they died, but they must be given the truth. Otherwise there could be no continuity and no science.

He looked at the Dictator before him – yes, it was a hysteric face. He would know how to deal with it in his classroom – but such faces should not rule countries or young men. One was willing to go through a great many meaningless ceremonies in order to do one's work – wear a uniform or salute or be president of the Academy. That did not matter; it was part of the due to Caesar. But not to tell lies to young men on one's own subject. After all, they had called him The Bear and said he carried improper post cards in his brief case. They had given him their terrible confidence – not for love or kindness, but because they had found him honest. It was too late to change.

The Dictator looked sharply at the General. "I thought this had been explained to Professor Malzius," he said.

"Why, yes," said Professor Malzius. "I will sign any papers. I assure you I am not interested in politics – a man like myself, imagine! One state is as good as another. And I miss my tobacco – I have not smoked in five months. But, you see, one cannot be a scientist and tell lies."

He looked at the two men.

"What happens if I do not?" he said, in a low voice. But, looking at the Dictator, he had his answer. It was a fanatic face.

"Why, we shall resume our conversations, Professor Malzius," said the General, with a simper.

"Then I shall be beaten again," said Professor Malzius. He stated what he knew to be a fact.

"The process of rehabilitation is obviously not quite complete," said the General, "but perhaps, in time – "

"It will not be necessary," said Professor Malzius. "I cannot be beaten again." He stared wearily around the room. His shoulders straightened – it was so he had looked in the classroom when they had called him The Bear. "Call your other officers in," he said in a clear voice. "There are papers for me to sign. I should like them all to witness."

"Why – " said the General. "Why – " He looked doubtfully at the Dictator.

An expression of gratification appeared on the lean, semi-Napoleonic face. A white hand, curiously limp, touched the hand of Professor Malzius.

"You will feel so much better, Gregor," said the hoarse, tense voice. "I am so very glad you have given in."

"Why, of course, I give in," said Gregor Malzius. "Are you not the Dictator? And besides, if I do not, I shall be beaten again. And I cannot – you understand? – I cannot be beaten again."

He paused, breathing a little. But already the room was full of other faces. He knew them well, the hard faces of the new regime. But youthful some of them too.

The Dictator was saying something with regard to receiving the distinguished scientist, Professor Gregor Malzius, into the service of the state.

"Take the pen," said the General in an undertone. "The inkwell is there, Professor Malzius. Now you may sign."

Professor Malzius stood, his fingers gripping the big old-fashioned inkwell. It was full of ink – the servants of the Dictator were very efficient. They could shoot small people with the eyes of fox terriers for treason, but their trains arrived on time and their inkwells did not run dry.

"The state," he said, breathing. "Yes. But science does not know about states. And you are a little man – a little, unimportant man."

Then, before the General could stop him, he had picked up the inkwell and thrown it in the Dictator's face. The next moment the General's fist caught him on the side of the head and he fell behind the desk to the floor. But lying there, through cracked glasses, he could still see the grotesque splashes of ink on the Dictator's face and uniform, and the small cut above his eye where the blood was gathering. They had not fired; he had thought he would be too close to the Dictator for them to fire in time.

"Take that man out and shoot him. At once," said the Dictator in a dry voice. He did not move to wipe the stains from his uniform – and for that Professor Malzius admired him. They rushed then, each anxious to be first. But Professor Malzius made no resistance.

As he was being hustled along the corridors, he fell now and then. On the second fall, his glasses were broken completely, but that did not matter to him. They were in a great hurry, he thought, but all the better – one did not have to think while one could not see.

Now and then he heard his voice make sounds of discomfort, but his voice was detached from himself. There was little Gregopolous – he could see him very plainly – and Williams, with his fresh English colouring – and all the men whom he had taught.

He had given them nothing but work and the truth; they had given him their terrible trust. If he had been beaten again, he might have betrayed them. But he had avoided that.

He felt a last weakness – a wish that someone might know. They would not, of course; he would have died of typhoid in the castle and there would be regretful notices in the newspapers. And then he would be forgotten, except for his work, and that was as it should be. He had never thought much of martyrs – hysterical people in the main. Though he'd like Bonnard to have known about the ink; it was in the coarse vein of humour that Bonnard could not appreciate. But then, he was a peasant; Bonnard had often told him so.

They were coming out into an open courtyard now; he felt the fresh air of outdoors. "Gently," he said. "A little gently. What's the haste?" But already they were tying him to the post. Someone struck him in the face and his eyes watered. "A schoolboy covered with ink," he muttered through his lost teeth. "A hysterical schoolboy too. But you cannot kill truth."

They were not good last words, and he knew that they were not. He must try to think of better ones – not shame Bonnard. But now they had a gag in his mouth; just as well; it saved him the trouble.

His body ached, bound against the post, but his sight and his mind were clearer. He could make out the evening sky, grey with fog, the sky that belonged to no country, but to all the world.

He could make out the grey high buttress of the castle. They had made it a jail, but it would not always be a jail. Perhaps in time it would not even exist. But if a little bit of truth were gathered, that would always exist, while there were men to remember and rediscover it. It was only the liars and the cruel who always failed.

Sixty years ago, he had been a little boy, eating black bread and thin cabbage soup in a poor house. It had been a bitter life, but he could not complain of it. He had had some good teachers and they had called him The Bear.

The gag hurt his mouth – they were getting ready now. There had been a girl called Anna once; he had almost forgotten her. And his rooms had smelt a certain way and he had had a dog. It did not matter what they did with the medals. He raised his head and looked once more at the grey foggy sky. In a moment there would be no thought, but, while there was thought, one must remember and note. His pulse rate was lower than he would have expected and his breathing oddly even, but those were not the important things. The important thing was beyond, in the grey sky that had no country, in the stones of the earth and the feeble human spirit. The important thing was truth.

"Ready!" called the officer. "Aim! Fire!" But Professor Malzius did not hear the three commands of the officer. He was thinking about the young men.

---

1. Imagine that you are Benét, planning "The Blood of the Martyrs." Explain what you hope to achieve with the first three paragraphs of the story. Show how specific words and images will prepare the reader for the narrative that follows.

2. a) In a group, consider the following details and determine what the author wishes them to convey to the reader:
   - the title of the story;
   - the eyeglasses and Malzius's eyesight;
   - the young men;
   - the inkwell and its contents;
   - the nickname *The Bear*;
   - the steel engraving of the execution of William Walker.

   b) The narrator says that Malzius "did not believe greatly in symbols." Write in your notebook an assessment of the validity of the statement in the context of the beginning and the end of the story.

c) "The reader is free to interpret a symbol or a story in whatever way she or he wishes." Decide whether or not you concur with this claim. Find a classmate who disagrees with you and conduct a brief argument in which each of you presents your point of view, referring to "The Blood of the Martyrs" to make your case. If you wish to extend your argument, use other selections in this book as evidence: "The Drowned Giant" (p. 312), "The Possibility of Evil" (p. 359), or "The Girl Next Door" (p. 59), for instance.

3. You are one of the prison guards, but secretly you are a member of the conspirators. You are in the General's office when The Bear performs his act of defiance. It is your responsibility to tell the other conspirators about Malzius's courage. Describe the incident in a pamphlet that would circulate among the underground.

OR

Malzius judges his last words harshly: "They were not good last words . . . He must try to think of better ones. . . . " Imagine that you are Malzius and that you have been given one minute to make a statement before your execution. Write what you would say and read it aloud for a classmate.

4. In the age of Star Wars, biological engineering, microsurgery, and chemical warfare, science wields a staggering amount of power. In a group of four, prepare and present a debate on the resolution "Science should always be at the service of the state."

5. If you have read the story of Antigone, indicate, in a brief essay, Benét's debt to that classical myth. You might also like to read "A West Coast Woman" (p. 78), a story patterned on Sophocles' *Antigone*.

6. Decide whether you like "The Blood of the Martyrs" and, in a piece of exploratory writing, examine the reasons for your decision. Look back at your evaluation after a few weeks to see if your opinion has modified. If it has, note the change.

T.J., like the giant Antaeus, knows the source
of his strength. Investigate the myth of
Antaeus and, as you read the following story,
note the places where your knowledge of the
myth complements Borden Deal's narrative.

ANTAEUS
Borden Deal

his was during the wartime, when lots of people were coming
North for jobs in factories and war industries, when people
moved around a lot more than they do now and sometimes
kids were thrown into new groups and new lives that were completely
different from anything they had ever known before. I remember this
one kid; T.J. his name was, from somewhere down South, whose family
moved into our building during that time. They'd come North with
everything they owned piled into the back seat of an old-model sedan
that you wouldn't expect could make the trip, with T.J. and his three
younger sisters riding shakily atop the load of junk.

Our building was just like all the others there, with families crowded
into a few rooms, and I guess there were twenty-five or thirty kids
about my age in that one building. Of course, there were a few of us
who formed a gang and ran together all the time after school, and I
was the one who brought T.J. in and started the whole thing.

The building right next door to us was a factory where they made
walking dolls. It was a low building with a flat, tarred roof that had a
parapet all around it about head-high and we'd found out a long time
before that no one, not even the watchman, paid any attention to the
roof because it was higher than any of the other buildings around. So

my gang used the roof as a headquarters. We could get up there by crossing over to the fire escape from our own roof on a plank and then going on up. It was a secret place for us, where nobody else could go without our permission.

I remember the day I first took T.J. up there to meet the gang. He was a stocky, robust kid with a shock of white hair, nothing sissy about him except his voice – he talked different from any of us and you noticed it right away. But I liked him anyway, so I told him to come on up.

We climbed up over the parapet and dropped down on the roof. The rest of the gang were already there.

"Hi," I said. I jerked my thumb at T.J. "He just moved into the building yesterday."

He just stood there, not scared or anything, just looking, like the first time you see somebody you're not sure you're going to like.

"Hi," Blackie said. "Where you from?"

"Marion County," T.J. said.

We laughed. "Marion County?" I said. "Where's that?"

He looked at me like I was a stranger, too. "It's in Alabama," he said, like I ought to know where it was.

"What's your name?" Charley said.

"T.J.," he said, looking back at him. He had pale blue eyes that looked washed-out but he looked directly at Charley, waiting for his reaction. He'll be all right, I thought. No sissy in him . . . except that voice. Who ever talked like that?

"T.J.," Blackie said. "That's just initials. What's your real name? Nobody in the world has just initials."

"I do," he said. "And they're T.J. That's all the name I got."

His voice was resolute with the knowledge of his rightness and for a moment no one had anything to say. T.J. looked around at the rooftop and down at the black tar under his feet. "Down yonder where I come from," he said, "we played out in the woods. Don't you-all have no woods around here?"

"Naw," Blackie said. "There's the park a few blocks over, but it's full of kids and cops and old women. You can't do a thing."

T.J. kept looking at the tar under his feet. "You mean you ain't got no fields to raise nothing in? No watermelons or nothing?"

"Naw," I said scornfully. "What do you want to grow something for? The folks can buy everything they need at the store."

He looked at me again with that strange, unknowing look. "In Marion County," he said, "I had my own acre of cotton and my own acre of corn. It was mine to plant ever' year."

He sounded like it was something to be proud of, and in some obscure way it made the rest of us angry. "Heck!" Blackie said. "Who'd want to have their own acre of cotton and corn? That's just work. What can you do with an acre of cotton and corn?"

T.J. looked at him. "Well, you get part of the bale offen your acre," he said seriously. "And I fed my acre of corn to my calf."

We didn't really know what he was talking about, so we were more puzzled than angry; otherwise, I guess, we'd have chased him off the roof and wouldn't let him be part of our gang. But he was strange and different and we were all attracted by his stolid sense of rightness and belonging, maybe by the strange softness of his voice contrasting our own tones of speech into harshness.

He moved his foot against the black tar. "We could make our own field right here," he said softly, thoughtfully. "Come spring we could raise us what we want to . . . watermelons and garden truck and no telling what all."

"You'd have to be a good farmer to make these tar roofs grow any watermelons," I said. We all laughed.

But T.J. looked serious. "We could haul us some dirt up here," he said. "And spread it out even and water it and before you know it we'd have us a crop in here." He looked at us intently. "Wouldn't that be fun?"

"They wouldn't let us," Blackie said quickly.

"I thought you said this was you-all's roof," T.J. said to me. "That you-all could do anything you wanted up here."

"They've never bothered us," I said. I felt the idea beginning to catch fire in me. It was a big idea and it took a while for it to sink in, but the more I thought about it the better I liked it. "Say," I said to the gang, "he might have something there. Just make us a regular roof garden, with flowers and grass and trees and everything. And all ours, too," I said. "We wouldn't let anybody up here except the ones we wanted to."

"It'd take a while to grow trees," T.J. said quickly, but we weren't paying any attention to him. They were all talking about it suddenly, all excited with the idea after I'd put it in a way they could catch hold of it. Only rich people had roof gardens, we knew, and the idea of our own private domain excited them.

"We could bring it up in sacks and boxes," Blackie said. "We'd have to do it while the folks weren't paying any attention to us. We'd have to come up to the roof of our building and then cross over with it."

"Where could we get the dirt?" somebody said worriedly.

"Out of those vacant lots over close to school," Blackie said. "Nobody'd notice if we scraped it up."

I slapped T.J. on the shoulder. "Man, you had a wonderful idea," I said, and everybody grinned at him, remembering he had started it. "Our own private roof garden."

He grinned back. "It'll be ourn," he said. "All ourn." Then he looked thoughtful again. "Maybe I can lay my hands on some cotton seed, too. You think we could raise us some cotton?"

We'd started big projects before at one time or another, like any gang of kids, but they'd always petered out for lack of organization and direction. But this one didn't . . . somehow or other T.J. kept it going all through the winter months. He kept talking about the watermelons and the cotton we'd raise, come spring, and when even that wouldn't work he'd switch around to my idea of flowers and grass and trees, though he was always honest enough to add that it'd take a while to get any trees started. He always had it on his mind and he'd mention it in school, getting them lined up to carry dirt that afternoon, saying, in a casual way, that he reckoned a few more weeks ought to see the job through.

Our little area of private earth grew slowly. T.J. was smart enough to start in one corner of the building, heaping up the carried earth two or three feet thick, so that we had an immediate result to look at, to contemplate with awe. Some of the evenings T.J. alone was carrying earth up to the building, the rest of the gang distracted by other enterprises or interests, but T.J. kept plugging along on his own and eventually we'd all come back to him again, and then our own little acre would grow more rapidly.

He was careful about the kind of dirt he'd let us carry up there and more than once he dumped a sandy load over the parapet into the areaway below because it wasn't good enough. He found out the kinds of earth in all the vacant lots for blocks around. He'd pick it up and feel it and smell it, frozen though it was sometimes, and then he'd say it was good growing soil or it wasn't worth anything and we'd have to go on somewhere else.

Thinking about it now, I don't see how he kept us at it. It was hard work, lugging paper sacks and boxes of dirt all the way up the stairs of our own building, keeping out of the way of the grown-ups so they wouldn't catch on to what we were doing. They probably wouldn't have cared, for they didn't pay much attention to us, but we wanted to keep it secret anyway. Then we had to go through the trapdoor to our roof, teeter over a plank to the fire escape, then climb two or three storeys to the parapet and drop down onto the roof. All that for a small pile of earth that sometimes didn't seem worth the effort. But T.J. kept the vision bright within us, his words shrewd and calculated toward the fulfilment of his dream; and he worked harder than any of us. He seemed driven toward a goal that we couldn't see, a particular point in time that would be definitely marked by signs and wonders that only he could see.

The laborious earth just lay there during the cold months, inert and lifeless, the clods lumpy and cold under our feet when we walked over it. But one day it rained, and afterward there was a softness in the air and the earth was alive and giving again with moisture and warmth. That evening T.J. smelled the air, his nostrils dilating with the odour of the earth under his feet.

"It's spring," he said, and there was a gladness rising in his voice that filled us all with the same feeling. "It's mighty late for it, but it's spring. I'd just about decided it wasn't never gonna get here at all."

We were all sniffing at the air, too, trying to smell it the way that T.J. did, and I can remember the sweet odour of the earth under our feet. It was the first time in my life that spring and spring earth had meant anything to me. I looked at T.J. then, knowing in a faint way the hunger within him through the toilsome winter months, knowing the dream that lay behind his plan. He was a new Antaeus, preparing his own bed of strength.

"Planting time," he said. "We'll have to find us some seed."

"What do we do?" Blackie said. "How do we do it?"

"First we'll have to break up the clods," T.J. said. "That won't be hard to do. Then we plant the seed, and after a while they come up. Then you got you a crop." He frowned. "But you ain't got it raised yet. You got to tend it and hoe it and take care of it and all the time it's growing and growing while you're awake and while you're asleep. Then you lay it by when it's growed and let it ripen and then you got you a crop."

"There's those wholesale seed houses over on Sixth," I said. "We could probably swipe some grass seed over there."

T.J. looked at the earth. "You-all seem mighty set on raising some grass," he said. "I ain't never put no effort into that. I spent all my life trying not to raise grass."

"But it's pretty," Blackie said. "We could play on it and take sun-baths on it. Like having our own lawn. Lots of people got lawns."

"Well," T.J. said. He looked at the rest of us, hesitant for the first time. He kept on looking at us for a moment. "I did have it in mind to raise some corn and vegetables. But we'll plant grass."

He was smart. He knew where to give in. And I don't suppose it made any difference to him, really. He just wanted to grow something, even if it was grass.

"Of course," he said, "I do think we ought to plant a row of watermelons. They'd be mighty nice to eat while we was a-laying on that grass."

We all laughed. "All right," I said. "We'll plant us a row of watermelons."

Things went very quickly then. Perhaps half the roof was covered with the earth, the half that wasn't broken by ventilators, and we swiped pocketfuls of grass seed from the open bins in the wholesale seed house, mingling among the buyers on Saturdays and during the school lunch hour. T.J. showed us how to prepare the earth, breaking up the clods and smoothing it and sowing the grass seed. It looked rich and black now with moisture, receiving of the seed, and it seemed that the grass sprang up overnight, pale green in the early spring.

We couldn't keep from looking at it, unable to believe that we had created this delicate growth. We looked at T.J. with understanding now, knowing the fulfilment of the plan he had carried alone within his mind. We had worked without full understanding of the task, but he had known all the time.

We found that we couldn't walk or play on the delicate blades, as we had expected to, but we didn't mind. It was enough just to look at it, to realize that it was the work of our own hands, and each evening the whole gang was there, trying to measure the growth that had been achieved that day.

One time a foot was placed on the plot of ground . . . one time only, Blackie stepping onto it with sudden bravado. Then he looked at the crushed blades and there was shame in his face. He did not do it again. This was his grass, too, and not to be desecrated. No one said anything, for it was not necessary.

T.J. had reserved a small section for watermelons and he was still trying to find some seed for it. The wholesale house didn't have any watermelon seed and we didn't know where we could lay our hands on them. T.J. shaped the earth into mounds, ready to receive them, three mounds lying in a straight line along the edge of the grass plot.

We had just about decided that we'd have to buy the seed if we were to get them. It was a violation of our principles, but we were anxious to get the watermelons started. Somewhere or other, T.J. got his hands on a seed catalogue and brought it one evening to our roof garden.

"We can order them now," he said, showing us the catalogue. "Look!"

We all crowded around, looking at the fat, green watermelons pictured in full colour on the pages. Some of them were split open, showing the red, tempting meat, making our mouths water.

"Now we got to scrape up some seed money," T.J. said, looking at us. "I got a quarter. How much you-all got?"

We made up a couple of dollars between us and T.J. nodded his head. "That'll be more than enough. Now we got to decide what kind to get. I think them Kleckley Sweets. What do you-all think?"

He was going into esoteric matters, beyond our reach. We hadn't even known there were different kinds of melons. So we just nodded our heads and agreed that yes, we thought the Kleckley Sweets, too.

"I'll order them tonight," T.J. said. "We ought to have them in a few days."

Then an adult voice said behind us: "What are you boys doing up here?"

It startled us, for no one had ever come up here before, in all the time we had been using the roof of the factory. We jerked around and saw three men standing near the trapdoor at the other end of the roof. They weren't policemen, or night watchmen, but three men in plump business suits, looking at us. They walked toward us.

"What are you boys doing up here?" the one in the middle said again.

We stood still, guilt heavy among us, levied by the tone of voice, and looked at the three strangers.

The men stared at the grass flourishing behind us. "What's this?" the man said. "How did this get up here?"

"Sure is growing good, ain't it?" T.J. said conversationally. "We planted it."

The men kept looking at the grass as if they didn't believe it. It was a thick carpet over the earth now, a patch of deep greenness startling in the sterile industrial surroundings.

"Yes, sir," T.J. said proudly. "We toted that earth up here and planted that grass." He fluttered the seed catalogue. "And we're just fixing to plant us some watermelon."

The man looked at him then, his eyes strange and faraway. "What do you mean, putting this on the roof of my building?" he said. "Do you want to go to jail?"

T.J. looked shaken. The rest of us were silent, frightened by the authority of his voice. We had grown up aware of adult authority, of policemen and night watchmen and teachers, and this man sounded like all the others. But it was a new thing to T.J.

"Well, you wan't using the roof," T.J. said. He paused a moment and added shrewdly, "So we just thought to pretty it up a little bit."

"And sag it so I'd have to rebuild it," the man said sharply. He turned away, saying to a man beside him, "See that all that junk is shovelled off by tomorrow."

"Yes, sir," the man said.

T.J. started forward. "You can't do that," he said. "We toted it up here and it's our earth. We planted it and raised it and toted it up here."

The man stared at him coldly. "But it's my building," he said. "It's to be shovelled off tomorrow."

"It's our earth," T.J. said desperately. "You ain't got no right!"

The men walked on without listening and descended clumsily through the trapdoor. T.J. stood looking after them, his body tense with anger, until they had disappeared. They wouldn't even argue with him, wouldn't let him defend his earth-rights.

He turned to us. "We won't let 'em do it," he said fiercely. "We'll stay up here all day tomorrow and the day after that and we won't let 'em do it."

We just looked at him. We knew that there was no stopping it. He saw it in our faces and his face wavered for a moment before he gripped it into determination.

"They ain't got no right," he said. "It's our earth. It's our land. Can't nobody touch a man's own land."

We kept on looking at him, listening to the words but knowing that it was no use. The adult world had descended on us even in our richest dream, and we knew there was no calculating the adult world, no fighting it, no winning against it.

We started moving slowly toward the parapet and the fire escape, avoiding a last look at the green beauty of the earth that T.J. had planted for us . . . had planted deeply in our minds as well as in our experience. We filed slowly over the edge and down the steps to the plank, T.J. coming last, and all of us could feel the weight of his grief behind us.

"Wait a minute," he said suddenly, his voice harsh with the effort of calling. We stopped and turned, held by the tone of his voice, and looked up at him standing above us on the fire escape.

"We can't stop them?" he said, looking down at us, his face strange in the dusky light. "There ain't no way to stop 'em?"

"No," Blackie said with finality. "They own the building."

We stood still for a moment, looking up at T.J., caught into inaction by the decision working in his face. He stared back at us and his face was pale and mean in the poor light, with a bald nakedness in his skin. . . .

"They ain't gonna touch my earth," he said fiercely. "They ain't gonna lay a hand on it! Come on."

He turned around and started up the fire escape again, almost running against the effort of climbing. We followed more slowly, not knowing what he intended. By the time we reached him, he had seized a board and thrust it into the soil, scooping it up and flinging it over the parapet into the areaway below. He straightened and looked us squarely in the face.

"They can't touch it," he said. "I won't let 'em lay a dirty hand on it!"

We saw it then. He stooped to his labour again and we followed it, the gusts of his anger moving in frenzied labour among us as we scattered along the edge of earth, scooping it and throwing it over the parapet, destroying with anger the growth we had nurtured with such tender care. The soil carried so laboriously upward to the light and the sun cascaded swiftly into the dark areaway, the green blades of grass crumpled and twisted in the falling.

It took less time than you would think . . . the task of destruction is infinitely easier than that of creation. We stopped at the end, leaving only a scattering of loose soil, and when it was finally over, a stillness stood among the group and over the factory building. We looked down at the bare sterility of black tar, felt the harsh texture of it under the soles of our shoes, and the anger had gone out of us, leaving only a sore aching in our minds like overstretched muscles.

T.J. stooped for a moment, his breathing slowing from anger and effort, caught into the same contemplation of destruction as all of us. He stooped slowly, finally, and picked up a lonely blade of grass left trampled under our feet, and put it between his teeth, tasting it, sucking the greenness out of it into his mouth. Then he started walking toward the fire escape, moving before any of us were ready to move, and disappeared over the edge while we stared after him.

We followed him but he was already halfway down to the ground, going on past the board where we crossed over, climbing down into the areaway. We saw the last section swing down with his weight and then he stood on the concrete below us, looking at the small pile of anonymous earth scattered by our throwing. Then he walked across the place where we could see him and disappeared toward the street without glancing back, without looking up to see us watching him.

They did not find him for two weeks. Then the Nashville police caught him just outside the Nashville freight yards. He was walking along the railroad track; still heading south, still heading home.

As for us, who had no remembered home to call us . . . none of us ever again climbed the escapeway to the roof.

---

1. a) In a small group, discuss the appropriateness of the title "Antaeus" for this story.
   b) The narrator tells a realistic tale that has none of the superhuman elements of the myth of Antaeus. Imagine, however, that T.J.'s endeavour becomes a local legend. With a classmate, brainstorm what sorts of transformations, exaggerations, and simplifications might occur with frequent retellings of the tale. Write the story as it might be told by children in the neighbourhood many years in the future. (You may wish to read two or three traditional myths and folk tales before you write.) You might wish to word-process or type the final draft of your story, illustrate it, and arrange to read it to a class of elementary school students.

2. T.J. and his project stand in stark contrast to the world in which he is forced to live. Write an interior monologue in T.J.'s voice as he heads south and ponders his experiences in the city.
   OR
   Write a letter as T.J. to a friend back in Alabama in which you describe your new home, your reactions to it, and your plans for transforming it.

3. a)" . . . the task of destruction is infinitely easier than that of creation." In the voices of T. (from "The Destructors," p. 268) and T.J., explore, in a diary format, your reactions to the above statement.
   b) In a piece of personal writing, tell about an incident from your own life that confirms or contradicts the quotation in (a).

Writing in the *Chicago Tribune*, 25 May 1916,
Henry Ford stated, "History is more or less
bunk." As you read the following portrait of
Ford and his famous Tin Lizzie, keep Ford's
comment in mind and decide whether Dos
Passos's mini-biography is history or bunk.

TIN LIZZIE

John Dos Passos

"M r. Ford the automobileer," *the featurewriter wrote in 1900,
"Mr. Ford the automobileer began by giving his steed three or four
sharp jerks with the lever at the righthand side of the seat; that is, he
pulled the lever up and down sharply in order, as he said, to mix air with
gasoline and drive the charge into the exploding cylinder. . . . Mr. Ford slipped
a small electric switch handle and there followed a puff, puff, puff. . . . The
puffing of the machine assumed a higher key. . . . She was flying along about
eight miles an hour. The ruts in the road were deep, but the machine certainly
went with a dreamlike smoothness. There was none of the bumping common
even to a steamer. . . . By this time the boulevard had been reached, and the
automobileer, letting a lever fall a little, let her out. Whiz! She picked up speed
with infinite rapidity. As she ran on there was a clattering behind, the new
noise of the automobile."*

For twenty years or more,
ever since he'd left his father's farm when he was sixteen to get a
job in a Detroit machineshop, Henry Ford had been nuts about machinery. First it was watches, then he designed a steamtractor, then
he built a horseless carriage with an engine adapted from the Otto gas-
engine he'd read about in *The World of Science*, then a mechanical buggy

with a onecylinder fourcycle motor, that would run forward but not back;

at last, in ninetyeight, he felt he was far enough along to risk throwing up his job with the Detroit Edison Company, where he'd worked his way up from night fireman to chief engineer, to put all his time into working on a new gasoline engine,

(in the late eighties he'd met Edison at a meeting of electriclight employees in Atlantic City. He'd gone up to Edison after Edison had delivered an address and asked him if he thought gasoline was practical as a motor fuel. Edison had said yes. If Edison said it, it was true. Edison was the great admiration of Henry Ford's life);

and in driving his mechanical buggy, sitting there at the lever jauntily dressed in a tightbuttoned jacket and a high collar and a derby hat, back and forth over the level illpaved streets of Detroit,

scaring the big brewery horses and the skinny trotting horses and the sleekrumped pacers with the motor's loud explosions,

looking for men scatterbrained enough to invest money in a factory for building automobiles.

He was the eldest son of an Irish immigrant who during the Civil War had married the daughter of a prosperous Pennsylvania Dutch farmer and settled down to farming near Dearborn in Wayne County, Michigan;

like plenty of other Americans, young Henry grew up hating the endless sogging through the mud about the chores, the hauling and pitching manure, the kerosene lamps to clean, the irk and sweat and solitude of the farm.

He was a slender, active youngster, a good skater, clever with his hands; what he liked was to tend the machinery and let the others do the heavy work. His mother had told him not to drink, smoke, gamble, or go into debt, and he never did.

When he was in his early twenties his father tried to get him back from Detroit, where he was working as mechanic and repairman for the Drydock Engine Company that built engines for steamboats, by giving him forty acres of land.

Young Henry built himself an uptodate square white dwellinghouse with a false mansard roof and married and settled down on the farm.

but he let the hired men do the farming;

he bought himself a buzzsaw and rented a stationary engine and cut the timber off the woodlots.

He was a thrifty young man who never drank or smoked or gambled or coveted his neighbour's wife, but he couldn't stand living on the farm.

He moved to Detroit, and in the brick barn behind his house tinkered for years in his spare time with a mechanical buggy that would be light enough to run over the clayey wagonroads of Wayne County, Michigan.

By 1900 he had a practicable car to promote.

He was forty years old before the Ford Motor Company was started and production began to move.

Speed was the first thing the early automobile manufacturers went after. Races advertised the makes of cars.

Henry Ford himself hung up several records at the track at Grosse Pointe and on the ice on Lake St. Clair. In his .999 he did the mile in thirtynine and fourfifths seconds.

But it had always been his custom to hire others to do the heavy work. The speed he was busy with was speed in production, the records, records in efficient output. He hired Barney Oldfield, a stunt bicyclerider from Salt Lake City, to do the racing for him.

Henry Ford had ideas about other things than designing of motors, carburetors, magnetos, jigs and fixtures, punches and dies; he had ideas about sales;

that the big money was in economical quantity production, quick turnover, cheap interchangeable easilyreplaced standardized parts;

it wasn't until 1909, after years of arguing with his partners, that Ford put out the first Model T.

Henry Ford was right.

That season he sold more than ten thousand tin lizzies, ten years later he was selling almost a million a year.

In these years the Taylor Plan was stirring up plantmanagers and manufacturers all over the country. Efficiency was the word. The same ingenuity that went into improving the performance of a machine could go into improving the performance of the workmen producing the machine.

In 1913 they established the assemblyline at Ford's. That season the profits were something like twentyfive million dollars, but they had trouble in keeping the men on the job, machinists didn't seem to like it at Ford's.

Henry Ford had ideas about other things than production.

He was the largest automobile manufacturer in the world; he paid high wages; maybe if the steady workers thought they were getting a cut (a very small cut) in the profits, it would give trained men an inducement to stick to their jobs,

wellpaid workers might save enough money to buy a tin lizzie; the first day Ford's announced that cleancut properlymarried American workers who wanted jobs had a chance to make five bucks a day (of course it turned out that there were strings to it; always there were strings to it)

such an enormous crowd waited outside the Highland Park plant
all through the zero January night
that there was a riot when the gates were opened; cops broke heads,
jobhunters threw bricks; property, Henry Ford's own property, was
destroyed. The company dicks had to turn on the firehose to beat back
the crowd.

The American Plan; automotive prosperity seeping down from above;
it turned out there were strings to it.
    But that five dollars a day
    paid to good, clean American workmen
    who didn't drink or smoke cigarettes or read or think,
    and who didn't commit adultery
    and whose wives didn't take in boarders,
    made America once more the Yukon of the sweated workers of the
world;
    made all the tin lizzies and the automotive age, and incidentally,
    made Henry Ford the automobileer, the admirer of Edison, the bird-
lover,
    the great American of his time.

But Henry Ford had ideas about other things besides assemblylines
and the livinghabits of his employees. He was full of ideas. Instead of
going to the city to make his fortune, here was a country boy who'd
made his fortune by bringing the city out to the farm. The precepts
he'd learned out of McGuffey's Reader, his mother's prejudices and
preconceptions, he had preserved clean and unworn as freshprinted
bills in the safe in a bank.
    He wanted people to know about his ideas, so he bought the *Dear-
born Independent* and started a campaign against cigarettesmoking.
    When war broke out in Europe, he had ideas about that too. (Sus-
picion of armymen and soldiering were part of the Mid-West farm
tradition, like thrift, stickativeness, temperance, and sharp practice in
money matters.) Any intelligent American mechanic could see that if
the Europeans hadn't been a lot of ignorant underpaid foreigners who
drank, smoked, were loose about women, and wasteful in their methods of production, the war could never have happened.
    When Rosika Schwimmer broke through the stockade of secretaries
and servicemen who surrounded Henry Ford and suggested to him
that he could stop the war,
    he said sure they'd hire a ship and go over and get the boys out of
the trenches by Christmas.
    He hired a steamboat, the *Oscar II*, and filled it up with pacifists and
socialworkers,
    to go over to explain to the princelings of Europe

that what they were doing was vicious and silly.

It wasn't his fault that Poor Richard's commonsense no longer rules the world and that most of the pacifists were nuts,

goofy with headlines.

When William Jennings Bryan went over to Hoboken to see him off, somebody handed William Jennings Bryan a squirrel in a cage; William Jennings Bryan made a speech with the squirrel under his arm. Henry Ford threw American Beauty roses to the crowd. The band played *I Didn't Raise My Boy to Be a Soldier*. Practical jokers let loose more squirrels. An eloping couple was married by a platoon of ministers in the saloon, and Mr. Zero, the flophouse humanitarian, who reached the dock too late to sail,

dove into the North River and swam after the boat.

The *Oscar II* was described as a floating Chautauqua; Henry Ford said it felt like a Middle-Western village, but by the time they reached Christiansand in Norway, the reporters had kidded him so that he had gotten cold feet and gone to bed. The world was too crazy outside of Wayne County, Michigan. Mrs. Ford and the management sent an Episcopal dean after him who brought him home under wraps,

and the pacifists had to speechify without him.

Two years later Ford's was manufacturing munitions, Eagle boats; Henry Ford was planning oneman tanks, and oneman submarines like the one tried out in the Revolutionary War. He announced to the press that he'd turn over his war profits to the government,

but there's no record that he ever did.

One thing he brought back from his trip

was the Protocols of the Elders of Zion.

He started a campaign to enlighten the world in the *Dearborn Independent*; the Jews were why the world wasn't like Wayne County, Michigan, in the old horse-and-buggy days;

the Jews had started the war, Bolshevism, Darwinism, Marxism, Nietzsche, short skirts and lipstick. They were behind Wall Street and the international bankers, and the whiteslave traffic and the movies and the Supreme Court and ragtime and the illegal liquor business.

Henry Ford denounced the Jews and ran for Senator and sued the *Chicago Tribune* for libel,

and was the laughingstock of the kept metropolitan press;

but when the metropolitan bankers tried to horn in on his business he thoroughly outsmarted them.

In 1918 he had borrowed on notes to buy out his minority stockholders for the picayune sum of seventyfive million dollars.

In February, 1920, he needed cash to pay off some of these notes that were coming due. A banker is supposed to have called on him and offered him every facility if the bankers' representative could be made a member of the board of directors. Henry Ford handed the banker his hat,

and went about raising the money in his own way:

he shipped every car and part he had in his plant to his dealers and demanded immediate cash payment. Let the other fellow do the borrowing had always been a cardinal principle. He shut down production and cancelled all orders from the supplyfirms. Many dealers were ruined, many supplyfirms failed, but when he reopened his plant,

he owned it absolutely,

the way a man owns an unmortgaged farm with the taxes paid up.

In 1922 there started the Ford boom for President (high wages, waterpower, industry scattered to the small towns) that was skillfully pricked behind the scenes

by another crackerbarrel philosopher,

Calvin Coolidge;

but in 1922 Henry Ford sold one million three hundred and thirty-two thousand two hundred and nine tin lizzies; he was the richest man in the world.

Good roads had followed the narrow ruts made in the mud by the Model T. The great automotive boom was on. At Ford's production was improving all the time; less waste, more spotters, strawbosses, stool-pigeons (fifteen minutes for lunch, three minutes to go to the toilet, the Taylorized speedup everywhere, reachunder, adjustwasher, screwdown bolt, shove in cotterpin, reachunder, adjustwasher, screwdown bolt, reachunderadjustscrewdownreachunderadjust, until every ounce of life was sucked off into production and at night the workmen went home grey shaking husks).

Ford owned every detail of the process from the ore in the hills until the car rolled off the end of the assemblyline under its own power; the plants were rationalized to the last tenthousandth of an inch as measured by the Johansen scale;

in 1926 the production cycle was reduced to eightyone hours from the ore in the mine to the finished salable car proceeding under its own power,

but the Model T was obsolete.

New Era prosperity and the American Plan

(there were strings to it, always there were strings to it)

had killed Tin Lizzie.

Ford's was just one of many automobile plants.

When the stockmarket bubble burst,

Mr. Ford the crackerbarrel philosopher said jubilantly,

"I told you so.

Serves you right for gambling and getting in debt.

The country is sound."

But when the country on cracked shoes, in frayed trousers, belts tightened over hollow bellies,

idle hands cracked and chapped with the cold of that coldest March day of 1932,

started marching from Detroit to Dearborn, asking for work and the American Plan, all they could think of at Ford's was machineguns.

The country was sound, but they mowed the marchers down.

They shot four of them dead.

Henry Ford as an old man

is a passionate antiquarian

(lives besieged on his father's farm embedded in an estate of thousands of millionaire acres, protected by an army of servicemen, secretaries, secret agents, dicks under orders of an English exprizefighter,

always afraid of the feet in broken shoes on the roads, afraid the gangs will kidnap his grandchildren,

that a crank will shoot him,

that Change and the idle hands out of work will break through the gates and the high fences;

protected by a private army against

the new America of starved children and hollow bellies and cracked shoes stamping on souplines,

that has swallowed up the old thrifty farmlands

of Wayne County, Michigan,

as if they had never been).

Henry Ford as an old man

is a passionate antiquarian.

He rebuilt his father's farmhouse and put it back exactly in the state he remembered it in as a boy. He built a village of museums for buggies, sleighs, coaches, old plows, waterwheels, obsolete models of motorcars. He scoured the country for fiddlers to play oldfashioned squaredances.

Even old taverns he bought and put back into their original shape, as well as Thomas Edison's early laboratories.

When he bought the Wayside Inn near Sudbury, Massachusetts, he had the new highway where the newmodel cars roared and slithered and hissed oilily past (*the new noise of the automobile*)

moved away from the door,

put back the old bad road,

so that everything might be

the way it used to be,

in the days of horses and buggies.

———————————————— ▶ •●• ◀ ————————————————

1. a)After you have finished reading the article, make notes on and describe for a classmate your initial reactions to the style of

"Tin Lizzie." Discuss whether the reader's understanding is enhanced or hindered by Dos Passos's technique.

b) Employing some of Dos Passos's stylistic devices, write a short autobiography, using the third person point of view. Analyse a classmate's autobiography and write a brief assessment of the image he or she conveyed. Your classmate will do the same with your work. Use your classmate's comments as the basis for your revisions.

2. a) Reread the selection carefully and determine Dos Passos's attitude towards Henry Ford.

b) Assume the voice of someone in the middle class. In a short interior monologue reveal what you think about Ford on the occasion of the purchase of your Tin Lizzie.

c) Script a dialogue between two Ford workers in the 1920s after a special day on the assembly line, a day that included a visit from Ford himself. Ensure that your feelings about Ford are revealed.

3. a) Using the information given by Dos Passos, and supplementing it with your own research, write a short biography of Henry Ford in which you pay special attention to the questions left open in "Tin Lizzie" (e.g., what was Ford's involvement in the war? In the presidential campaign?)

b) You are Henry Ford, and you are staging a final press conference not long before your death. Deliver a short speech telling of your thoughts as you reflect on the course of your life. Afterwards, answer any questions the reporters (your classmates) might have.

4. Compose an obituary for Henry Ford in which you pay due respect to the man and his accomplishments.

In a small group, share your perceptions of the advantages of a multi-ethnic, multi-racial society. Consider also what the citizens of such a society must do in order to preserve the equality to which all are entitled. You may want to discuss such issues as affirmative action programs and laws against hate literature.

A BLACK VIEW OF CANADA
Mary Janigan

In Gwen Robinson's yellowing photographs, the blacks pose self-consciously for the camera, prosperous and proud. There is James (Gunsmith) Jones, the son of a slave, who moved to Chatham, Ontario, in 1849 and who won prizes for his firearms at a Montreal exhibition in 1860. There is Jones's daughter, Sophia, solemn and self-possessed, who went to Michigan to study medicine. There are the members of the Chatham Knights Templar, a 19th-century Masonic society of black community leaders, who stand in a row, shoulders thrown back beneath capes, the plumes of their hats floating in the breeze.

But as Robinson, 53, thumbs those photographs, she also sees reminders of the brutal discrimination of the past – and the subtle racism of the present. "We blacks have been largely eliminated from the history books," declared the Chatham hairdresser and amateur local historian. Added her husband John, 59, a postal clerk: "Blacks have been left out of the Canadian mosaic."

Racism: That conviction was echoed by many black Canadians across the nation last week as, along with American blacks, they struggled to assess how far they have come – and how much farther they have to go. As the United States prepared to celebrate a new national holiday named after America's pre-eminent modern black leader, the late Dr. Martin Luther King Jr., many Canadian blacks told *Maclean's* that overt discrimination is lessening. Many added that they drew comfort from the fact that black communities in 1986 face challenges and opportunities that seemed impossible only a generation ago. But many also stressed that subtle discrimination – in schools, housing and the job markets – confines thousands to the role of second-class citizens. "This country has changed dramatically – Canada is doing quite well on civil rights," said Windsor, Ontario, New Democrat Howard McCurdy, the nation's only black MP. "But there is still not a single black in this country who has not been subjected to racism."

Their tales of pride and of prejudice also underlined the fact that blacks in Canada are united only by their colour – and by their desire for the new generation to achieve success. Indeed, the current black community is one of the least cohesive of Canada's minority groups. And unlike its American counterpart, it still lacks political strength and a firm political agenda. Some blacks, including Gwen Robinson, trace their Canadian roots back into the mid-19th century. Others, including Lincoln Alexander, Ontario's new lieutenant-governor, are the children of more recent immigrants from the Caribbean. "The only thing we have in common is that we are black," Alexander told *Maclean's*. Added McCurdy: "We are talking about different cultures, different backgrounds."

Complaints: One measure of those differences is that Statistics Canada does not know the number of black Canadians – because the category "Black" was not listed in the 1981 census. That survey did indicate that there are about 240 000 blacks in several categories: 31 000 Haitians, 160 000 of other Caribbean origin, and 48 000 African and Canadian-born blacks. But government officials admit that large numbers of Canadian-born blacks – especially those in Metropolitan Toronto and Nova Scotia – were simply overlooked if they did not write the word "Black" on the census form. This year's scheduled census corrects that omission by adding the category "Black" under a question about ethnic origin. But until that census is tabulated there are only rough estimates of the size of Canada's three largest black communities: 30 000 in Nova Scotia, the vast majority Canadian-born; 115 000 in Montreal, including 35 000 Haitians, 35 000 West Indians, and 40 000 Canadian-born; and at least 70 000 in Toronto, the majority from the West Indies.

The three communities feature different ethnic and cultural strains but share disturbing complaints of discrimination. The most accurate reflection of that discontent appeared last summer when pollster Martin Goldfarb interviewed 200 Toronto blacks about their experiences in Canada. Although 76 per cent said they were "very satisfied" with opportunities for their children in Canada, roughly 65 per cent declared that they have less opportunity than other Canadians to obtain senior positions in business or to win election to political office. And almost as many blacks felt that prejudice is increasing as believed that it is decreasing.

Indeed, Toronto's Urban Alliance on Race Relations and the Social Planning Council of Metro Toronto released a study last year disclosing that white job applicants receive three offers for every one obtained by blacks. A follow-up survey showed that only nine per cent of 199 Toronto employers in firms with more than 50 employees believed firmly in racial equality. Fully 28 per cent said that nonwhites lack the ability to compete, 13 per cent viewed them as threatening and seven per cent expressed "outright contempt" for them.

Drinking: Many blacks told *Maclean's* that they feel – and fight – racism in every facet of their lives. In Nova Scotia last week the provincial court referred to the judicial council a dispute over comments about blacks by Digby provincial court judge John Nichols. The remarks followed a four-day trial last October when an all-white jury acquitted a 29-year-old white, Jeff Mullen, on a second-degree murder charge for the shooting of Graham Jarvis, a 32-year-old black. Last month Nichols, the presiding judge at Mullen's preliminary hearing, told *The Toronto Star* that he would not have sent the case to trial if he had known all the facts. Said Nichols: "You know what happens when those black guys start drinking."

Blacks also say that discrimination spills into the educational system. Iona Crawley, the program director at a senior citizens' home in Windsor, N.S., is a single parent who has raised four children – a vocational school graduate and three university graduates. But she notes that there are no black high school teachers or guidance counsellors in Halifax. And for his part, Halifax lawyer H.A.J. (Gus) Wedderburn credits his career to the role models and motivation in his native Jamaica. Declared Wedderburn: "If I had been born here, I doubt if I would be a lawyer today."

Even students who do not perceive overt discrimination cite examples of racial stereotyping. Guyana-born June Ann Nobrega, 19, says that her Toronto teachers have always pushed her to go further than the Grade 12 academic course in which she is enrolled. But black males, she conceded, are encouraged to devote more time to sports than to academic work. "I remember another thing that seemed strange to me," Nobrega told *Maclean's*. "They put me straight into the choir – no auditions like the other kids. I wondered how they knew that I could sing."

Stereotyping often pursues blacks into the job market. Gwen Lord, 50, is the black principal of Montreal's Northmount high school, a school with a 55-per-cent black population. Frequently – and candidly – she tells her students about the problems of discrimination. "I tell them that they are going to be treated differently than other people," she explained. "Traditionally, we are the last hired and the first released." Montreal's Tommy Kane, 22, has a four-year athletic scholarship in football to Syracuse University in New York. After he graduates, Kane intends to remain in the United States. Employment opportunities for blacks, he says, are better. "All my [Montreal black] friends are doing is getting older," he said. "For them, time is just passing. I try to encourage them, but they just see a straight tunnel to nowhere."

Slavery: Indeed, the history of blacks in Canada is an extraordinary chronicle of dashed hopes and brave spirits. The first recorded black resident of Canada was a six-year-old slave from Madagascar, Olivier LeJeune, who arrived on a British ship in New France in 1628. LeJeune was a rarity, since the law of France officially forbade slavery. But in 1689 King Louis XIV permitted his New France colonists to hold slaves as field hands and household servants. By 1749 the British were using black slaves to build Halifax. And after their conquest of Québec in 1760 the British hastily assured the residents that they could keep their slaves. During the American Revolution the British offered to free any slaves who would join their forces. When the war ended in 1783 many of those blacks fled or were transported to Canada: about 10 per cent of Nova Scotia's 30 000 United Empire Loyalists were black. And many of the 10 000 Loyalists who settled in Central Canada held black slaves. The slavery system was gradually phased out as first the British and then the Americans after the Civil War abolished it, but the social stigmas that attached to it linger even now.

Southern Ontario's history is rich with their sagas. Among them: Dresden's Rev. Josiah Henson, the model for Harriet Beecher Stowe's powerful antislavery novel, *Uncle Tom's Cabin*; American abolitionist John Brown, who planned in Chatham to overthrow the governments of the slaveholding states and was hanged for treason in 1859 after leading an attack on the U.S. federal armoury at Harpers Ferry in West Virginia; and Harriet Tubman, the underground railroad's organizing genius, who funnelled hundreds of escaped slaves into St. Catharines.

In the wake of the U.S. Civil War and Abraham Lincoln's 1863 Emancipation Proclamation, many blacks returned to the United States. The result was a net loss of black citizens until the start of the First World War. The 1921 census showed about 18 300 blacks in Canada, a population that remained stable for the next 30 years. That pattern changed with the first surges in migration from the West Indies. Between 1950 and the mid 1960s Canada's black population doubled to about 40 000 with approximately 90 per cent of the new arrivals from the Caribbean. Since then about 10 000 West Indian immigrants have arrived each year. And the number of African immigrants has occasionally reached an annual high of 5000. Most of the new immigrants possess educational and professional skills surpassing those of the Canadian-born blacks. And those gaps have added to the strains between communities.

Other experts say that what blacks need are better schools, a co-ordinated job strategy and more support for black business ventures.

Halifax physician Anthony Sebastian came to Canada from St. Kitts in 1968 and is still astonished by the passivity of Canadian-born blacks. He says blacks must push harder to get an education and into local politics. "Blacks are their own worst enemies here," Sebastian told *Maclean's*. And in a speech last fall Rick Joseph, executive director of Nova Scotia's Black United Front, cautioned, "If we do not move quickly, we will see our grandchildren trying to fare well on welfare."

Strength: That sense of urgency is tempered by the knowledge that the black community has come a long way in a short time. Thirty-four years ago Chatham's Robinson could not eat in the dining room of a local hotel – even though her place in the community could be traced back to her great-great-grandfather, Abraham Shadd. Toronto senior public school principal Wilson Brooks, 61, recounts that when he applied for a department store job 30 years ago, "I was told to my face that they did not want blacks waiting on their customers." Now, racists are more subtle, and blacks are more determined. Ontario Housing Minister Alvin Curling, who came to Canada in 1965 from Jamaica, told a black audience last month to seek – and find – unity. "When one man pulls, he has only the strength of one," Curling said. "But when two pull together, they have much more than the strength of two. And when all of us, hundreds of thousands of black people, pull together, our strength shall be a strength beyond any human measure." That lyrical prayer is the challenge – and could be the salvation – for Canadian blacks.

---

1. a) With a classmate, reread the article and determine the ideas that the writer would most like readers to remember. Present these ideas in a few statements.
   b) Make a précis of the article, reducing it to about 250 words. Working with a classmate, examine each other's précis, noting whether they agree in essential points and what sort of information you have omitted.

2. Identify, and list with an example for each, the techniques used by the writer of "A Black View of Canada" to present factual information (e.g., references to well-known personalities, use of statistics). You may wish to add to your list by analysing other examples of current journalism. Compare your list with a classmate's and discuss
   • the purpose and relative effectiveness of the techniques;
   • the reasons for repeating information several times in several different ways;
   • whether it is possible to present information in a totally objective manner.

3. In a small group, share an experience in which someone made you feel like an outsider. As well, share an experience in which someone was made to feel welcome in spite of differences between you and him or her. As a group, you may wish to compile a short anthology of personal memoirs, either recorded on tape or written. You may find that reading "The Hallowe'en Party," the next selection in this book, will trigger additional insights.

THE HALLOWE'EN PARTY
Miriam Waddington

The year that I was twelve my father came home one day and announced that he had bought a farm. My sister Helen and I could hardly wait to see the farm which, according to my father, consisted of twenty-six acres in St. Vital, just beyond the outskirts of Winnipeg. There were twenty acres of bush with buildings, and six acres of meadow beside the river. My father had dreamed of such a farm all the years he was shut up in the dark greasy machine shop where he earned his living.

My mother was appeased by the knowledge that my father had no intention of giving up his job to move his family onto the land. That would come later. At this point he would begin to talk about his dream of a Jewish settlement on the banks of the Red River, an ideal farm community that would prove a thing or two to the world. And in his vision, we, the Lurias, were always the strongest, the busiest and the most ardent pioneers.

Now as I look back, I can understand my father's deep hunger for land. Separated from his native Russia he searched without knowing it for landscapes that were like his old home. That is why he chose to settle on the windswept plains of Manitoba.

The first sight of our farm was a disappointment, coming as it did after the exciting upgrade of the old Salter Street bridge, the golden statues and church spires of St Boniface, and further along, the noise and smell of the abattoir. We saw nothing but a few fields, a whitewashed hut and an old barn. We couldn't share my father's enthusiasm for a mushroom bed behind the stable, or a cucumber garden beside the river. So we left him to plan his crops while we wandered down to the river's edge. There was nothing to interest us here either, and so we decided to go frog-hunting.

Our frog hunt brought us to a wooded grove, and after winding in and out, we found ourselves looking down into a gully. We skirted it, and as we came around the curve we could see ahead of us a tiny cottage set back in the trees. We stopped in amazement. It was so quiet and strange, finding the cottage in just that spot.

We stood there in silence and watched some chicks wander out of the coop to scratch in the garden. From around the corner came a kitten, and then the barking of a dog, followed by a woman's voice.

The voice was old and sturdy like its owner. Over her face, to shade it from the sun, she wore a stringy straw hat, and under it, her eyes looked out as clear and flawless as aquamarines. She smiled at us, greeted us in a neighbourly way, and almost before we knew it, we were talking like old friends. She told us her name was Miss MacNeill and that she kept house for her brother Dan.

Helen and I followed her into the house. It was dark and cool inside and had a pleasant musty smell. There were braided rugs on the floor, and bright calendar pictures on the walls.

Miss MacNeill had a little trouble pronouncing our last name and rolled it over her tongue experimentally. "Luria, Luria. Now would that be some foreign name?"

"Well," I told her, "Not exactly; that is, we aren't, but my father, well, he wasn't born here, he comes from Russia." "And besides," said Helen, as though she were revealing some terrible secret, "We're Jewish."

Miss MacNeill nodded, "Well now, that'll be like Dan and me – born in Scotland we were, and ever since we've been away we're always scheming to get back."

And she sighed in the same way my mother used to when she had finished telling us about her father's mill in Russia. It almost seemed to me at that moment that Miss MacNeill and my mother looked alike.

But that was foolishness, of course, for here was Miss MacNeill talking about their farm in Scotland, and how she had left it to keep house for her brother Dan. So there they were, the two of them, alone except for a boarder called John, who was cook for the construction crew working up the road. And that was how we came to know the MacNeills.

As the summer deepened we visited them often. Although we always called her Miss MacNeill, it wasn't long before Dan was Dan to us, and as for John, we never knew his surname at all. We soon found out that Dan worked for Mr. Marshall, whose land bordered my father's, and we pestered the life out of him to let us play in the new-stacked hay, and to take us along whenever he went to tap the fishing lines he had strung up across the river.

It was such a summer as we had never lived before. Helen and I tramped, dug, and explored. Inevitably, we would end up in the clearing where the cottage always waited for us as it had that first time, strange and magical.

And then September came and we were sitting in the garden in front of the cottage, Dan whittling away at something, and Miss MacNeill busy cutting geranium slips for us to take home to our mother. Helen caught sight of the ripening pumpkins and asked Dan if he would help her make a jack o'lantern for Hallowe'en.

Then Dan was off on one of his stories, talking and whittling, whittling and talking. Pretty soon, John, who had been mending a pair of boots in the parlour, came out and joined us. John was no talker, but he always knew to nod in the right places. He nodded several times, and after a bit he took his pipe out of his mouth and said it would be nice if Helen and I could get my father to bring us out to the cottage on Hallowe'en night. We could then have a real old-fashioned party – and there'd be no lack of company either. Here John reeled off the names of a dozen children from the surrounding farms.

It all sounded wonderful until I remembered that Helen and I probably wouldn't be allowed to come. Apart from the fact that my father might not want to drive us out to a party so far from home, he was sure to object because Hallowe'en was not a Jewish holiday.

And sure enough when we brought it up that evening, my father took the position that we ought not to celebrate a Christian holiday. Although Helen and I both pointed out that Hallowe'en had nothing to do with religion my father insisted that it was a culture symbol.

The MacNeills were almost as disappointed as we were. Miss MacNeill thought it a shame that my father would let a thing like being Jewish stand in the way of our having fun with other children, but Dan puffed thoughtfully on his pipe and surprised us all by saying that women couldn't understand such things, but a man could see how another man wouldn't want to lose the one thing he had lived for all his life.

This seemed deep coming from Dan, and I probably wouldn't have paid much attention to it if he hadn't followed it up by announcing that he intended to see my father himself.

It was lucky for Helen and me that we happened to be hunting for a couple of pails in the barn when Dan ran into my father. We didn't even try to resist the temptation to eavesdrop, and we heard Dan say,

"Mr. Luria, there's something I want to talk to you about."

"Yes sure, and what may it be?" that was my father.

"Well, it's about your children. I guess you know that we'd like to have them come to our Hallowe'en party along with the others from the farms hereabouts."

We peered through a crack in the barn and could just see my father smile.

"I know you mean well, Mr. MacNeill. You and your sister, you must be kind people. Helen and David tell us how they enjoy it at your house – and I don't want you to think it is anything we have against you as people."

Dan didn't seem to have any trouble understanding my father's accent, and said right off that he was glad it was nothing like that. "We won't keep the children late, and if it's that you're worried about, why you and Mrs. Luria are more than welcome to come too!"

My father laughed,

"But thank you, no – what would we do at a Hallowe'en party? No, it isn't that either." And here his voice came slower. He began to frown the way he usually did when he was serious.

"You look to me like an honest man, Mr. MacNeill, so I'm going to tell you the truth. I don't want to start this kind of thing. I don't want my children celebrating Christmas or going to Hallowe'en parties. Once you begin, even with a little Hallowe'en party, everything is lost. You see, we are Jewish, and I have suffered because of it. I don't want them to forget who they are, where they belong. And here, in this country, it is easy to forget. There are so many who are forgetting. You think I like to make problems for my children, Mr. MacNeill?"

Dan said "No, I don't think you are trying to make it hard. I guess you maybe figure that it is hard – I guess I know what you mean – you want them to face it."

My father said with a sigh, "That's right, they don't know yet, but there will be many problems."

Dan nodded. He went on to tell my father that he knew it wasn't easy, that he himself had left home and come to a new country. It was true that the language was the same, but a hundred little things were different – the songs, the food, the people.

"What I keep wondering about is whether it's outside things like Hallowe'en that matter – can that change what's inside a person? Gosh, it's like asking a preacher to put religion into a soul when religion isn't there already. Or like telling the devil to take it away when it is there. No sir – if you'll excuse the example – you can't put religion into a lad just by showing him the inside of a church."

"You mean that if my children don't feel what I want them to feel inside themselves, then keeping them away from a Hallowe'en party isn't going to teach them?"

"Something like that. These things go deep, lots deeper than a Hallowe'en party. After all is said and done, in years to come they'll only remember the fun they had at MacNeill's one Hallowe'en. And if you don't let them come, it'll be childish grief that'll stay in their minds forever."

My father listened and rubbed his chin. We knew when he started that he was about to give in. So we crept out of the barn and made for the cottage to bring Miss MacNeill the good news.

And as it turned out, Dan was right. We went to the Hallowe'en party, and bobbed for apples with the other children. Miss MacNeill told our fortunes and John produced an orange pie with licorice trimming. We played games, pulled molasses taffy and drank punch. And later, riding home in the back of my father's truck, sleepy and tired, my mind blurred with excitement, I kept thinking of the cottage with its festoons of coloured streamers, and grinning jack o'lanterns, and I clutched my witch's broom with a feeling of happiness.

1. With a classmate, examine Mr. Luria's motives for not wanting his children to attend the Hallowe'en party. Take turns role-playing Mr. Luria and Dan MacNeill as they discuss the matter. Analyse your reactions to the role-playing. If you found one of the roles or points of view easier to assume, try to account for the reason.

2. David, the twelve-year-old narrator of "The Hallowe'en Party," states near the end of the story: "And as it turned out, Dan was right." Examine the imagery and diction of the final paragraph, and decide whether Waddington means the reader to take David's statement at face value. Argue your opinion in a concise paragraph, giving reasons for your view. Share opinions in a small group.

3. a) In a small group, compile a list of holidays commonly celebrated in Canada, including the cultural or religious symbols associated with each.
   b) Compile another list of holidays celebrated by individual ethnic or cultural groups, along with the history behind the holidays.
   c) Discuss the effects of having one official pattern of celebration and several unofficial patterns, considering both favourable and unfavourable aspects.

4. In a team of four or six, stage a parliamentary debate on the resolution "A society deriving from a multi-cultural mosaic has distinct advantages over a society deriving from a melting pot."

5. Write a poem about one of the themes you perceive in Waddington's story. Include your poem in your writing folder.

Our culture is intoxicated with the idea of progress, particularly technological progress. Before reading "A Trip Abroad," make a list of ways in which "we have dominated and overruled nature." Make another list of the aspects of nature not under our control. Exchange lists with two or three classmates, and then consider this statement by Lewis Thomas, scientist, philosopher, and essayist: "We will have everything under control, managed. Then what do we do?"

A TRIP ABROAD
Lewis Thomas

I do not believe for a minute that we are nearing the end of human surprise, despite resonantly put arguments by wonderfully informed scientists who tell us that after molecular biology and astrophysics there is really very little more to learn of substance. Except, they always add, for the nature of human consciousness, and that, they always add, is placed beyond our reach by the principle of indeterminacy; that is, our thought is so much at the centre of life that it cannot sit still while we examine it.

But there may be a way out of this; it may turn out that consciousness is a much more generalized mechanism, shared round not only among ourselves but with all the other conjoined things of the biosphere. Thus, since we are not, perhaps, so absolutely central, we may be able to get a look at it, but we will need a new technology for this kind of neurobiology; in which case we will likely find that we have a whole eternity of astonishment stretching out ahead of us. Always assuming, of course, that we're still here.

We must rely on our scientists to help us find the way through the near distance, but for the longer stretch of the future we are dependent on the poets. We should learn to question them more closely, and listen more carefully. A poet is, after all, a sort of scientist, but engaged in a qualitative science in which nothing is measurable. He lives with data that cannot be numbered, and his experiments can be done only once. The information in a poem is, by definition, not reproducible. His pilot runs involve a recognition of things that pop into his head. The skill consists in his capacity to decide quickly which things to retain, which to eject. He becomes an equivalent of scientist, in the act of examining and sorting the things popping in, finding the marks of remote similarity, points of distant relationship, tiny irregularities that indicate that this one is really the same as that one over there only more important. Gauging the fit, he can meticulously place pieces of the universe together, in geometric configurations that are as beautiful and balanced as crystals. Musicians and painters listen, and copy down what they hear.

I wish that poets were able to give straight answers to straight questions, but that is like asking astrophysicists to make their calculations on their fingers, where we can watch the process. What I would like to know is: how should I feel about the earth, these days? Where has all the old nature gone? What became of the wild, writhing, unapproachable mass of the life of the world, and what happened to our old, panicky excitement about it? Just in fifty years, since I was a small boy in a suburban town, the world has become a structure of steel and plastic, intelligible and diminished. Mine was a puzzling maple grove of a village on the outskirts of New York City, and it vanished entirely, trees and all. It is now a syncytium of apartment houses, sprouting out of a matrix of cement flooded and jelled over an area that once contained 25,000 people who walked on grass. Now I live in another, more distant town, on a street with trees and lawns, and at night I can hear the soft sound of cement, moving like incoming tide, down the Sunrise Highway from New York.

If you fly around the earth and keep looking down, you will see that we have inserted ourselves everywhere. All fields are tilled. All mountains have been climbed and are being covered with concrete and plastic; some mountains, like the Appalachians, are simply cut down like trees. The fish are all trapped and domesticated, farmed in zoned undersea pastures. As for the animals, we will never have enough plastic bags for the bodies; soon the only survivors will be the cattle and sheep for the feeding of us, and the dogs and cats in our houses, fed while it lasts on the flesh of whales. And the rats and roaches, and a few reptiles.

The winged insects are vanishing, the calcium in the shells of eggs, and the birds.

We have dominated and overruled nature, and from now on the earth is ours, a kitchen garden until we learn to make our own chlorophyll and float it out in the sun inside plastic membranes. We will build Scarsdale on Mount Everest.

We will have everything under control, managed. Then what do we do? On long Sunday afternoons, what do we do, when there is nobody to talk to but ourselves?

It is because of these problems that we are now engaged in scrutinizing with such intensity the dark, bare flanks of Mars, hideous with lifelessness as it seems to be. We are like a family looking through travel brochures.

There is such a thing as too much of this. Because of our vast numbers and the rapidity with which we have developed prosthetic devices enabling us to hear and see each other, in person, all around the earth, we have become obsessed with ourselves. You'd think, to hear us think, that there was nothing else of significance on the earth except us.

Perhaps we should try to get away, for a while anyway. A change of scene might do us a world of good.

The trouble is, the barrenness of all the local planets. Perhaps we will be unlucky with our green thumbs, unable to create or maintain the faintest gasp of life on Mars or Titan. What's to stop us from looking elsewhere, farther on? If we can learn to navigate before the solar wind, we could, out there, hoist sail and tack our way out to where the wind fades off, practising free-falls all the while, probing for gravity, trusting to luck, taking our chances. It would be like old times.

---

1. Reduce the ideas of the first two paragraphs into two clear sentences of your own. Compare your sentences with those of a classmate to check how closely your interpretations correlate.

2. In a small group assess the suitability of the essay's title. Make up other titles that would be appropriate and defend your choices.

3. a) In a small group discuss and evaluate Thomas's description of poets.
   b) The poet P.B. Shelley wrote a famous essay titled "In Defence of Poetry"; using Thomas's ideas and your own, write a personal "Defence of Poetry" (or an attack upon its lack of relevance in today's world.) In your group, share and discuss your essays.

4. If you are unfamiliar with the word *hyperbole*, look it up and write the definition in your notes in your own words. With a classmate, discuss whether Thomas's predictions about humanity's ability to control nature are hyperbolic.
   b) Write a response to "A Trip Abroad" in the form of an editorial, a letter to a magazine, or a letter to the author himself.

5. Using some of the information alluded to in paragraphs four to seven, and adding material from your own knowledge and

research, prepare a speech in which you either condemn or defend humanity's treatment of earth. (You may find it helpful to read "Bio-engineering Gone Wrong," p. 351, and the excerpt from "Northing," p. 346.) Present your speech to a small group of your classmates.

OR

In a personal memoir relate an experience, as Thomas does in paragraph four, that made you aware of the encroachment of humankind on a place you had considered natural and untouched.

On Language

THE INVENTOR OF THE PERIOD
K. Jason Sitewell

*S*oon there will occur an event of profound importance to the lit-
eratures of all languages. I refer to the 2,500th birthday of Kohmar
Pehriad (544-493 B.C.), inventor of punctuation in written language.
He also figures prominently in the development of copyright law, which
I shall discuss in a moment. Pehriad was the leading literary figure of
Macedonia in the pre-Christian era. His writings ranged from poetry
to speculations on astronomy and physics. Few of these writings remain. What does remain, however, is his successful reform of written
language in virtually all tongues.

In those days written language was continuous. There were no sentence or paragraph breaks. Pehriad's own writings represent the first
recorded use of the small round dot to indicate the end of a completed
unit of expression. More important than that is the fact that he gave
thirty years of his life, travelling throughout ancient Greece, Rome,
Persia, North Africa, and Asia, in the effort to obtain local acceptance
of the small dot that has since done so much for literature.

His first great success outside his country came when he was able
to persuade some Greek scholars to issue a complete version of Homer's
Odyssey and *Iliad*, with the small round dots in the proper places. Up
to that time Homer had had a limited following in Greece. With the
reformed version, however, his work gained widespread acceptance.
Pehriad's next success came in Constantinople, where he was directly
responsible for the first manuscript of the Hebrew Torah containing
periods.

As he travelled from place to place the logic of Pehriad's argument
became increasingly accepted. It was not necessary, he reasoned, for
each language to devise its own mark to denote a proper pause. The
small round dot could be used in all languages. The stark simplicity
of this idea, amounting virtually to genius, is doubtless responsible for
the fact that every written language in the world today uses the small

round dot. Thus, Pehriad's contribution is not only to his own country but to mankind.

Pehriad's reward, of course, is that the small round dot has been named after him, our spelling of his name having been anglicized. Even in a country as remote as Nepal the influence of Pehriad today is to be found in the fact that the sentence dot is called a "puhyed." In China it is called "pi-yen." In Malaya, "pee-yeed." In New Guinea the capital P is used as a gesture of respect to the inventor in its word, "Peeliod."

Pehriad's efforts did not stop with the period. He was also concerned with the need for an appropriate marking that might correspond to the pause in a person's speech in the middle of an incompleted sentence. This led him to devise what we now know as the comma, also named after him (Kohmar). It is interesting to read in his "Journal" that he later felt he had made a mistake in not using the comma marking instead of the period and vice-versa. "The dot with the curved descending tail is the more impressive and visible mark and should therefore have been used for the more important purpose of indicating the end of a sentence," he wrote. "The dot slows up the reader and should therefore have been used to indicate a pause." Pehriad, in his declining years, sought to bring about this shift in comma-period usage, but by this time the custom had hardened.

It remained for Pehriad's son to devise yet other markings for the purpose of strengthening the written language. Apos-Trophe Pehriad felt that the comma was adaptable to a wide variety of purposes, so long as its position could be varied. He used it inside a word to denote the abbreviation; at the end of a word to denote possession; in tandem to denote quotation, with the mark inverted at the end of the quotation. As in the case of his father, his invention bears his name.

There is no evidence that the Pehriads, father or son, invented either the question mark or the exclamation point. The younger Pehriad, however, did attempt to indicate emphasis inside a sentence. If the emotion registered in the pronunciation of a word was scorn or anger he placed a concave curve atop the key word so emphasized. If a person wished to give a sorrowful or sad expression to a word the marking was a convex curve below the word. If a person's speech was staccato or jerky, young Pehriad required the writer to put down each word slantwise. One shudders at the difficulties this would have caused printers had the reform been generally adopted.

The historical verdict on young Pehriad must be that, outside of his juggling of commas so that they became apostrophes or quotation marks, he lacked the simple directness and the judgment that made his father the only literary figure in history whose contribution is visible in almost every piece of writing anywhere in the world, except, of course, in the poetry of ee cummings and other modern innovators.

But the significance of the Pehriads is not confined to the small round dot or the comma. I wrote at the start that they figured indirectly in the development of copyright law. What happened was that a descendant of Apos-Trophe and of Pehriad moved to Rome, where he became a highly successful counselor-at-law. Pehriad Apullus had proper pride in the family name but had always felt that his ancestors had been inexcusably amateurish and unbusinesslike. Apullus set out to earn for himself the tangible rewards that he felt the old folks had overlooked. Under old Roman law direct descendants could obtain legal rights to inventions if their forbears had neglected to take out patents.

Apullus had considerable influence in the Roman courts. He contended that the period was an invention and therefore subject to royalties. To demonstrate his highmindedness he informed the court that, though he would insist on full rights to the period, he would make a gift of the comma to the state. Impressed by the fairness of the man, the Court granted him a copyright on the period, and prescribed a fee of one drachma for any piece of writing containing more than 100 periods. Manuscripts containing upwards of 500 periods were to bring a flat royalty of ten drachmas. This marked the beginning of the short essay in ancient Rome.

Apullus discreetly waited several years before moving for an extension of his copyright to include any piece of writing, whatever the length and whatever the nature. Even private letters were to be subject to royalty for the use of periods. By this time he had insinuated himself into the circle of those closest to Octavius. Rome was sorely pressed for funds and it was Apullus's ingenious proposal to Octavius that, in addition to extending his royalty to include any use of periods, the Government itself should collect a modest tax.

Serious consideration was given to this idea but it was eventually discarded because of the tremendous increase it would require in the number of tax investigators. There was also some apprehension in Government quarters that many citizens would circumvent the law by using substitute markings instead of periods.

In any event, during the period of the debate general fear spread through the populace. Suetonius, in his *Lives of the Twelve Caesars*, writes that the general citizenry came close to giving up writing altogether for fear that some retroactive law would be passed compelling them to pay both royalty and tax on every period they had ever used in their lifetimes. As might be expected, this led to incredibly involved, non-stop sentences, clear traces of which are still discernible in modern times.

In an attempt to ridicule the proposed law some people exclaimed "period" in the proper places during their conversation. This habit has persisted to the present day.

Eventually the situation in ancient Rome was straightened out. In the course of so doing, Roman law devised what Anglo-Saxon law commonly accepts as the basis for copyright. Recognizing that some time limit ought to be set to the benefits Apullus would derive from his copyright, the Roman courts decreed that beyond Apullus's generation no royalties would be paid. A complicating factor, of course, in terms of precedent, involved the original inventor of the period, who had received no rewards for his work. This is what led the Roman courts to decree that the benefits of copyright should be limited to a single generation, or twenty-six years, except where a son may wish to extend it, in which case it would run for another twenty-six years. But the absolute limit was fixed at fifty-two years.

Outside his native Macedonia and, to a lesser extent, Italy, the inventor of the period is not generally recognized. The 2,500th anniversary of his birth (April 1, A.F.D.) gives all of us a long-deferred opportunity to pay homage to a man who has made written language not only intelligible but possible. The period did not come about by accident. Someone had to invent it and fight for it.

THE URGE FOR DESTRUCTION

The urge for destruction is also a creative urge!
Michael Bakunin

The selections in this unit examine "the urge for
destruction" in a variety of guises. It can be seen in
its familiar and maligned forms, warfare and human
cruelty. Less familiarly, it appears also in the forms of
self-destructive inertia, exhilarating mayhem, natural
imperative, and kinetic art. Bakunin's statement seems
paradoxical but, as you will find in reading this unit, the
destructive urge is vastly more complex than a simple
impulse to smash.

It seems that few people deface insignificant objects – small rocks, saplings, lampposts, ugly buildings, private residences. People deface cathedrals, government buildings and property, works of art, forts, mighty oaks, and virtually inaccessible rock faces and bridges. In a small group, discuss the proposition that vandalism is a bizarre compliment to that which is destroyed.

THE DESTRUCTORS
Graham Greene

1

It was on the eve of August Bank Holiday that the latest recruit became the leader of the Wormsley Common Gang. No one was surprised except Mike, but Mike at the age of nine was surprised by everything. "If you don't shut your mouth," somebody once said to him, "you'll get a frog down it." After that Mike had kept his teeth tightly clamped except when the surprise was too great.

The new recruit had been with the gang since the beginning of the summer holidays, and there were possibilities about his brooding silence that all recognized. He never wasted a word even to tell his name until that was required of him by the rules. When he said "Trevor" it was a statement of fact, not as it would have been with the others a statement of shame or defiance. Nor did anyone laugh except Mike, who finding himself without support and meeting the dark gaze of the newcomer opened his mouth and was quiet again. There was every reason why T., as he was afterwards referred to, should have been an object of mockery – there was his name (and they substituted the initial because otherwise they had no excuse not to laugh at it), the fact that his father, a former architect and present clerk, had "come down in the world," and that his mother considered herself better than the neighbours. What but an odd quality of danger, of the unpredictable, established him in the gang without any ignoble ceremony of initiation?

The gang met every morning in an impromptu car-park, the site of the last bomb of the first blitz. The leader, who was known as Blackie, claimed to have heard it fall, and no one was precise enough in his dates to point out that he would have been one year old and fast asleep on the down platform of Wormsley Common Underground Station. On one side of the car-park leant the first occupied house, No. 3, of the shattered Northwood Terrace – literally leant, for it had suffered from the blast of the bomb and the side walls were supported on wooden struts. A smaller bomb and some incendiaries had fallen beyond, so that the house stuck up like a jagged tooth and carried on the further wall relics of its neighbour, a dado, the remains of a fireplace. T., whose words were almost confined to voting "Yes" or "No" to the plan of operations proposed each day by Blackie, once startled the whole gang by saying broodingly, "Wren built that house, father says."

"Who's Wren?"

"The man who built St. Paul's."

"Who cares?" Blackie said. "It's only Old Misery's."

Old Misery – whose real name was Thomas – had once been a builder and decorator. He lived alone in the crippled house, doing for himself: once a week you could see him coming back across the common with bread and vegetables, and once as the boys played in the car-park he put his head over the smashed wall of his garden and looked at them.

"Been to the loo," one of the boys said, for it was common knowledge that since the bombs fell something had gone wrong with the pipes of the house and Old Misery was too mean to spend money on the property. He could do the redecorating himself at cost price, but he had never learnt plumbing. The loo was a wooden shed at the bottom of the narrow garden with a star-shaped hole in the door: it had escaped the blast which had smashed the house next door and sucked out the window-frames of No. 3.

The next time the gang became aware of Mr. Thomas was more surprising. Blackie, Mike, and a thin yellow boy, who for some reason was called by his surname Summers, met him on the common coming back from the market. Mr. Thomas stopped them. He said glumly, "You belong to the lot that play in the car-park?"

Mike was about to answer when Blackie stopped him. As the leader he had responsibilities. "Suppose we are?" he said ambiguously.

"I got some chocolates," Mr. Thomas said. "Don't like 'em myself. Here you are. Not enough to go round, I don't suppose. There never is," he added with sombre conviction. He handed over three packets of Smarties.

The gang were puzzled and perturbed by this action and tried to explain it away. "Bet someone dropped them and he picked 'em up,'' somebody suggested.

"Pinched 'em and then got in a bleeding funk,'' another thought aloud.

"It's a bribe,'' Summers said. "He wants us to stop bouncing balls on his wall.''

"We'll show him we don't take bribes,'' Blackie said, and they sacrificed the whole morning to the game of bouncing that only Mike was young enough to enjoy. There was no sign from Mr. Thomas.

Next day T. astonished them all. He was late at the rendezvous, and the voting for that day's exploit took place without him. At Blackie's suggestion the gang was to disperse in pairs, take buses at random and see how many free rides could be snatched from unwary conductors (the operation was to be carried out in pairs to avoid cheating). They were drawing lots for their companions when T. arrived.

"Where you been, T.?" Blackie asked. "You can't vote now. You know the rules.''

"I've been *there*," T. said. He looked at the ground, as though he had thoughts to hide.

"Where?''

"At Old Misery's.'' Mike's mouth opened and then hurriedly closed again with a click. He had remembered the frog.

"At Old Misery's?'' Blackie said. There was nothing in the rules against it, but he had a sensation that T. was treading on dangerous ground. He asked hopefully, "Did you break in?''

"No. I rang the bell.''

"And what did you say?''

"I said I wanted to see his house.''

"What did he do?''

"He showed it me.''

"Pinch anything?''

"No.''

"What did you do it for then?''

The gang had gathered round: it was as though an impromptu court were about to form and to try some case of deviation. T. said, "It's a beautiful house,'' and still watching the ground, meeting no one's eyes, he licked his lips first one way, then the other.

"What do you mean, a beautiful house?'' Blackie asked with scorn.

"It's got a staircase two hundred years old like a corkscrew. Nothing holds it up.''

"What do you mean, nothing holds it up. Does it float?''

"It's to do with opposite forces, Old Misery said.''

"What else?''

"There's panelling.''

"Like in the Blue Boar?''

"Two hundred years old."

"Is Old Misery two hundred years old?"

Mike laughed suddenly and then was quiet again. The meeting was in a serious mood. For the first time since T. had strolled into the car-park on the first day of the holidays his position was in danger. It only needed a single use of his real name and the gang would be at his heels.

"What did you do it for?" Blackie asked. He was just, he had no jealousy, he was anxious to retain T. in the gang if he could. It was the word "beautiful" that worried him – that belonged to a class world that you could still see parodied at the Wormsley Common Empire by a man wearing a top hat and a monocle, with a haw-haw accent. He was tempted to say, "My dear Trevor, old chap," and unleash his hell hounds. "If you'd broken in," he said sadly – that indeed would have been an exploit worthy of the gang.

"This was better," T. said. "I found out things." He continued to stare at his feet, not meeting anybody's eye, as though he were ab-sorbed in some dream he was unwilling – or ashamed – to share.

"What things?"

"Old Misery's going to be away all tomorrow and Bank Holiday."

Blackie said with relief, "You mean we could break in?"

"And pinch things?" somebody asked.

Blackie said, "Nobody's going to pinch things. Breaking in – that's good enough, isn't it? We don't want any court stuff."

"I don't want to pinch anything," T. said. "I've got a better idea."

"What is it?"

T. raised eyes, as grey and disturbed as the drab August day. "We'll pull it down," he said. "We'll destroy it."

Blackie gave a single hoot of laughter and then, like Mike, fell quiet, daunted by the serious implacable gaze. "What'd the police be doing all the time?" he said.

"They'd never know. We'd do it from inside. I've found a way in." He said with a sort of intensity, "We'd be like worms, don't you see, in an apple. When we came out again there'd be nothing there, no staircase, no panels, nothing but just walls, and then we'd make the walls fall down – somehow."

"We'd go to jug," Blackie said.

"Who's to prove? and anyway we wouldn't have pinched anything." He added without the smallest flicker of glee, "There wouldn't be anything to pinch after we'd finished."

"I've never heard of going to prison for breaking things," Summers said.

"There wouldn't be time," Blackie said. "I've seen housebreakers at work."

"There are twelve of us," T. said. "We'd organize."

"None of us know how . . . "

"I know," T. said. He looked across at Blackie, "Have you got a better plan?"

"Today," Mike said tactlessly, "we're pinching free rides . . . "

"Free rides," T. said. "You can stand down, Blackie, if you'd rather . . . "

"The gang's got to vote."

"Put it up then."

Blackie said uneasily, "It's proposed that tomorrow and Monday we destroy Old Misery's house."

"Hear, hear," said a fat boy called Joe.

"Who's in favour?"

T. said, "It's carried."

"How do we start?" Summers asked.

"He'll tell you," Blackie said. It was the end of his leadership. He went away to the back of the car-park and began to kick a stone, dribbling it this way and that. There was only one old Morris in the park, for few cars were left there except lorries: without an attendant there was no safety. He took a flying kick at the car and scraped a little paint off the rear mudguard. Beyond, paying no more attention to him than to a stranger, the gang had gathered round T.; Blackie was dimly aware of the fickleness of favour. He thought of going home, of never returning, of letting them all discover the hollowness of T.'s leadership, but suppose after all what T. proposed was possible – nothing like it had ever been done before. The fame of the Wormsley Common car-park gang would surely reach around London. There would be head-lines in the papers. Even the grown-up gangs who ran the betting at the all-in wrestling and the barrow-boys would hear with respect of how Old Misery's house had been destroyed. Driven by the pure, simple and altruistic ambition of fame for the gang, Blackie came back to where T. stood in the shadow of Misery's wall.

T. was giving his orders with decision: it was as though this plan had been with him all his life, pondered through the seasons, now in his fifteenth year crystallized with the pain of puberty. "You," he said to Mike, "bring some big nails, the biggest you can find, and a hammer. Anyone else who can better bring a hammer and a screwdriver. We'll need plenty of them. Chisels too. We can't have too many chisels. Can anybody bring a saw?"

"I can," Mike said.

"Not a child's saw," T. said. "A real saw."

Blackie realized he had raised his hand like any ordinary member of the gang.

"Right, you bring one, Blackie. But now there's a difficulty. We want a hacksaw."

"What's a hacksaw?" someone asked.

"You can get 'em at Woolworth's," Summers said.

The fat boy called Joe said gloomily, "I knew it would end in a collection."

"I'll get one myself," T. said. "I don't want your money. But I can't buy a sledge-hammer."

Blackie said, "They are working on No. 15. I know where they'll leave their stuff for Bank Holiday."

"Then that's all," T. said. "We meet here at nine sharp."

"I've got to go to church," Mike said.

"Come over the wall and whistle. We'll let you in."

2

On Sunday morning all were punctual except Blackie, even Mike. Mike had had a stroke of luck. His mother felt ill, his father was tired after Saturday night, and he was told to go to church alone with many warnings of what would happen if he strayed. Blackie had had difficulty in smuggling out the saw, and then in finding the sledge-hammer at the back of No. 15. He approached the house from a lane at the rear of the garden, for fear of the policeman's beat along the main road. The tired evergreens kept off a stormy sun: another wet Bank Holiday was being prepared over the Atlantic, beginning in swirls of dust under the trees. Blackie climbed the wall into Misery's garden.

There was no sign of anybody anywhere. The loo stood like a tomb in a neglected graveyard. The curtains were drawn. The house slept. Blackie lumbered nearer with the saw and the sledge-hammer. Perhaps after all nobody had turned up: the plan had been a wild invention: they had woken wiser. But when he came close to the back door he could hear a confusion of sound, hardly louder than a hive in swarm: a clickety-clack, a bang bang bang, a scraping, a creaking, a sudden painful crack. He thought: it's true, and whistled.

They opened the back door to him and he came in. He had at once the impression of organization, very different from the old happy-go-lucky ways under his leadership. For a while he wandered up and down stairs looking for T. Nobody addressed him: he had a sense of great urgency, and already he could begin to see the plan. The interior of the house was being carefully demolished without touching the outer walls.

Summers with hammer and chisel was ripping out the skirting-boards in the ground floor dining-room: he had already smashed the panels of the door. In the same room Joe was heaving up the parquet blocks, exposing the soft wood floor-boards over the cellar. Coils of wire came out of the damaged skirting and Mike sat happily on the floor, clipping the wires.

On the curved stairs two of the gang were working hard with an inadequate child's saw on the banisters – when they saw Blackie's big saw they signalled for it wordlessly. When he next saw them a quarter of the banisters had been dropped into the hall. He found T. at last in the bathroom – he sat moodily in the least cared-for room in the house, listening to the sounds coming up from below.

"You've really done it," Blackie said with awe. "What's going to happen?"

"We've only just begun," T. said. He looked at the sledge-hammer and gave his instructions. "You stay here and break the bath and the wash-basin. Don't bother about the pipes. They come later."

Mike appeared at the door. "I've finished the wire, T.," he said.

"Good. You've just got to go wandering round now. The kitchen's in the basement. Smash all the china and glass and bottles you can lay hold of. Don't turn on the taps – we don't want a flood – yet. Then go into all the rooms and turn out drawers. If they are locked get one of the others to break them open. Tear up any papers you find and smash all the ornaments. Better take a carving-knife with you from the kitchen. The bedroom's opposite here. Open the pillows and tear up the sheets. That's enough for the moment. And you, Blackie, when you've finished in here crack the plaster in the passage up with your sledge-hammer."

"What are you going to do?" Blackie asked.

"I'm looking for something special," T. said.

It was nearly lunch-time before Blackie had finished and went in search of T. Chaos had advanced. The kitchen was a shambles of broken glass and china. The dining-room was stripped of parquet, the skirting was up, the door had been taken off its hinges, and the destroyers had moved up a floor. Streaks of light came in through the closed shutters where they worked with the seriousness of creators – and destruction after all is a form of creation. A kind of imagination had seen this house as it had now become.

Mike said, "I've got to go home for dinner."

"Who else?" T. asked, but all the others on one excuse or another had brought provisions with them.

They squatted in the ruins of the room and swapped unwanted sandwiches. Half an hour for lunch and they were at work again. By the time Mike returned, they were on the top floor, and by six the superficial damage was completed. The doors were all off, all the skirtings raised, the furniture pillaged and ripped and smashed – no one could have slept in the house except on a bed of broken plaster. T. gave his orders – eight o'clock next morning, and to escape notice they climbed singly over the garden wall, into the car-park. Only Blackie and T. were left: the light had nearly gone, and when they touched a switch, nothing worked – Mike had done his job thoroughly.

"Did you find anything special?" Blackie asked.

T. nodded. "Come over here," he said, "and look." Out of both pockets he drew bundles of pound notes. "Old Misery's savings," he said. "Mike ripped out the mattress, but he missed them."

"What are you going to do? Share them?"

"We aren't thieves," T. said. "Nobody's going to steal anything from this house. I kept these for you and me – a celebration." He knelt down on the floor and counted them out – there were seventy in all. "We'll burn them," he said, "one by one," and taking it in turns they held a note upwards and lit the top corner, so that the flame burnt slowly towards their fingers. The grey ash floated above them and fell on their heads like age. "I'd like to see Old Misery's face when we are through," T. said.

"You hate him a lot?" Blackie asked.

"Of course I don't hate him," T. said. "There'd be no fun if I hated him." The last burning note illuminated his brooding face. "All this hate and love," he said, "it's soft, it's hooey. There's only things, Blackie," and he looked round the room crowded with the unfamiliar shadows of half things, broken things, former things. "I'll race you home, Blackie," he said.

3

Next morning the serious destruction started. Two were missing – Mike and another boy whose parents were off to Southend and Brighton in spite of the slow warm drops that had begun to fall and the rumble of thunder in the estuary like the first guns of the old blitz. "We've got to hurry," T. said.

Summers was restive. "Haven't we done enough?" he said. "I've been given a bob for slot machines. This is like work."

"We've hardly started," T. said. "Why, there's all the floors left, and the stairs. We haven't taken out a single window. You voted like the others. We are going to *destroy* this house. There won't be anything left when we've finished."

They began again on the first floor picking up the top floor-boards next the outer wall, leaving the joists exposed. Then they sawed through the joists and retreated into the hall, as what was left of the floor heeled and sank. They had learnt with practice, and the second floor collapsed more easily. By the evening an odd exhilaration seized them as they looked down the great hollow of the house. They ran risks and made mistakes: when they thought of the windows it was too late to reach them. "Cor," Joe said, and dropped a penny down into the dry rubble-filled well. It cracked and span among the broken glass.

"Why did we start this?" Summers asked with astonishment; T. was already on the ground, digging at the rubble, clearing a space along the outer wall. "Turn on the taps," he said. "It's too dark for anyone to see now, and in the morning it won't matter." The water overtook them on the stairs and fell through the floorless rooms.

It was then they heard Mike's whistle at the back. "Something's wrong," Blackie said. They could hear his urgent breathing as they unlocked the door.

"The bogies?" Summers asked.

"Old Misery," Mike said. "He's on his way." He put his head between his knees and retched. "Ran all the way," he said with pride.

"But why?" T. said. "He told me . . ." He protested with the fury of the child he had never been, "It isn't fair."

"He was down at Southend," Mike said, "and he was on the train coming back. Said it was too cold and wet." He paused and gazed at the water. "My, you've had a storm here. Is the roof leaking?"

"How long will he be?"

"Five minutes. I gave Ma the slip and ran."

"We better clear," Summers said. "We've done enough, anyway."

"Oh no, we haven't. Anybody could do this – " "this" was the shattered hollowed house with nothing left but the walls. Yet walls could be preserved. Façades were valuable. They could build inside again more beautifully than before. This could again be a home. He said angrily, "We've got to finish. Don't move. Let me think."

"There's no time," a boy said.

"There's got to be a way," T. said. "We couldn't have got thus far . . ."

"We've done a lot," Blackie said.

"No. No, we haven't. Somebody watch the front."

"We can't do any more."

"He may come in at the back."

"Watch the back too." T. began to plead. "Just give me a minute and I'll fix it. I swear I'll fix it." But his authority had gone with his ambiguity. He was only one of the gang. "Please," he said.

"Please," Summers mimicked him, and then suddenly struck home with the fatal name. "Run along home, Trevor."

T. stood with his back to the rubble like a boxer knocked groggy against the ropes. He had no words as his dreams shook and slid. Then Blackie acted before the gang had time to laugh, pushing Summers backward. "I'll watch the front, T.," he said, and cautiously he opened the shutters of the hall. The grey wet common stretched ahead, and the lamps gleamed in the puddles. "Someone's coming, T. No, it's not him. What's your plan, T.?"

"Tell Mike to go out to the loo and hide close beside it. When he hears me whistle he's got to count ten and start to shout."

"Shout what?"

"Oh, 'Help', anything."

"You hear, Mike," Blackie said. He was the leader again. He took a quick look between the shutters. "He's coming, T."

"Quick, Mike. The loo. Stay here, Blackie, all of you till I yell."

"Where are you going, T.?"

"Don't worry. I'll see to this. I said I would, didn't I?"

Old Misery came limping off the common. He had mud on his shoes and he stopped to scrape them on the pavement's edge. He didn't

want to soil his house, which stood jagged and dark between the bomb-
sites, saved so narrowly, as he believed, from destruction. Even the
fanlight had been left unbroken by the bomb's blast. Somewhere somebody whistled. Old Misery looked sharply round. He didn't trust whistles. A child was shouting: it seemed to come from his own garden.
Then a boy ran into the road from the car-park. "Mr. Thomas," he
called, "Mr. Thomas."

"What is it?"

"I'm terribly sorry, Mr. Thomas. One of us got taken short, and we
thought you wouldn't mind, and now he can't get out."

"What do you mean, boy?"

"He's got stuck in your loo."

"He'd no business . . . Haven't I seen you before?"

"You showed me your house."

"So I did. So I did. That doesn't give you the right to . . . "

"Do hurry, Mr. Thomas. He'll suffocate."

"Nonsense. He can't suffocate. Wait till I put my bag in."

"I'll carry your bag."

"Oh no, you don't. I carry my own."

"This way, Mr. Thomas."

"I can't get in the garden that way. I've got to go through the house."

"But you *can* get in the garden this way, Mr. Thomas. We often do."

"You often do?" He followed the boy with a scandalized fascination.
"When? What right? . . . "

"Do you see . . . ? the wall's low."

"I'm not going to climb walls into my own garden. It's absurd."

"This is how we do it. One foot here, one foot there, and over."
The boy's face peered down, an arm shot out, and Mr. Thomas found
his bag taken and deposited on the other side of the wall.

"Give me back my bag," Mr. Thomas said. From the loo a boy yelled
and yelled. "I'll call the police."

"Your bag's all right. Mr. Thomas. Look. One foot there. On your
right. Now just above. To your left." Mr. Thomas climbed over his
own garden wall. "Here's your bag, Mr. Thomas."

"I'll have the wall built up," Mr. Thomas said, "I'll not have you
boys coming over here, using my loo." He stumbled on the path, but
the boy caught his elbow and supported him. "Thank you, thank you,
my boy," he murmured automatically. Somebody shouted again through
the dark. "I'm coming, I'm coming," Mr. Thomas called. He said to
the boy beside him, "I'n not unreasonable. Been a boy myself. As long
as things are done regular. I don't mind you playing round the place
Saturday mornings. Sometimes I like company. Only it's got to be
regular. One of you asks leave and I say Yes. Sometimes I'll say No.
Won't feel like it. And you come in at the front door and out at the
back. No garden walls."

"Do get him out, Mr. Thomas."

"He won't come to any harm in my loo," Mr. Thomas said, stumbling slowly down the garden. "Oh, my rheumatics," he said. "Always get 'em on Bank Holiday. I've got to go careful. There's loose stones here. Give me your hand. Do you know what my horoscope said yesterday? 'Abstain from any dealings in first half of week. Danger of serious crash.' That might be on this path," Mr. Thomas said. "They speak in parables and double meanings." He paused at the door of the loo. "What's the matter in there?" he called. There was no reply.

"Perhaps he's fainted," the boy said.

"Not in my loo. Here, you, come out," Mr. Thomas said, and giving a great jerk at the door he nearly fell on his back when it swung easily open. A hand first supported him and then pushed him hard. His head hit the opposite wall and he sat heavily down. His bag hit his feet. A hand whipped the key out of the lock and the door slammed. "Let me out," he called, and heard the key turn in the lock. "A serious crash," he thought, and felt dithery and confused and old.

A voice spoke to him softly through the star-shaped hole in the door. "Don't worry, Mr. Thomas," it said, "we won't hurt you, not if you stay quiet."

Mr. Thomas put his head between his hands and pondered. He had noticed that there was only one lorry in the car-park, and he felt certain that the driver would not come for it before the morning. Nobody could hear him from the road in front, and the lane at the back was seldom used. Anyone who passed there would be hurrying home and would not pause for what they would certainly take to be drunken cries. And if he did call 'Help,' who, on a lonely Bank Holiday evening, would have the courage to investigate? Mr. Thomas sat on the loo and pondered with the wisdom of age.

After a while it seemed to him that there were sounds in the silence – they were faint and came from the direction of his house. He stood up and peered through the ventilation-hole – between the cracks in one of the shutters he saw a light, not the light of a lamp, but the wavering light that a candle might give. Then he thought he heard the sound of hammering and scraping and chipping. He thought of burglars – perhaps they had employed the boy as a scout, but why should burglars engage in what sounded more and more like a stealthy form of carpentry? Mr. Thomas let out an experimental yell, but nobody answered. The noise could not even have reached his enemies.

4

Mike had gone home to bed, but the rest stayed. The question of leadership no longer concerned the gang. With nails, chisels, screwdrivers, anything that was sharp and penetrating they moved around the inner walls worrying at the mortar between the bricks. They started too high, and it was Blackie who hit on the damp course and realized the work could be halved if they weakened the joints immediately above. It was a long, tiring, unamusing job, but at last it was finished. The gutted house stood there balanced on a few inches of mortar between the damp course and the bricks.

There remained the most dangerous task of all, out in the open at the edge of the bomb-site. Summers was sent to watch the road for passers-by, and Mr. Thomas, sitting on the loo, heard clearly now the sound of sawing. It no longer came from his house, and that a little reassured him. He felt less concerned. Perhaps the other noises too had no significance.

A voice spoke to him through the hole. "Mr. Thomas."

"Let me out," Mr. Thomas said sternly.

"Here's a blanket," the voice said, and a long grey sausage was worked through the hole and fell in swathes over Mr. Thomas's head.

"There's nothing personal," the voice said. "We want you to be comfortable to-night."

"To-night," Mr. Thomas repeated incredulously.

"Catch," the voice said. "Penny buns – we've buttered them, and sausage-rolls. We don't want you to starve, Mr. Thomas."

Mr. Thomas pleaded desperately. "A joke's a joke, boy. Let me out and I won't say a thing. I've got rheumatics. I got to sleep comfortable."

"You wouldn't be comfortable, not in your house, you wouldn't. Not now."

"What do you mean, boy?" but the footsteps receded. There was only the silence of night: no sound of sawing. Mr. Thomas tried one more yell, but he was daunted and rebuked by the silence – a long way off an owl hooted and made away again on its muffled flight through the soundless world.

At seven next morning the driver came to fetch his lorry. He climbed into the seat and tried to start the engine. He was vaguely aware of a voice shouting, but it didn't concern him. At last the engine responded and he backed the lorry until it touched the great wooden shore that supported Mr. Thomas's house. That way he could drive right out and down the street without reversing. The lorry moved forward, was momentarily checked as though something were pulling it from be-hind, and then went on to the sound of a long rumbling crash. The driver was astonished to see bricks bouncing ahead of him, while stones hit the roof of his cab. He put on his brakes. When he climbed out the whole landscape had suddenly altered. There was no house beside the car-park, only a hill of rubble. He went round and examined the back of his car for damage, and found a rope tied there that was still twisted at the other end round part of a wooden strut.

The driver again became aware of somebody shouting. It came from the wooden erection which was the nearest thing to a house in that desolation of broken brick. The driver climbed the smashed wall and unlocked the door. Mr. Thomas came out of the loo. He was wearing a grey blanket to which flakes of pastry adhered. He gave a sobbing cry. "My house," he said. "Where's my house?"

"Search me," the driver said. His eye lit on the remains of a bath and what had once been a dresser and he began to laugh. There wasn't anything left anywhere.

"How dare you laugh," Mr. Thomas said. "It was my house. My house."

"I'm sorry," the driver said, making heroic efforts, but when he remembered the sudden check to his lorry, the crash of bricks falling, he became convulsed again. One moment the house had stood there with such dignity between the bomb-sites like a man in a top hat, and then, bang, crash, there wasn't anything left – not anything. He said, "I'm sorry. I can't help it, Mr. Thomas. There's nothing personal, but you got to admit it's funny."

---

1. a) Identify a number of the words and phrases that suggest that the gang treats the demolition as a serious work project, perhaps even as a work of kinetic sculpture.
   b) Choose one section of the story and alter the diction to present Trevor and the gang in a different light. Exchange your version for a classmate's. Analyse your classmate's work and write a short statement of what, in your opinion, she or he wanted you to feel about the boys. Discuss each other's evaluations and together edit and revise your work.

2. a) With a classmate, talk about what motivates Trevor to suggest the destruction of Old Misery's house.
   b) Imagine that you are a social worker or a teacher, and write a short letter to the local authorities in which you either defend or attack Trevor's actions, bearing in mind his initial motives.

3. "There's nothing personal . . . " says the lorry driver to Old Misery.
   a) Identify incidents in the story where the characters' actions reflect the statement above.
   b) Vandalism involves the wilful destruction of property, particularly works of art. Some vandalism is an indirect attack against the person who values the thing that is destroyed; other vandalism is aimed solely at the thing and what it represents. In a group, discuss the implications for society of "personal" and "impersonal" vandalism.
   c) In a piece of personal writing, explore your thoughts and feelings about which kind of vandalism is more frightening and dangerous.

4. In a group, discuss whether or not the story has a happy ending. Achieve a consensus if you can and report your conclusions to the rest of the class.

5. Write an interior monologue in the persona of Old Misery either as he sits in the loo during the night or when he sees the hill of rubble in the morning. (For an example of an interior monologue, see "But the One on the Right," p. 96.)

CLEAN FUN AT RIVERHEAD
Tom Wolfe

*T*he inspiration for the demolition derby came to Lawrence Mendelsohn one night in 1958 when he was nothing but a spareribbed twenty-eight-year-old stock-car driver halfway through his 10th lap around the Islip, Long Island, Speedway and taking a curve too wide. A lubberly young man with a Chicago boxcar haircut came up on the inside in a 1949 Ford and caromed him 12 rows up into the grandstand, but Lawrence Mendelsohn and his entire car did not hit one spectator.

"That was what got me," he said, "I remember I was hanging upside down from my seat belt like a side of Jersey bacon and wondering why no one was sitting where I hit. 'Lousy promotion,' I said to myself.

"Not only that, but everybody who *was* in the stands forgot about the race and came running over to look at me gift-wrapped upside down in a fresh pile of junk."

At that moment occurred the transformation of Lawrence Mendelsohn, racing driver, into Lawrence Mendelsohn, promoter, and, a few transactions later, owner of the Islip Speedway, where he kept seeing more of this same underside of stock car racing that everyone in the industry avoids putting into words. Namely, that for every purist who comes to see the fine points of the race, such as who is going to win, there are probably five waiting for the wrecks to which stock car racing is so gloriously prone.

The pack will be going into a curve when suddenly two cars, three cars, four cars tangle, spinning and splattering all over each other and the retaining walls, upside down, right side up, inside out and in pieces, with the seams bursting open and discs, rods, wires and gasoline spewing out and yards of sheet metal shearing off like Reynolds Wrap and crumpling into the most baroque shapes, after which an ash-blue smoke starts seeping up from the ruins and a thrill begins to spread over the stands like Newburg sauce.

So why put up with the monotony between crashes?

Such, in brief, is the early history of what is culturally the most important sport ever originated in the United States, a sport that ranks with the gladiatorial games of Rome as a piece of national symbolism. Lawrence Mendelsohn had a vision of an automobile sport that would be all crashes. Not two cars, not three cars, not four cars, but 100 cars would be out in an arena doing nothing but smashing each other into shrapnel. The car that outrammed and outdodged all the rest, the last car that could still move amid the smoking heap, would take the prize money.

So at 8:15 at night at the Riverhead Raceway, just west of Riverhead, Long Island, on Route 25, amid the quaint tranquillity of the duck and turkey flatlands of eastern Long Island, Lawrence Mendelsohn stood up on the back of a flat truck in his red neon warmup jacket and lectured his 100 drivers on the rules and niceties of the new game, the "demolition derby." And so at 8:30 the first 25 cars moved out onto the raceway's quarter-mile stock car track. There was not enough room for 100 cars to mangle each other. Lawrence Mendelsohn's dream would require four heats. Now the 25 cars were placed at intervals all about the circumference of the track, making flatulent revving noises, all headed not around the track but toward a point in the centre of the infield.

Then the entire crowd, about 4,000, started chanting a countdown, "Ten, nine, eight, seven, six, five, four, three, two," but it was impossible to hear the rest because right after "two" half the crowd went into a strange whinnying wail. The starter's flag went up, and the 25 cars took off, roaring into second gear with no mufflers, all headed toward that same point in the centre of the infield, converging nose on nose.

The effect was exactly what one expects that many simultaneous crashes to produce: the unmistakable tympany of automobiles colliding and cheap-gauge sheet metal buckling; front ends folding together at the same cock-eyed angles police photographs of night-time wreck scenes capture so well on grainy paper; smoke pouring from under the hoods and hanging over the infield like a howitzer cloud; a few of the surviving cars lurching eccentrically on bent axles. At last, after four heats, there were only two cars moving through the junk, a 1953 Chrysler and a 1958 Cadillac. In the Chrysler a small fascia of muscles named Skip Ligon who smoked a cigar while he drove, had the Cadillac cornered up against a guard rail in front of the main grandstand. He dispatched it by swinging around and backing full throttle through the left side of its grille and radiator.

By now the crowd was quite beside itself. Spectators broke through a gate in the retaining screen. Some rushed to Spider Ligon's car, hoisted him to their shoulders and marched off the field, howling. Others clambered over the stricken cars of the defeated, enjoying the details of their ruin, and howling. The good, full cry of triumph and annihilation rose from Riverhead Raceway, and the demolition derby was over.

That was the 154th demolition derby in two years. Since Lawrence Mendelsohn staged the first one at Islip Speedway in 1961, they have been held throughout the United States at the rate of one every five days, resulting in the destruction of about 15,000 cars. The figures alone indicate a gluttonous appetite for the sport. Sports writers, of course, have managed to ignore demolition derbies even more successfully than they have ignored stock car racing and drag racing. All in all, the new automobile sports have shown that the sports pages, which on the surface appear to hum with life and earthiness, are at bottom pillars of gentility. This drag racing and demolition derbies and things, well, there are too many kids in it with sideburns, tight Levis and winkle-picker boots.

Yet the demolition derbies keep growing on word-of-mouth publicity. The "nationals" were held last month at Langhorne, Pennsylvania, with 50 cars in the finals, and demolition derby fans everywhere know that Don McTavish, of Dover, Massachusetts, is the new world's champion. About 1,250,000 spectators have come to the 154 contests held so far. More than 75 per cent of the derbies have drawn full houses.

The nature of their appeal is clear enough. Since the onset of the Christian era, i.e., since about 500 A.D., no game has come along to fill the gap left by the abolition of the purest of all sports, gladiatorial combat. As late as 300 A.D. these bloody duels, usually between men but sometimes between women and dwarfs, were enormously popular not only in Rome but throughout the Roman Empire. Since then no game, not even boxing, has successfully acted out the underlying motifs of most sport, that is, aggression and destruction.

Boxing, of course, is an aggressive sport, but one contestant has actually destroyed the other in a relatively small percentage of matches. Other games are progressively more sublimated forms of sport. Often, as in the case of football, they are encrusted with oddments of passive theology and metaphysics to the effect that the real purpose of the game is to foster character, teamwork, stamina, physical fitness and the ability to "give-and-take."

But not even those wonderful clergymen who pray in behalf of Congress, expressway ribbon-cuttings, urban renewal projects and testimonial dinners for ethnic aldermen would pray for a demolition derby. The demolition derby is, pure and simple, a form of gladiatorial combat for our times.

As hand-to-hand combat has gradually disappeared from our civilization, even in wartime, and competition has become more and more sophisticated and abstract, Americans have turned to the automobile to satisfy their love of direct aggression. The mild-mannered man who turns into a bear behind the wheel of a car – i.e., who finds in the power of the automobile a vehicle for the release of his inhibitions – is part of American folklore. Among teen-agers the automobile has become the symbol, and in part the physical means, of triumph over family and community restrictions. Seventy-five per cent of all car thefts in the United States are by teen-agers out for "joy rides."

The symbolic meaning of the automobile tones down but by no means vanishes in adulthood. Police traffic investigators have long been convinced that far more accidents are purposeful crashes by belligerent drivers than they could ever prove. One of the heroes of the era was the Middle Eastern diplomat who rammed a magazine writer's car from behind in the Kalorama embassy district of Washington two years ago. When the American bellowed out the window at him, he backed up and smashed his car again. When the fellow leaped out of his car to pick a fight, he backed up and smashed his car a third time, then drove off. He was recalled home for having "gone native."

The unabashed, undisguised, quite purposeful sense of destruction of the demolition derby is its unique contribution. The aggression, the battering, the ruination are there to be enjoyed. The crowd at a demolition derby seldom gasps and often laughs. It enjoys the same full-throated participation as Romans at the Colosseum. After each trial or heat at a demolition derby, two drivers go into the finals. One is the driver whose car was still going at the end. The other is the driver the crowd selects from among the 24 vanquished on the basis of his courage, showmanship or simply the awesomeness of his crashes. The numbers of the cars are read over loudspeakers, and the crowd chooses one with its cheers. By the same token, the crowd may force a driver out of competition if he appears cowardly or merely cunning. This is the sort of driver who drifts around the edge of the battle avoiding crashes with the hope that the other cars will eliminate one another. The umpire waves a yellow flag at him and he must crash into someone within 30 seconds or run the risk of being booed off the field in dishonour and disgrace.

The frank relish of the crowd is nothing, however, compared to the kick the contestants get out of the game. It costs a man an average of $50 to retrieve a car from a junk yard and get it running for a derby. He will only get his money back – $50 – for winning a heat. The chance of being smashed up in the madhouse first 30 seconds of a round are so great, even the best of drivers faces long odds in his shot at the $500 first prize. None of that matters to them.

Tommy Fox, who is nineteen, said he entered the demolition derby because, "You know, it's fun. I like it. You know what I mean?" What was fun about it? Tommy Fox had a way of speaking that was much like the early Marlon Brando. Much of what he had to say came from the trapezii, which he rolled quite a bit, and the forehead, which he cocked, and the eyebrows, which he could bring together expressively from time to time. "Well," he said, "you know, like when you hit 'em, and all that. It's fun."

Tommy Fox had a lot of fun in the first heat. Nobody was bashing around quite like he was in his old green Hudson. He did not win, chiefly because he took too many chances, but the crowd voted him into the finals as the best showman.

"I got my brother," said Tommy. "I came in from the side and he didn't even see me."

His brother is Don Fox, thirty-two, who owns the junk yard where they both got their cars. Don likes to hit them, too, only he likes it almost too much. Don drives with such abandon, smashing into the first car he can get a shot at and leaving himself wide open, he does not stand much chance of finishing the first three minutes.

For years now sociologists have been calling upon one another to undertake a serious study of America's "car culture." No small part of it is the way the automobile has, for one very large segment of the population, become the focus of the same sort of quasi-religious dedication as art is currently for another large segment of a higher social order. Tommy Fox is unemployed, Don Fox runs a junk yard, Spider Ligon is a maintenance man for Brookhaven Naval Laboratory, but to categorize them as such is getting no closer to the truth than to have categorized William Faulkner in 1926 as a clerk at Lord & Taylor, although he was.

Tommy Fox, Don Fox and Spider Ligon are acolytes of the car culture, an often esoteric world of arts and sciences that came into its own after World War II and now has believers of two generations. Charlie Turbush, thirty-five, and his son, Buddy, seventeen, were two more contestants, and by no stretch of the imagination can they be characterized as bizarre figures or cultists of the death wish. As for the dangers of driving in a demolition derby, they are quite real by all physical laws. The drivers are protected only by crash helmets, seat belts and the fact that all glass, interior handles, knobs and fixtures have been removed. Yet Lawrence Mendelsohn claims that there have been no serious injuries in 154 demolition derbies and now gets his insurance at a rate below that of stock car racing.

The sport's future may depend in part on word getting around about its relative safety. Already it is beginning to draw contestants here and there from social levels that could give the demolition derby the cachet of respectability. In eastern derbies so far two doctors and three young men of more than passable connections in eastern society have entered under whimsical *noms de combat* and emerged neither scarred nor victorious. Bull fighting had to win the same social combat.

All of which brings to mind that fine afternoon when some high-born Roman women were out in Nero's box at the Colosseum watching this sexy Thracian carve an ugly little Samnite up into prime cuts, and one said, darling, she had an inspiration, and Nero, needless to say, was all for it. Thus began the new vogue of Roman socialites fighting as gladiators themselves, for kicks. By the second century A.D. even the Emperor Commodus was out there with a tiger's head as a helmet hacking away at some poor dazed fall guy. He did a lot for the sport. Arenas sprang up all over the empire like shopping centre bowling alleys.

The future of the demolition derby, then, stretches out over the face of America. The sport draws no lines of gender, and post-debs may reach Lawrence Mendelsohn at his office in Deer Park.

---

1. a) State, in a sentence for each, the major theses that Wolfe argues in his essay.
   b) Defend or refute one of the theses in a short essay, using material drawn from research or from your own experience.

2. a) Wolfe's vocabulary is a mixture of the everyday and the sophisticated. Discuss with a classmate how the blend affects the reader and how it reflects Wolfe's attitude to his subject.
   b) The writer also uses a wide range of figurative language in this essay: "tympany of automobiles colliding," "like a howitzer cloud," "gasoline spewing out," and so on. Select five other examples and examine each, discussing how it
   • affects the reader;
   • helps create the tone of the piece;
   • contributes to Wolfe's purpose.
   c) On your own, summarize your discussion in a piece of expository writing that could be used as a preface to "Clean Fun at Riverhead," introducing the reader to Wolfe's prose style. Ask the classmate you worked with earlier to help you revise and proofread the draft. You may wish to put the final draft in your writing folder.

3. Write an editorial for a sports magazine in which you attempt to persuade the readers that the demolition derby (or some other sensational or dangerous sport, such as boxing, the roller derby, or wrestling) deserves the "cachet of respectability."

4. a) Read Graham Greene's "The Destructors," (p. 268), and then, in a small group, discuss the paradox of destruction as an art form or creative enterprise.

 b) Drawing on the ideas raised in your discussion, write an extended piece of personal writing that explains how an act of destruction may be creative and, if you can, describe an incident that you have witnessed or experienced that exemplifies this paradox.

5. Patterning your style on Wolfe's, write a description of a sporting event in which you have participated or that you have witnessed. Ask a classmate to read your work and to evaluate how successful you were in imitating Wolfe's style.

In a small group, brainstorm the
characteristics of Gothic literature, paying
particular attention to the traditional
presentation of the haunted house and its
customary tenants. As you read "The House on
the Esplanade," note any elements of Hébert's
indebtedness to the genre.

THE HOUSE ON THE ESPLANADE

Anne Hébert

tephanie de Bichette was a curious little creature with frail limbs that seemed badly put together. Only her starched collarette kept her head from falling over on her shoulder; it was too heavy for her long, slender neck. If the head of Stephanie de Bichette looked so heavy, it was because all the pomp of her aristocratic ancestors was symbolized in her coiffure, a high up-swept style, with padded curls arranged in rows on her narrow cranium, an architectural achievement in symmetrical silvery blobs.

Mademoiselle de Bichette had passed, without transition period, without adolescence, from the short frocks of her childhood to this everlasting ash-grey dress, trimmed at neck and wrists with a swirl of lilac braiding. She owned two parasols with carved ivory handles – one lilac and the other ash-grey. When she went out driving in the carriage she chose her parasol according to the weather, and everyone in the little town could tell the weather by the colour of Mademoiselle de Bichette's parasol. The lilac one appeared on days of brilliant sunshine, the ash-grey one whenever it was slightly cloudy. In winter, and when it rained, Stephanie simply never went out at all.

I have spoken at length about her parasols because they were the outward and visible signs of a well-regulated life, a perfect edifice of regularity. Unchanging routine surrounded and supported this innocent old creature. The slightest crack in this extraordinary construction, the least change in this stern program would have been enough to make Mademoiselle de Bichette seriously ill.

Fortunately, she had never had to change her maid. Geraldine served and cared for her mistress with every evidence of complete respect for tradition. The whole life of Stephanie de Bichette was a tradition, or rather a series of traditions, for apart from the tradition of the well-known parasols and the complicated coiffure, there was the ritual of getting up, of going to bed, of lace-making, of mealtimes, and so on.

Stephanie Hortense Sophie de Bichette lived facing the Esplanade, in a grey stone house dating back to the days of the French occupation. You know the sort of house *that* implies – a tall, narrow edifice with a pointed roof and several rows of high windows, where the ones at the top look no bigger than swallows' nests, a house with two or three large attics that most old maids would have delighted in. But, believe it or not, Mademoiselle de Bichette never climbed up to her attics to sentimentalize over souvenirs, to caress treasured old belongings, or to plan meticulous orgies of housecleaning amid the smell of yellowing paper and musty air that even the best-kept attics seem to possess.

No, she occupied the very heart of the house, scarcely one room on each floor. On the fourth story, only Geraldine's room remained open, among the rooms of all the former servants. It was part of the family tradition to close off rooms that were no longer used. One after another, bedroom after bedroom had been condemned: the room where the little brothers had died of scarlet fever, when Stephanie was only ten years old; the bedroom of their mother, who had passed away soon after her two children; the room of Irénée, the elder brother who had been killed in an accident, out hunting; the room of the elder sister, Desneiges, who had entered the Ursuline convent; then the bedroom of Monsieur de Bichette, the father, who had succumbed to a long illness; to say nothing of the room belonging to Charles, the only surviving brother, which had been closed ever since his marriage.

The ritual was always the same: once the occupant of the room had departed for the cemetery, the convent, or the adventure of matrimony, Geraldine would tidy everything away, carefully leaving each piece of furniture exactly in place; then she would draw the shutters, put dust-covers on the arm-chairs, and lock the door for good. No one ever set foot in that room again. One more member of the family was finally disposed of.

Geraldine took a distinct pleasure in this solemn, unvarying rite, just as a gravedigger may take pride in a neat row of graves, with well-kept mounds and smoothly raked grass above them. Sometimes she remembered that one day she would have to close Mademoiselle Stephanie's room, too, and live on for a while, the only living creature among all the dead. She looked forward to that moment, not with horror, but with pleasant anticipation, as a rest and a reward. After so many years of housework in that great house, all its rooms would be fixed at last in order, for all eternity. Mildew and dust could take possession then; Geraldine would have no more cleaning to do then. The rooms of the dead are not "done up."

This was not the calculation of a lazy woman. Geraldine dreamed of the last door closed and the last key turned in the lock just as the harvester dreams of the last sheaf of corn, or the needlewoman of the last stitch in her embroidery. It would be the crowning achievement of her long life, the goal of her destiny.

It was strange that the old servant reckoned two living people among the dead: Mademoiselle Desneiges, the nun, and Monsieur Charles, a married man and the father of a family. They had both left the family roof, that was enough for Geraldine to class them as non-existent. The heavy door of the cloister had closed forever on one, while Charles, by marrying a common little seamstress from the Lower Town, had so grieved his father that the old house and all it contained had been left to Stephanie. Charles came to see his sister every evening, but Geraldine never spoke a word to him. For her, Stephanie was the whole of the de Bichette family.

On the third floor, all the bedrooms were closed, with the exception of Mademoiselle de Bichette's. On the second, only the small blue boudoir lived on, a life of dimness and disuse. On the first floor, an immense drawing-room stretched from front to back, cluttered with furniture of different periods, each piece bristling with fussy, elaborate knick-knacks. The ground-floor doors were always open, with high, carved portals to the vestibule, the parlour, the dining-room. In the basement was the old-fashioned kitchen, uncomfortable and always damp. Geraldine was the cook as well as the maid-of-all-work, but was never addressed as such.

If her mistress lived by tradition until it became a religion, Geraldine, too had her tradition, the collecting of bright-coloured buttons. Her black skirt and her white apron never changed, but she used her imagination in trimming her blouses. Red buttons sparkled on blue blouses, yellow ones on green, and so on, not to mention buttons in gold and silver and crystal. In the attic, she had discovered great chests of ancient garments which she stripped, shamelessly, of their trimmings. Apart from this innocent craze for buttons, the big woman with the ruddy complexion made no objection to touring the wine cellar every evening before going to bed, as the last of her duties, conscientiously and even devotedly performed. But where she excelled, was in the observance of tradition where her mistress was concerned.

Every morning, at seven o'clock in summer and eight in winter, she climbed the three flights of stairs and knocked at the bedroom door . . . . Two taps, two firm, decided taps, no more, no less. This was the signal for the ceremonial to begin.

Geraldine opened the bed curtains, then the window curtains, and finally the shutters. Her aging mistress preferred to sleep in complete darkness, requiring several thicknesses of material and polished wood between herself and the wicked witchcraft of the night. She was afraid of the first rays of sunlight as well, not knowing what to do about them, since they might easily wake you long before the proper time for getting up.

Then Geraldine would return to the passage to fetch a kind of wagon equipped with everything Stephanie might need for the first few hours of the day. Two white pills in a glass of water, coffee and toast, tooth-brush and toothpowder, a copper bathtub, white towels, white, starched underwear. Also a feather duster, a broom, a dust-pan . . . all that she used for tidying up the room. This wagon was as wide as a single bed, four feet wide, with three shelves. Geraldine had made it herself out of old packing cases.

When Stephanie's breakfast was finished, the maid would bathe, dress, and powder her mistress, then do her hair. Stephanie allowed her to do everything, silent, inert, trusting. After that, there was some-times a moment of painful indecision, an anguished knot in the brain of Mademoiselle de Bichette, when Geraldine leaned over to look out of the window, examining the sky and frowning as she declared:

"I really don't know what sort of weather we're going to have today."

Then the old lady would stare at her maid with such forlorn eyes that Geraldine would say, hurriedly:

"It's going to rain. You're not going to be able to go out this morning. I'll let the coachman know."

Stephanie would grow calm again after that, but she would not be entirely herself until Geraldine had settled her carefully in the blue drawing-room, on her high-backed chair of finely carved wood, near the window, her half-finished lace on her knee and her crochet hook in her hand. Only then would the idea take firm root in her brain:

"It's going to rain. I can't go out. . . . All I have to do is to handle this hook and this thread as my mother taught me to do when I was seven years old. . . . If it had been a fine day, it would have been different, I would have gone out in the carriage. There are only two realities in the world . . . only two realities I can rely on . . . and close my eyes, deep inside them: the reality of going out in the carriage, the reality of making my lace. . . . How lost and strange I am when Ger-aldine cannot tell what the weather is going to do, and I am left in suspense with no solid ground beneath my feet. . . . It just *wracks* my brain! Oh! Not to have to think about it, to let myself be carried away by one or the other of these my only two sure and certain realities, going out for a drive or sitting here, making my lace. . . . "

Even if the day turned out fine in the end, Geraldine never said so. It would have been too much of a shock for her mistress. Imagine what confusion in such a patterned existence if someone had suddenly announced a change, after she had firmly established herself for the day in the reality of lace-making, and dared to tell her she had taken the wrong road? She could never again have believed in any reality at all.

Since her childhood, Mademoiselle de Bichette had been making lace doilies of different sizes, which Geraldine used in many different ways. These doilies flowed from her fingers at the steady rate of four per week, small pieces of white lace that resembled each other like peas in a pod. They were everywhere in the house – five or six on the piano, seven or eight on all the tables, as many as ten on every armchair, one or two on all the smaller chairs. Every knick-knack rested on a piece of delicate openwork, so that the furniture all seemed powdered with snowflakes, enlarged as if under a microscope.

In winter, and in summer, on the days when Geraldine had decided the weather was not fit for going out, Mademoiselle de Bichette would crochet all the morning, in her blue boudoir, sitting up so straight and still that she scarcely seemed real, her feet resting on a stool covered by something that was strangely like the work the old lady held in her hands.

At five minutes to twelve, Geraldine would announce: "Mademoiselle Stephanie's luncheon is served."

At the mention of her name, the old lady would rise at once; the ritual phrase had touched a switch somewhere within her, so that without effort, without thinking, without even understanding, she would put herself slowly and ceremoniously in motion, descend the staircase, and take her place at the table.

If Stephanie did go out, she invariably returned home at a quarter to twelve, so she had ample time to receive the announcement that luncheon was served with the necessary calm.

The outings of Mademoiselle de Bichette were governed by just as incredible a routine. She came out on the sidewalk with tiny steps, her frail little body bending under the weight of that enormous pile of scaffolded curls. Geraldine helped her mistress into the carriage, the coachman whipped up his horse, and the victoria started on its slow, quiet drive, invariably the same, through the streets of the little town. The horse knew the road by heart, so the coachman seized the opportunity for a short nap, his cap pulled down over his eyes, his legs stretched out, his hands folded on his stomach. He always woke up in time, as if by magic, when the drive came to an end, crying out and stretching himself, with a jolly air of surprise:

"Well, well, Mamzelle, here we are back again!"

Just as if the old fellow, when he went to sleep as the drive started, had not been quite sure he would come back when he awoke, or if his return would be to the country of the living!

Mademoiselle de Bichette would disappear into the house, on Geraldine's arm; the coachman would unharness the horse and put the carriage away; and it was all over. With regret, the townsfolk watched the disintegration of this strange conveyance, like a ghostly apparition cutting through the clear morning light . . . the ancient nag, pulling an antique carriage, with a sleeping coachman and a tiny figure like a mummy, swathed in ash-grey and lilac.

After luncheon, Geraldine would lead her mistress into the long drawing-room on the first floor, where, without ever laying her crochet aside, Stephanie would receive a few callers, and the maid would serve dandelion wine and madeleines.

The old lady never left her chair, forcing herself to hold her head high, though her neck felt as if it were breaking under the weight of her monumental coiffure. Sometimes, this constant, painful effort was betrayed by a twitch of the lips, the only change of expression that callers could ever distinguish upon that small, powdered face. Then Stephanie would ask: "How is Madame your mother?" in a voice so white and colourless that it might have come from one of the closed rooms, where, according to the gossips of the town, some of the original inhabitants still lived on.

This phrase of Stephanie's had to do for greeting, for farewell, for conversation; indeed, it had to do for everything, for the wine was sour and the madeleines stale and hard as stones. The callers were all so aged and unsteady that the most utter stranger would have had the tact never to ask that preposterous question, but Mademoiselle de Bichette knew no other formula, and in any case, she attached no importance whatever to the words she was saying. If she finished a lace doily while her callers were present, she simply let it fall at her feet, like a pebble into a pool, and began another identical piece of lace. The visiting ladies never stayed very long, and Stephanie seemed to notice their departure as little as she did their presence.

At a quarter past six, Geraldine would announce that Monsieur Charles was waiting below. The program of the day was ticking on like the mechanism of a good Swiss watch, and the invisible wheels of Mademoiselle de Bichette responded perfectly, warning the limbs of this strange little creature that they must immediately convey her to the ground floor.

Her brother would kiss her brow and smile, rubbing his stubby-fingered hands together and remarking:

"Um-phm! It feels good in the house."

Then he would hang his overcoat up on a hall stand, while Geraldine followed his every movement with her look of triumphant disdain.

With her arms crossed upon her swelling chest, she doubtless thought she looked like the statue of the Commendatore, bound on revenge. She would cast a glance of scorn on the thread-bare coat, as if to say:

"Well, what did you expect? Monsieur Charles *would* get married to a chit of a girl from the Lower Town, so naturally, his father cut him off, and I locked up his room as if he were dead. If Mademoiselle Stephanie wants him here every evening, it's her own business, but *I'm* going to let him know that I'm *glad* he was thrown out, if I *am* only the servant. I know he's poor, and that's his punishment for disobeying his father. He comes here because there isn't enough to eat at home. So he gobbles up our dinners and carries away on his nasty skin a bit of the warmth from our fires. . . . The good-for-nothing!"

If it were true that Charles had only one decent meal a day, it was astonishing that he was not at all thin. He was even fat, very fat, flabby and yellow-complexioned, with a bald head and a shiny face, colourless lips and almost colourless eyes. Geraldine said he had eyes like a codfish and his clothes always smelt of stale grease. Apart from that, she could not forgive a de Bichette for forgetting his table manners.

"To think that his slut of a wife has made him lose all he ever learned in decent society. . . . You wouldn't believe it possible," she would grumble to herself.

As dinner-time drew near, Charles became more and more noisily jolly. He never stopped rubbing his hands together; he got up, sat down, got up again, went from window to door and back a dozen times, while Stephanie's eyes ignored him. Then the brother and sister took their places, one at each end of the long table in the dining-room. There was no gas chandelier in this room so it seemed even longer and darker, lit only by two tall candles in silver candlesticks. The corners of the room disappeared into the dimness, and the shadows of the brother and sister danced like black flames on the curiously carved oak panelling of the walls.

Every evening, the atmosphere of this dining-room seemed more impressive to Charles. Perhaps he felt unseen forms hiding in the darkness, invisible spectators of this singular repast; perhaps he feared to find the ghosts that haunted the bedrooms above, to see them take their places at the huge dining-table, where an old creature presided, small as a cat, white as the table-linen, who seemed already to be living in the uneasy world of phantoms.

As soon as Stephanie's brother had swallowed a few mouthfuls of soup, his good humour fell away, lifeless, utterly destroyed. When he entered the house, the smell of cooking would stimulate him, would intoxicate him with its marvellous promise, but now that the promise was kept, the man became gloomy again. Through his own bitter thoughts, he stared at the lace cloth, the heavy silverware, the fine china, and at this sister of his, who was still alive, in spite of her look of belonging to some other world. What mysterious thread was keeping Stephanie here on earth? To look at her, you would have thought the slightest breath might carry her away, yet there she was, still alive.

Geraldine came and went around the table and her sharp eyes seemed to plumb the very depths of the man's thoughts. The brother sat there, knowing himself watched and understood, telling himself, in his embarrassment, that his sister would have joined her ancestors long ago had it not been for this fiendish servant, who by some diabolical process had contrived to keep the dying thing alive in her father's mansion, simply in order to enjoy as long as possible the spectacle of his own failure. In what dread "No Man's Land" of the spirit had the old witch made a pact with Monsieur de Bichette – and with Satan himself? Geraldine had inherited all the father's anger against his son, and faithful to that anger as if to a sacred promise, she was constantly reminding Charles of the curse that lay heavy upon him. At that moment he raised his head, resenting the eyes he felt fixed upon his every movement, but Geraldine was no longer there, Charles could hear the tinkle of her keys, in the passage between the staircase and the kitchen. He shuddered, for he knew very well which keys she carried at her waist. No cupboard, no inhabited room possessed a key. It chilled his heart strangely to know that the key of his room was there, along with those of the rooms of the dead. It scared him. Then he took hold of himself again and muttered:

"This damned house! . . . Enough to drive a man crazy to sit here night after night with two cracked old fools of women. . . . The wine must have gone to my head."

But Stephanie had just got up from the table, and Charles followed her as usual.

The evening began like all the rest. Stephanie took up her lace again, while her brother walked to and fro in the long drawing-room, his hands behind his back.

And so, night after night, in complete silence, without a single word exchanged between brother and sister, the time passed until the old clock chimed ten. Then Charles, having laid up a store of warmth for the night, kissed his sister's brow, slipped on his overcoat, and with his hands in his pockets, made for Ireland Street, walking slowly along, like an idle fellow accustomed to musing as he walked.

The man followed his shadow as it flickered on the walls. The same thoughts were turning and twisting in his brain; he was used to them, as a man gets used to animals he tends every day. He knew them too well to be surprised by them; he had stopped looking at them straight in the face; they passed to and fro behind his pale eyes without ever changing his passive stare.

As he came near his own home, Charles thought of his wife. He was going back to her, in no hurry, but with a certain feeling of security, as if to a piece of property he knew belonged to him.

Suddenly, he noticed that he was nearly there. Two low houses, identical twins in misery and poverty, stood waiting for him, their tumbledown grey "stoops" jutting out to meet the sidewalk. He rented rooms on the second floor of one of these houses.

He climbed the stairs, lit a candle, and went into the bedroom. A hoarse, veiled voice, a well-known voice, that could still charm him in spite of himself, said wearily:

"That you Charles?"

He set the candle on the night table. The woman shaded her eyes with her hand. He sat down on the foot of the bed.

"How's your sister?"

"Just the same."

This question, this reply, as on every other night, fell heavily into a dull silence. Beneath the words was stirring in the shadows the real meaning, unexpressed:

"Do you think your sister will last much longer?"

"Fraid so. . . . She's still hanging on. . . . "

At that moment, in the house on the Esplanade, Stephanie de Bichette was crossing her tiny cold hands on her breast and abandoning to the great empty gulf of night the small emptiness that was herself, ridiculous as an old fashion plate and dry as a pressed fig.

And Geraldine lay awake, dreaming that death had closed the last door in the old house.

Translated by Morna Scott Stoddart

---

1. In a paragraph or two, and with specific references to the text, explain how Mlle. Stephanie and her house complement each other.

2. Write Geraldine's interior monologue, using stream-of-consciousness narrative, as she lies in bed "dreaming" at the end of the day. Read your monologue to a classmate.

3. Working with a classmate, script and role-play for the class a conversation between Charles and his wife before he sets out for supper in the house on the esplanade.

4. a) Reread the story and jot down the diction Hébert uses to create the impression that Stephanie de Bichette is one of the "living dead."
b) You have been chosen to direct the film version of "The House on the Esplanade." Choose one scene or paragraph in the story, and write detailed instructions for your film crew. Tell them how you want the set to appear, how you want to use sound and silence, and how you intend to shoot the scene.

5. a) In a small group discuss how Hébert makes use of colours and silence in her story. Compare your group's findings with those of another group and together make an outline for a short essay on the topic.
b) On your own, decide on a thesis for the essay and then write the introductory paragraph. For each paragraph of the body of your essay, write a topic sentence and a point-form outline of the content of the paragraph.

6. In a few written paragraphs, prove to a classmate that self-destruction need not be a violent act. Use the characters in the story to demonstrate your point. Compare arguments to see whether you and your classmate have chosen to highlight the same details.

"It has 30 000 quills, an irritable back, and a propensity for isolation. It is capable of the most hideous of wails, particularly when in love. But it is the porcupine's appetite for young trees that raises the hackles of its staunchest opponent: humanity." In a group, jot down anything else you know about porcupines. Check the accuracy of your notes as you read this article.

WHAT GETS A PORCUPINE'S BACK UP?
Bruce Obee

It seems a case of overkill for a nugatory rodent like the porcupine to be equipped with such notorious defences. A full-grown porcupine, twice as heavy as a Canada goose and as long as a polar bear's arm, protects its lumpish body with 30 000 needle-sharp quills. The tips are barbed and arranged like layers of shakes on a roof. The most horrific quills, covering the critter's back, are the length of your index finger.

Loosely attached to the porcupine's skin, the quills gather like burrs on any animal, or person, who touches them. Slowly, painfully they work their way into a victim, a millimetre an hour, until they emerge or become lodged against bone or other hard tissue. They can be removed only by tearing the flesh.

The porcupine, however, is a poky, mild-mannered mammal that prefers undisturbed solitude over battle. When threatened, the animal would rather retreat to some protective cover than fight. It moves with a speed which belies its sluggish form, sometimes crashing into stumps or fallen logs. In a frenzied dash, a porcupine may dive headlong into a rushing stream, then swim against the current to shore, buoyed by the air in its quills.

But when combat is inevitable, the porcupine mobilizes its defence system. The muscles under its skin contract, bristling the quills like the hairs on an angry cat's shoulders. With its bow-legged, pigeon-toed forelegs firmly on the ground it pivots around, presenting its back to the intruder. It slashes menacingly with a 20-cm tail, delivering 50 or 100 quills with a single well-placed swat.

One of the few animals which seems almost invulnerable to wounds inflicted by porcupine quills is the fisher, a weasel-like carnivore less than half the size of a porcupine. The fisher is particularly adept at killing its prickly prey, small enough to stand at eye-level to a porcupine, yet agile enough to avoid a swipe from the quill-covered tail. It's the porcupine's most formidable foe and kills by repeatedly biting the porcupine's face, then flipping the animal over to chew through the soft underbelly.

The fisher's resistance to the porcupine's defences makes it a valuable asset to foresters who must vigilantly guard porcupine-infested timberlands. "The problem is really serious," says Ralph Archibald, a research biologist with the B.C. Wildlife Branch. "Look up from the shore there," he said, gesturing to a wooded slope of an isolated inlet in northern B.C. "We've got a tremendous amount of brown forest there – dead trees interspersed with live."

The area is, or was until the fishers came, a predator-free haven where porcupines had proliferated to unprecedented numbers. The population burgeoned when the habitat was altered by logging. Slash areas, created by current logging operations, are attractive to porcupines during summer when they feed on succulent vegetation that sprouts up in newly opened areas. When those foraging grounds are covered with snow, porcupines turn to 30- and 40-year-old second-growth trees. They'll stay in a tree for days at a time, gnawing at the bark to get at the cambium, or inner layer of growing tissue. Eventually they'll girdle the tree, stifling the flow of nutrients up from the ground.

The porcupine's continuously growing incisors are similar to those of a beaver, the only larger Canadian rodent. Where food is abundant, most porcupines stay within an area of about 12 hectares for their entire nine- or 10-year lives. In fact, 13 porcupines tagged in one American survey moved less than a kilometre from the tagging point in a year. Many travel less than 100 m a day, spending their nights munching on trees. In the newly created foraging grounds on B.C.'s north coast, there's little reason to move.

"It really is an ideal porcupine habitat," says Archibald. "It's a porcupine heaven in there."

During the past decade more than half of a 2400 hectare forest of sitka spruce, hemlock, cedar, and balsam has been damaged or destroyed. The number of trees lost to porcupines is growing by some 360 000 trees a year. It's estimated the value of stumpage – royalties paid to the Crown by logging companies – for the lost trees is $6 million. The value of the timber to forest companies and workers is substantially higher.

The idea of controlling burgeoning porcupine populations biologically as an alternative to bounties, poisoning, or trapping, was the brainwave of Bill Jackson, a protection officer for the B.C. Ministry of Forests. He'd seen the success of similar control programs in Montana, Ontario, Alberta, and other parts of North America. Nobody's sure why fishers don't naturally inhabit the forests of northern coastal B.C. but there is good reason to believe that fishers transplanted from other parts of the province will thrive with the abundance of prey. Detailed surveys have not been done but it is believed porcupine densities around the inlet are between five and 12 per hectare, extremely high by North American standards.

The forests above the inlet are extremely dense, Jackson says, and fishers will be able to penetrate areas which are inaccessible to people.

"We've been through there four times in two years and still haven't seen a porcupine," says Jackson. "They hear us coming and take off." Still, Jackson will not name the inlet for fear the fishers will be trapped for their valuable fur. Two fishers – a male and a pregnant female – were released last winter after radio transmitters were surgically inserted in their abdomens. Ten more are to be released next winter and six will be fitted with transmitters, allowing researchers to monitor their movements for up to nine months.

It is hoped that eight of the 12 transplanted fishers will be pregnant, carrying an average of three offspring each. If six are pregnant and survival is high there could be a total of 30 fishers in the area by the end of next spring. Each fisher would likely eat 30 porcupines a year. With porcupines producing only one offspring, occasionally two a year, it won't be long before an acceptable balance between predator and prey is established. That is, of course, if the fishers decide to stay.

Foresters are not the only ones frustrated by the porcupine's epicurean preferences. Cottage owners, farmers, campers, and others who travel in porcupine territory are often disgruntled by the porcupine's voracity. Plywood building materials, fences, wooden bridges, even plastic irrigation pipes and communication lines are fair fodder to a porcupine.

Naturalist Sheila Thomson has watched porcupines on Mount St. Patrick in the Madawaska Hills of Renfrew County, Ontario. "They also eat aluminum!" she writes in *Trail and Landscape*. "Incredible as it sounds, the evidence is that in the spring of 1977 a porcupine actually consumed hand-sized patches of aluminum sheeting on our makeshift cabin. No scraps, splinters, or fragments of metal were found anywhere near the damaged aluminum walls. Corroborating this observation, a neighbour 20 km through the bush to the west of us keeps on exhibit what is left of an aluminum boat 'eaten, not just chewed' by porcupines."

Aluminum, plastic and wood may be tasty but to a porcupine, the pièce de résistance is salt, one of the reasons for the abundance of lifeless roadside porcupines. They gravitate to highways, where salt sprinkled for snow removal accumulates. If traffic is too heavy to lick the road, porcupines turn to parked cars, attacking rubber tires and brake systems to get at the salt. They search out things moistened by human sweat and eat them ravenously – farm implements, canoe gunnels, paddles, glass bottles, or frying pans.

Writer David Costello was camped in Idaho's Bitter Root Mountains when he awoke to the sound of a porcupine gnawing at the leg of his cot. It had been stored in a smoke-house where salt was used for curing. Another night he chased off five porcupines trying to eat the same cot.

Even pet porcupines can't be trusted to eat only what they're fed. Maynard Cummings, a biologist with the U.S. Fish and Wildlife Service, had a porcupine named Boris. It was particularly fond of potato chips which it often shared with Cummings's children. But after devouring portions of rosebushes and an elm tree in the yard, it developed a taste for furniture and shoes. Cummings eventually released it in the wild.

The porcupine's appetite is well nigh impossible to curb. Yet despite its infuriating habits, it is the porcupine's intriguing armour that has set it apart as an oddball among Canadian wildlife. And like oddballs everywhere, it has attracted widespread attention. It is no real surprise to find a magnificent set of hills on the Manitoba-Saskatchewan border named after the porcupine. The prairies have a healthy population of the creatures, and they are celebrated as well in Saskatchewan's Porcupine River and the town called Porcupine Plain. In the Yukon, one of the country's largest caribou herds is named after the Porcupine River, a tributary of the Yukon River. Porcupine Bay and Cape Porcupine are on the Labrador Sea, across from the porcupine-less province of Newfoundland.

The porcupine's image is impossible to ignore. It is respected for its weaponry, cursed for its appetite, and admired for its sheer eccentricity. Of the world's 600 rodents, the porcupine may well be the most peculiar.

---

1. Reduce the article to a précis of about 300 words. Exchange your version with a classmate's to compare the elements that you considered to be of most importance. Take into account your classmate's comments when you revise your work.

2. Obee's writing is expository rather than argumentative. Imagine that you are to deliver a speech arguing for either the extermination or the protection of the porcupine in a forested recreation area. Using the material in the selection and your own resources, develop a thesis, organize the content, and reach a conclusion;

deliver your speech to a small group. A classmate should present the opposite point of view.

3. Write a letter to the editor of an appropriate periodical, such as a real estate developer's journal, a nature magazine, a hunting and fishing magazine, or a conservation publication. Ensure that your point of view is clear and that your content is detailed. Your topic might be one of the following or one of your own choice:
   • Wild animals in cities should be destroyed/protected.
   • Commercial exploitation of land should/should not be dependent upon environmental considerations.

4. Write a humorous or absurd story in which a porcupine plays an important role. Compose a suitable title. Read your story aloud to a group of your classmates.
   OR
   In a serio-comic tone, write an article proposing that Canada adopt the porcupine, rather than the beaver, as its national symbol. Present your proposal orally to a group of classmates.

po•grom *n.* [Russ., devastation], 1. an organized massacre of Jews, as in Czarist Russia. 2. any similar attack – *Webster's New World Dictionary*

Auschwitz. Belsen. Treblinka. Dachau. The names reverberate in the consciousness of people in the latter half of the twentieth century. Before reading "No News from Auschwitz," discuss in a small group what you have learned about the mass-murder of the Jews during World War II. If you know of any first-hand accounts, whether told in a book or related by a friend or relative, share them with your classmates.

NO NEWS FROM AUSCHWITZ
A. M. Rosenthal

he most terrible thing of all, somehow, was that at Brzezinka the sun was bright and warm, the rows of graceful poplars were lovely to look upon and on the grass near the gates children played.

It all seemed frighteningly wrong, as in a nightmare, that at Brzezinka the sun should ever shine or that there should be light and greenness and the sound of young laughter. It would be fitting if at Brzezinka the sun never shone and the grass withered because this is a place of unutterable terror.

And yet, every day, from all over the world, people come to Brzezinka, quite possibly the most grisly tourist centre on earth. They come for a variety of reasons – to see if it could really have been true, to remind themselves not to forget, to pay homage to the dead by the simple act of looking upon their place of suffering.

Brzezinka is a couple of miles from the better-known southern Polish town of Oswiecim. Oswiecim has about 12,000 inhabitants, is situated about 171 miles from Warsaw and lies in a damp, marshy area at the eastern end of the pass called the Moravian Gate. Brzezinka and Oswiecim together formed part of that minutely organized factory of torture and death that the Nazis called Konzentrationslager Auschwitz.

By now, fourteen years after the last batch of prisoners was herded naked into the gas chambers by dogs and guards, the story of Auschwitz has been told a great many times. Some of the inmates have written of those events of which sane men cannot conceive. Rudolf Franz Ferdinand Hoess, the superintendent of the camp, before he was executed wrote his detailed memoirs of mass exterminations and the experiments on living bodies. Four million people died here, the Poles say.

And so there is no news to report about Auschwitz. There is merely the compulsion to write something about it, a compulsion that grows out of a restless feeling that to have visited Auschwitz and then turned away without having said or written anything would be a most grievous act of discourtesy to those who died there.

Brzezinka and Oswiecim are very quiet places now; the screams can no longer be heard. The tourist walks silently, quickly at first to get it over with and then, as his mind peoples the barracks and the chambers and the dungeons and flogging posts, he walks draggingly. The guide does not say much either, because there is nothing much for him to say after he has pointed.

For every visitor, there is one particular bit of horror that he knows he will never forget. For some it is seeing the rebuilt gas chamber at Oswiecim and being told that this is the "small one." For others it is the fact that at Brzezinka, in the ruins of the gas chambers and the crematoria the Germans blew up when they retreated, there are daisies growing.

There are visitors who gaze blankly at the gas chambers and the furnaces because their minds simply cannot encompass them, but stand shivering before the great mounds of human hair behind the plate glass window or the piles of babies' shoes or the brick cells where men sentenced to death by suffocation were walled up.

One visitor opened his mouth in a silent scream simply at the sight of boxes – great stretches of three-tiered wooden boxes in the women's barracks. They were about six feet wide, about three feet high, and into them from five to ten prisoners were shoved for the night. The guide walks quickly through the barracks. Nothing more to see here.

A brick building where sterilization experiments were carried out on women prisoners. The guide tries the door – it's locked. The visitor is grateful that he does not have to go in, and then flushes with shame.

A long corridor where rows of faces stare from the walls. Thousands of pictures, the photographs of prisoners. They are all dead now, the men and women who stood before the cameras, and they all knew they were to die.

They all stare blank-faced, but one picture, in the middle of a row, seizes the eye and wrenches the mind. A girl, 22 years old, plumply pretty, blonde. She is smiling gently, as at a sweet, treasured thought. What was the thought that passed through her young mind and is now her memorial on the wall of the dead at Auschwitz?

Into the suffocation dungeons the visitor is taken for a moment and feels himself strangling. Another visitor goes in, stumbles out, and crosses herself. There is no place to pray at Auschwitz.

The visitors look pleadingly at each other and say to the guide, "Enough."

There is nothing new to report about Auschwitz. It was a sunny day and the trees were green and at the gates the children played.

———————————◆◆◆◆———————————

1. a) Describe in writing how "No News from Auschwitz" made you feel, and explain why those particular feelings were aroused.
   b) Rosenthal wants to evoke a strong reaction in his readers, even readers who are familiar with the information in his essay. In a small group, share the explanations you wrote in 1(a) and discuss your responses. Consider the appropriateness of the use of restraint, dispassion, and irony in handling such an emotional topic as the persecution of the Jews.
   c) Write a passage about an atrocity such as the Holocaust in which one emotion dominates, e.g., anger, outrage, horror. Read your passage aloud to a few classmates and ask for their opinions on whether you have effectively conveyed the mood you intended.

2. In a few paragraphs, and with specific references to the text, argue that the subject of Rosenthal's essay is universal rather than limited to one time and one group of people.

3. In paragraph six, Rosenthal speaks of his "compulsion to write," attributing it to his desire to treat the dead courteously. Discuss with a classmate what Rosenthal means. Clip a newspaper article that reports on the loss of human life and talk about whether the newspaper's motives are similar to or different from Rosenthal's. When you have come to a conclusion, summarize your views in a paragraph and read it aloud for another group.

London in 1940 was under constant aerial
bombardment. Ask your history teacher or
librarian to help you locate a film or tape
recording made in London during the blitz.
(Ed Murrow's radio broadcasts are well known
examples of such reporting.) Read Bowen's
memoir "London, 1940" and compare her
observations with what you saw or heard.

LONDON, 1940
Elizabeth Bowen

Early September morning in Oxford Street. The smell of charred
dust hangs on what should be crystal pure air. Sun, just up,
floods the once more innocent sky, strikes silver balloons and
the intact building-tops. The whole length of Oxford Street, west to
east, is empty, looks polished like a ballroom, glitters with smashed
glass. Down the distances, natural mists of morning are brown with
the last of smoke. Fumes still come from the shell of a shop. At this
corner where the burst gas main flaming floors high made a scene like
a hell in the night, you still feel heat. The silence is now the enormous
thing – it appears to amaze the street. Sections and blocks have been
roped off; there is no traffic; the men in the helmets say not a person
may pass (but some sneak through). Besides the high explosives that
did the work, this quarter has been seeded with timebombs – so we
are herded, waiting for those to go off. This is the top of Oxford Street,
near where it joins the corner of Hyde Park at Marble Arch.

We people have come up out of the ground, or out from the bottom
floors of the damaged houses: we now see what we heard happen
throughout the night. Roped away from the rest of London we seem
to be on an island – when shall we be taken off? Standing, as might
the risen dead in the doors of tombs, in the mouths of shelters, we

have nothing to do but yawn at each other or down the void of streets, meanwhile rubbing the smoke-smart deeper into our eyes with our dirty fists. . . . It has been a dirty night. The side has been ripped off one near block – the open gash is nothing but dusty, colourless. (As bodies shed blood, buildings shed mousey dust.) Up there the sun strikes a mirror over a mantelpiece; shreds of a carpet sag out over the void. An A.R.P. man, like a chamois, already runs up the debris; we stare. The charred taint thickens everyone's lips and tongues – what we want is bacon and eggs, coffee. We attempt little sorties – "Keep BACK, please! Keep OFF the street!" The hungry try to slake down with smoking. "PLEASE – that cigarette *out!* Main gone – gas all over the place – d'*you* want to blow up London?" Cigarette trodden guiltily into the trodden glass. We loaf on and on in our cave-mouths; the sun goes on and on up. Some of us are dressed, some of us are not: pyjama-legs show below overcoats. There are some Poles, who having lost everything all over again sit down whenever and wherever they can. They are our seniors in this experience; we cannot but watch them. There are two or three unmistakable pairs of disturbed lovers – making one think "Oh yes, how odd – love." There are squads of ageless "residents" from aquarium-like private hotels just round the corner. There are the nomads of two or three nights ago who, having been bombed out of where they were, pitched on this part, to be bombed out again. There is the very old gentleman wrapped up in the blanket, who had been heard to say, humbly, between the blasts in the night, "The truth is, I have outlived my generation. . . . " We are none of us – except perhaps the Poles? – the very very poor: our predicament is not a great predicament. The lady in the fur coat has hair in two stiff little bedroomy grey plaits. She appeals for hair pins: most of us have short hair – pins for her are extracted from one of the Poles' heads. Girls stepping further into the light look into pocket mirrors. "Gosh," they say remotely. Two or three people have, somehow, begun walking when one time-bomb goes off at Marble Arch. The street puffs itself empty; more glass splinters. Everyone laughs.

It is a fine morning and we are still alive.

This is the buoyant view of it – the theatrical sense of safety, the steady breath drawn. We shall be due, at tonight's siren, to feel our hearts once more tighten and sink. Soon after black-out we keep that date with fear. The howling ramping over the darkness, the lurch of the barrage opening, the obscure throb in the air. We *can* go under-ground – but for this to be any good you have to go very deep, and a number of us, fearful of being buried, prefer not to. Our own "things" – tables, chairs, lamps – give one kind of confidence to us who stay in our own paper rooms. But when tonight the throb gathers over the roof we must not remember what we looked at this morning – these fuming utter glissades of ruin. No, these nights in September nowhere is pleasant. Where you stay is your own choice, how you feel is your fight.

However many people have crowded together, each has, while air whistles and solids rock, his or her accesses of solitude. We can do much for each other, but not all. Between bomb and bomb we are all together again: we all guess, more or less, what has been happening to all the others. Chatter bubbles up; or there is a cosy plumping sideways, to doze. Fear is not cumulative: each night it starts from scratch. On the other hand, resistance becomes a habit. And, better, it builds up a general fund.

Autumn seems a funny time to be bombed. By nature it is the hopeful start of the home year. The colours burning in the trees and weed-fires burning in the gardens ought to be enough. Autumn used to be a slow sentimental fête, with an edge of melancholy – the children going back to school, the evenings drawing in. Windows lit up earlier. Lanes in the country, squares in the city crisp with leaves. (This year, leaves are swept up with glass in them.) In autumn, where you live touches the heart – it is the worst time not to be living anywhere. This is the season in which to honour safety.

London feels all this this year most. To save something, she contracts round her wounds. Transport stoppages, roped-off districts, cut-off communications and "dirty" nights now make her a city of villages – almost of village communes. Marylebone is my village. Friends who live outside it I think about but seldom see: *they* are sunk in the life of their own villages. We all have new friends: our neighbours. In Marylebone, shopping just before the black-out or making for home before the bombers begin to fill up the sky, we say, "Well, good luck!" to each other. And every morning after the storm we go out to talk. News comes filtering through from the other villages. They say St. John's Wood had it worse than we did. Camden Town, on the other hand, got off light. Chelsea, it seems, was hot again. They say they brought "one" down on Paddington Green. Has anybody been over to Piccadilly? A man from Hampstead was here a minute ago; he said . . . Mrs. X is a Pimlico woman; she's quite upset. Anybody know how it was in Kilburn? Somebody had a letter from Finsbury Park.

For one bad week, we all turned out on account of time-bombs: exiled. We camped about London in other villages. (That was how I happened to be in Oxford Street, only to be once more dislodged from there.) When we were let home again we were full of stories, spent another morning picking up all the threads. The fishmonger said he had caught sight of me buying milk in Paddington. "What, you were there too?" I asked. "No," he replied, "I've got Finchley people; I was only over in Paddington looking after a friend." We had all detested our week away: for instance, I had been worrying about my typewriter left uncovered in the dust blowing through our suddenly-emptied house;

the fishmonger had been worrying about all that fish of his in the frig, with the power off. It had been necessary for several of us to slip through the barricades from time to time in order to feed cats.

Regent's Park where I live is still, at the time of writing, closed: officially, that is to say, we are not here. Just inside the gates an unexploded bomb makes a boil in the tarmac road. Around three sides of the Park, the Regency terraces look like scenery in an empty theatre: in the silence under the shut facades a week's drift of leaves flitters up and down. At nights, at my end of my terrace, I feel as though I were sleeping in one corner of a deserted palace. I had always placed this Park among the most civilized scenes on earth; the Nash pillars look as brittle as sugar – actually, which is wonderful, they have not cracked; though several of the terraces are gutted – blown-in shutters swing loose, ceilings lie on floors and a premature decay-smell comes from the rooms. A pediment has fallen on to a lawn. Illicitly, leading the existence of ghosts, we overlook the locked park.

Through the railings I watch dahlias blaze out their colour. Leaves fill the empty deck-chairs; in the sunshine water-fowl, used to so much attention, mope round the unpeopled rim of the lake. One morning a boy on a bicycle somehow got inside and bicycled round and round the silence, whistling "It's a Happy, Happy Day." The tune was taken up by six soldiers digging out a bomb. Now and then everything rips across; a detonation rattles remaining windows. The R.E. "suicide squad" detonate, somewhere in the hinterland of this park, bombs dug up elsewhere.

We have no feeling to spare.

---

1. a) Bowen conveys an overall impression of London in 1940 by focussing upon specific details. Select several details and in a group discussion explore how they contribute to the tone of the memoir.
   b) "We have no feeling to spare," writes Bowen. Find two passages that demonstrate the author's assertion, and explain to your group why you chose those particular incidents.
   c) Imagine that you are visiting London in 1940. Write to your family in Canada about your impressions of London and Londoners during the blitz, referring to Bowen's record for information.

2. Bowen often contrasts wartime and peacetime London. Isolate three contrasts and, in a short passage for each, explain their impact.

3. Using your school and community libraries, do some research and

give a short oral presentation to the class (or make a small photo-journal) on the effects of bombing on two of the following: London, Coventry, Berlin, Dresden, Tokyo, Hiroshima, or Shanghai.

4. a) A photograph of a sign proclaiming "We can take it!" is often used to exemplify the attitude of people in wartime London. Cite four passages that express defiance and work them into a radio broadcast that Londoners might have listened to in 1940. Read your broadcast for a small group.

b) Form a group and appoint two members to do research and report on why the German and British governments chose to attack civilian as well as military centres. Was the strategy effective? Discuss the morality of destroying cities and their inhabitants during war.

People have long been fascinated by giants:
Goliath, Cyclops, Antaeus, Jack's giant at the
top of the beanstalk. Working in a small
group, list as many giants as you can and
identify any recurrent elements in the stories
about them. Speculate on what J.G. Ballard
will mention about his drowned giant; compare
your predictions with the story as you read.

THE DROWNED GIANT
J.G. Ballard

On the morning after the storm the body of a drowned giant was washed ashore on the beach five miles to the north-west of the city. The first news of its arrival was brought by a nearby farmer and subsequently confirmed by the local newspaper reporters and the police. Despite this the majority of people, myself among them, remained sceptical, but the return of more and more eye-witnesses attesting to the vast size of the giant was finally too much for our curiosity. The library where my colleagues and I were carrying out our research was almost deserted when we set off for the coast shortly after two o'clock, and throughout the day people continued to leave their offices and shops as accounts of the giant circulated around the city.

By the time we reached the dunes above the beach a substantial crowd had gathered, and we could see the body lying in the shallow water two hundred yards away. At first the estimates of its size seemed greatly exaggerated. It was then at low tide, and almost all the giant's body was exposed, but he appeared to be a little larger than a basking shark. He lay on his back with his arms at his sides, in an attitude of repose, as if asleep on the mirror of wet sand, the reflection of his blanched skin fading as the water receded. In the clear sunlight his body glistened like the white plumage of a sea-bird.

Puzzled by this spectacle, and dissatisfied with the matter-of-fact explanations of the crowd, my friends and I stepped down from the dunes on to the shingle. Everyone seemed reluctant to approach the giant, but half an hour later two fishermen in wading boots walked out across the sand. As their diminutive figures neared the recumbent body a sudden hubbub of conversation broke out among the spectators. The two men were completely dwarfed by the giant. Although his heels were partly submerged in the sand, the feet rose to at least twice the fishermen's height, and we immediately realized that this drowned leviathan had the mass and dimensions of the largest sperm whale.

Three fishing smacks had arrived on the scene and with keels raised remained a quarter of a mile off-shore, the crews watching from the bows. Their discretion deterred the spectators on the shore from wading out across the sand. Impatiently everyone stepped down the dunes and waited on the shingle slopes, eager for a closer view. Around the margins of the figure the sand had been washed away, forming a hollow, as if the giant had fallen out of the sky. The two fishermen were standing between the immense plinths of the feet, waving to us like tourists among the columns of some water-lapped temple on the Nile. For a moment I feared that the giant was merely asleep and might suddenly stir and clap his heels together, but his glazed eyes stared skywards, unaware of the minuscule replicas of himself between his feet.

The fishermen then began a circuit of the corpse, strolling past the long white flanks of the legs. After a pause to examine the fingers of the supine hand, they disappeared from sight between the arm and chest, then re-emerged to survey the head, shielding their eyes as they gazed up at its Grecian profile. The shallow forehead, straight high-bridged nose, and curling lips reminded me of a Roman copy of Praxiteles, and the elegantly formed cartouches of the nostrils emphasized the resemblance to monumental sculpture.

Abruptly there was a shout from the crowd, and a hundred arms pointed towards the sea. With a start I saw that one of the fishermen had climbed on to the giant's chest and was now strolling about and signalling to the shore. There was a roar of surprise and triumph from the crowd, lost in a rushing avalanche of shingle as everyone surged forward across the sand.

As we approached the recumbent figure, which was lying in a pool of water the size of a field, our excited chatter fell away again, subdued by the huge physical dimensions of this moribund colossus. He was stretched out at a slight angle to the shore, his legs carried nearer the beach, and this foreshortening had disguised his true length. Despite the two fishermen standing on his abdomen, the crowd formed itself into a wide circle, groups of three or four people tentatively advancing towards the hands and feet.

My companions and I walked around the seaward side of the giant, whose hips and thorax towered above us like the hull of a stranded ship. His pearl-coloured skin, distended by immersion in salt water, masked the contours of the enormous muscles and tendons. We passed below the left knee, which was flexed slightly, threads of damp sea-weed clinging to its sides. Draped loosely across the midriff, and pre-serving a tenuous propriety, was a shawl of heavy open-weaved material, bleached to a pale yellow by the water. A strong odour of brine came from the garment as it steamed in the sun, mingled with the sweet but potent scent of the giant's skin.

We stopped by his shoulder and gazed up at the motionless profile. The lips were parted slightly, the open eye cloudy and occluded, as if injected with some blue milky liquid, but the delicate arches of the nostrils and eyebrows invested the face with an ornate charm that belied the brutish power of the chest and shoulders.

The ear was suspended in mid-air over our heads like a sculptured doorway. As I raised my hand to touch the pendulous lobe someone appeared over the edge of the forehead and shouted down at me. Startled by this apparition, I stepped back, and then saw that a group of youths had climbed up on to his face and were jostling each other in and out of the orbits.

People were now clambering all over the giant, whose reclining arms provided a double stairway. From the palms they walked along the forearms to the elbow and then crawled over the distended belly of the biceps to the flat promenade of the pectoral muscles which covered the upper half of the smooth hairless chest. From here they climbed up on to the face, hand over hand along the lips and nose, or forayed down the abdomen to meet others who had straddled the ankles and were patrolling the twin columns of the thighs.

We continued our circuit through the crowd, and stopped to examine the outstretched right hand. A small pool of water lay in the palm, like the residue of another world, now being kicked away by the people ascending the arm. I tried to read the palm-lines that grooved the skin, searching for some clue to the giant's character, but the distension of the tissues had almost obliterated them, carrying away all trace of the giant's identity and his last tragic predicament. The huge muscles and wrist-bones of the hand seemed to deny any sensitivity to their owner, but the delicate flexion of the fingers and the well-tended nails, each cut symmetrically to within six inches of the quick, argued a certain refinement of temperament, illustrated in the Grecian features of the face, on which the townsfolk were now sitting like flies.

One youth was even standing, arms wavering at his sides, on the very tip of the nose, shouting down at his companions, but the face of the giant still retained its massive composure.

Returning to the shore, we sat down on the shingle, and watched the continuous stream of people arriving from the city. Some six or seven fishing boats had collected off-shore, and their crews waded in through the shallow water for a closer look at this enormous storm-catch. Later a party of police appeared and made a half-hearted attempt to cordon off the beach, but after walking up to the recumbent figure any such thoughts left their minds, and they went off together with bemused backward glances.

An hour later there were a thousand people present on the beach, at least two hundred of them standing or sitting on the giant, crowded along his arms and legs or circulating in a ceaseless mêlée across his chest and stomach. A large gang of youths occupied the head, toppling each other off the cheeks and sliding down the smooth planes of the jaw. Two or three straddled the nose, and another crawled into one of the nostrils, from which he emitted barking noises like a dog.

That afternoon the police returned, and cleared a way through the crowd for a party of scientific experts – authorities on gross anatomy and marine biology – from the university. The gang of youths and most of the people on the giant climbed down, leaving behind a few hardy spirits perched on the tips of the toes and on the forehead. The experts strode around the giant, heads nodding in vigorous consultation, preceded by the policemen who pushed back the press of spectators. When they reached the outstretched hand the senior officer offered to assist them up on to the palm, but the experts hastily demurred.

After they returned to the shore, the crowd once more climbed on to the giant, and was in full possession when we left at five o'clock, covering the arms and legs like a dense flock of gulls sitting on the corpse of a large fish.

I next visited the beach three days later. My friends at the library had returned to their work, and delegated to me the task of keeping the giant under observation and preparing a report. Perhaps they sensed my particular interest in the case, and it was certainly true that I was eager to return to the beach. There was nothing necrophilic about this, for to all intents the giant was still alive for me, indeed more alive than many of the people watching him. What I found so fascinating was partly his immense scale, the huge volumes of space occupied by his arms and legs, which seemed to confirm the identity of my own miniature limbs, but above all the mere categorical fact of his existence. Whatever else in our lives might be open to doubt, the giant, dead or alive, existed in an absolute sense, providing a glimpse into a world of similar absolutes of which we spectators on the beach were such imperfect and puny copies.

When I arrived at the beach the crowd was considerably smaller, and some two or three hundred people sat on the shingle, picnicking and watching the groups of visitors who walked out across the sand. The successive tides had carried the giant nearer the shore, swinging his head and shoulders towards the beach, so that he seemed doubly to gain in size, his huge body dwarfing the fishing boats beached beside his feet. The uneven contours of the beach had pushed his spine into a slight arch, expanding his chest and tilting back the head, forcing him into a more expressly heroic posture. The combined effects of seawater and the tumefaction of the tissues had given the face a sleeker and less youthful look. Although the vast proportions of the features made it impossible to assess the age and character of the giant, on my previous visit his classically modelled mouth and nose suggested that he had been a young man of discreet and modest temper. Now, however, he appeared to be at least in early middle age. The puffy cheeks, thicker nose and temples, and narrowing eyes gave him a look of well-fed maturity that even now hinted at a growing corruption to come.

This accelerated post-mortem development of the giant's character, as if the latent elements of his personality had gained sufficient momentum during his life to discharge themselves in a brief final resumé, continued to fascinate me. It marked the beginning of the giant's surrender to that all-demanding system of time in which the rest of humanity finds itself, and of which, like the million twisted ripples of a fragmented whirlpool, our finite lives are the concluding products. I took up my position on the shingle directly opposite the giant's head, from where I could see the new arrivals and the children clambering over the legs and arms.

Among the morning's visitors were a number of men in leather jackets and cloth caps, who peered up critically at the giant with a professional eye, pacing out his dimensions and making rough calculations in the sand with spars of driftwood. I assumed them to be from the public works department and other municipal bodies, no doubt wondering how to dispose of this gargantuan piece of jetsam.

Several rather more smartly attired individuals, circus proprietors and the like, also appeared on the scene, and strolled slowly around the giant, hands in the pockets of their long overcoats, saying nothing to one another. Evidently its bulk was too great even for their matchless enterprise. After they had gone the children continued to run up and down the arms and legs, and the youths wrestled with each other over the supine face, the damp sand from their feet covering the white skin.

The following day I deliberately postponed my visit until the late afternoon, and when I arrived there were fewer than fifty or sixty people sitting on the shingle. The giant had been carried still closer to the shore, and was now little more than seventy-five yards away, his feet crushing the palisade of a rotting breakwater. The slope of the firmer sand tilted his body towards the sea, and the bruised face was averted in an almost conscious gesture. I sat down on a large metal winch which had been shackled to a concrete caisson above the shingle, and looked down at the recumbent figure.

His blanched skin had now lost its pearly translucence and was spattered with dirty sand which replaced that washed away by the night tide. Clumps of seaweed filled the intervals between the fingers and a collection of litter and cuttle bones lay in the crevices below the hips and knees. But despite this, and the continuous thickening of his features, the giant still retained his magnificent Homeric stature. The enormous breadth of the shoulders, and the huge columns of the arms and legs, still carried the figure into another dimension, and the giant seemed a more authentic image of one of the drowned Argonauts or heroes of the Odyssey than the conventional human-sized portrait previously in my mind.

I stepped down on to the sand, and walked between the pools of water towards the giant. Two small boys were sitting in the well of the ear, and at the far end a solitary youth stood perched high on one of the toes, surveying me as I approached. As I had hoped when delaying my visit, no one else paid any attention to me, and the people on the shore remained huddled beneath their coats.

The giant's supine right hand was covered with broken shells and sand, in which a score of footprints were visible. The rounded bulk of the hip towered above me, cutting off all sight of the sea. The sweetly acrid odour I had noticed before was now more pungent, and through the opaque skin I could see the serpentine coils of congealed blood vessels. However repellent it seemed, this ceaseless metamorphosis, a visible life in death, alone permitted me to set foot on the corpse.

Using the jutting thumb as a stair-rail, I climbed up on to the palm and began my ascent. The skin was harder than I expected, barely yielding to my weight. Quickly I walked up the sloping forearm and the bulging balloon of the biceps. The face of the drowned giant loomed to my right, the cavernous nostrils and huge flanks of the cheeks like the cone of some freakish volcano.

Safely rounding the shoulder, I stepped out on to the broad promenade of the chest, across which the bony ridges of the rib-cage lay like huge rafters. The white skin was dappled by the darkening bruises of countless footprints, in which the patterns of individual heel-marks were clearly visible. Someone had built a small sandcastle on the centre of the sternum, and I climbed on to this partly demolished structure to give myself a better view of the face.

The two children had now scaled the ear and were pulling themselves into the right orbit, whose blue globe, completely occluded by some milk-coloured fluid, gazed sightlessly past their miniature forms. Seen obliquely from below, the face was devoid of all grace and repose, the drawn mouth and raised chin propped up by its gigantic slings of muscles resembling the torn prow of a colossal wreck. For the first time I became aware of the extremity of this last physical agony of the giant, no less painful for his unawareness of the collapsing musculature and tissues. The absolute isolation of the ruined figure, cast like an abandoned ship upon the empty shore, almost out of sound of the waves, transformed his face into a mask of exhaustion and helplessness.

As I stepped forward, my foot sank into a trough of soft tissue, and a gust of fetid gas blew through an aperture between the ribs. Retreating from the fouled air, which hung like a cloud over my head, I turned towards the sea to clear my lungs. To my surprise I saw that the giant's left hand had been amputated.

I stared with bewilderment at the blackening stump, while the solitary youth reclining on his aerial perch a hundred feet away surveyed me with a sanguinary eye.

This was only the first of a sequence of depredations. I spent the following two days in the library, for some reason reluctant to visit the shore, aware that I had probably witnessed the approaching end of a magnificent illusion. When I next crossed the dunes and set foot on the shingle the giant was litle more than twenty yards away, and with this close proximity to the rough pebbles all traces had vanished of the magic which once surrounded his distant wave-washed form. Despite his immense size, the bruises and dirt that covered his body made him appear merely human in scale, his vast dimensions only increasing his vulnerability.

His right hand and foot had been removed, dragged up the slope and trundled away by cart. After questioning the small group of people huddled by the breakwater, I gathered that a fertilizer company and a cattle food manufacturer were responsible.

The giant's remaining foot rose into the air, a steel hawser fixed to the large toe, evidently in preparation for the following day. The surrounding beach had been disturbed by a score of workmen, and deep ruts marked the ground where the hands and foot had been hauled away. A dark brackish fluid leaked from the stumps, and stained the sand and the white bones of the cuttlefish. As I walked down the shingle I noticed that a number of jocular slogans, swastikas and other signs had been cut into the grey skin, as if the mutilation of this motionless colossus had released a sudden flood of repressed spite. The lobe of one of the ears was pierced by a spear of timber, and a small fire had burnt out in the centre of the chest, blackening the surrounding skin. The fine wood ash was still being scattered by the wind.

A foul smell enveloped the cadaver, the undisguisable signature of putrefaction, which had at last driven away the usual gathering of youths. I returned to the shingle and climbed up on to the winch. The giant's swollen cheeks had now almost closed his eyes, drawing the lips back in a monumental gape. The once straight Grecian nose had been twisted and flattened, stamped into the ballooning face by countless heels.

When I visited the beach the following day I found, almost with relief, that the head had been removed.

Some weeks elapsed before I made my next journey to the beach, and by then the human likeness I had noticed earlier had vanished again. On close inspection the recumbent thorax and abdomen were unmistakably manlike, but as each of the limbs was chopped off, first at the knee and elbow, and then at shoulder and thigh, the carcass resembled that of any headless sea-animal – whale or whale-shark. With this loss of identity, and the few traces of personality that had clung tenuously to the figure, the interest of the spectators expired, and the foreshore was deserted except for an elderly beachcomber and the watchman sitting in the doorway of the contractor's hut.

A loose wooden scaffolding had been erected around the carcass, from which a dozen ladders swung in the wind, and the surrounding sand was littered with coils of rope, long metal-handled knives and grappling irons, the pebbles oily with blood and pieces of bone and skin.

I nodded to the watchman, who regarded me dourly over his brazier of burning coke. The whole area was pervaded by the pungent smell of huge squares of blubber being simmered in a vat behind the hut.

Both the thigh-bones had been removed, with the assistance of a small crane draped in the gauze-like fabric which had once covered the waist of the giant, and the open sockets gaped like barn doors. The upper arms, collar bones and pudenda had likewise been dispatched. What remained of the skin over the thorax and abdomen had been marked out in parallel strips with a tar brush, and the first five or six sections had been pared away from the midriff, revealing the great arch of the rib-cage.

As I left, a flock of gulls wheeled down from the sky and alighted on the beach, picking at the stained sand with ferocious cries.

Several months later, when the news of his arrival had been generally forgotten, various pieces of the body of the dismembered giant began to reappear all over the city. Most of these were bones, which the fertilizer manufacturers had found too difficult to crush, and their massive size, and the huge tendons and discs of cartilage attached to their joints, immediately identified them. For some reason, these disembodied fragments seemed better to convey the essence of the giant's original magnificence than the bloated appendages that had been subsequently amputated. As I looked across the road at the premises of the largest wholesale merchants in the meat market, I recognized the two enormous thighbones on either side of the doorway. They towered over the porters' heads like the threatening megaliths of some primitive druidical religion, and I had a sudden vision of the giant climbing to his knees upon these bare bones and striding away through the streets of the city, picking up the scattered fragments of himself on his return journey to the sea.

A few days later I saw the left humerus lying in the entrance to one of the shipyards (its twin for several years lay on the mud among the piles below the harbour's principal commercial wharf). In the same week the mummified right hand was exhibited on a carnival float during the annual pageant of the guilds.

The lower jaw, typically, found its way to the museum of natural history. The remainder of the skull has disappeared, but is probably still lurking in the waste grounds or private gardens of the city – quite recently, while sailing down the river, I noticed two ribs of the giant forming a decorative arch in a waterside garden, possibly confused with the jaw-bones of a whale. A large square of tanned and tattooed skin, the size of an Indian blanket, forms a backcloth to the dolls and masks in a novelty shop near the amusement park, and I have no doubt that elsewhere in the city, in the hotels or golf clubs, the mummified nose or ears of the giant hang from the wall above a fireplace. As for the immense pizzle, this ends its days in the freak museum of a circus which travels up and down the north-west. This monumental apparatus, stunning in its proportions and sometime potency, occupies a complete booth to itself. The irony is that it is wrongly identified as that of a whale, and indeed most people, even those who first saw him cast up on the shore after the storm, now remember the giant, if at all, as a large sea beast.

The remainder of the skeleton, stripped of all flesh, still rests on the sea-shore, the clutter of bleached ribs like the timbers of a derelict ship. The contractor's hut, the crane and the scaffolding have been removed, and the sand being driven into the bay along the coast has buried the pelvis and backbone. In the winter the high curved bones are deserted, battered by the breaking waves, but in the summer they provide an excellent perch for the sea-wearying gulls.

1. Write your personal response to the story, exploring how it made you feel and the possible origins of your feelings.

2. The narrator's report covers the span of several weeks. Working with a classmate, role-play a series of conversations between the narrator and one of his "friends at the library," in which you reveal the narrator's feelings about the giant and his gradual decay.

3. In this story, the author adopts a matter-of-fact tone that seems at odds with the peculiarity he is describing. With a classmate, discuss, with specific references to the text, the effects Ballard achieves through the tone he has chosen. Include your piece in your writing folder.

4. The corpse of the giant is subjected to progressively worse indignities.

a) Make note of these and find appropriate quotations for each stage in the corpse's degeneration.

b) In a group, discuss the author's reason for cataloguing so specifically the effects of people and time upon the giant.

c) Extend your discussion to consider whether Ballard has a purpose, other than to entertain, in writing "The Drowned Giant." If you think that the story has a theme or themes, state them and write an argument for your decision.

5. a) Ballard leaves much unsaid in "The Drowned Giant." Write down five questions about events in the story that you would like to have answered.

b) Work with a classmate and try to answer each other's questions. Together, compare your answers, discuss whether they satisfy your curiosity, and speculate on why the author has left many details to the reader's imagination.

HISTORY LESSON
Arthur C. Clarke

No one could remember when the tribe had begun its long journey. The land of great rolling plains that had been its first home was now no more than a half-forgotten dream.

For many years Shann and his people had been fleeing through a country of low hills and sparkling lakes, and now the mountains lay ahead. This summer they must cross them to the southern lands. There was little time to lose. The white terror that had come down from the Poles, grinding continents to dust and freezing the very air before it, was less than a day's march behind.

Shann wondered if the glaciers could climb the mountains ahead, and within his heart he dared to kindle a little flame of hope. This might prove a barrier against which even the remorseless ice would batter in vain. In the southern lands of which the legends spoke, his people might find refuge at last.

It took weeks to discover a pass through which the tribe and the animals could travel. When midsummer came, they had camped in a lonely valley where the air was thin and the stars shone with a brilliance no one had ever seen before.

The summer was waning when Shann took his two sons and went ahead to explore the way. For three days they climbed, and for three nights slept as best they could on the freezing rocks, and on the fourth morning there was nothing ahead but a gentle rise to a cairn of grey stones built by other travellers, centuries ago.

Shann felt himself trembling, and not with cold, as they walked toward the little pyramid of stones. His sons had fallen behind. No one spoke, for too much was at stake. In a little while they would know if all their hopes had been betrayed.

To east and west, the wall of mountains curved away as if embracing the land beneath. Below lay endless miles of undulating plain, with a great river swinging across it in tremendous loops. It was a fertile land; one in which the tribe could raise crops knowing that there would be no need to flee before the harvest came.

Then Shann lifted his eyes to the south, and saw the doom of all his hopes. For there at the edge of the world glimmered that deadly light he had seen so often to the north – the glint of ice below the horizon.

There was no way forward. Through all the years of flight, the glaciers from the south had been advancing to meet them. Soon they would be crushed beneath the moving walls of ice . . .

Southern glaciers did not reach the mountains until a generation later. In that last summer the sons of Shann carried the sacred treasures of the tribe to the lonely cairn overlooking the plain. The ice that had once gleamed below the horizon was now almost at their feet. By spring it would be splintering against the mountain walls.

No one understood the treasures now. They were from a past too distant for the understanding of any man alive. Their origins were lost in the mists that surrounded the Golden Age, and how they had come at last into the possession of this wandering tribe was a story that now would never be told. For it was the story of a civilization that had passed beyond recall.

Once, all these pitiful relics had been treasured for some good reason, and now they had become sacred though their meaning had long been lost. The print in the old books had faded centuries ago though much of the lettering was still visible – if there had been any to read it. But many generations had passed since anyone had had a use for a set of seven-figure logarithms, an atlas of the world, and the score of Sibelius's Seventh Symphony printed, according to the fly-leaf, by H. K. Chu and Sons, at the City of Pekin in the year 2371 A.D.

The old books were placed reverently in the little crypt that had been made to receive them. There followed a motley collection of fragments – gold and platinum coins, a broken telephoto lens, a watch, a cold-light lamp, a microphone, the cutter from an electric razor, some midget radio tubes, the flotsam that had been left behind when the great tide of civilization had ebbed forever.

All these treasures were carefully stowed away in their resting place. Then came three more relics, the most sacred of all because the least understood.

The first was a strangely shaped piece of metal, showing the colouration of intense heat. It was, in its way, the most pathetic of all these symbols from the past, for it told of man's greatest achievement and of the future he might have known. The mahogany stand on which it was mounted bore a silver plate with the inscription:

Auxiliary Igniter from Starboard Jet
Spaceship "Morning Star"
Earth-Moon, A.D. 1985

Next followed another miracle of the ancient science – a sphere of transparent plastic with strangely shaped pieces of metal imbedded in it. At its centre was a tiny capsule of synthetic radio-element, surrounded by the converting screens that shifted its radiation far down the spectrum. As long as the material remained active, the sphere would be a tiny radio transmitter, broadcasting power in all directions. Only a few of these spheres had ever been made. They had been designed as perpetual beacons to mark the orbits of the asteroids. But man had never reached the asteroids and the beacons had never been used.

Last of all was a flat, circular tin, wide in comparison with its depth. It was heavily sealed, and rattled when shaken. The tribal lore predicted that disaster would follow if it was ever opened, and no one knew that it held one of the great works of art of nearly a thousand years before.

The work was finished. The two men rolled the stones back into place and slowly began to descend the mountainside. Even to the last, man had given some thought to the future and had tried to preserve something for posterity.

That winter the great waves of ice began their first assault on the mountains, attacking from north and south. The foothills were overwhelmed in the first onslaught, and the glaciers ground them into dust. But the mountains stood firm, and when the summer came the ice retreated for a while.

So, winter after winter, the battle continued, and the roar of the avalanches, the grinding of rock and the explosions of splintering ice filled the air with tumult. No war of man's had been fiercer than this, and even man's battles had not quite engulfed the globe as this had done.

At last the tidal waves of ice began to subside and to creep slowly down the flanks of the mountains they had never quite subdued. The valleys and passes were still firmly in their grip. It was stalemate. The glaciers had met their match, but their defeat was too late to be of any use to man.

So the centuries passed, and presently there happened something that must occur once at least in the history of every world in the universe, no matter how remote and lonely it may be.

The ship from Venus came five thousand years too late, but its crew knew nothing of this. While still many millions of miles away, the telescopes had seen the great shroud of ice that made Earth the most brilliant object in the sky next to the sun itself.

Here and there the dazzling sheet was marred by black specks that revealed the presence of almost buried mountains. That was all. The rolling oceans, the plains and forests, the deserts and lakes – all that had been the world of man was sealed beneath the ice, perhaps forever.

The ship closed in to Earth and established an orbit less than a thousand miles away. For five days it circled the planet, while cameras recorded all that was left to see and a hundred instruments gathered information that would give the Venusian scientists many years of work.

An actual landing was not intended. There seemed little purpose in it. But on the sixth day the picture changed. A panoramic monitor, driven to the limit of its amplification, detected the dying radiation of the five-thousand-year-old beacon. Through all the centuries, it had been sending out its signals with ever-failing strength as its radioactive heart steadily weakened.

The monitor locked on the beacon frequency. In the control room, a bell clamoured for attention. A little later, the Venusian ship broke free from its orbit and slanted down toward Earth, toward a range of mountains that still towered proudly above the ice, and to a cairn of grey stones that the years had scarcely touched . . . .

The great disk of the sun blazed fiercely in a sky no longer veiled with mist, for the clouds that had once hidden Venus had now completely gone. Whatever force had caused the change in the sun's radiation had doomed one civilization, but had given birth to another. Less than five thousand years before, the half-savage people of Venus had seen sun and stars for the first time. Just as the science of Earth had begun with astronomy, so had that of Venus, and on the warm, rich world that man had never seen progress had been incredibly rapid.

Perhaps the Venusians had been lucky. They never knew the Dark Age that held man enchained for a thousand years. They missed the long detour into chemistry and mechanics but came at once to the more fundamental laws of radiation physics. In the time that man had taken to progress from the Pyramids to the rocket-propelled spaceship, the Venusians had passed from the discovery of agriculture to antigravity itself – the ultimate secret that man had never learned.

The warm ocean that still bore most of the young planet's life rolled its breakers languidly against the sandy shore. So new was this continent that the very sands were coarse and gritty. There had not yet been time enough for the sea to wear them smooth.

The scientists lay half in the water, their beautiful reptilian bodies gleaming in the sunlight. The greatest minds of Venus had gathered on this shore from all the islands of the planet. What they were going to hear they did not know, except that it concerned the Third World and the mysterious race that had peopled it before the coming of the ice.

The Historian was standing on the land, for the instruments he wished to use had no love of water. By his side was a large machine which attracted many curious glances from his colleagues. It was clearly concerned with optics, for a lens system projected from it toward a screen of white material a dozen yards away.

The Historian began to speak. Briefly he recapitulated what little had been discovered concerning the Third Planet and its people.

He mentioned the centuries of fruitless research that had failed to interpret a single word of the writings of Earth. The planet had been inhabited by a race of great technical ability. That, at least, was proved by the few pieces of machinery that had been found in the cairn upon the mountain.

"We do not know why so advanced a civilization came to an end," he observed. "Almost certainly, it had sufficient knowledge to survive an Ice Age. There must have been some other factors of which we know nothing. Possibly disease or racial degeneration may have been responsible. It has even been suggested that the tribal conflicts endemic to our own species in prehistoric times may have continued on the Third Planet after the coming of technology.

"Some philosophers maintain that knowledge of machinery does not necessarily imply a high degree of civilization, and it is theoretically possible to have wars in a society possessing mechanical power, flight, and even radio. Such a conception is alien to our thoughts, but we must admit its possibility. It would certainly account for the downfall of the lost race.

"It has always been assumed that we should never know anything of the physical form of the creatures who lived on Planet Three. For centuries our artists have been depicting scenes from the history of the dead world, peopling it with all manner of fantastic beings. Most of these creations have resembled us more or less closely, though it has often been pointed out that because *we* are reptiles it does not follow that all intelligent life must necessarily be reptilian.

"We now know the answer to one of the most baffling problems of history. At last, after hundreds of years of research, we have discovered the exact form and nature of the ruling life on the Third Planet."

There was a murmur of astonishment from the assembled scientists. Some were so taken aback that they disappeared for a while into the comfort of the ocean, as all Venusians were apt to do in moments of stress. The Historian waited until his colleagues re-emerged into the element they so disliked. He himself was quite comfortable, thanks to the tiny sprays that were continually playing over his body. With their help he could live on land for many hours before having to return to the ocean.

The excitement slowly subsided and the lecturer continued:

"One of the most puzzling of the objects found on Planet Three was a flat metal container holding a great length of transparent plastic material, perforated at the edges and wound tightly into a spool. This transparent tape at first seemed quite featureless, but an examination with the new subelectronic microscope has shown that this is not the case. Along the surface of the material, invisible to our eyes but perfectly clear under the correction radiation, are literally thousands of tiny pictures. It is believed that they were imprinted on the material by some chemical means, and have faded with the passage of time.

"These pictures apparently form a record of life as it was on the Third Planet at the height of its civilization. They are not independent. Consecutive pictures are almost identical, differing only in the detail of movement. The purpose of such a record is obvious. It is only necessary to project the scenes in rapid succession to give an illusion of continuous movement. We have made a machine to do this, and I have here an exact reproduction of the picture sequence.

"The scenes you are now going to witness take us back many thousands of years, to the great days of our sister planet. They show a complex civilization, many of whose activities we can only dimly understand. Life seems to have been very violent and energetic, and much that you will see is quite baffling.

"It is clear that the Third Planet was inhabited by a number of different species, none of them reptilian. That is a blow to our pride, but the conclusion is inescapable. The dominant type of life appears to have been a two-armed biped. It walked upright and covered its body with some flexible material, possibly for protection against the cold, since even before the Ice Age the planet was at a much lower temperature than our own world. But I will not try your patience any further. You will now see the record of which I have been speaking."

A brilliant light flashed from the projector. There was a gentle whirring, and on the screen appeared hundreds of strange beings moving rather jerkily to and fro. The picture expanded to embrace one of the creatures, and the scientists could see that the Historian's description had been correct.

The creature possessed two eyes, set rather close together, but the other facial adornments were a little obscure. There was a large orifice in the lower portion of the head that was continually opening and closing. Possibly it had something to do with the creature's breathing.

The scientists watched spellbound as the strange being became involved in a series of fantastic adventures. There was an incredibly violent conflict with another, slightly different creature. It seemed certain that they must both be killed, but when it was all over neither seemed any the worse.

Then came a furious drive over miles of country in a four-wheeled mechanical device which was capable of extraordinary feats of locomotion. The ride ended in a city packed with other vehicles moving in all directions at breathtaking speeds. No one was surprised to see two of the machines meet head-on with devastating results.

After that, events became even more complicated. It was now quite obvious that it would take many years of research to analyse and understand all that was happening. It was also clear that the record was a work of art, somewhat stylized, rather than an exact reproduction of life as it actually had been on the Third Planet.

Most of the scientists felt themselves completely dazed when the sequence of pictures came to an end. There was a final flurry of motion, in which the creature that had been the centre of interest became involved in some tremendous but incomprehensible catastrophe. The picture contracted to a circle, centred on the creature's head.

The last scene of all was an expanded view of its face, obviously expressing some powerful emotion. But whether it was rage, grief, defiance, resignation, or some other feeling could not be guessed. The picture vanished. For a moment some lettering appeared on the screen, then it was all over.

For several minutes there was complete silence, save for the lapping of the waves upon the sand. The scientists were too stunned to speak. The fleeting glimpse of Earth's civilization had had a shattering effect on their minds. Then little groups began to start talking together, first in whispers and then more and more loudly as the implications of what they had seen became clearer. Presently the Historian called for attention and addressed the meeting again.

"We are now planning," he said, "a vast program of research to extract all available knowledge from this record. Thousands of copies are being made for distribution to all workers. You will appreciate the problems involved. The psychologists in particular have an immense task confronting them.

"But I do not doubt that we shall succeed. In another generation, who can say what we may not have learned of this wonderful race? Before we leave, let us look again at our remote cousins, whose wisdom may have surpassed our own but of whom so little has survived."

Once more the final picture flashed on the screen, motionless this time, for the projector had been stopped. With something like awe, the scientists gazed at the still figure from the past, while in turn the little biped stared back at them with its characteristic expression of arrogant bad temper.

For the rest of time it would symbolize the human race. The psychologists of Venus would analyse its actions and watch its every movement until they could reconstruct its mind. Thousands of books would be written about it. Intricate philosophies would be contrived to account for its behaviour.

But all this labour, all this research, would be utterly in vain. Perhaps the proud and lonely figure on the screen was smiling sardonically at the scientists who were starting on their age-long fruitless quest.

Its secret would be safe as long as the universe endured, for no one now would ever read the lost language of Earth. Millions of times in the ages to come those last few words would flash across the screen, and none could ever guess their meaning:

A Walt Disney Production

---

1. a) Although Clarke's title refers to one history lesson, there are clearly several lessons to be learned from the story. In a small group, identify the lessons and decide, in your view, which is the most significant.

   b) Choose one of the lessons your group has identified and plan an essay that argues for or against the idea. Your outline should include a thesis paragraph and supporting arguments in point form.

2. a) Shann's descendants place a miscellany of items under the cairn. In a small group, talk about why Clarke selected those particular items as the "flotsam" of "the great tide of civilization."

   b) Make a list of ten items that, as the flotsam of our civilization, would make an ironic comment upon its accomplishments. Justify your choice in a group discussion, and then as a group decide upon a mutually acceptable list of ten objects. Compare your list with those of other groups.

3. "History Lesson" concludes with a "twist in the tale" – a surprise ending. In a short expository piece, state which elements of the story are clarified by its ending and describe the significance they have assumed.

4. Identify the different stages of the narrative and, in a paragraph, explain how the "cairn of grey stones" is used as a unifying device.

5. Watch a cartoon of your own choice. Taking the stance of a Venusian scientist, write a learned paper about your interpretation

of life on the "Third Planet" based on what you see in the cartoon. (You may first wish to read Bergen Evans's "Nursery
Crimes," p. 161, a mock-learned paper on children's verse.)
Present your paper to an assembly of your colleagues, answering
any questions they may have about your theories.

WILL SOMEONE PLEASE HICCUP MY PAT?

William Spooner Donald

*O*ne afternoon nearly a hundred years ago the October wind gusted merrily down Oxford's High Street. Hatless and helpless, a white-haired clergyman with pink cherubic features uttered his plaintive cry for aid. As an athletic youngster chased the spinning topper, other bystanders smiled delightedly – they had just heard at first hand the latest "Spoonerism."

My revered relative William Archibald Spooner was born in 1844, the son of a Staffordshire county court judge. As a young man, he was handicapped by a poor physique, a stammer, and weak eyesight; at first, his only possible claim to future fame lay in the fact that he was an albino, with very pale blue eyes and white hair tinged slightly yellow.

But nature compensated the weakling by blessing him with a brilliant intellect. By 1868 he had been appointed a lecturer at New College, Oxford. Just then he would have been a caricaturist's dream with his freakish looks, nervous manner, and peculiar mental kink that caused him – in his own words – to "make occasional felicities in verbal diction."

Victorian Oxford was a little world of its own where life drifted gently by; a world where splendid intellectuals lived in their ivory towers of Latin, Euclid, and Philosophy; a world where it was always a sunny summer afternoon in a countryside, where Spooner admitted he loved to "pedal gently round on a well-boiled icicle."

As the years passed, Spooner grew, probably without himself being aware of the fact, into a "character." A hard worker himself, he detested idleness and is on record as having rent some lazybones with the gem, "You have hissed all my mystery lessons, and completely tasted two whole worms."

With his kindly outlook on life, it was almost natural for him to take holy orders; he was ordained a deacon in 1872 and a priest in 1875. His unique idiosyncrasy never caused any serious trouble and merely made him more popular. On one occasion, in New College chapel in 1879, he announced smilingly that the next hymn would be "Number One seven five – Kinkering Kongs their Titles Take." Other congregations were treated to such jewels as " . . . Our Lord, we know, is a shoving Leopard . . . " and " . . . All of us have in our hearts a half-warmed fish to lead a better life . . . . "

Spooner often preached in the little village churches around Oxford and once delivered an eloquent address on the subject of Aristotle. No doubt the sermon contained some surprising information for his rustic congregation. For after Spooner had left the pulpit, an idea seemed to occur to him, and he hopped back up the steps again.

"Excuse me, dear brethren," he announced brightly, "I just want to say that in my sermon whenever I mentioned Aristotle, I should have said Saint Paul."

By 1885 the word "Spoonerism" was in colloquial use in Oxford circles, and a few years later, in general use all over England. If the dividing line between truth and myth is often only a hairsbreadth, does it really matter? One story that has been told concerns an optician's shop in London. Spooner is reputed to have entered and asked to see a "signifying glass." The optician registered polite bewilderment.

"Just an ordinary signifying glass," repeated Spooner, perhaps surprised at the man's obtuseness.

"I'm afraid we haven't one in stock, but I'll make inquiries right away, sir," said the shopkeeper, playing for time.

"Oh, don't bother, it doesn't magnify, it doesn't magnify," said Spooner airily, and walked out.

Fortunately for Spooner, he made the right choice when he met his wife-to-be. He was thirty-four years old when he married Frances Goodwin in 1878. The marriage was a happy one, and they had one son and four daughters. Mrs. Spooner was tall, good-looking girl, and on one occasion the family went on a short holiday in Switzerland. The "genial Dean," as he was then called, took a keen interest in geology, and in no time at all he had mastered much information and many technical definitions on the subject of glaciers.

One day at lunchtime the younger folk were worried because their parents had not returned from a long walk. When Spooner finally appeared with his wife, his explanation was: "We strolled up a long valley, and when we turned a corner we found ourselves completely surrounded by erotic blacks."

He was, of course, referring to "erratic blocks," or large boulders left around after the passage of a glacier.

In 1903 Spooner was appointed Warden of New College, the highest possible post for a Fellow. One day walking across the quadrangle, he met a certain Mr. Casson, who had just been elected a Fellow of New College.

"Do come to dinner tonight," said Spooner, "we are welcoming our new Fellow, Mr. Casson."

"But, my dear Warden, I *am* Casson," was the surprised reply.

"Never mind, never mind, come along all the same," said Spooner tactfully.

On another occasion in later years when his eyesight was really very bad, Spooner found himself seated next to a most elegant lady at dinner. In a casual moment the latter put her lily-white hand onto the polished table, and Spooner, in an even more casual manner, pronged her hand with his fork, remarking genially, "My bread, I think."

In 1924 Spooner retired as Warden. He had established an astonishing record of continuous residence at New College for sixty-two years first as undergraduate, then as Fellow, then Dean, and finally as Warden. His death in 1930, at the age of eighty-six, was a blushing crow to collectors of those odd linguistic transpositions known by then throughout the English-speaking world as Spoonerisms.

THE POSSIBILITY OF ANYTHING

I am too much of a sceptic to deny the possibility of anything.
                        T.H. Huxley

Most of us have wished for a glimpse of the future so that we might know how our hopes and plans will turn out. The fiction and non-fiction you will read in this unit have in common a similar concern with possibility and consequence. Our culture is full of little truisms that offer common-sense advice about how to achieve desired consequences – work hard, persevere, be moderate. There is always room, however, for the intrusion of the unexpected and the miraculous. As a reader, you will probably catch yourself trying to predict the outcomes of the following stories and articles. You will find two rewards: the satisfaction of a guess well made, and the delight of the unforeseen twist. Consider, also, the lesson of Huxley's remark: scepticism leads not to closed-mindedness, but to receptiveness to the possibility of anything.

A BOLT OF WHITE CLOTH
Leon Rooke

 man came by our road carrying an enormous bolt of white cloth on his back. Said he was from the East. Said whoever partook of this cloth would come to know true happiness. Innocence without heartbreak, he said, if that person proved worthy. My wife fingered his cloth, having in mind something for new curtains. It was good quality, she said. Beautifully woven, of a fine, light texture, and you certainly couldn't argue with the colour.

"How much is it?" she asked.

"Before I tell you that," the man said, "you must tell me truthfully if you've ever suffered."

"Oh, I've suffered," she said. "I've known suffering of some description every day of my natural life."

I was standing over by the toolshed, with a big smile. My wife is a real joker, who likes nothing better than pulling a person's leg. She's known hardships, this and that upheaval, but nothing I would call down-and-out suffering. Mind you, I don't speak for her. I wouldn't pretend to speak for another person.

This man with the bolt of cloth, however, he clearly had no sense of my wife's brand of humour. She didn't get an itch of a smile out of him. He kept the cloth neatly balanced on his shoulder, wincing a little from the weight and from however far he'd had to carry it, staring hard and straight at my wife the whole time she fooled with him, as if he hoped to peer clear through to her soul. His eyes were dark and brooding and hollowed out some. He was like no person either my wife or me had ever seen before.

"Yes," he said, "but suffering of what kind?"

"Worse than I hope forever to carry, I'll tell you that," my wife said. "But why are you asking me these questions? I like your cloth and if the price is right I mean to buy it."

"You can only buy my cloth with love," he said.

We began right then to understand that he was some kind of oddity. He was not like anybody we'd ever seen and he didn't come from around here. He'd come from a place we'd never heard of, and if that was the East, or wherever, then he was welcome to it.

"Love?" she said. "Love? There's *love* and there's *love*, mister. What kind are you talking about?" She hitched a head my way, rolling her eyes, as if to indicate that if it was *passionate* love he was talking about then he'd first have to do something with me. He'd have to get me off my simmer and onto full boil. That's what she was telling him, with this mischief in her eyes.

I put down my pitchfork about here, and strolled nearer. I liked seeing my wife dealing with difficult situations. I didn't want to miss anything. My life with that woman has been packed with the unusual. Unusual circumstances, she calls them. Any time she's ever gone out anywhere without me, whether for a day or an hour or for five minutes, she's come back with whopping good stories about what she's seen and heard and what's happened to her. She's come back with reports on these unusual circumstances, these little adventures in which so many people have done so many extraordinary things or behaved in such fabulous or foolish ways. So what was rare this time, I thought, was that it had come visiting. She hadn't had to go out and find it.

"Hold these," my wife told me. And she put this washtub of clothes in my hands, and went back to hanging wet pieces on the line, which is what she'd been doing when this man with the bolt of cloth ventured up into our yard.

"Love," she told him. "You tell me what kind I need, if I'm to buy that cloth. I got good ears and I'm listening."

The man watched her stick clothespins in her mouth, slap out a good wide sheet, and string it up. He watched her hang two of these, plus a mess of towels, and get her mouth full again before he spoke. He looked about the unhappiest I've ever seen any man look. He didn't have any joy in him. I wondered why he didn't put down that heavy bolt of cloth, and why he didn't step around into a spot of shade. The sun was lick-killing bright in that yard. I was worried he'd faint.

"The ordinary kind," he said. "Your ordinary kind of love will buy this cloth."

My wife flapped her wash and laughed. He was really tickling her. She was having herself a wonderful time.

"What's ordinary?" she said. "I've never known no *ordinary* love."

He jumped right in. He got excited just for a second.

"The kind such as might exist between the closest friends," he said. "The kind such as might exist between a man and his wife or between parents and children or for that matter the love a boy might have for his dog. That kind of love."

"I've got that," she said. "I've had all three. Last year this time I had me a fourth, but it got run over. Up on the road there, by the tall trees, by a man in a car who didn't even stop."

"That would have been your cat," he said. "I don't know much about cats."

I put down the washtub. My wife let her arms drop. We looked at him, wondering how he knew about that cat. Then I laughed, for I figured someone down the road must have told him of my wife's mourning over that cat. She'd dug it a grave under the grapevine and said sweet words over it. She sorely missed that cat.

"What's wrong with loving cats?" she asked him. "Or beasts of the fields? I'm surprised at you."

The man shifted his burden and worked one shoe into the ground. He stared off at the horizon. He looked like he knew he'd said something he shouldn't.

She pushed me out of the way. She wanted to get nearer to him. She had something more to say.

"Now listen to me," she said. "I've loved lots of things in my life. Lots and lots. *Him!*" she said (pointing at me), *"it"* (pointing to our house), *"them!"* (pointing to the flower beds), *"that!"* (pointing to the sky), *"those"* (pointing to the woods), *"this"* (pointing to the ground) – "practically *everything*! There isn't any of it I've hated, and not much I've been indifferent to. Including cats. So put that in your pipe and smoke it."

Then swooping up her arms and laughing hard, making it plain she bore no grudge but wasn't just fooling.

Funny thing was, hearing her say it, I felt the same way. *It, them, that, those* – they were all beautiful. I couldn't deny it was love I was feeling.

The man with the cloth had turned each way she'd pointed. He'd staggered a time or two but he'd kept up. In fact, it struck me that he'd got a little ahead of her. That he knew where her arm was next going. Some trickle of pleasure was showing in his face. And something else was happening, something I'd never seen. He had his face lifted up to this burning sun. It was big and orange, that sun, and scorching-hot, but he was staring smack into it. He wasn't blinking or squinting. His eyes were wide open.

Madness or miracle, I couldn't tell which.

He strode over to a parcel of good grass.

"I believe you mean it," he said. "How much could you use?"

He placed the bolt of white cloth down on the grass and pulled out shiny scissors from his back pocket.

"I bet he's blind," I whispered to my wife. "I bet he's got false eyes."

My wife shushed me. She wasn't listening. She had her excitement hat on; her *unusual circumstances* look. He was offering free cloth for love, ordinary love, and she figured she'd go along with the gag.

How much?

"Oh," she said, "maybe eight yards. Maybe ten. It depends on how many windows I end up doing, plus what hang I want, plus the pleating I'm after."

"You mean to make these curtains yourself?" he asked. He was already down on his knees, smoothing the bolt. Getting set to roll it out.

"Why, sure," she said. "I don't know who else would do it for me. I don't know who else I would ask."

He nodded soberly, not thinking about it. "That's so," he said casually. "Mend your own fences first." He was perspiring in the sun, and dishevelled, as though he'd been on the road a long time. His shoes had big holes in them and you could see the blistered soles of his feet, but he had an air of exhilaration now. His hair fell down over his eyes and he shoved the dark locks back. I got the impression that some days he went a long time between customers; that he didn't find cause to give away this cloth every day.

He got a fair bit unrolled. It certainly did look like prime goods, once you saw it spread out on the grass in that long expanse.

"It's so pretty!" My wife said. "Heaven help me, but I think it is *prettier* than grass!"

"It's pretty, all right," he said. "It's a wing-dinger. Just tell me when to stop," he said. "Just shout yoo-hoo."

"Hold up a minute," she said. "I don't want to get greedy. I don't want you rolling off more than we can afford."

"You can afford it," he said.

He kept unrolling. He was up past the well house by now, whipping it off fast, though the bolt didn't appear to be getting any smaller. My wife had both hands up over her mouth. Half of her wanted to run into the house and get her purse so she could pay; the other half wanted to stay and watch this man unfurl his beautiful cloth. She whipped around to me, all agitated.

"I believe he means it," she said. "He means us to have this cloth. What do I do?"

I shook my head. This was her territory. It was the kind of adventure constant to her nature and necessary to her well-being.

"Honey," I said, "you deal with it."

The sun was bright over everything. It was whipping-hot. There wasn't much wind but I could hear the clothes flapping on the line. A woodpecker had himself a pole somewhere and I could hear him pecking. The sky was wavy blue. The trees seemed to be swaying.

He was up by the front porch now, still unrolling. It surprised us both that he could move so fast.

"Yoo-hoo," my wife said. It was no more than a peep, the sound you might make if a butterfly lands on your hand.

"Wait," he said. "One thing. One question I meant to ask. All this talk of love, your *it*, your *those* and *them*, it slipped my mind."

"Let's hear it," my wife said. "Ask away." It seemed to me that she spoke out of a trance. That she was as dazzled as I was.

"You two got no children," he said. "Why is that? You're out here on this nice farm, and no children to your name. Why is that?"

We hadn't expected this query from him. It did something to the light in the yard and how we saw it. It was as if some giant dark bird had fluttered between us and the sun. Without knowing it, we sidled closer to each other. We fumbled for the other's hand. We stared off every which way. No one on our road had asked that question in a long, long time; they hadn't asked it in some years.

"We're not able," we said. Both of us spoke at the same time. It seemed to me that it was my wife's voice which carried; mine was some place down in my chest, and dropping, as if it meant to crawl on the ground.

"We're not able," we said. That time it came out pure, without any grief to bind it. It came out the way we long ago learned how to say it.

"Oh," he said. "I see." He mumbled something else. He kicked the ground and took a little walk back and forth. He seemed angry, though not at us. "Wouldn't you know it?" he said. "Wouldn't you know it?"

He swore a time or two. He kicked the ground. He surely didn't like it.

"We're over that now," my wife said. "We're past that caring."

"I bet you are," he said. "You're past that little misfortune."

He took to unrolling his bolt again, working with his back to the sun. Down on his knees, scrambling, smoothing the material. Sweating and huffing. He was past the front porch now, and still going, getting on toward that edge where the high weeds grew.

"About here, do you think?" he asked.

He'd rolled off about fifty yards.

My wife and I slowly shook our heads, not knowing what to think.

"Say the word," he told us. "I can give you more if more is what you want.

"I'd say you were giving us too much," my wife said. "I'd say we don't need nearly that much."

"Never mind that," he said. "I'm feeling generous today."

He nudged the cloth with his fingers and rolled off a few yards more. He would have gone on unwinding his cloth had the weeds not stopped him. He stood and looked back over the great length he had unwound.

"Looks like a long white road, don't it?" he said. "You could walk that road and your feet never get dirty."

My wife clenched my hand; it was what we'd both been thinking.

SnipSnipSnip. He began snipping. His scissors raced over the material. *SnipSnipSnip.* The cloth was sheared clear and clean of his bolt, yet it seemed to me the size of that bolt hadn't lessened any. My wife saw it too.

"He's got cloth for all eternity," she said. "He could unroll that cloth till doomsday."

The man laughed. We were whispering this, but way up by the weeds he heard us. "There's doom and there's doom," he said. "*Which* doomsday?"

I had the notion he'd gone through more than one. That he knew the picture from both sides.

"It *is* smart as grass," he said. "Smarter. It never needs watering." He chuckled at that, spinning both arms. Dancing a little. "You could make *nighties* out of this," he said. "New bedsheets. Transform your whole bedroom."

My wife made a face. She wasn't too pleased, talking *nighties* with another man.

Innocence without heartbreak, I thought. That's what we're coming to.

He nicely rolled up the cloth he'd sheared off and presented it to my wife. "I hope you like it," he said. "No complaints yet. Maybe you can make yourself a nice dress as well. Maybe two or three. Make him some shirts. I think you'll find there's plenty here."

"Goodness, it's light," she said.

"Not if you've been carrying it long as I have," he said. He pulled a blue bandanna from his pocket and wiped his face and neck. He ran his hand through his hair and slicked it back. He looked up at the sky. His dark eyes seemed to have cleared up some. They looked less broody. "Gets hot," he said, "working in this sun. But a nice day. I'm glad I found you folks home."

"Oh, we're most always home," my wife said.

I had to laugh at that. My wife almost never *is* home. She's forever gallivanting over the countryside, checking up on this person and that, taking them her soups and jams and breads.

"We're homebodies, us two."

She kept fingering the cloth and sighing over it. She held it up against her cheek and with her eyes closed rested herself on it. The man hoisted his own bolt back on his shoulder; he seemed ready to be going. I looked at my wife's closed lids, at the soft look she had.

I got trembly, fearful of what might happen if that cloth didn't work out.

"Now look," I said to him, "what's wrong with this cloth? Is it going to rot inside a week? Tomorrow is some *other* stranger going to knock on our door saying we owe him a hundred or five hundred dollars for this cloth? Mister, I don't understand you," I said.

He hadn't bothered with me before; now he looked me dead in the eye. "I can't help being a stranger," he said. "If you never set eyes on me before, I guess that's what I would have to be. Don't you like strangers? Don't you trust them?"

My wife jumped in. Her face was fiery, like she thought I had wounded him. "We like strangers just fine," she said. "We've helped out many a-one. No, I can't say our door has ever been closed to whoever it is comes by. Strangers can sit in our kitchen just the same as our friends."

He smiled at her but kept his stern look for me. "As to your questions," he said, "You're worried about the golden goose, I can see that. Fair enough. No, your cloth will not rot. It will not shred, fade, or tear. Nor will it ever need cleaning, either. This cloth requires no upkeep whatsoever. Though a sound heart helps. A sweet disposition, too. Innocence without heartbreak, as I told you. And your wife, if it's her making the curtains or making herself a dress, she will find it to be an amazingly easy cloth to work with. It will practically do the job itself. No, I don't believe you will ever find you have any reason to complain of the quality of that cloth."

My wife had it up to her face again. She had her face sunk in it.

"Goodness," she said. "it's *soft*! It smells so fresh. It's like someone singing a song to me."

The man laughed. "It *is* soft," he said. "But it can't sing a note, or has never been known to."

It was my wife singing. She had this little hum under the breath.

"This is the most wonderful cloth in the world," she said.

He nodded. "I can't argue with you on that score," he said. Then he turned again to me. "I believe your wife is satisfied," he said. "But if you have any doubts, if you're worried someone is going to knock on your door tomorrow asking you for a hundred or five hundred dollars, I suppose I could write you up a guarantee. I could give you a PAID IN FULL."

He was making me feel ashamed of myself. They both were. "No, no," I said, "if she's satisfied then I am. And I can see she's tickled pink. No, I beg your pardon. I meant no offence."

"No offence taken," he said.

But his eyes clouded a token. He gazed off at our road and up along the stand of trees and his eyes kept roaming until they snagged the sun. He kept his eyes there, unblinking, open, staring at the sun. I could see the red orbs reflected in his eyes.

"There is one thing," he said.

I caught my breath and felt my wife catch hers. The hitch? A hitch, after all? Coming so late?

We waited.

He shuffled his feet. He brought out his bandanna and wiped his face again. He stared at the ground.

"Should you ever stop loving," he said, "you shall lose this cloth and all else. You shall wake up one morning and it and all else will no longer be where you left it. It will all be gone and you will not know where you are. You will not know what to do with yourself. You will wish you'd never been born."

My wife's eyes went saucer-size.

He had us in some kind of spell.

Hocus-pocus, I thought. He is telling us some kind of hocus-pocus. Yet I felt my skin shudder; I felt the goose bumps rise.

"That's it?" my wife said. "That's the only catch?"

He shrugged. "That's it," he said. "Not much, is it? Not a whisper of menace for a pair such as yourselves."

My wife's eyes were gauzed over; there was a wetness in them.

"Hold on," she said. "Don't you be leaving yet. Hold this, honey."

She put the cloth in my arms. Then she hastened over to the well, pitched the bucket down, and drew it up running over with fresh water.

"Here," she said, coming back with a good dipperful. "Here's a nice drink of cool water. You need it on a day like this."

The man drank. He held the dipper in both hands, with the tips of his fingers, and drained the dipper dry, then wiped his chin with the back of his hand.

"I did indeed," he said. "That's very tasty water. I thank you."

"That's good water," she said. "That well has been here lo a hundred years. You could stay on for supper," she said. "It's getting on toward that time and I have a fine stew on the stove, with plenty to spare."

"That's kind of you," he said back, "and I'm grateful. But I'd best pass on up your road while there's still daylight left, and see who else might have need of this cloth."

My wife is not normally a demonstrative woman, not in public. Certainly not with strangers. You could have knocked me over with a feather when she up and kissed him full on the mouth, with a nice hug to boot.

"There's payment," she said, "if our money's no good."

He blushed, trying to hide his pleasure. It seemed to me she had him wrapped around her little finger . . . or the other way around.

"You kiss like a woman," he said. "Like one who knows what kissing is for, and can't hardly stop herself."

It was my wife's turn to blush.

I took hold of her hand and held her down to grass, because it seemed to me another kiss or two and she'd fly right away with him.

He walked across the yard and up by the well house, leaving by the same route he had come. Heading for the road. At the turn, he spun around and waved.

"You could try the Hopkins place!" my wife called. "There's a fat woman down that road got a sea of troubles. She could surely use some of that cloth."

He smiled and again waved. Then we saw his head and his bolt of white cloth bobbing along the weeds as he took the dips and rises in the road. Then he went on out of sight.

"There's that man with some horses down that road!" my wife called. "You be careful of him."

It seemed we heard some sound come back, but whether it was his we couldn't say.

My wife and I stood a long time in the yard, me holding the dipper and watching her, while she held her own bolt of cloth in her arms, staring off to where he'd last been.

Then she sighed dreamily and went inside.

I went on down to the barn and looked after the animals. Getting my feeding done. I talked a spell to them. Talking to animals is soothing to me, and they like it too. They pretend to stare at the walls or the floor as they're munching their feed down, but I know they listen to me. We had us an *unusual circumstances* chat. "That man with the cloth," I said. "Maybe you can tell me what you make of him."

Thirty minutes later I heard my wife excitedly calling me. She was standing out on the back doorstep, with this incredulous look.

"I've finished," she said. "I've finished the windows. *Nine* windows. It beats me how."

I started up to the house. Her voice was all shaky. Her face flushed, flinging her arms about. Then she got this new look on.

"Wait!" she said. "Stay there! Give me ten minutes!"

And she flung herself back inside, banging the door. I laughed. It always gave me a kick how she ordered me around.

I got the milk pail down under the cow. Before I'd touched and drained all four teats she was calling again.

"Come look, come look, oh come look!"

She was standing in the open doorway, with the kitchen to her back. Behind her, through the windows, I could see the streak of a red sunset and how it lit up the swing of trees. But I wasn't looking there. I was looking at her. Looking and swallowing hard and trying to remember how a body produced human speech. I had never thought of white as a colour she could wear. White, it pales her some. It leaves her undefined and washes out what parts I like best. But she looked beautiful now. In her new dress she struck me down to my bootstraps. She made my chest break.

"Do you like it?" she said.

I went running up to her. I was up against her, hugging her and lifting her before she'd even had a chance to get set. I'd never held on so tightly or been so tightly held back.

Truth is, it was the strangest thing. Like we were both so innocent we hadn't yet shot up out of new ground.

"Come see the curtains," she whispered. "Come see the new sheets. Come see what else I've made. You'll see it all. You'll see how our home has been transformed."

I crept inside. There was something holy about it. About it and about us and about those rooms and the whole wide world. Something radiant. Like you had to put your foot down easy and hold it down or you'd float on up.

"That's it," she said. "That's how I feel too."

That night in bed, trying to figure it out, we wondered how Ella Mae down the road had done. How the people all along our road had made out.

"No worry," my wife said. "He'll have found a bonanza around here. There's heaps of decent people in this neck of the woods."

"Wonder where he is now?" we said.

"Wonder where he goes next?"

"Where he gets that cloth?"

"Who he *is*?"

We couldn't get to sleep, wondering about that.

---

1. a) With a couple of classmates, summarize in your notebooks the characteristics of the man with the bolt of cloth, supporting your analysis with specific references to the story.
   b) Considering other legendary or mythic figures, speculate on possible replies to the narrator's musings: "That man with the cloth – maybe you can tell me what you make of him." Share your suggestions with another group.

2. Working in a small group, prepare a dramatization of a scene from the story.
   OR
   In a small group, discuss what might happen to the couple in the future. Using your discussion as a base, improvise a future moment in the couple's lives.

3. "A Bolt of White Cloth" has much to say about love. Develop a thesis on Rooke's treatment of the theme and write the introductory paragraph for an essay on the topic.

4. True happiness is "innocence without heartbreak." Use the phrase as the title of a piece of personal writing: a story, a memoir, or a poem, for example.

Here is what Annie Dillard says about the term *northing*.

"A kind of northing is what I wish to accomplish, a single-minded trek toward that place where any shutter left open to the zenith at night will record the wheeling of all the sky's stars as a pattern of perfect, concentric circles. I seek a reduction, a shedding, a sloughing off." As you read the excerpt that follows, consider how the experience Dillard describes is a step toward northing.

from "NORTHING"
Annie Dillard

few days later the monarchs hit. I saw one, and then another, and then others all day long, before I consciously understood that I was witnessing a migration, and it wasn't until another two weeks had passed that I realized the enormity of what I had seen.

Each of these butterflies, the fruit of two or three broods of this summer, had hatched successfully from one of those emerald cases that Teale's caterpillar had been about to form when the parasitic larvae snapped it limp, eating their way out of its side. They had hatched, many of them, just before a thunderstorm, when winds lifted the silver leaves of trees and birds sought the shelter of shrubbery, uttering cries. They were butterflies, going south to the Gulf states or farther, and some of them had come from Hudson's Bay.

Monarchs were everywhere. They skittered and bobbed, rested in the air, lolled on the dust – but with none of their usual insouciance. They had but one unwearying thought: South. I watched from my study window: three, four . . . eighteen, nineteen, one every few seconds, and some in tandem. They came fanning straight towards my window from the northwest, and from the northeast, materializing from behind the tips of high hemlocks, where Polaris hangs by night.

They appeared as Indian horsemen appear in movies: first dotted, then massed, silent, at the rim of a hill.

Each monarch butterfly had a brittle black body and deep orange wings limned and looped in black bands. A monarch at rest looks like a fleck of tiger, stilled and wide-eyed. A monarch in flight looks like an autumn leaf with a will, vitalized and cast upon the air from which it seems to suck some thin sugar of energy, some leaf-life or sap. As each one climbed up the air outside my window, I could see the more delicate, ventral surfaces of its wings, and I had a sense of bunched legs and straining thorax, but I could never focus well into the flapping and jerking before it vaulted up past the window and out of sight over my head.

I walked out and saw a monarch do a wonderful thing: it climbed a hill without twitching a muscle. I was standing at the bridge over Tinker Creek, at the southern foot of a very steep hill. The monarch beat its way beside me over the bridge at eye level, and then, flailing its wings exhaustedly, ascended straight up in the air. It rose vertically to the enormous height of a bankside sycamore's crown. Then, fixing its wings at a precise angle, it glided *up* the steep road, losing altitude extremely slowly, climbing by checking its fall, until it came to rest at a puddle in front of the house at the top of the hill.

I followed. It panted, skirmished briefly westward, and then, returning to the puddle, began its assault on the house. It struggled almost straight up the air next to the two-storey brick wall, and then scaled the roof. Wasting no effort, it followed the roof's own slope, from a distance of two inches. Puff, and it was out of sight. I wondered how many more hills and houses it would have to climb before it could rest. From the force of its will it would seem it could flutter through the walls.

Monarchs are "tough and powerful, as butterflies go." They fly over Lake Superior without resting; in fact, observers there have discovered a curious thing. Instead of flying directly south, the monarchs crossing high over the water take an inexplicable turn towards the east. Then when they reach an invisible point, they all veer south again. Each successive swarm repeats this mysterious dogleg movement, year after year. Entomologists actually think that the butterflies might be "remembering" the position of a long-gone, looming glacier. In another book I read the geologists think that Lake Superior marks the site of the highest mountain that ever existed on this continent. I don't know. I'd like to see it. Or I'd like to be it, to feel when to turn. At night on land migrating monarchs slumber on certain trees, hung in festoons with wings folded together, thick on the trees and shaggy as bearskin.

Monarchs have always been assumed to taste terribly bitter, because of the acid milkweed on which the caterpillars feed. You always run into monarchs and viceroys when you read about mimicry: viceroys look enough like monarchs that keen-eyed birds who have tasted monarchs once will avoid the viceroys as well. New studies indicate that milkweed-fed monarchs are not so much evil-tasting as literally nauseating, since milkweed contains "heart poisons similar to digitalis" that make the bird ill. Personally, I like an experiment performed by an entomologist with real spirit. He had heard all his life, as I have, that monarchs taste unforgettably bitter, so he tried some. "To conduct what was in fact a field experiment the doctor first went south, and he ate a number of monarchs in the field. . . . The monarch butterfly, Dr. Urquhart learned, has no more flavour than dried toast." Dried toast? It was hard for me, throughout the monarch migration, in the middle of all that beauty and real splendour, to fight down the thought that what I was really seeing in the air was a vast and fluttering tea tray for shut-ins.

It is easy to coax a dying or exhausted butterfly onto your finger. I saw a monarch walking across a gas station lot; it was walking south. I placed my index finger in its path, and it clambered aboard and let me lift it to my face. Its wings were faded but unmarked by hazard; a veneer of velvet caught the light and hinted at the frailest depth of lapped scales. It was a male; his legs clutching my finger were short and atrophied; they clasped my finger with a spread fragility, a fineness as of some low note of emotion or pure strain of spirit, scarcely perceived. And I knew that those feet were actually tasting me, sipping with sensitive organs the vapour of my finger's skin: butterflies taste with their feet. All the time he held me, he opened and closed his glorious wings, senselessly, as if sighing.

The closing of his wings fanned an almost imperceptible redolence at my face, and I leaned closer. I could barely scent a sweetness, I could almost name it . . . fireflies, sparklers – honeysuckle. He smelled like honeysuckle; I couldn't believe it. I knew that many male butterflies exuded distinctive odours from special scent glands, but I thought that only laboratory instruments could detect those odours compounded of many, many butterflies. I had read a list of the improbable scents of butterflies: sandalwoods, chocolate heliotrope, sweet pea. Now this live creature here on my finger had an odour that even I could sense – this flap actually smelled, this chip that took its temperature from the air like any envelope or hammer, this programmed wisp of spread horn. And he smelled of honeysuckle. Why not caribou hoof or Labrador tea, tundra lichen or dwarf willow, the brine of Hudson's Bay or the vapour of rivers milky with fine-ground glacial silt? This honeysuckle was an odour already only half-remembered, a breath of the summer past, the Lucas cliffs and overgrown fence by Tinker Creek, a drugged sweetness that had almost cloyed on those moisture-laden nights, now refined to a wary trickle in the air, a distillation pure and rare, scarcely known and mostly lost, and heading south.

I walked him across the gas station lot and lowered him into a field. He took to the air, pulsing and gliding; he lighted on sassafras, and I lost him.

For weeks I found paired monarch wings, bodiless, on the grass or on the road. I collected one such wing and freed it of its scales; first I rubbed it between my fingers, and then I stroked it gently with the tip of an infant's silver spoon. What I had at the end of this delicate labour is lying here on this study desk: a kind of resilient scaffolding, like the webbing over a hot-air balloon, black veins stretching the merest something across the nothingness it plies. The integument itself is perfectly transparent; through it I can read the smallest print. It is as thin as the skin peeled from sunburn, and as tough as a parchment of flensed buffalo hide. The butterflies that were eaten here in the valley, leaving us their wings, were, however, few: most lived to follow the valley south.

The migration lasted in full force for five days. For those five days I was inundated, drained. The air was alive and unwinding. Time itself was a scroll unravelled, curved and still quivering on a table or altar stone. The monarchs clattered in the air, burnished like throngs of pennies, here's one, and here's one and more, and more. They flapped and floundered; they thrust, splitting the air like the keels of canoes, quickened and fleet. It looked as though the leaves of the autumn forest had taken flight, and were pouring down the valley like a waterfall, like a tidal wave, all the leaves of hardwoods from here to Hudson's Bay. It was as if the season's colour were draining away like lifeblood, as if the year were moulting and shedding. The year was rolling down, and a vital curve had been reached, the tilt that gives way to headlong rush. And when the monarchs had passed and were gone, the skies were vacant, the air poised. The dark night into which the year was plunging was not a sleep but an awakening, a new and necessary austerity, the sparer climate for which I longed. The shed trees were brittle and still, the creek light and cold, and my spirit holding its breath.

---

1. a) In a short piece of personal writing, record your initial response to the piece and to the personality of the narrator.
   b) Compare your response with a classmate's and, using quotations and specific details in the text, explain to each other why you responded the way you did.
   c) Contrast Dillard's purpose and tone with those of a naturalist writing for a scientific journal or a geographic magazine. (You may wish to read "What Gets a Porcupine's Back Up?", p. 299, for a light-hearted example.)

2. a) Read Franklin Russell's "A Madness of Nature" (p. 194). In

your notebook, propose at least three bases upon which the two essays might be constructively compared.

b) Write the introductory and concluding paragraphs of a comparative essay on the two pieces.

3. Choose a natural phenomenon that intrigues you and express your thoughts and feelings about it in a short personal essay or a poem.

4. Annie Dillard, who has lived in the Roanoke Valley in the Blue Ridge Mountains of Virginia since 1965, is both a naturalist and a poet. In her voice, write a letter responding to these questions posed by Lewis Thomas in "A Trip Abroad" (p. 258): "What I would like to know is: how should I feel about the earth, these days? Where has all the old nature gone? What became of the wild, writhing, unapproachable mass of the life of the world, and what happened to our old, panicky excitement about it?"

Go to the library and find one or two
newspaper or magazine clippings about
disasters that resulted from human attempts to
modify the environment. Try to decide whether
the misfortunes were unforseeable or whether
the perpetrators were obviously foolish.

BIO-ENGINEERING GONE WRONG
Sheila Kulka and Barry Estabrook

In 1890 few Americans would have guessed that the seemingly innocuous lines from Shakespeare's *Henry IV*, "Nay, I'll have a starling shall be taught to speak nothing but 'Mortimer'," would eventually lead to the deaths of 62 persons aboard a Lockheed Electra aircraft.

But for the misguided efforts of Eugene Scheifflin, a New York drug manufacturer and leading force in the American Acclimatization Society, the 10 000-bird-strong flock of starlings with which the ill-fated aircraft collided just after takeoff from Boston, would have never been found in North American skies.

Scheifflin had spent idle hours pursuing a perplexing avocation: it was his goal to bring all birds mentioned by Shakespeare to America's deprived shores.

But only 10 years after its 1890 introduction, the starling began showing clear signs that it was one species the New World would have been better off without.

Scheifflin's starlings spread rapidly from their first New World roost – ironically – beneath the eaves of the American Museum of Natural History in New York's Central Park.

Within six years the black marauders were seen regularly in Brooklyn and Long Island. Spurred forward by a territorial nature that forces young starlings to seek new foraging areas, those first tentative New York flocks had spread to Halifax within 15 years, and by 1945 had become commonplace as far afield as British Columbia. Today starlings can claim title to being the most numerous of all bird species in North America.

Although some people thought the birds would benefit North America by eating insects, it fast became evident that Mr. Scheifflin's starlings preferred a varied menu of feedlot grain, corn, sorghum, rice, truck crops and fruit. Voracious, starlings consume up to twice their own body weight daily – an appetite that costs North American agriculture millions of dollars each year. And there is evidence that starlings are key villains in the spread of swine disease from feedlot to feedlot.

As pugnacious as they are voracious, starlings have no trouble out-competing less aggressive native birds. Flickers, wrens, bluebirds and martins – birds eating only insects – were forced from favourite haunts as starlings bullied their way to prominence.

But no one understands the nuisance of starlings as well as citizens of Waterbury, Connecticut, a town whose police force once staged a dawn shotgun war against the 250 000 starlings that called Waterbury townhall their home.

Citizens of Waterbury had to turn on windshield wipers when driving through town at dusk. Sidewalks were slippery from accumulated starling dung, and the downtown area was characterized by an irksome odour reminiscent of an ill-kept chicken coop.

Bestial Ramifications: Since Noah filled his ark, man has been afflicted with an insatiable desire to shift animals far beyond their natural range. All of man's meddling has been backed by near total ignorance of the ramifications, and although some bestial transfers have met with (at best) marginal success, far too often they have resulted in irreversible natural disasters.

The most monumental meddling failure occurred in 1859 when the merchant vessel *Lightning* pulled into an Australian port with a shipment of 24 European rabbits destined for the sheep ranch of Thomas Austin.

Mr. Austin's desire to bring this delectable, long-eared native of his homeland to Australia was perhaps understandable, but the gentleman farmer would shudder to hear the contempt with which his name is held in that country today.

For a time, however, Austin was happy. Only six years after the first rabbits hopped from their cages onto his ranch, Austin was bagging as many as 20 000 per year. But within a decade rabbits had leapt the borders of Austin's estate and Australians were beginning to wonder whether they had a monstrous problem on their hands.

They did. On the dry Australian plains, it was found that five of

Mr. Austin's fertile bunnies could consume the same amount of valuable grass as one sheep. One ranch, which supported 20 000 plump ewes before the first rabbit cast hungry eyes on its grassy hills, saw its capacity reduced to 2000 sheep within four years.

In 1887 angry outbackers in New South Wales killed 20 million rabbits. By 1901 the problem had become so acute that Australians erected 2000 miles of buried, rabbit-proof fence in a futile gesture aimed at stopping the spread of these pests.

Man fought a losing battle against these nimble foes until 1950, when germ warfare was called into the fray. Australian biologists inoculated several laboratory rabbits with a deadly South American rabbit disease. Released, these rabbits spread germs that killed 995 out of every 1000 Australian bunnies. With the rabbits decimated, deserts once again became productive pastures.

But Australians could soon face a second, escalated battle. It is now speculated that the rabbits may be developing an immunity to the South American disease.

Espeut's Mongoose: A Jamaican planter named W.B. Espeut, in 1876, released nine mongooses (recently shipped from India) on his sugar plantation. Rats that had accompanied Europeans to this tropical island had become serious pests in sugar cane fields, consuming as much as one-fifth of the crop.

By importing the squirrel-sized mongoose to Jamaica, Espeut hoped to solve the rat problem. His plan worked. Those nine mongooses contentedly disappeared into his cane fields and, well-fed on rat meat, began to multiply.

Other planters, noting Espeut's fields were no longer plagued by rats, grew eager to get their hands on mongooses. Soon the little beasts were transported not only all over Jamaica, but to every sugar island in the West Indies.

By this time, however, the mongoose began to show his true colours. Noted for the speed and agility that permit them to kill cobras in their native India (although mongooses do lose the occasional battle), Espeut's introduction quickly devoured all Jamaica's rats and then turned its attention to other animals – chickens, piglets, goat kids, lambs, kittens, puppies.

Before the mongooses' rampage was stemmed by natural forces, they had not only made it nearly impossible to raise small domestic animals in Jamaica, but had eliminated virtually all the island's native animals.

It is only by virtue of a miracle that these pests did not gain a foothold in North America. In the 1890's, western ranchers, plagued by gophers, had begun to introduce mongooses. By then aware of the dangers of these pests, scientists managed to stop the newcomers before populations became established.

Sparrow Pie: When British farmers found that a new market had sprung up for live specimens of the thousands of house sparrows they had been killing each year to protect crops, they were understandably delighted – if not a little perplexed.

Once again, it was the Acclimatization Society movement of homesick Europeans and this time they were attempting to introduce these chirping little birds to a new homeland in America.

Originally from southern Europe, house sparrows fast learned the ease of pilfering from man, and they have faithfully followed him everywhere he has gone.

By the spring of 1853, Mr. John Hooper of the Brooklyn Institute could proudly report to members of his organization that fifty sparrows released in a New York cemetery had done well and multiplied. "I have original notes taken from time to time of their increase and colonization over our great country," he wrote.

In Strathroy, Ontario, a Mr. L.H. Smith could claim that he had procured a good bargain on the 12 sparrows he had purchased for the princely sum of one dollar each. Not only were there now thousands of the little birds in his home town, but they had spread to become plentiful in "every town, city and village in this part of Ontario."

Once these fast-breeding birds became numerous in North America, they began to show some of the less desirable traits that made them so detested in their homeland. In orchards, they ate blossoms, buds and ripe fruit. They moved into ripening wheat fields in huge flocks, heavily damaging crops. In cities their droppings began to kill decorative plants.

Philadelphians, who had only recently cheered the release of 1000 house sparrows, were called upon in 1883 "to kill or otherwise destroy the small bird known as the English sparrow." Michigan offered a one-penny bounty for dead sparrows in lots of 25 or more. Meanwhile, one enterprising New York landlady put the newfound pests to good use by serving sparrow pie to her lodgers, who reported favourably on the delicacy.

Carp-Barrelling: Each year fish and wildlife authorities in Canada and the United States spend millions of dollars on programs aimed at cutting back numbers of carp in our waters.

These hungry bottom feeders, with their unpleasant habit of devouring aquatic weeds and stirring mud on lake bottoms in search of food, can quickly render formerly clear waters unfit for habitation by any other fish species.

Shunned almost universally for both poor eating quality and inept fighting abilities, the carp now ranks as one of the worst plagues in North American waterways.

This, however, was not true in 1877 when Rudolph Hessel stood proudly before the United States Congress to receive applause for his successful planting of a breeding stock of carp in a pond near Boston.

Rumours spread that this supposedly fine-tasting European battler was now living on this continent, and it wasn't long before every constituent in the United States was clamouring for carp to be introduced in his area. Rising to the call, legislators made carp stocking a first-rate, pork-barrel issue. An election promise of carp for all was bound to garner votes.

But carp would have proliferated without extensive stocking programs. All they really needed was a lift across the salty Atlantic. During spring floods they moved from watershed to watershed, gorging themselves on valuable aquatic plants and the spawn of gamefish as they travelled.

As fast as the carp fad had swept the land, it died. People, disappointed at the loss of native fish and no longer waxing eloquent about the carp's culinary and angling merits, began to demand elimination. But it was too late. By 1901 an American biologist studying carp for the federal government concluded that the best thing to do was to learn to live with the carp; it was here to stay. The biologist was correct.

Georgia-Bound: The angler's world is rife with tall stories, but the eyes of Florida Game and Freshwater Fish authorities must really have rolled one autumn morning in 1968 when a bartender, holding three bizarre, pale-skinned catfish, started telling a story about how he was driving along this road north of Fort Lauderdale at 2 a.m. when he came across hundreds of these fish – all of them walking across the pavement.

The bartender must have exercised some of the fast talk for which his profession is noted. At any rate, he convinced the government men to go out to the scene where they found several more of the mobile fish crushed on the pavement.

Today this scenario is no longer cause for raised eyebrows in the Sunshine State. The walking catfish has comfortably established itself as a Florida resident.

North America can thank Thailand for the walking catfish. These talented fish were originally introduced to Florida as five-centimetre-long aquarium novelties, but no one thought to inform unsuspecting Americans of the strange little specimen's unfish-like manners.

Their perambulatory prowess went unrecognized until one day, during a heavy rainstorm, some catfish got out of their tank and crawled down to a nearby pond. They have never looked back.

The walking catfish is now at home throughout southern Florida, and has begun to turn its steps northward. Scientists speculate that walking catfish might (using stiff spines on their pectoral fins to draw themselves forward in a series of steps) someday move as far north as Georgia. Without natural enemies, they are over-running Florida waters by out-competing native large-mouth bass and bluegills, vital to Florida's important freshwater sport fishery. But not only do these Thai introductions walk, they fight. Walking catfish have been known to kill conventional catfish in fin-to-fin combat, and have forced piranhas to turn tail in observation aquariums.

Attempts to eradicate the walking catfish by poisoning have met with no success. Equipped with a lung-like organ, walking catfish can live out of water for 12 hours. Should the water of a particular pond drop to an uncomfortable level or become poisoned, walking catfish resident in that pond merely get up and move to another more to their liking.

Further south, another biological disaster is fast marching this way. In 1957, an uninformed beekeeper wandered into the experimental beeyard of Warwick Kerr, a Brazilian geneticist who had set out to improve the honey-producing capacity of Brazil's traditional European bees through crossbreeding with an African strain.

The unknowing beekeeper removed devices Kerr had installed on hives in his experimental beeyard to retain queens, and by the time the blunder was discovered, 26 swarms had escaped. The western world got its first taste of killer bees.

Leaving a trail of at least 150 dead humans and thousands of dead domestic animals, the released bees began to move away from Sao Paulo (the site of Kerr's experiment) at a rate of 322 km per year. By 1990 they will have arrived at the southern borders of the United States, and no one is sure what will result. One positive hope is that they will cross with gentler European strains during the course of their travels and arrive on this continent somewhat mollified.

But by no means has all man's meddling moved animals from the Old World to the new. Britons are still cursing the Duke of Bedford for releasing 10 American grey squirrels on his estate in 1890. The North American roughnecks made short work of displacing Britain's more mild-mannered red squirrels.

In the early 1900's, muskrats were sent from North America to Czechoslovakia in the hope of starting a new fur industry for Europe. The aquatic rodents took an immediate liking to their new home, and within 20 years escapees from fur farms had spread across the continent into areas where their affinity for constructing dens in dikes, embankments and roadbeds assured them a solid position on the exotic pest list.

Canada Goose Vs. Sheep: Canadians, too, have had a hand in ecological meddling. Several Canada geese – those proud waterfowl whose seasonal migration stirs all of our hearts – were sent to gooseless New Zealand where they are now viewed with disdain. The unruly Canadians have become so numerous in some areas that they compete with sheep for food.

Man persists in his folly. Just over a decade ago, an Ohio Beagle club released thousands of those European rabbits of Australian renown, hoping to bolster hunts.

In the southern United States, fish and game men jealous of the North's ring necked pheasant (a Chinese introduction) are still attempting to convince a host of oriental gamebirds that Dixie isn't such a bad place after all.

New Mexican gunners are keenly eyeing a protected herd of wild Moroccan mountain sheep introduced to the state a dozen years ago. In Arizona there is worry about the new sheep competing with threatened native bighorns, and wildlife authorities have given the order to shoot the Moroccan immigrants on sight.

Meanwhile in Florida, pressure groups are springing up to encourage the introduction of 45-kg-plus Chinese weed-eating carp to help control the man-introduced water hyacinths that clog many inland waterways.

Hopefully Floridians will heed the words of naturalist George Laycock before introducing yet another exotic animal:

"Release of wildlife into territory foreign to it involves, not a calculated risk, but a risk too great to calculate."

---

1. a) With a classmate, determine from the content, style, and tone of this article its purpose and the audience to whom it is directed.
   b) In your notebook, support your conclusions with specific references to the article.

2. Write a concise summary (one paragraph) of "Bio-engineering Gone Wrong" that could be used as the abstract for the article.

3. Locate the thesis statement in "Bio-engineering Gone Wrong." Read the first section of the article aloud to a partner, but begin it with the statement you identified. Together, assess how the new beginning changes the effect of the anecdote about the starlings. State in writing the version you prefer, and write a brief defence of your choice.

4. Your small group will take the role of your teacher for one class. For your classmates, prepare a comparison of "Bio-engineering Gone Wrong" and "A Madness of Nature" (p. 194) in terms of
   • the writer's purpose;
   • the writer's use of language.
   Present your comparison to the students and be prepared to answer their questions.

5. Kulka and Estabrook state that all human attempts to improve nature have been "backed by near total ignorance of the

ramifications." The authors of "Time to Ban Surrogate Motherhood" (p. 22) and "Sinning Bravely: The Case of Baby Fae" (p. 17) express similar concerns. Read these two essays and write a page or two of personal response, expressing your own thoughts and feelings on the benefits and/or hazards of human intervention in natural processes. You may wish to focus on one issue that particularly interests or worries you.

"Honi soit qui mal y pense." – *Motto of the Order of the Garter*

In a small group, discuss the possible interpretations of the motto above, and then read Shirley Jackson's story about Miss Strangeworth of Pleasant Street.

THE POSSIBILITY OF EVIL
Shirley Jackson

Miss Adela Strangeworth came daintily along Main Street on her way to the grocery. The sun was shining, the air was fresh and clear after the night's heavy rain and everything in Miss Strangeworth's little town looked washed and bright. Miss Strangeworth took deep breaths and thought that there was nothing in the world like a fragrant summer day.

She knew everyone in town, of course; she was fond of telling strangers – tourists who sometimes passed through the town and stopped to admire Miss Strangeworth's roses – that she had never spent more than a day outside this town in all her long life. She was seventy-one, Miss Strangeworth told the tourists, with a pretty little dimple showing by her lip, and she sometimes found herself thinking that the town belonged to her. "My grandfather built the first house on Pleasant Street," she would say, opening her blue eyes wide with the wonder of it. "This house, right here. My family has lived here for better than a hundred years. My grandmother planted these roses, and my mother tended them, just as I do. I've watched my town grow; I can remember when Mr. Lewis, Senior, opened the grocery store, and the year the river flooded out the shanties on the low road, and the excitement when some young folks wanted to move the park over to the space in front of where the new post office is today. They wanted to put up a statue of Ethan Allen" – Miss Strangeworth would frown a little and sound stern – "but it should have been a statue of my grandfather. There wouldn't have been a town here at all if it hadn't been for my grandfather and the lumber mill."

Miss Strangeworth never gave away any of her roses, although the tourists often asked her. The roses belonged on Pleasant Street, and it bothered Miss Strangeworth to think of people wanting to carry them away, to take them into strange towns and down strange streets. When the new minister came, and the ladies were gathering flowers to decorate the church, Miss Strangeworth sent over a great basket of gladioli; when she picked the roses at all, she set them in bowls and vases around the inside of the house her grandfather had built.

Walking down Main Street on a summer morning, Miss Strangeworth had to stop every minute or so to say good morning to someone or to ask after someone's health. When she came into the grocery, half a dozen people turned away from the shelves and the counters to wave at her or call out good morning.

"And good morning to you, too, Mr. Lewis," Miss Strangeworth said at last. The Lewis family had been in the town almost as long as the Strangeworths; but the day young Lewis left high school and went to work in the grocery, Miss Strangeworth had stopped calling him Tommy and started calling him Mr. Lewis, and he had stopped calling her Addie and started calling her Miss Strangeworth. They had been in high school together, and had gone to picnics together, and to high-school dances and basketball games; but now Mr. Lewis was behind the counter in the grocery, and Miss Strangeworth was living alone in the Strangeworth house on Pleasant Street.

"Good morning," Mr. Lewis said, and added politely, "Lovely day."

"It is a very nice day," Miss Strangeworth said, as though she had only just decided that it would do after all. "I would like a chop, please, Mr. Lewis, a small, lean veal chop. Are those strawberries from Arthur Parker's garden? They're early this year."

"He brought them in this morning," Mr. Lewis said.

"I shall have a box," Miss Strangeworth said. Mr. Lewis looked worried, she thought, and for a minute she hesitated, but then she decided that he surely could not be worried over the strawberries. He looked very tired indeed. He was usually so chipper, Miss Strangeworth thought, and almost commented, but it was far too personal a subject to be introduced to Mr. Lewis, the grocer, so she only said, "And a can of cat food and, I think, a tomato."

Silently, Mr. Lewis assembled her order on the counter and waited. Miss Strangeworth looked at him curiously and then said, "It's Tuesday, Mr. Lewis. You forgot to remind me."

"Did I? Sorry."

"Imagine your forgetting that I always buy my tea on Tuesday,"

Miss Strangeworth said gently. "A quarter pound of tea, please, Mr. Lewis."

"Is that all, Miss Strangeworth?"

"Yes, thank you. Mr. Lewis. Such a lovely day, isn't it?"

"Lovely," Mr. Lewis said.

Miss Strangeworth moved slightly to make room for Mrs. Harper at the counter. "Morning, Adela," Mrs. Harper said, and Miss Strangeworth said, "Good morning, Martha."

"Lovely day," Mrs. Harper said, and Miss Strangeworth said, "Yes, lovely," and Mr. Lewis, under Mrs. Harper's glance, nodded.

"Ran out of sugar for my cake frosting," Mrs. Harper explained. Her hand shook slightly as she opened her pocketbook. Miss Strangeworth wondered, glancing at her quickly, if she had been taking proper care of herself. Martha Harper was not as young as she used to be, Miss Strangeworth thought. She probably could use a good strong tonic.

"Martha," she said, "you don't look well."

"I'm perfectly all right," Mrs. Harper said shortly. She handed her money to Mr. Lewis, took her change and her sugar, and went out without speaking again. Looking after her, Miss Strangeworth shook her head slightly. Martha definitely did *not* look well.

Carrying her little bag of groceries, Miss Strangeworth came out of the store into the bright sunlight and stopped to smile down on the Crane baby. Don and Helen Crane were really the two most infatuated young parents she had ever known, she thought indulgently, looking at the delicately embroidered baby cap and the lace-edged carriage cover.

"That little girl is going to grow up expecting luxury all her life," she said to Helen Crane.

Helen laughed. "That's the way we want her to feel," she said. "Like a princess."

"A princess can see a lot of trouble sometimes," Miss Strangeworth said dryly. "How old is Her Highness now?"

"Six months next Tuesday," Helen Crane said, looking down with rapt wonder at her child. "I've been worrying, though, about her. Don't you think she ought to move around more? Try to sit up, for instance?"

"For plain and fancy worrying," Miss Strangeworth said, amused, "give me a new mother every time."

"She just seems – slow," Helen Crane said.

"Nonsense. All babies are different. Some of them develop much more quickly than others."

"That's what my mother says." Helen Crane laughed, looking a little bit ashamed.

"I suppose you've got young Don all upset about the fact that his daughter is already six months old and hasn't yet begun to learn to dance?"

"I haven't mentioned it to him. I suppose she's just so precious that I worry about her all the time."

"Well, apologize to her right now," Miss Strangeworth said. "*She* is probably worrying about why you keep jumping around all the time." Smiling to herself and shaking her old head, she went on down the sunny street, stopping once to ask little Billy Moore why he wasn't out riding in his daddy's shiny new car, and talking for a few minutes outside the library with Miss Chandler, the librarian, about the new novels to be ordered and paid for by the annual library appropriation. Miss Chandler seemed absentminded and very much as though she were thinking about something else. Miss Strangeworth noticed that Miss Chandler had not taken much trouble with her hair that morning, and sighed. Miss Strangeworth hated sloppiness.

Many people seemed disturbed recently, Miss Strangeworth thought. Only yesterday the Stewarts' fifteen-year-old Linda had run crying down her own front walk and all the way to school, not caring who saw her. People around town thought she might have had a fight with the Harris boy, but they showed up together at the soda shop after school as usual, both of them looking grim and bleak. Trouble at home, people concluded, and sighed over the problems of trying to raise kids right these days.

From halfway down the block Miss Strangeworth could catch the heavy scent of her roses, and she moved a little more quickly. The perfume of roses meant home, and home meant the Strangeworth House on Pleasant Street. Miss Strangeworth stopped at her own front gate, as she always did, and looked with deep pleasure at her house, with the red and pink and white roses massed along the narrow lawn, and the rambler going up along the porch; and the neat, the unbelievably trim lines of the house itself, with its slimness and its washed white look. Every window sparkled, every curtain hung stiff and straight, and even the stones of the front walk were swept and clear. People around town wondered how old Miss Strangeworth managed to keep the house looking the way it did and there was a legend about a tourist once mistaking it for the local museum and going all through the place without finding out about his mistake. But the town was proud of Miss Strangeworth and her roses and her house. They had all grown together.

Miss Strangeworth went up her front steps, unlocked her front door with her key and went into the kitchen to put away her groceries. She debated about having a cup of tea and then decided that it was too close to midday dinner time; she would not have the appetite for her little chop if she had tea now. Instead she went into the light, lovely sitting room, which still glowed from the hands of her mother and her grandmother, who had covered the chairs with bright chintz and hung the curtains. All the furniture was spare and shining, and the round hooked rugs on the floor had been the work of Miss Strangeworth's grandmother and her mother. Miss Strangeworth had put a bowl of her red roses on the low table before the window, and the room was full of their scent.

Miss Strangeworth went to the narrow desk in the corner and unlocked it with her key. She never knew when she might feel like writing letters, so she kept her notepaper inside and the desk locked. Miss Strangeworth's usual stationery was heavy and cream-coloured, with "Strangeworth House" engraved across the top, but, when she felt like writing her other letters, Miss Strangeworth used a pad of various-coloured paper bought from the local newspaper shop. It was almost a town joke, that coloured paper, layered in pink and green and blue and yellow; everyone in town bought it and used it for odd, informal notes and shopping lists. It was usual to remark, upon receiving a note written on a blue page, that so-and-so would be needing a new pad soon – here she was, down to the blue already. Everyone used the matching envelopes for tucking away recipes, or keeping odd little things in, or even to hold cookies in the school lunch boxes. Mr. Lewis sometimes gave them to the children for carrying home penny candy.

Although Miss Strangeworth's desk held a trimmed quill pen which had belonged to her grandfather, and a gold-frosted fountain pen which had belonged to her father, Miss Strangeworth always used a dull stub of pencil when she wrote her letters, and she printed them in a childish block print. After thinking for a minute, although she had been phrasing the letter in the back of her mind all the way home, she wrote on a pink sheet: DIDN'T YOU EVER SEE AN IDIOT CHILD BEFORE? SOME PEOPLE JUST SHOULDN'T HAVE CHILDREN, SHOULD THEY?

She was pleased with the letter. She was fond of doing things exactly right. When she made a mistake, as she sometimes did, or when the letters were not spaced nicely on the page, she had to take the discarded page to the kitchen stove and burn it at once. Miss Strangeworth never delayed when things had to be done.

After thinking for a minute, she decided that she would like to write another letter, perhaps to go to Mrs. Harper, to follow up the ones she had already mailed. She selected a green sheet this time and wrote quickly: HAVE YOU FOUND OUT YET WHAT THEY WERE ALL LAUGHING ABOUT AFTER YOU LEFT THE BRIDGE CLUB ON THURSDAY? OR IS THE WIFE REALLY ALWAYS THE LAST ONE TO KNOW?

Miss Strangeworth never concerned herself with facts; her letters all dealt with the more negotiable stuff of suspicion. Mr. Lewis would never have imagined for a minute that his grandson might be lifting petty cash from the store register if he had not had one of Miss Strangeworth's letters. Miss Chandler, the librarian, and Linda Stewart's parents would have gone unsuspectingly ahead with their lives, never aware of possible evil lurking nearby, if Miss Strangeworth had not sent letters opening their eyes. Miss Strangeworth would have been genuinely shocked if there *had* been anything between Linda Stewart and the Harris boy, but, as long as evil existed unchecked in the world, it was Miss Strangeworth's duty to keep her town alert to it. It was far more sensible for Miss Chandler to wonder what Mr. Shelley's first wife had really died of than to take a chance on not knowing. There were so many wicked people in the world and only one Strangeworth left in the town. Besides, Miss Strangeworth liked writing her letters.

She addressed an envelope to Don Crane after a moment's thought, wondering curiously if he would show the letter to his wife, and using a pink envelope to match the pink paper. Then she addressed a second envelope, green, to Mrs. Harper. Then an idea came to her and she selected a blue sheet and wrote: YOU NEVER KNOW ABOUT DOCTORS. REMEMBER THEY'RE ONLY HUMAN AND NEED MONEY LIKE THE REST OF US. SUPPOSE THE KNIFE SLIPPED ACCIDENTALLY. WOULD DOCTOR BURNS GET HIS FEE AND A LITTLE EXTRA FROM THAT NEPHEW OF YOURS?

She addressed the blue envelope to old Mrs. Foster, who was having an operation next month. She had thought of writing one more letter, to the head of the school board, asking how a chemistry teacher like Billy Moore's father could afford a new convertible, but, all at once, she was tired of writing letters. The three she had done would do for one day. She could write more tomorrow; it was not as though they all had to be done at once.

She had been writing her letters – sometimes two or three every day for a week, sometimes no more than one in a month – for the past year. She never got any answers, of course, because she never signed her name. If she had been asked, she would have said that her name, Adela Strangeworth, a name honoured in the town for so many years, did not belong on such trash. The town where she lived had to be kept clean and sweet, but people everywhere were lustful and evil and degraded, and needed to be watched; the world was so large, and there was only one Strangeworth left in it. Miss Strangeworth sighed, locked her desk and put the letters into her big black leather pocketbook, to be mailed when she took her evening walk.

She broiled her little chop nicely, and had a sliced tomato and a good cup of tea ready when she sat down to her midday dinner at the table in her dining room, which could be opened to seat twenty-two, with a second table, if necessary, in the hall. Sitting in the warm sunlight that came through the tall windows of the dining room, seeing her roses massed outside, handling the heavy, old silverware and the fine, translucent china, Miss Strangeworth was pleased; she would not have cared to be doing anything else. People must live graciously, after all, she thought, and sipped her tea. Afterward, when her plate and cup and saucer were washed and dried and put back onto the shelves where they belonged, and her silverware was back in the mahogany silver chest, Miss Strangeworth went up the graceful staircase and into her bedroom, which was the front room overlooking the roses, and had been her mother's and her grandmother's. Their Crown Derby dresser set and furs had been kept here, their fans and silverbacked brushes and their own bowls of roses; Miss Strangeworth kept a bowl of white roses on the bed table.

She drew the shades, took the rose-satin spread from the bed, slipped out of her dress and her shoes, and lay down tiredly. She knew that no doorbell or phone would ring; no one in town would dare to disturb Miss Strangeworth during her afternoon nap. She slept, deep in the rich smell of roses.

After her nap she worked in her garden for a little while, sparing herself because of the heat; then she came in to her supper. She ate asparagus from her own garden, with sweet-butter sauce and a soft-boiled egg, and, while she had her supper, she listened to a late-evening news broadcast and then to a program of classical music on her small radio. After her dishes were done and her kitchen set in order, she took up her hat – Miss Strangeworth's hats were proverbial in the town; people believed that she had inherited them from her mother and her grandmother – and, locking the front door of her house behind her, set off on her evening walk, pocketbook under her arm. She nodded to Linda Stewart's father, who was washing his car in the pleasantly cool evening. She thought that he looked troubled.

There was only one place in town where she could mail her letters, and that was the new post office, shiny with red brick and silver letters. Although Miss Strangeworth had never given the matter any particular thought, she had always made a point of mailing her letters very secretly; it would, of course, not have been wise to let anyone see her mail them. Consequently, she timed her walk so she could reach the post office just as darkness was starting to dim the outlines of the trees and the shapes of people's faces, although no one could ever mistake Miss Strangeworth, with her dainty walk and her rustling skirts.

There was always a group of young people around the post office, the very youngest roller-skating upon its driveway, which went all the way around the building and was the only smooth road in town; and the slightly older ones already knowing how to gather in small groups and chatter and laugh and make great, excited plans for going across the street to the soda shop in a minute or two. Miss Strangeworth had never had any self-consciousness before the children. She did not feel that any of them were staring at her unduly or longing to laugh at her; it would have been most reprehensible for their parents to permit their children to mock Miss Strangeworth of Pleasant Street. Most of the children stood back respectfully as Miss Strangeworth passed, silenced briefly in her presence, and some of the older children greeted her, saying soberly, "Hello, Miss Strangeworth."

Miss Strangeworth smiled at them and quickly went on. It had been a long time since she had known the name of every child in town. The mail slot was in the door of the post office. The children stood away as Miss Strangeworth approached it, seemingly surprised that anyone should want to use the post office after it had been officially closed up for the night and turned over to the children. Miss Strangeworth stood by the door, opening her black pocketbook to take out the letters, and heard a voice which she knew at once to be Linda Stewart's. Poor little Linda was crying again, and Miss Strangeworth listened carefully. This was, after all, her town, and these were her people; if one of them was in trouble she ought to know about it.

"I can't tell you, Dave," Linda was saying – so she *was* talking to the Harris boy, as Miss Strangeworth had supposed – "I just *can't*. It's just *nasty*."

"But why won't your father let me come around any more? What on earth did I do?"

"I can't tell you. I just wouldn't tell you for *any*thing. You've got to have a dirty, dirty mind for things like that."

"But something's happened. You've been crying and crying, and your father is all upset. Why can't *I* know about it, too? Aren't I like one of the family?"

"Not any more, Dave, not any more. You're not to come near our house again; my father said so. He said he'd horsewhip you. That's all I can tell you: You're not to come near our house any more."

"But I didn't *do* anything."

"Just the same, my father said . . ."

Miss Strangeworth sighed and turned away. There was so much evil in people. Even in a charming little town like this one, there was still so much evil in people.

She slipped her letters into the slot, and two of them fell inside. The third caught on the edge and fell outside, onto the ground at Miss Strangeworth's feet. She did not notice it because she was wondering whether a letter to the Harris boy's father might not be of some service in wiping out this potential badness. Wearily Miss Strangeworth turned to go home to her quiet bed in her lovely house, and never heard the Harris boy calling to her to say that she had dropped something.

"Old lady Strangeworth's getting deaf," he said, looking after her and holding in his hand the letter he had picked up.

"Well, who cares?" Linda said. "Who cares any more, anyway?"

"It's for Don Crane," the Harris boy said, "this letter. She dropped a letter addressed to Don Crane. Might as well take it on over. We pass his house anyway." He laughed. "Maybe it's got a cheque or something in it and he'd be just as glad to get it tonight instead of tomorrow."

"Catch old lady Strangeworth sending anybody a cheque," Linda said. "Throw it in the post office. Why do anyone a favour?" She sniffled. "Doesn't seem to me anybody around here cares about us," she said. "Why should we care about them?"

"I'll take it over anyway," the Harris boy said. "Maybe it's good news for them. Maybe they need something happy tonight, too. Like us."

Sadly, holding hands, they wandered off down the dark street, the Harris boy carrying Miss Strangeworth's pink envelope in his hand.

Miss Strangeworth awakened the next morning with a feeling of intense happiness and, for a minute, wondered why, and then remembered that this morning three people would open her letters. Harsh, perhaps, at first, but wickedness was never easily banished, and a clean heart was a scoured heart. She washed her soft, old face and brushed her teeth, still sound in spite of her seventy-one years, and dressed herself carefully in her sweet, soft clothes and buttoned shoes. Then, coming downstairs and reflecting that perhaps a little waffle would be agreeable for breakfast in the sunny dining room, she found the mail on the hall floor and bent to pick it up. A bill, the morning paper, a letter in a green envelope that looked oddly familiar. Miss Strangeworth stood perfectly still for a minute, looking down at the green envelope with the pencilled printing, and thought: It looks like one of my letters. Was one of my letters sent back? No, because no one would know where to send it. How did this get here?

Miss Strangeworth was a Strangeworth of Pleasant Street. Her hand did not shake as she opened the envelope and unfolded the sheet of green paper inside. She began to cry silently for the wickedness of the world when she read the words: LOOK OUT AT WHAT USED TO BE YOUR ROSES.

---

1. Reread "The Possibility of Evil," noting particularly the many references to Miss Strangeworth's roses. With a classmate, analyse the significance that the flowers assume as the story progresses.

2. Most of "The Possibility of Evil" is told from the third-person-limited point of view, but in one passage the author deviates from that perspective.
a) Identify the lines in which the point of view changes.
b) Talk with three or four classmates to see if their answer for (a) corresponds with yours. If not, discuss the discrepancies and arrive at a consensus.
c) Together, write an explanation of why the author might have chosen the third-person-limited point of view, and what she gained by briefly altering her narrative stance.

3. In a short expository piece, evaluate the effectiveness of the story's final paragraph.

4. The angry townspeople take Miss Strangeworth to court. Prepare the arguments you, as her lawyer, might use to defend her against a charge of public mischief. Compare your tactics with those of a classmate.

OR

With a classmate, read "The Destructors" by Graham Greene
(p. 268) and compare it with "The Possibility of Evil."
Examine how the writer in each case makes an unusual moral
position plausible.

In a small group, investigate the legend of the
Pied Piper of Hamelin. As you read the
following excerpt from Agnes deMille's
autobiography, consider how it is illuminated
by the title "Dance to the Piper."

from DANCE TO THE PIPER
Agnes deMille

We went down for our audition on a summer morning. The studio
was an enormous bare room with folding chairs pushed against
the white walls for the mothers to sit on while they watched
their daughters sweat. Across one end of the hall hung a large mirror.
Around the other three sides stretched the traditional barre. I gave my
audition in a bathing suit. Kosloff himself put me through the test. He
did not say how talented I was or how naturally graceful. He said my
knees were weak, my spine curved, that I was heavy for my age and
had "no juice." By this he meant, I came to learn, that my muscles
were dry, stubborn and unresilient. He said I was a bit old to start
training; I was at the time thirteen. I looked at him in mild surprise. I
hardly knew what emotion to give way to, the astonishment of hurt
vanity or gratitude for professional help. I was sent off (I keep saying
"I" – my sister of course was with me but from the start I took for
granted that these lessons were mine. She just came along). We were
sent off to buy blocked toe slippers, fitted right to the very ends of our
toes, and to prepare proper practice dresses.

The first lesson was a private one conducted by Miss Fredova. Miss
Fredova was born Winifred Edwards and had received her training in
London from Anna Pavlova. She was as slim as a sapling and always

wore white like a trained nurse. She parted her dark hair in the centre and drew it to the nape of her neck in glossy wings, Russian style. She was shod in low-heeled sandals. She taught standing erect as a guardsman, and beat time with a long pole. First she picked up a watering can and sprinkled water on the floor in a sunny corner by the barre. This she explained was so that we should not slip. Then she placed our hands on the barre and showed us how to turn out our feet ninety degrees from their normal walking stance into first position. Then she told us to *plier* or bend our knees deeply, keeping our heels as long as possible on the floor. I naturally stuck out behind. I found the pole placed rigidly against my spine. I naturally pressed forward on my insteps. Her leg and knee planted against my foot curbed this tendency. "I can't move," I said, laughing with winning helplessness.

"Don't talk," she said. "Down-ee, two-ee, three-ee, four-ee. Down the heels, don't rock on your feet."

At the end of ten minutes the sweat stuck in beads on my forehead. "May I sit down?" I asked.

"You must never sit during practice. It ruins the thigh muscles. If you sit down you may not continue with class." I of course would have submitted to a beating with whips rather than stop. I was taking the first steps into the promised land. The path might be thorny but it led straight to Paradise. "Down-ee, two-ee, three-ee, four-ee. *Nuca.* Give me this fourth position. Repeat the exercise."

So she began every lesson. So I have begun every practice period since. It is part of the inviolable ritual of ballet dancing. Every ballet student that has ever trained in the classic technique in any part of the world begins just this way, never any other. They were dreary exercises and I was very bad at them but these were the exercises that built Taglioni's leg. These repeated stretches and pulls gave Pavlova her magic foot and Legnani hers and Kchessinska hers. This was the very secret of how to dance, the tradition handed down from teacher to pupil for three hundred years. A king had patterned the style and named the steps, the king who built Versailles. Here was an ancient and enduring art whose technique stood like the rules of harmony. All other kinds of performance in our Western theatre had faded or changed. What were movies to this? Or Broadway plays?

I, a complacent child, who had been flattered into believing I could do without what had gone before, now inherited the labour of centuries. I had come into my birthright. I was fourteen, and I had found my life's work. I felt superior to other adolescents as I stood beside the adults serene and strong, reassured by my vision.

I bent to the discipline. I learned to relax with my head between my knees when I felt sick or faint. I learned how to rest my insteps by lying on my back with my feet vertically up against the wall. I learned how to bind up my toes so that they would not bleed through the satin shoes. But I never sat down. I learned the first and all-important dictate of ballet dancing – never to miss the daily practice, hell or high water, sickness or health, never to miss the barre practice; to miss meals, sleep, rehearsals even but not the practice, not for one day ever under any circumstances, except on Sundays and during childbirth.

I seemed, however, to have little aptitude for the business. What had all this talk about God-given talent amounted to? It was like trying to wiggle my ears. I strained and strained. Nothing perceptible happened. A terrible sense of frustration drove me to striving with masochistic frenzy. Twice I fainted in class. My calves used to ache until tears stuck in my eyes. I learned every possible manipulation of the shoe to ease the aching tendons of my insteps. I used to get abominable stitches in my sides from attempting continuous jumps. But I never sat down. I learned to cool my forehead against the plaster of the walls. I licked the perspiration off from around my mouth. I breathed through my nose though my eyes bugged. But I did not sit and I did not stop.

Ballet technique is arbitrary and very difficult. It never becomes easy; it becomes possible. The effort involved in making a dancer's body is so long and relentless, in many instances so painful, the effort to maintain the technique so gruelling that unless a certain satisfaction is derived from the disciplining and punishing, the pace could not be maintained. Most dancers are to an extent masochists. "What a good pain! What a profitable pain!" said Miss Fredova as she stretched her insteps in her two strong hands. "I have practised for three hours. I am exhausted, and I feel wonderful."

My strongest impression of the Kosloff studio was, beside the sunlight on the floor and the white walls, the smell of sweat, the salty smell of clean sweat, the musty smell of old sweat on unwashed dresses. Every dance studio smells of this – moist flesh, moist hair, hot glue in the shoes, hot socks and feet, and soap.

Paradoxically enough ballet dancing is designed to give the impression of lightness and ease. Nothing in classic dancing should be convulsive or tormented. Derived from the seventeenth- and eighteenth-century court dances the style is kingly, a series of harmonious and balanced postures linked by serene movement. The style involves a total defiance of gravity, and because this must perforce be an illusion, the effect is achieved first by an enormous strengthening of the legs and feet to produce great resilient jumps and second by a co-ordination of arms and head in a rhythm slower than the rhythm of the legs which have no choice but to take the weight of the body when the body falls. But the slow relaxed movement of head and arms gives the illusion of sustained flight, gives the sense of effortless ease. The lungs may be bursting, the heart pounding in the throat, sweat springing from every pore, but hands must float in repose, the head stir gently as though swooning in delight. The diaphragm must be lifted to expand the chest fully, proudly; the abdomen pulled in flat. The knees must be taut and flat to give the extended leg every inch of length. The leg must be turned outward forty-five degrees in the hip socket so that the side of the knee and the long unbroken line of the leg are presented to view and never the lax, droopy line of a bent knee. The leg must look like a sword. The foot arches to prolong the line of extension. The supporting foot turns out forty-five degrees to enhance the line of the supporting leg, to keep the hips even, and to ensure the broadest possible base for the support and balancing of the body.

It should always be remembered that the court, and therefore the first, ballet dances were performed by expert swordsmen and derive much of their style from fencing positions. The discipline embraces the whole deportment. The lifted foot springs to attention the minute it leaves the floor. The supporting foot endures all; the instep must never give way even when the whole weight of the body drops and grinds on the single slim arch. The legs can be held in their turned position by the great muscles across the buttocks only by pulling the buttocks in flat. The spine should be steady, the expression of the face noble, the face of a king to whom all things are possible. The eyebrows may not go up, the shoulders may not lift, the neck may not stiffen, nor the mouth open like a hooked fish.

The five classic positions and the basic arm postures and steps were named at the request of Louis XIV by his great ballet master, Pécourt, Lully's collaborator, codified, described and fixed in the regimen of daily excercise which has become almost ceremonial with time. Since then the technique has expanded and diversified but the fundamental steps and nomenclature remain unchanged. The "Royale" is still the faked beaten jump it was when Louis XIV, not as nimble in the legs as he would have liked to appear, failed to achieve a proper *entrechat quatre*.

The ideal ballet body is long limbed with a small compact torso. This makes for beauty of line; the longer the arms and legs the more exciting the body line. The ideal ballet foot has a high taut instep and a wide stretch in the Achilles tendon. This tendon is the spring on which a dancer pushes for his jump, the hinge on which he takes the shock of landing. If there is one tendon in a dancer's body more important than any other, it is this tendon. It is, I should say, the prerequisite for all great technique. When the heel does not stretch easily and softly like a cat's, as mine did not, almost to the point of malformation, the shock of running or jumping must be taken somewhere in the spine by sticking out behind, for instance, in a sitting posture after every jump. I seemed to be all rusty wire and safety pins. My torso was long with unusually broad hips, my legs and arms abnormally short, my hands and feet broad and short. I was besides fat. What I did not know was that I was constructed for endurance and that I developed through effort alone a capacity for outperforming far, far better technicians. Because I was built like a mustang, stocky, mettlesome and sturdy, I became a good jumper, growing special compensating muscles up the front of my shins for the lack of a helpful heel. But the long, cool, serene classic line was forever denied me.

———————————————◆•••◆———————————————

1. Condense the selection into a concise but detailed point-form outline that the author might have used as a guide for her writing.

2. In a small group, brainstorm for words that describe deMille's writing style. Discuss how deMille's style reflects her character as it is revealed in the selection.

3. "Most dancers are to an extent masochists." In a succinct paragraph, assess how masochism was necessary for deMille's development as a dancer.

4. DeMille alternates between anecdotes of her early training in dance and passages about the history and technique of ballet. Choose one of your interests or hobbies and write a similar autobiographical sketch, combining personal experience with more general background information about your subject. Ask a classmate to read your work and to help you edit and revise it into a polished version for your writing folder.

5. Do some research into deMille's life and accomplishments and write a capsule biography of the highlights. Present your biography to the class or to a small group that has read the deMille excerpt in this book.

Bishop Berkeley, 18th century cleric and philosopher, argued that we could never be sure of the existence of anything outside ourselves. His reasonings led him to question the existence of all matter. Here is a passage from Boswell's biography of the great man of letters Samuel Johnson. "After we came out of the church, we stood talking for some time together of Bishop Berkeley's ingenious sophistry to prove the non-existence of matter, and that every thing in the universe is merely ideal. I observed, that though we are satisfied his doctrine is not true, it is impossible to refute it. I never shall forget the alacrity with which Johnson answered, striking his foot with mighty force against a large stone, till he rebounded from it, 'I refute it *thus*.' " – *James Boswell*, The Life of Samuel Johnson

THUS I REFUTE BEELZY
John Collier

"There goes the tea bell," said Mrs. Carter. "I hope Simon hears it."

They looked out from the window of the drawing-room. The long garden, agreeably neglected, ended in a waste plot. Here a little summer-house was passing close by beauty on its way to complete decay. This was Simon's retreat. It was almost completely screened by the tangled branches of the apple tree and the pear tree, planted too close together, as they always are in the suburbs. They caught a glimpse of him now and then, as he strutted up and down, mouthing and gesticulating, performing all the solemn mumbo-jumbo of small boys who spend long afternoons at the forgotten ends of long gardens.

"There he is, bless him!" said Betty.

"Playing his game," said Mrs. Carter. "He won't play with the other children any more. And if I go down there – the temper! And comes in tired out!"

"He doesn't have his sleep in the afternoon?" asked Betty.

"You know what Big Simon's ideas are," said Mrs. Carter. " 'Let him choose for himself,' he says. That's what he chooses, and he comes in as white as a sheet."

"Look! He's heard the bell," said Betty. The expression was justified, though the bell had ceased ringing a full minute ago. Small Simon stopped in his parade exactly as if its tinny dingle had at that moment reached his ear. They watched him perform certain ritual sweeps and scratchings with his little stick, and come lagging over the hot and flaggy grass toward the house.

Mrs. Carter led the way down to the play-room, or garden-room, which was also the tea-room for hot days. It had been the huge scullery of this tall Georgian house. Now the walls were cream-washed, there was coarse blue net in the windows, canvas-covered armchairs on the stone floor, and a reproduction of Van Gogh's *Sunflowers* over the mantelpiece.

Small Simon came drifting in, and accorded Betty a perfunctory greeting. His face was an almost perfect triangle, pointed at the chin, and he was paler than he should have been. "The little elf-child!" cried Betty.

Simon looked at her. "No," said he.

At that moment the door opened, and Mr. Carter came in, rubbing his hands. He was a dentist, and washed them before and after everything he did. "You!" said his wife. "Home already!"

"Not unwelcome, I hope," said Mr. Carter, nodding to Betty. "Two people cancelled their appointments: I decided to come home. I said, I hope I am not unwelcome."

"Silly!" said his wife. "Of course not."

"Small Simon seems doubtful," continued Mr. Carter. "Small Simon, are you sorry to see me at tea with you?"

"No, Daddy."

"No, what?"

"No, Big Simon."

"That's right. Big Simon and Small Simon. That sounds more like friends, doesn't it? At one time little boys had to call their father 'sir.' If they forgot – a good spanking. On the bottom, Small Simon! On the bottom!" said Mr. Carter, washing his hands once more with his invisible soap and water.

The little boy turned crimson with shame or rage.

"But now, you see," said Betty, to help, "you can call your father whatever you like."

"And what," asked Mr. Carter, "has Small Simon been doing this afternoon? While Big Simon has been at work."

"Nothing," muttered his son.

"Then you have been bored," said Mr. Carter. "Learn from experience, Small Simon. Tomorrow, do something amusing, and you will not be bored. I want him to learn from experience, Betty. That is my way, the new way."

"I have learned," said the boy, speaking like an old, tired man as little boys so often do.

"It would hardly seem so," said Mr. Carter, "if you sit on your behind all the afternoon, doing nothing. Had *my* father caught me doing nothing, I should not have sat very comfortably."

"He played," said Mrs. Carter.

"A bit," said the boy, shifting on his chair.

"Too much," said Mrs. Carter. "He comes in all nervy and dazed. He ought to have his rest."

"He is six," said her husband. "He is a reasonable being. He must choose for himself. But what game is this, Small Simon, that is worth getting nervy and dazed over? There are very few games as good as all that."

"It's nothing," said the boy.

"Oh, come," said his father. "We are friends, are we not? You can tell me. I was a Small Simon once, just like you, and played the same games you play. Of course there were no aeroplanes in those days. With whom do you play this fine game? Come on, we must all answer civil questions, or the world would never go round. With whom do you play?"

"Mr. Beelzy," said the boy, unable to resist.

"Mr. Beelzy?" said his father, raising his eyebrows inquiringly at his wife.

"It's a game he makes up," said she.

"Not makes up!" cried the boy, "Fool!"

"That is telling stories," said his mother. "And rude as well. We had better talk of something different."

"No wonder he is rude," said Mr. Carter, "if you say he tells lies, and then insist on changing the subject. He tells you his fantasy: you implant a guilt feeling. What can you expect? A defence mechanism. Then you get a real lie."

"Like in *These Three*," said Betty. "Only different, of course. *She* was an unblushing little liar."

"I would have made her blush," said Mr. Carter, "in the proper part of her anatomy. But Small Simon is in the fantasy stage. Are you not, Small Simon? You just make things up."

"No, I don't," said the boy.

"You do," said his father. "And because you do, it is not too late to reason with you. There is no harm in a fantasy, old chap. There is no harm in a bit of make-believe. Only you have to know the difference between day dreams and real things, or your brain will never grow. It will never be the brain of a Big Simon. So come on. Let us hear about this Mr. Beelzy of yours. Come on. What is he like?"

"He isn't like anything," said the boy.

"Like nothing on earth?" said his father. "That's a terrible fellow."

"I'm not frightened of him," said the child, smiling. "Not a bit."

"I should hope not," said his father. "If you were, you would be frightening yourself. I am always telling people, older people than you are, that they are just frightening themselves. Is he a funny man? Is he a giant?"

"Sometimes he is," said the little boy.

"Sometimes one thing, sometimes another," said his father. "Sounds pretty vague. Why can't you tell us just what he's like?"

"I love him," said the small boy. "He loves me."

"That's a big word," said Mr. Carter. "That might be better kept for real things, like Big Simon and Small Simon."

"He is real," said the boy, passionately. "He's not a fool. He's real."

"Listen," said his father. "When you go down the garden there's nobody there. Is there?"

"No," said the boy.

"Then you think of him inside your head, and he comes."

"No," said Small Simon. "I have to make marks. On the ground. With my stick."

"That doesn't matter."

"Yes, it does."

"Small Simon, you are being obstinate," said Mr. Carter. "I am trying to explain something to you. I have been longer in the world than you have, so naturally I am older and wiser. I am explaining that Mr. Beelzy is a fantasy of yours. Do you hear? Do you understand?"

"Yes, Daddy."

"He is a game. He is a let's-pretend."

The little boy looked down at his plate, smiling resignedly.

"I hope you are listening to me," said his father. "All you have to do is to say, 'I have been playing a game of let's-pretend. With someone I make up, called Mr. Beelzy.' Then no one will say you tell lies, and you will know the difference between dreams and reality. Mr. Beelzy is a day dream."

The little boy still stared at his plate.

"He is sometimes there and sometimes not there," pursued Mr. Carter. "Sometimes he's like one thing, sometimes another. You can't really see him. Not as you see me. I am real. You can't touch him. You can touch me. I can touch you." Mr. Carter stretched out his big, white, dentist's hand, and took his little son by the nape of the neck. He stopped speaking for a moment and tightened his hand. The little boy sank his head still lower.

"Now you know the difference," said Mr. Carter, "between a pretend and a real thing. You and I are one thing; he is another. Which is the pretend? Come on. Answer me. What is the pretend?"

"Big Simon and Small Simon," said the little boy.

"Don't!" cried Betty, and at once put her hand over her mouth, for why should a visitor cry "Don't!" when a father is explaining things in a scientific and modern way? Besides, it annoys the father.

"Well, my boy," said Mr. Carter, "I have said you must be allowed to learn from experience. Go upstairs. Right up to your room. You shall learn whether it is better to reason, or to be perverse and obstinate. Go up. I shall follow you."

"You are not going to beat the child?" cried Mrs. Carter.

"No," said the little boy. "Mr. Beelzy won't let him."

"Go on up with you!" shouted his father.

Small Simon stopped at the door. "He said he wouldn't let anyone hurt me," he whimpered. "He said he'd come like a lion, with wings on, and eat them up."

"You'll learn how real he is!" shouted his father after him. "If you can't learn it at one end, you shall learn it at the other. I'll have your breeches down. I shall finish my cup of tea first, however," said he to the two women.

Neither of them spoke. Mr. Carter finished his tea, and unhurriedly left the room, washing his hands with his invisible soap and water.

Mrs. Carter said nothing. Betty could think of nothing to say. She wanted to be talking for she was afraid of what they might hear.

Suddenly it came. It seemed to tear the air apart. "Good God!" she cried. "What was that? He's hurt him." She sprang out of her chair, her silly eyes flashing behind her glasses. "I'm going up there!" she cried, trembling.

"Yes, let us go up," said Mrs. Carter. "Let us go up. That was not Small Simon."

It was on the second-floor landing that they found the shoe, with the man's foot still in it, like that last morsel of a mouse which sometimes falls unnoticed from the side of the jaws of the cat.

---

1. In a small group, examine the ending of the story. Begin by jotting down the details that make the ending unusual. Discuss the ending's impact on the reader and how Collier prepares the reader for it.

2. With a classmate, assess Big Simon's views on child-rearing, considering both his words and his behaviour. Write your assessment in a paragraph, referring to the story to explain how you reached your conclusions.

3. Take the role of a newspaper reporter who covers Big Simon's remarkable death and interview all the witnesses.

4. Make preliminary notes as the director of a proposed film or video-taped version of "Thus I Refute Beelzy." Consider interpretation of the various roles, camera work, and special effects. You may wish to work with another student and, if the equipment is available, to select a cast and make the film or tape.

HIGH TECH CAN MEAN WEALTH AND JOBS
Stuart L. Smith

*C*anada is a modern, advanced country that has always had all the science and technology it has needed. Why all the fuss now about new technology and its importance to Canada's future?

The concern is there because we are, as the saying goes, in a new ball game. The old patterns, so successful in the past, cannot sustain us in the future. Ironically, technology is, at one and the same time, a major reason our old game won't work and the very means by which we might succeed in the new one.

Throughout our short history, nations of the advanced world have beaten a path to our door seeking vital raw materials with which to expand industry, build shelter, feed people, fuel machines and, on several occasions, fight wars. We learned how to operate such a natural resource economy, sometimes brilliantly, sometimes wastefully and often with only a short term view. Still, we learned and we have been very successful.

Using our natural resource wealth as the base, we built a manufacturing sector mainly to produce goods for our own Canadian market. These goods cost more than they needed to, but such industries offered jobs suitable for an advanced nation and kept our exports and imports in reasonable balance. Although these industries were seldom innovative and were often mere branch plant operations, they did employ people, provide training, and reduce our dependency upon imports.

Outdated Strategy: Critics warned us about the dangers of an economy so reliant upon natural resources and a manufacturing sector so dominated by foreign ownership and so lacking in innovation. Still, the fact is that, until recent times, this combination has provided a very high standard of living for Canadians. So rewarding have been these habits that the previous government tried to base the economic strategy of the country on natural resource "mega projects" and the present government seems to want more branch plants for Canada.

New technology means this traditional strategy won't work. We must add new elements to our economy if we are to avoid gradual economic decline.

With new technology, Canada's competitors can find and exploit their own natural resources. Among these competitors are many poorer nations that are prepared to sell at low prices to get foreign currency for repaying debts. As these nations gain experience, they become even stronger competitors.

Technology also reduces the demand for certain raw materials. The microchip permits much smaller, lighter, more efficient devices to do work that used to require large, bulky machines. All of this means that less raw material is required for each car, house, or clothes dryer. The new machines use less energy and that has an impact on our oil, coal, or natural gas industries. In summary, we can get more function out of less raw material.

Furthermore, new technology has created cheaper substitutes for our natural resource materials. Plastics, fibre optics, composites, ceramics, and other advanced industrial materials are now replacing metals and might eventually replace wood as well. Electronics could still replace newsprint as time goes by.

The natural resource sector has other problems, apart from the effect of technology. There is the mismanagement of the fishery, the short-term attitude in forest management, the effect of acid rain on trees, fish and crops, and the matter of soil erosion and salinity affecting farmland.

On the other hand, there are certainly important strengths in the resource sector, especially in agriculture (which has become a knowledge-intensive industry). Energy resources should also enjoy a pretty good market for years to come. Even at worst, the market for natural resources is not going to disappear overnight.

We are not facing a sharp drop but rather a gradual decline. Still, even when our resources were in strong demand, such as during the seventies, our economy was outpaced by other countries who concentrated on manufacturing. Canada must now rely less on the resource sector, given the trends that are apparent for the eighties and nineties.

If our resource exports won't carry us, then we must become better at manufacturing. We must modernize our manufacturing sector so that it can fight effectively for the home market and, more importantly, can compete for new markets abroad. Technology is a vital factor in this change.

Since it is easy to place modern technology in the hands of low wage workers in developing countries, we simply cannot compete in traditional, labour-intensive products. Advanced countries can only hope to succeed by producing the kinds of products that the newly industrializing countries cannot themselves produce but which they will want to consume, using their newly acquired wealth.

Examples of such advanced products are modern electronically operated machinery, satellite-based telecommunications systems, laser cutting tools, optical disc information storage systems, industrial ceramics, composites and engineered plastics, modern medical devices, new diagnostic and therapeutic pharmaceuticals, membrane technology for purification of drinking water, software to permit computerized mapping and resource exploration, software and systems for adult education programs, and so on and so forth.

There is a vast, virtually unlimited array of new products and services that the whole world will need and that advanced nations can supply.

High Tech Imports: Unfortunately, Canadian manufacturing rarely enters these new, innovative areas. We tend to import most of the products that are based on up-to-the-minute research and new knowledge. In fact, among manufactured goods, the higher the amount of new technology required, the higher Canada's trade deficit happens to be.

What new technology does, therefore, to our manufacturing sector is to make it more vulnerable to overwhelming foreign competition. This points up Canada's relative absence from those areas of manufacturing that will enjoy the greatest growth in the future.

Canadian scientists and engineers are as good as any in the world; technology holds no special mystery for our trained people. Where Canadians have had the freedom to innovate, we have done extremely well. Canadian successes in telecommunications, space technology, modern agriculture, remote sensing, and large scale construction, to name but a few areas, have been recognized around the world. We have no reason to feel inferior to other advanced nations where technology is concerned. Our inability lies not in the capacity to compete but rather in the will to do so and in the way we organize our human and financial capital.

What must we do? In the first place, we need leadership and consensus building; we must agree on the need to diversify Canada's economy. We must set targets for improving our international trade performance in modern goods and services. Policies then need to be adopted to achieve these targets and to reduce our dependence upon the export of raw or partially finished materials. Most of this shift must occur in the private sector but there is still a major role for government in helping to bring the change about.

Government must support the training of experts and the performance of excellent research at our universities. Government must ensure that all our businesses, traditional or modern, have the information they require to become competitive and up-to-date in their products, their equipment, and their management.

A more specific role for government is to share the financial risks so that Canadians will enter businesses that are based on new knowledge and advanced research. Government may not wish to "pick winners" but it certainly has a responsibility to make sure we have enough horses in the right races so that some winners might emerge from the marketplace. Right now we are virtually unrepresented in pharmaceuticals, fine chemicals, precision machinery, medical devices, advanced industrial materials, and many other areas.

We are only barely present in microelectronics, advanced software, biotechnology, modern aquaculture, and advanced production machinery. General measures to encourage the private sector are important but they are useless if there is no private sector representation to respond! Government makes decisions all the time in support of our existing industries – what is required are some decisions to help create some new industries.

Creating Jobs: If new technology creates new wealth, there is nothing to prevent us from distributing that wealth in the form of jobs. We should not expect the same enterprise that applies the technology, however, to be the one that directly creates the jobs. If a new automated factory brings wealth to a given community, jobs will be created in that community and in the country generally.

In the past, the jobs were created by the mere fact that people spent their wages and profits, thus hiring other people to do work of various kinds, usually in the service sector. Since successful enterprises are likely to have fewer workers to spend wages, it may be necessary to tax the profits and use the proceeds to create service sector jobs.

Technology is also reducing the need for people in the service sector, as we notice any time we use a banking machine or an automated check-out counter. We may therefore need deliberate policies to increase employment in those parts of the service sector where human beings can do the job better than machines, namely all forms of care giving, individual instruction, rehabilitation and so on.

There should also be a reduction in the number of hours or days worked per year so that we can share the work that exists. One useful way of doing this would be to give people paid leave each year during which they would take some form of education or training.

In any case, we need to clarify the distinction between policies for wealth creation and policies for job creation. They are no longer the same thing.

Enormous benefits await Canadians who are ready to participate in the new opportunities brought about by the advance of science and technology. Change is always difficult and there will always be those who are more desperate to hang on to what they have than to move into promising new fields. Still, technology leaves us no choice but to compete in a new way. Fortunately, it also provides the means by which we can be successful. What we need is the courage and leadership to accept our changed circumstances and use them as a springboard to greater achievements.

———————————————◆•••◄———————————————

1. "Ironically, technology is, at one and the same time, a major reason our old game won't work and the very means by which we might succeed in the new one."
   a) Write a précis of the arguments that Smith advances to defend the above thesis.
   b) Compare your outline of key ideas with that of a classmate, discussing each point in order to clarify your understanding.

2. a) In a small group, prepare a list of questions you might ask Smith about Canada's economic future.
   b) Incorporate some or all of the questions you formulated in part (a) into a letter to Smith (or the current chair of the Science Council). Ask another group to help you proofread your letter before you mail it.

3. Smith suggests that, in Canada's future, anything is possible – dependency and decline, or prosperity. Imagine that you are a well-known social critic and consultant who has been asked to give a brief speech on Canada's future to a group of businesspeople from across the country. Taking an optimistic or a pessimistic view, write a two-minute address and present it to a small group. Your listeners should be prepared to take notes on and question your arguments.

tattoo, – permanent mark or design made on the body by the introduction of pigment through ruptures in the skin. . . . Tattooed designs are thought by various peoples to provide magical protection against sickness or misfortune, or they serve to identify the wearer's rank, status, or membership in a group. Decoration is perhaps the commonest motive for tattooing.
– *Encyclopaedia Britannica Micropaedia*

Keep in mind all the details of the above description as you read Roald Dahl's short story "Skin."

SKIN
Roald Dahl

 hat year – 1946 – winter was a long time going. Although it was April, a freezing wind blew through the streets of the city, and overhead the snow clouds moved across the sky.

The old man who was called Drioli shuffled painfully along the sidewalk of the Rue de Rivoli. He was cold and miserable, huddled up like a hedgehog in a filthy black coat, only his eyes and the top of his head visible above the turned-up collar.

The door of a café opened and the faint whiff of roasting chicken brought a pain of yearning to the top of his stomach. He moved on, glancing without any interest at the things in the shopwindows – perfume, silk ties and shirts, diamonds, porcelain, antique furniture, finely bound books. Then a picture gallery. He had always liked picture galleries. This one had a single canvas on display in the window. He stopped to look at it. He turned to go on. He checked, looked back; and now, suddenly, there came to him a slight uneasiness, a movement of the memory, a distant recollection of something, somewhere, he had seen before. He looked again. It was a landscape, a clump of trees leaning madly over to one side as if blown by a tremendous wind, the sky swirling and twisting all around. Attached to the frame there was a little plaque, and on this it said: "CHAÏM SOUTINE (1894-1943)."

Drioli stared at the picture, wondering vaguely what there was about it that seemed familiar. Crazy painting, he thought. Very strange and crazy – but I like it . . . Chaïm Soutine . . . Soutine . . . He cried suddenly, "My little Kalmuck, that's who it is! My little Kalmuck with a picture in the finest shop in Paris! Just imagine that!"

The old man pressed his face closer to the window. He could remember the boy – yes, quite clearly he could remember him. But when? When? The rest of it was not so easy to recollect. It was so long ago. How long? Twenty – no, more like thirty years, wasn't it? Wait a minute. Yes – it was the year before the war, the first war, 1913. That was it. And this Soutine, this ugly little Kalmuck, a sullen brooding boy whom he had liked – almost loved – for no reason at all that he could think of except that he could paint.

And how he could paint! It was coming back more clearly now – the street, the line of refuse cans along the length of it, the rotten smell, the brown cats walking delicately over the refuse, and then the women, moist fat women sitting on the doorsteps with their feet upon the cobblestones of the street. Which street? Where was it the boy had lived?

The Cité Falguière, that was it! The old man nodded his head several times, pleased to have remembered the name. Then there was the studio with the single chair in it, and the filthy red couch that the boy had used for sleeping; the drunken parties, the cheap white wine, the furious quarrels, and always, always the bitter sullen face of the boy brooding over his work.

It was odd, Drioli thought, how easily it all came back to him now, how each single small remembered fact seemed instantly to remind him of another.

There was that nonsense with the tattoo, for instance. Now, *that* was a mad thing if ever there was one. How had it started? Ah, yes – he had got rich one day, that was it, and he had bought lots of wine. He could see himself now as he entered the studio with the parcel of bottles under his arm – the boy sitting before the easel, and his (Drioli's) own wife standing in the centre of the room, posing for her picture.

"Tonight we shall celebrate," he said. "We shall have a little celebration, us three."

"What is it that we celebrate?" the boy asked, without looking up. "Is it that you have decided to divorce your wife so she can marry me?"

"No," Drioli said. "We celebrate because today I have made a great sum of money with my work."

"And I have made nothing. We can celebrate that also."

"If you like." Drioli was standing by the table unwrapping the parcel. He felt tired and he wanted to get at the wine. Nine clients in one day was all very nice, but it could play havoc with a man's eyes. He had never done as many as nine before. Nine boozy soldiers – and the remarkable thing was that no fewer than seven of them had been able to pay in cash. This had made him extremely rich. But the work was terrible on the eyes. Drioli's eyes were half closed from fatigue, the whites streaked with little connecting lines of red; and about an inch behind each eyeball there was a small concentration of pain. But it was evening now and he was wealthy as a pig, and in the parcel there were three bottles – one for his wife, one for his friend, and one for him. He had found the corkscrew and was drawing the corks from the bottles, each making a small plop as it came out.

The boy put down his brush and said, "How can one work with all this going on?"

The girl came across the room to look at the painting. Drioli came over also, holding a bottle in one hand, a glass in the other.

"No!" the boy shouted, blazing up suddenly. "Please – no!" He snatched the canvas from the easel and stood it against the wall. But Drioli had seen it.

"I like it."

"It's terrible."

"It's marvellous. Like all the others that you do, it's marvellous. I love them all."

"The trouble is," the boy said, scowling, "that in themselves they are not nourishing. I cannot eat them."

"But still they are marvellous." Drioli handed him a tumbler full of the pale-yellow wine. "Drink it," he said. "It will make you happy."

Never, he thought, had he known a more unhappy person, or one with a gloomier face. He had spotted him in a café some seven months before, drinking alone, and because he had looked like a Russian or some sort of an Asiatic, Drioli had sat down at his table and talked.

"You are a Russian?"

"Yes."

"Where from?"

"Minsk."

Drioli had jumped up and embraced him, crying that he too had been born in that city.

"It wasn't actually Minsk," the boy had said. "But quite near."

"Where?"

"Smilovichi, about twelve miles away."

"Smilovichi!" Droili had shouted, embracing him again. "I walked there several times when I was a boy." Then he had sat down again, staring affectionately at the other's face. "You know," he had said, "you don't look like a western Russian. You're like a Tartar, or a Kalmuck. You look exactly like a Kalmuck."

Now, standing in the studio, Drioli looked again at the boy as he took the glass of wine and tipped it down his throat in one swallow. Yes, he did have a face like a Kalmuck – very broad and high-cheeked, with a wide coarse nose. This broadness of the cheeks was accentuated by the ears which stood out sharply from the head. And then he had the narrow eyes, the black hair, the thick sullen mouth of a Kalmuck; but the hands – the hands were always a surprise, so small and white like a lady's with tiny thin fingers.

"Give me some more," the boy said. "If we are to celebrate, then let us do it properly."

Drioli distributed the wine and sat himself on a chair. The boy sat on the old couch with Drioli's wife. The three bottles were placed on the floor between them.

"Tonight we shall drink as much as we possibly can," Drioli said. "I am exceptionally rich. I think perhaps I should go out now and buy some more bottles. How many shall I get?"

"Six more," the boy said. "Two for each."

"Good. I shall go now and fetch them."

"And I will help you."

In the nearest café Drioli bought six bottles of white wine, and they carried them back to the studio. They placed them on the floor in two rows, and Drioli fetched the corkscrew and pulled the corks, all six of them; then they sat down again and continued to drink.

"It is only the very wealthy," Drioli said, "who can afford to celebrate in this manner."

"That is true," the boy said. "Isn't that true, Josie?"

"Of course."

"How do you feel, Josie?"

"Fine."

"Will you leave Drioli and marry me?"

"No."

"Beautiful wine," Drioli said. "It is a privilege to drink it."

Slowly, methodically, they set about getting themselves drunk. The process was routine, but all the same there was a certain ceremony to be observed, and a gravity to be maintained, and a great number of things to be said, then said again – and the wine must be praised, and the slowness was important too, so that there would be time to savour the three delicious stages of transition, especially (for Drioli) the one when he began to float and his feet did not really belong to him. That was the best period of them all – when he could look down at his feet and they were so far away that he would wonder what crazy person they might belong to and why they were lying around on the floor like that, in the distance.

After a while, he got up to switch on the light. He was surprised to see that the feet came with him when he did this, especially because he couldn't feel them touching the ground. It gave him a pleasant sensation of walking on air. Then he began wandering around the room, peeking slyly at the canvases stacked against the walls.

"Listen," he said at length. "I have an idea." He came across and stood before the couch, swaying gently. "Listen, my little Kalmuck."

"What?"

"I have a tremendous idea. Are you listening?"

"I'm listening to Josie."

"Listen to me, *please*. You are my friend – my ugly little Kalmuck from Minsk – and to me you are such an artist that I would like to have a picture, a lovely picture – "

"Have them all. Take all you can find, but do not interrupt me when I am talking with your wife."

"No, no. Now listen. I mean a picture that I can have with me always . . . forever . . . wherever I go . . . whatever happens . . . but always with me . . . a picture by you." He reached forward and shook the boy's knee. "Now listen to me, *please*."

"Listen to him," the girl said.

"It is this. I want you to paint a picture on my skin, on my back. Then I want you to tattoo over what you have painted so that it will be there always."

"You have crazy ideas."

"I will teach you how to use the tattoo. It is easy. A child could do it."

"I am not a child."

"*Please* . . ."

"You are quite mad. What is it you want?" The painter looked up into the slow, dark, wine-bright eyes of the other man. "What in heaven's name is it you want?"

"You could do it easily! You could! You could!"

"You mean with the tattoo?"

"Yes, with the tattoo! I will teach you in two minutes!"

"Impossible!"

"Are you saying I don't know what I'm talking about?"

No, the boy could not possibly be saying that because if anyone knew about the tattoo it was he – Drioli. Had he not, only last month, covered a man's whole belly with the most wonderful and delicate design composed entirely of flowers? What about the client who had had so much hair upon his chest that he had done him a picture of a grizzly bear so designed that the hair on the chest became the furry coat of the bear? Could he not draw the likeness of a lady and position it with such subtlety upon a man's arm that when the muscle of the arm was flexed the lady came to life and performed some astonishing contortions?

"All I am saying," the boy told him, "is that you are drunk and this is a drunken idea."

"We could have Josie for a model. A study of Josie upon my back. Am I not entitled to a picture of my wife upon my back?"

"Of Josie?"

"Yes." Drioli knew he only had to mention his wife and the boy's thick brown lips would loosen and begin to quiver.

"No," the girl said.

"Darling Josie, *please*. Take this bottle and finish it, then you will feel more generous. It is an enormous idea. Never in my life have I had such an idea before."

"What idea?"

"That he should make a picture of you upon my back. Am I not entitled to that?"

"A picture of me?"

"A nude study," the boy said. "It is an agreeable idea."

"Not nude," the girl said.

"It is an enormous idea," Drioli said.

"It's a very crazy idea," the girl said.

"It is in any event an idea," the boy said. "It is an idea that calls for a celebration."

They emptied another bottle among them. Then the boy said, "It is no good. I could not possibly manage the tattoo. Instead, I will paint this picture on your back and you will have it with you so long as you do not take a bath and wash it off. If you never take a bath again in your life then you will have it always, as long as you live."

"No," Drioli said.

"Yes – and on the day that you decide to take a bath I will know that you do not any longer value my picture. It will be a test of your admiration of my art."

"I do not like the idea," the girl said. "His admiration for your art is so great that he would be unclean for many years. Let us have the tattoo. But not nude."

"Then just the head," Drioli said.

"I could not manage it."

"It is immensely simple. I will undertake to teach you in two minutes. You will see. I shall go now and fetch the instruments. The needles and the inks. I have inks of many different colours – as many different colours as you have paints, and far more beautiful. . . ."

"It is impossible."

"I have many inks. Have I not many different colours of inks, Josie?"

"Yes."

"You will see," Drioli said. "I will go now and fetch them." He got up from his chair and walked unsteadily, but with determination, out of the room.

In half an hour Drioli was back. "I have brought everything," he cried, waving a brown suitcase. "All the necessities of the tattooist are here in this bag."

He placed the bag on the table, opened it, and laid out the electric needles and the small bottles of coloured inks. He plugged in the electric needle, then he took the instrument in his hand and pressed a switch. It made a buzzing sound and the quarter inch of needle that projected from the end of it began to vibrate swiftly up and down. He threw off his jacket and rolled up his left sleeve. "Now look. Watch me and I will show you how easy it is. I will make a design on my arm, here."

His forearm was already covered with blue markings, but he selected a small clear patch of skin upon which to demonstrate.

"First, I choose my ink – let us use ordinary blue – and I dip the point of my needle in the ink . . . so . . . and I hold the needle up straight and I run it lightly over the surface of the skin . . . like this . . . and with the little motor and the electricity, the needle jumps up and down and punctures the skin and the ink goes in and there you are . . . See how easy it is . . . see how I draw a picture of a greyhound here upon my arm . . ."

The boy was intrigued. "Now let *me* practise a little – on your arm."

With the buzzing needle he began to draw blue lines upon Drioli's arm. "It is simple," he said. "It is like drawing with pen and ink. There is no difference except that it is slower."

"There is nothing to it. Are you ready? Shall we begin?"

"At once."

"The model!" cried Drioli. "Come on, Josie!" He was in a bustle of enthusiasm now, tottering around the room arranging everything, like a child preparing for some exciting game. "Where will you have her? Where shall she stand?"

"Let her be standing there, by my dressing table. Let her be brushing her hair. I will paint her with her hair down over her shoulders and her brushing it."

"Tremendous. You are a genius."

Reluctantly, the girl walked over and stood by the dressing table, carrying her glass of wine with her.

Drioli pulled off his shirt and stepped out of his trousers. He retained only his underpants and his socks and shoes, and he stood there swaying gently from side to side, his small body firm, whiteskinned, almost hairless. "Now," he said, "I am the canvas. Where will you place your canvas?"

"As always, upon the easel."

"Don't be crazy. I am the canvas."

"Then place yourself upon the easel. That is where you belong."

"How can I?"

"Are you the canvas or are you not the canvas?"

"I am the canvas. Already I begin to feel like a canvas."

"Then place yourself upon the easel. There should be no difficulty."

"Truly, it is not possible."

"Then sit on the chair. Sit back to front, then you can lean your drunken head against the back of it. Hurry now, for I am about to commence."

"I am ready. I am waiting."

"First," the boy said, "I shall make an ordinary painting. Then, if it pleases me, I shall tattoo over it." With a wide brush he began to paint upon the naked skin of the man's back.

"Ayee! Ayee!" Drioli screamed. "A monstrous centipede is marching down my spine!"

"Be still now! Be still!" The boy worked rapidly, applying the paint only in a thin blue wash so that it would not afterward interfere with the process of tattooing. His concentration, as soon as he began to paint, was so great that it appeared somehow to supersede his drunkenness. He applied the brush strokes with quick short jabs of the arm, holding the wrist stiff, and in less than half an hour it was finished.

"All right. That's all," he said to the girl, who immediately returned to the couch, lay down, and fell asleep.

Drioli remained awake. He watched the boy take up the needle and dip it in the ink; then he felt the sharp tickling sting as it touched the skin of his back. The pain, which was unpleasant but never extreme, kept him from going to sleep. By following the track of the needle and by watching the different colours of ink that the boy was using, Drioli amused himself trying to visualize what was going on behind him. The boy worked with an astonishing intensity. He appeared to have become completely absorbed in the little machine and in the unusual effects it was able to produce.

Far into the small hours of the morning the machine buzzed and the boy worked. Drioli could remember that when the artist finally stepped back and said, "It is finished," there was daylight outside and the sound of people walking in the street.

"I want to see it," Drioli said. The boy held up a mirror, at an angle, and Drioli craned his neck to look.

"Mon Dieu!" he cried. It was a startling sight. The whole of his back, from the top of the shoulders to the base of the spine, was a blaze of colour – gold and green and blue and black and scarlet. The tattoo was applied so heavily it looked almost like an impasto. The boy had followed as closely as possible the original brush stokes, filling them in solid, and it was marvellous the way he had made use of the spine and the protrusion of the shoulder blades so that they became part of the composition. What is more, he had somehow managed to achieve – even with this slow process – a certain spontaneity. The portrait was quite alive; it contained much of that twisted, tortured quality so characteristic of Soutine's other work. It was not a good likeness. It was a mood rather than a likeness, the model's face vague and tipsy, the background swirling around her head in a mass of dark-green curling strokes.

"It's tremendous!"

"I rather like it myself." The boy stood back, examining it critically. "You know," he added, "I think it's good enough for me to sign." And taking up the buzzer again, he inscribed his name in red ink on the right-hand side, over the place where Drioli's kidney was.

The old man who was called Drioli was standing in a sort of trance, staring at the painting in the window of the picture-dealer's shop. It had been so long ago, all that – almost as though it had happened in another life.

And the boy? What had become of him? He could remember now that after returning from the war – the first war – he had missed him and had questioned Josie.

"Where is my little Kalmuck?"

"He is gone," she had answered. "I do not know where, but I heard it said that a dealer had taken him up and sent him away to Céret to make more paintings."

"Perhaps he will return."

"Perhaps he will. Who knows?"

That was the last time they had mentioned him. Shortly afterward they had moved to Le Havre where there were more sailors and business was better. The old man smiled as he remembered Le Havre. Those were the pleasant years, the years between the wars, with the small shop near the docks and the comfortable rooms and always enough work, with every day three, four, five sailors coming and wanting pictures on their arms. Those were truly the pleasant years.

Then had come the second war, and Josie being killed, and the Germans arriving, and that was the finish of his business. No one had wanted pictures on their arms any more after that. And by that time he was too old for any other kind of work. In desperation he had made his way back to Paris, hoping vaguely that things would be easier in the big city. But they were not.

And now, after the war was over, he possessed neither the means nor the energy to start up his small business again. It wasn't very easy for an old man to know what to do, especially when one did not like to beg. Yet how else could he keep alive?

Well, he thought, still staring at the picture. So that is my little Kalmuck. And how quickly the sight of one small object such as this can stir the memory. Up to a few moments ago he had even forgotten that he had a tattoo on his back. It had been ages since he had thought about it. He put his face closer to the window and looked into the gallery. On the walls he could see many other pictures and all seemed to be the work of the same artist. There were a great number of people strolling around. Obviously it was a special exhibition.

On a sudden impulse, Drioli turned, pushed open the door of the gallery and went in.

It was a long room with a thick wine-coloured carpet, and how beautiful and warm it was! There were all these people strolling about looking at the pictures, well-washed, dignified people, each of whom held a catalogue in the hand. Drioli stood just inside the door, nervously glancing around, wondering whether he dared go forward and mingle with this crowd. But before he had had time to gather his courage, he heard a voice beside him saying, "What is it you want?"

The speaker wore a black morning coat. He was plump and short and had a very white face. It was a flabby face with so much flesh upon it that the cheeks hung down on either side of the mouth in two fleshy collops, spanielwise. He came up close to Drioli and said again, "What is it you want?"

Drioli stood still.

"If you please," the man was saying, "take yourself out of my gallery."

"Am I not permitted to look at the pictures?"

"I have asked you to leave."

Drioli stood his ground. He felt suddenly, overwhelmingly outraged.

"Let us not have trouble," the man was saying. "Come on now, this way." He put a fat white paw on Drioli's arm and began to push him firmly to the door.

That did it. "Take your wretched hands off me!" Drioli shouted. His voice rang clear down the long gallery and all the heads jerked around as one – all the startled faces stared down the length of the room at the person who had made this noise. A flunky came running over to help, and the two men tried to hustle Drioli through the door. The people stood still, watching the struggle. Their faces expressed only a mild interest, and seemed to be saying, "It's all right. There's no danger to us. It's being taken care of."

"I, too!" Drioli was shouting. "I, too, have a picture by this painter! He was my friend and I have a picture which he gave me!"

"He's mad."

"A lunatic. A raving lunatic."

"Someone should call the police."

With a rapid twist of the body Drioli suddenly jumped clear of the two men, and before anyone could stop him he was running down the gallery shouting, "I'll show you! I'll show you! I'll show you!" He flung off his overcoat, then his jacket and shirt, and he turned so that his naked back was toward the people.

"There!" he cried, breathing quickly. "You see? There it is!"

There was a sudden absolute silence in the room, each person arrested in what he was doing, standing motionless in a kind of shocked, uneasy bewilderment. They were staring at the tattooed picture. It was still there, the colours as bright as ever, but the old man's back was thinner now, the shoulder blades protruded more sharply, and the effect, though not great, was to give the picture a curiously wrinkled, squashed appearance.

Somebody said, "Mon Dieu, but it is!"

Then came the excitement and the noise of voices as the people surged forward to crowd around the old man.

"It is unmistakable!"

"His early manner, yes?"

"It is fantastic, fantastic!"

"And look, it is signed!"

"Bend your shoulders forward, my friend, so that the picture stretches out flat."

"Old one, when was this done?"

"In 1913," Drioli said, without turning around. "In the autumn of 1913."

"Who taught Soutine to tattoo?"

"I taught him."

"And the woman?"

"She was my wife."

The gallery owner was pushing through the crowd toward Drioli. He was calm now, deadly serious, making a smile with his mouth. "Monsieur," he said, "I will buy it." Drioli could see the loose fat upon the face vibrating as he moved his jaw. "I said I will buy it, Monsieur."

"How can you buy it?" Drioli asked softly.

"I will give two hundred thousand francs for it." The dealer's eyes were small and dark, the wings of his broad nose-base were beginning to quiver.

"Don't do it!" someone murmured in the crowd. "It is worth twenty times as much."

Drioli opened his mouth to speak. No words came, so he shut it; then he opened it again and said slowly, "But how can I sell it?" He lifted his hands, let them drop loosely to his sides. "Monsieur, how can I possibly sell it?" All the sadness in the world was in his voice.

"Yes!" they were saying in the crowd. "How can he sell it? It is a part of himself!"

"Listen," the dealer said, coming up close. "I will help you. I will make you rich. Together we shall make some private arrangement over this picture, no?"

Drioli watched him with slow, apprehensive eyes. "But how can you buy it, Monsieur? What will you do with it when you have bought it? Where will you keep it? Where will you keep it tonight? And where tomorrow?"

"Ah, where will I keep it? Yes, where will I keep it? Now, where will I keep it? Well, now . . ." The dealer stroked the bridge of his nose with a fat white finger. "It would seem," he said, "that if I take the picture, I take you also. That is a disadvantage." He paused and stroked his nose again. "The picture itself is of no value until you are dead. How old are you, my friend?"

"Sixty-one."

"But you are perhaps not very robust, no?" The dealer lowered the hand from his nose and looked Drioli up and down, slowly, like a farmer appraising an old horse.

"I do not like this," Drioli said, edging away. "Quite honestly, Monsieur, I do not like it." He edged straight into the arms of a tall man who put out his hands and caught him gently by the shoulders. Drioli glanced around and apologized. The man smiled down at him, patting one of the old fellow's naked shoulders reassuringly with a hand encased in a canary-coloured glove.

"Listen, my friend," the stranger said, still smiling. "Do you like to swim and to bask yourself in the sun?"

Drioli looked up at him, rather startled.

"Do you like fine food and red wine from the great châteaux of Bordeaux?" The man was still smiling, showing strong white teeth with a flash of gold among them. He spoke in a soft coaxing manner, one gloved hand still resting on Drioli's shoulder. "Do you like such things?"

"Well – yes," Drioli answered, still greatly perplexed. "Of course."

"And the company of beautiful women?"

"Why not?"

"And a cupboard full of suits and shirts made to your own personal measurements? It would seem that you are a little lacking for clothes."

Drioli watched this suave man, waiting for the rest of the proposition.

"Have you ever had a shoe constructed especially for your own foot?"

"No."

"You would like that?"

"Well . . ."

"And a man who will shave you in the morning and trim your hair?"

Drioli simply stood and gaped.

"And a plump attractive girl to manicure the nails of your fingers?"

Someone in the crowd giggled.

"And a bell beside your bed to summon a maid to bring your breakfast in the morning? Would you like these things, my friend? Do they appeal to you?"

Drioli stood still and looked at him.

"You see, I am the owner of the Hotel Bristol in Cannes. I now invite you to come down there and live as my guest for the rest of your life in luxury and comfort." The man paused, allowing his listener time to savour this cheerful prospect.

"Your only duty – shall I call it your pleasure – will be to spend your time on my beach in bathing trunks, walking among my guests, sunning yourself, swimming, drinking cocktails. You would like that?"

There was no answer.

"Don't you see – all the guests will thus be able to observe this fascinating picture by Soutine. You will become famous, and men will say, 'Look, there is the fellow with ten million francs upon his back.' You like this idea, Monsieur? It pleases you?"

Drioli looked up at the tall man in the canary gloves, still wondering whether this was some sort of joke. "It is a comical idea," he said slowly. "But do you really mean it?"

"Of course I mean it."

"Wait," the dealer interrupted. "See here, old one. Here is the answer to our problem. I will buy the picture, and I will arrange with a surgeon to remove the skin from your back, and then you will be able to go off on your own and enjoy the great sum of money I shall give you for it."

"With no skin on my back?"

"No, no please! You misunderstand. This surgeon will put a new piece of skin in the place of the old one. It is simple."

"Could he do that?"

"There is nothing to it."

"Impossible!" said the man with the canary gloves. "He's too old for such a major skin-grafting operation. It would kill him. It would kill you, my friend."

"It would kill me?"

"Naturally. You would never survive. Only the picture would come through."

"Nom de Dieu!" Drioli cried. He looked around aghast at the faces of the people watching him, and in the silence that followed, another man's voice, speaking quietly from the back of the group, could be heard saying, "Perhaps if one were to offer this old man enough money, he might consent to kill himself on the spot. Who knows?" A few people sniggered. The dealer moved his feet uneasily on the carpet.

Then the hand in the canary glove was tapping Drioli again upon the shoulder. "Come on," the man was saying, smiling his broad white smile. "You and I will go and have a good dinner and we can talk about it some more while we eat. How's that? Are you hungry?"

Drioli watched him, frowning. He didn't like the man's long flexible neck, or the way he craned it forward at you when he spoke, like a snake.

"Roast duck and Chambertin," the man was saying. He put a rich succulent accent on the words, splashing them out with his tongue. "And perhaps a soufflé aux marrons, light and frothy."

Drioli's eyes turned up toward the ceiling, his lips became loose and wet. One could see the poor old fellow beginning literally to drool at the mouth.

"How do you like your duck?" the man went on. "Do you like it very brown and crisp outside, or shall it be . . ."

"I am coming," Drioli said quickly. Already he had picked up his shirt and was pulling it frantically over his head. "Wait for me, Monsieur. I am coming." And within a minute he had disappeared out of the gallery with his new patron.

It wasn't more than a few weeks later that a picture by Soutine, of a woman's head, painted in an unusual manner, nicely framed and heavily varnished, turned up for sale in Buenos Aires. That – and the fact that there is no hotel in Cannes called Bristol – causes one to wonder a little, and to pray for the old man's health, and to hope fervently that wherever he may be at this moment, there is a plump attractive girl to manicure the nails of his fingers, and a maid to bring him his breakfast in bed in the mornings.

---

1. Various details in the story foreshadow its conclusion. With a classmate, identify three or four such details and specify, in one or two sentences, how each one prepares the reader for the ending.

2. In a personal piece of writing, describe your reaction to the final paragraph of "Skin." Include an analysis of the writer's tone and state how you were affected by it.

3. a) In a small group, discuss the use of stereotypes and clichés in "Skin," considering both characters and themes.
   b) " 'Skin' is stereotyped and trite." Divide your group into two and argue for and against the above statement. One member of the group should act as recorder, jotting down the arguments presented on both sides. Analyse the record and determine which side was most convincing.

4. You are Drioli, and you have just left the gallery with the canary-gloved man. Write your diary of the next few weeks of your life. Let a classmate read your work, or, if you wish, read it aloud for him or her.

5. You are a wealthy connoisseur of art who purchases Soutine's painting of a woman's head when it appears for sale in Buenos Aires. After prolonged scrutiny, you are disturbed by some of the painting's unusual features. Write a formal letter to the art dealer who sold you the Soutine, expressing your concerns and requesting details concerning the painting's provenance.

THE OXFORD ENGLISH DICTIONARY AWAKENS TO A COMPUTER'S KISS

Martin Bronstein

his year marks the centenary of the Oxford English Dictionary. What, asked the editors of Oxford University Press a couple of years ago, will they do with the world's most famous dictionary?

Inevitably, the words "electronic" and "computerized" were placed before the initials OED. It became apparent that despite its solid reputation, the 21 000 pages, 660 million words and two million quotations of the OED was an intellectual sleeping beauty and an electronic kiss would awaken it to more people in the next 10 years than in its previous 100.

Timothy Benbow, the energetic and articulate manager of the New Oxford English Dictionary project – the NOED – describes his thinking this way: "Do we put out another supplement or do we do something more radical? We put together a document called A Future For The OED. We set out what the dictionary did, what it contains, how significant it is, how different from any other dictionary, and we circulated that fairly widely, mainly in Britain."

The document was, in effect, an invitation to tender.

The tender – the computer prize of the century – was won by the University of Waterloo, famed for its computer expertise. For the past 18 months Waterloo has been trying to grasp how many different ways the NOED data base can be used.

It was an English civil engineer, E. Michael Brookes, who was responsible for the NOED connection between the University of Waterloo and Oxford University Press. Brookes, director of planning when the University of Waterloo was built back in the early fifties, was the land agent for Oxford University in 1982, when Waterloo president Douglas

Wright dropped in to say hello to his old friend. Brookes told Wright about the project, knowing Waterloo's enviable world reputation in computer software. Wright lost no time bidding to take part in the project.

The project was conceived in two phases. Phase one was to integrate the 12 volumes, four supplements and new material onto magnetic tape. The massive task of keystroking was given to International Computaprint Corporation in the United States, and is expected to be completed by early 1986. After checking and rechecking by pairs of proofreaders and teams of lexicographers, the electronic text will be transferred to type by photo typesetter and, in 1988, the first new version of the OED in 100 years will be available.

There has only been one set of type, and this was broken up in 1933. Since then, all printing has been from plates taken from moulds of that original type. Now, even those moulds have been destroyed (Benbow has one on his desk as an objet d'art). The only way a new printing could be undertaken would be to photograph the existing plates.

It is the second phase, the preparation of an electronic version of the dictionary and data base, that is staggering in its range. "The dictionary is a great source of information, but not one which you can easily use in printed form," says John Stubbs, a 41-year-old Waterloo history professor who is working on the project. "In its electronic form it is suddenly going to become a tool for all kinds of people who have never looked at it before."

The OED is virtually a history of the English language which reaches back into the middle of the eleventh century. It is so envied the world over that the French are desperately preparing an equivalent.

Ironically, it was the success of a French dictionary that helped get the OED off the ground in 1877, when Henry Sweet, of the London Philological Society, persuaded the Clarendon Press to publish the results of 19 years of work by the society's members. He wrote: "We are not asking to subsidize an unremunerative undertaking, but are rather offering a share in what promises to be a safe and remunerative one . . . a dictionary which will have a full number of citations from every period of the language arranged so as to exhibit the history of each word . . . . Proof of success is afforded by Littré's French Dictionary, due entirely to its fullness of citation and its historical and scientific character. Upward of 4000 copies have been sold."

Even in 1877 they were thinking on a grand scale. The first dictionary of 6400 pages would have to be considered an abridgement of their original plans for 18 000 quarto pages.

The first editor was James Murray, who had, in his own words, "a sort of mania for learning languages; every new language was a new delight, no matter what it was, Hebrew, Tongan, Russian or Caffre, I swallowed them all. . . . I at one time or another could read in a sort of way 25 or more languages."

The first volume, A to AND, was published in 1884; the 12th and final volume 44 years later. In 1933 it was decided to publish a supplement which would update a work that was, in parts, already 50 years old. Once more in 1957, Oxford decided on a further updating with a four-volume supplement, the first of which appeared in 1972 with the fourth due out in 1986. It was while preparing this last volume in 1982 that the future was considered.

To understand how the University of Waterloo captured this computer prize, a study of its remarkable – if short – history is in order. If Oxford is all dreaming spires, then Waterloo is a nightmarish concrete design. The North American efficiency starts at the main gate, where a beautiful printed map of the campus is given out free by the uniformed attendant, with precise instructions on where to go and exactly which car park to use.

In almost every endeavour, Waterloo's business acumen has been nothing short of brilliant. It has managed to combine the academic aims of a university with the commercial aims of the corporate world. The Dean of Computing, Dr. Wes Graham, has been there from the time the doors opened in 1957 and must take much of the credit for its computer leadership.

"The tube computers were just going out and our first computer was transistorized. I don't think you could find anywhere in the world a university that was using a computer in the classroom then. I've often speculated that Waterloo was the first and nobody has ever challenged it," says Graham.

Although Waterloo has concentrated on software, it did develop its own eight-bit microcomputer, at one time the most advanced available. "We developed it because we couldn't buy one," says Graham. That computer was taken over by Commodore, became known as the Super Pet and sold tens of thousands around the world.

It's Waterloo's constantly growing understanding and expertise that encourage the larger corporations to breathtaking gestures of largesse. Digital Equipment Corporation donated $25 million in equipment. Over the last three years, IBM has given at least $12 million in equipment. And the Canadian government has given $400 000 to the NOED project at Waterloo.

The NOED would certainly benefit from the relationship between big business and the university, as Tim Benbow freely admits. "If we went to a commercial software house, they would charge us about $3.4 million. The university is doing it on a royalty basis on the software they will produce."

The project's headquarters in the basement of the arts library is not, as one would expect, a hive of activity in front of banks of computers. A small team, directed by Stubbs, is undertaking a survey in an attempt to find out what potential users might require.

Frank Tompa, who has been in the project as long as Stubbs, likens the major problem of the survey to that of a motor car designer in the nineteenth century asking horse-and-buggy drivers what they would like in their future automobile: "He says, 'Would you like to steer with your feet or your hands and would you like the clutch on the left or in the middle?' and the response is 'Well, we hold the reins in our hands so we'd like to steer with our hands, but what is a clutch?' "

"What I'm doing within the university," says Stubbs, "is encouraging people to come forward and say, 'This is what I'd like to be able to do with the dictionary if it were available in this form. Could I do it?' "

Stubbs says the aim is to understand the complex problem of "tagging" to allow the recovery of specialized information. For instance, someone interested in medical terms from the fifteenth century could go to the local library in 1995 and get that information in a day or two, a task that would now take three months of poring over the printed version.

In a paper written in November, Stubbs and Tompa attempted to give some idea of the scope of an electronic OED: "It is certainly conceivable that the computerized dictionary will change the nature of word games such as Scrabble. One will simply type in the available letters and possible words using those letters will appear on the screen. The second simple example depends on the dictionary for traditional assistance – spelling. One would enter a word phonetically, for example 'sykologie', from which the computer would determine its pronunciation and thus derive the word 'psychology'."

In a more complicated vein, they quote the work of Prof. Neil Hultin, who is researching the state of English in the fifteenth century, a significant point in the movement of Middle English to Modern English. "This is a period scanted in the OED largely because of the poverty of texts from that period at the time of the creation of the dictionary, but also apparently because of certain subjective judgments by the Oxford editors about the worth of the period. The availability of the NOED in electronic form will allow the influence of the fifteenth-century English to be studied much more efficiently than was previously possible."

The project has already elicited a wide range of inquiries from other dictionaries, encyclopedias and software houses to discuss sharing operations, knowledge and common goals. Waterloo has been associated for some time with Prof. Ashley Amos of the University of Toronto, which is producing a Dictionary of Old English.

The countless trans-Atlantic crossings by staff from Waterloo and Oxford so far have been to establish a standard grammar in parsing the entries. Howard Johnson, a Waterloo faculty member, has designed a collection of software tools which transforms the defined grammar into a parser-translator, which in turn processes the dictionary text to produce a text with enhanced tagging.

By tagging, the question "How many eighteenth-century authors referred to Buddha in sociological rather than religious terms in works set in the sixteenth century using Greek word roots?" will become a 1990 reality rather than a line from a student sketch. The answer would be available at your local library at minimal cost, because despite the estimated £6.6 million ($11.2 million) cost of the NOED, ownership will be within the reach of more people.

The present cost of 12 volumes and four supplements in English is just less than £900, or about $1530 (in 1933, the cost of 10 volumes was £90). When the NOED is published in 1988, it will cost at least $1700. "The cost of buying a printed version is going beyond the means of a reasonably well-off person," says Benbow. "The cost of an optical visual disc would be substantially lower, so we would get a larger market. And by the time we are ready to go to market, optical disc readers will be as common as micros."

"The OED, one scholar has written, has 'staked out England's claim to be the keeper of our language'," says John Stubbs. "That a Canadian university is to have an important role in maintaining and modernizing this central archive of the English language is, indeed, a great honour as well as a major intellectual challenge."

ACTIVITIES FOR
INDEPENDENT STUDY

I ndependent study is a requirement of most senior English programs. The following activities for independent study are linked to the writings in *The Arch of Experience* so that you can, if you wish, study in more depth a theme, an idea, an author, or a style of writing that intrigued you when you were reading the selections.

The activities suggest not only ideas for research and exploration, but also formats for presentation: research essay, literary essay, oral presentation, seminar, video, short story, dramatization, and so on. You may use an activity as it stands, or adapt the topic or format to suit your own preferences. Another possibility is for you to take an activity that accompanies one of the selections and use it as a springboard into an independent study project.

The organization of your independent study unit will require careful planning and extensive consultation with your teacher, and probably with classmates as well. You may be required to keep a writing folder, to hand in project plans, to negotiate a contract with your teacher, to make progress reports, and to use audio-visual materials, for example. It is our hope that the selections in this book will have given you a range of possible starting points, and that your independent study will be a source of satisfaction for you and also provide you with an opportunity to share your interests and learning with others.

LOOK TO THE ESSENCE

1. Analyse the craft of the persuasive writer. Select three essays or articles: one from Look to the Essence, one from another unit in the book, and one from your own reading outside of class. Ensure that the three pieces differ from one another in tone and technique. For your reader, explain the purpose of each selection and the writer's intended audience. You should also describe the characteristics of each piece and the techniques employed by the author. Include your evaluation of the successfulness of the essays, i.e., their coherence and persuasiveness. Your analysis should contain specific references to the materials you are investigating.

2. Select a moral or ethical dilemma addressed in any of the essays in Look to the Essence and, for your writing folder, write a short story using that dilemma as a theme. You should take your story through all the stages in the writing process: pre-writing planning (including notes and possibly an outline); first draft; editing and revision (with the help of a classmate); second draft; polished version. You should also keep a diary in which you record the date you complete each stage, the sources of your ideas, and the reasoning behind your revisions.

OR

Compile an anthology of seven to ten short stories that put the reader in the position of moral arbiter. Write a general introduction for your anthology and devise one or two good questions for each story to encourage the reader to focus on the values at issue. You may wish to use one of the stories in another unit of this anthology as a start: for example, "The Destructors" (p. 268), "Antaeus" (p. 229), or "We Have to Sit Opposite" (p. 115).

THE WEB OF OUR LIFE

1. Dorothy Parker's amusing story "But the One on the Right" (p. 96) is written in the form of an interior monologue. The monologue is a flexible literary device that has been used in a variety of contexts. Write a research essay on different kinds of monologues, concentrating on the form and purpose of each. Refer to
   - the soliloquies of Shakespeare;
   - the dramatic monologues of Robert Browning;
   - the stream-of-consciousness style of Virginia Woolf;

- the work of a contemporary Canadian writer, e.g., Anne Hébert (*Kamouraska*).

2. If Dylan Thomas's unique style appeals to you, you may wish to learn something about his background and his life. Working on your own, or with one or two classmates, read at least two biographies of Thomas in order to achieve a balanced view. Take notes on what you read, using index cards with appropriate headings to help you organize your observations. Selecting highlights from the biographical material you have accumulated, prepare a multi-media presentation on Dylan Thomas for your class. Make use of any or all of
   - biographical notes and summaries you have composed;
   - readings from Thomas's literary work;
   - slides or pictures;
   - music;
   - dramatic role play.

PERIPETEIA

1. "*Peripeteia* is the change . . . from one state of things within the play to its opposite. . . . A Discovery is, as the very word implies, a change from ignorance to knowledge, and thus to either love or hate, in the personages marked for good or evil fortune. The finest form of Discovery is one attended by Peripeteia." – Aristotle's *Poetics*

   In a literary essay, reveal how discovery and *peripeteia* figure in two pieces of writing. One piece should be a selection from the *Peripeteia* unit; the other piece may be any other work of literature you have read. Your essay should briefly explain what Aristotle meant by the terms. (You may wish to ask your teacher for help with the concepts.) As well, speculate on what the writers you have chosen achieve by making use of discovery and *peripeteia*, and on how that pattern of narrative affects the reader.

2. In works of art, the sea is many things. It may be, for example, an isolator or a destroyer; it may represent chaos or endless possibility and adventure. Write the script for a documentary about the significance of the sea in art. Your documentary should show how the sea figures in several different works of art – stories, novels, plays, films, poems, and paintings, for example – including at least one of the selections in the *Peripeteia* unit. Your documentary should have a clear introduction and conclusion, as well as a thesis statement that suggests the specific focus of your investigation. You may wish

to accompany your documentary with photographs and/or slides. Present your documentary to the class.

HEROES AND IDEALISTS

1. "I say to you in all sadness of conviction, that to think great thoughts you must be heroes as well as idealists." – *Oliver Wendell Holmes Jr.*

   In a small group, discuss the above quotation and clarify Holmes's meaning. Together, make a list of ten historical figures who you feel have been both heroes and idealists. On your own, read a biography or autobiography of one of the figures. (Each group member should choose someone different.) Take notes as you read, using them to help you share what you have learned from your reading with the other members of your group.

2. In a group, select a format for a visual presentation – e.g., a bulletin board, a pamphlet, a photo-journal, a video, a series of skits – and present a gallery of ten Canadian heroes and idealists. All the people in your gallery should have something in common (all are doctors, for example, or athletes, or rebels). To accompany the visual material you find or create, write brief biographies highlighting each person's accomplishments. You should also explain why in your view each person belongs in your gallery. You might offer to present your gallery to a social studies class in a junior grade.

THE URGE FOR DESTRUCTION

1. Working with a classmate, present a pair of seminars on the topic of destruction. You are responsible for one of the seminars, your classmate for the other. The seminars should present opposing points of view. Each person should clearly articulate a thesis and use specific references to material the class has studied and material garnered from personal reading and research. The seminars will be more interesting and effective if the opposing viewpoints are argued on the basis of the same material. After the seminars are presented, open up the topic to the class for questions, comments, and new arguments.

2. In a group, prepare a video presentation on the subject of the human urge for destruction. Your video may take any number of forms – a documentary, a newscast, a dramatization, or an interview, for example. Before you shoot the video, your group should make a detailed plan, including the equipment you will need, the specific focus of your work, the settings and personnel required, and an

outline of the finished product. Show your video to the class, and ask them for their feedback. You may wish to appoint two or three classmates to be reviewers.

THE POSSIBILITY OF ANYTHING

1. Joseph Conrad, novelist, asserts that the artist, including the writer of fiction, appeals to

> that part of our being which is not dependent on wisdom; to that in us which is a gift and not an acquisition – and, therefore, more permanently enduring. He speaks to our capacity for delight and wonder, to the sense of mystery surrounding our lives; to our sense of pity, and beauty, and pain. – Preface to *The Nigger of the "Narcissus"*

In a literary essay, consider any two stories from this unit, plus one additional fictional work (a novel, play, film, or short story with which you are familiar), in light of Conrad's aesthetic theory. The introduction to your essay should indicate whether you agree or disagree with Conrad's assertion and what you intend to show in your analysis. You may find it helpful to read the whole of Conrad's Preface before you begin.

2. Will technology be the salvation or the damnation of humankind? Draw up a proposal for an independent research project to examine the question. Include a list of intended readings, a description of the form your report will take, and a time-frame for your work, with projected dates for completion of the various stages. Your proposal might take the form of a contract that both you and your teacher sign. To begin your project, read some of the following relevant selections in this anthology:
   - "Bio-engineering Gone Wrong";
   - "Can TV Tell the Truth?";
   - "High Tech Can Mean Wealth and Jobs";
   - "The *Oxford English Dictionary* Awakens to a Computer's Kiss";
   - "Tin Lizzie";
   - "A Trip Abroad";
   - "Sinning Bravely: The Case of Baby Fae";
   - "Time to Ban Surrogate Motherhood";
   - "Surrogate Motherhood: Why It Should Be Permitted."

ON LANGUAGE

1. Conduct some lexicographical research on the use of the word "man" and masculine pronouns. (Begin by reading the excerpts from "Man

as a False Generic," p. 67.) Compile examples from writing and speaking in current media to show how the words are now being used, and keep a log of the frequency of various usages. Introduce your findings to your audience by explaining the issues underlying this particular question of usage, the importance of the issues, and the options available. Draw conclusions from the data you have gathered and end your report by making your own recommendations.

2. Use Lewis Thomas's "Notes on Punctuation" (p. 124) as a springboard into a project about the history of punctuation. Look through grammar and style books of the past and present to see how rules have changed. Select examples of how various writers use punctuation. (Your teacher or librarian may help you find conventional as well as unconventional examples.) Present your findings in the form of an oral report to the class; making overheads of your examples will help the class to follow your discussion. Before you begin your research, you may wish to read K. Jason Sitewell's "The Inventor of the Period" (p. 261) for a humorous speculation on the origin of punctuation.

ACKNOWLEDGMENTS

Care has been taken to trace the ownership of copyright material used in this text. The publishers will welcome any information enabling them to rectify any reference or credit in subsequent editions.

LOOK TO THE ESSENCE

How Do You Know It's Good?: From *But Will It Sell?* © 1964 by Marya Mannes.

Essence of Marigold: By Elizabeth Brewster is reprinted from *A House Full of Women* by permission of Oberon Press.

Sinning Bravely: The Case of Baby Fae: By Charles Krauthammer. Copyright 1984 Time Inc. All rights reserved. Reprinted by permission from *Time*. Published December 3, 1984.

Time to Ban Surrogate Motherhood: By Lynda Hurst. Reprinted with permission – *The Toronto Star* Syndicate. Published 1985.

Surrogate Motherhood: Why It Should Be Permitted: By Allan C. Hutchinson. Reprinted by permission of Allan C. Hutchinson. *The Globe and Mail*, Toronto. Published July 12, 1985.

A Little Cloud: From *Dubliners*, by James Joyce. Copyright 1916 by B.W. Huebsch. Definitive text copyright © 1967 by The Estate of James Joyce. Reprinted by permission of Viking Penguin, Inc.

Is War Inevitable?: By Julian Huxley. Published February 10, 1946.

And May the Best Cheater Win: © Harry Bruce/Reprinted by permission of Bella Pomer Agency Inc. Published November, 1984.

Can TV Tell the Truth?: By Morris Wolfe. First published by *Toronto Life*, November 1985. Reprinted with permission of Morris Wolfe.

The Girl Next Door: By Norman Levine. Written as commission for CBC-Radio series *Anthology*. Originally published in Canada by Deneau & Greenberg in *Thin Ice*, 1979. And in *Champagne Barn* by Penguin Canada, Penguin UK, and Viking Penguin, 1984 & 1985. Copyright © 1979 by Norman Levine. All rights reserved. Reprinted by arrangement with the author.

Man as a False Generic: Excerpted and abridged from *The Handbook of Non-Sexist Writing for Writers, Editors and Speakers*. Published by The Women's Press. Copyright © 1980 by Casey Miller and Kate Swift. All Rights Reserved. Reprinted by permission of the authors.

THE WEB OF OUR LIFE

A West Coast Woman: By Jan Hopaklyissumqwa Gould. Reprinted with permission of the author.

Of a Dancing Girl: By Lafcadio Hearn. From *119 Years of the Atlantic* published by Little, Brown and Company. Published 1893.

Just a Little Japanese: By Eric Patrick. Reprinted with permission of the author. Published 1983.

But the One on the Right: By Dorothy Parker. Copyright 1929, renewed © 1957 by Dorothy Parker. Originally published in *The New Yorker*. Reprinted by permission of Viking Penguin, Inc.

Amnesty International: An Address: By Margaret Atwood, from *Second Words: Selected Critical Prose* (Toronto: House of Anansi Press, 1982). Reprinted by permission. Address delivered 1981.

Nurses' New Role: Patients' Advocate: By Professor Arthur Schafer, reprinted from *The Globe & Mail*, April 19, 1985.

Holiday Memory: By Dylan Thomas from *Collected Stories*, published by Dent. Reprinted with permission of David Higham Associates Ltd. Broadcast on BBC Wales Radio October, 1946. Published November, 1946.

We Have to Sit Opposite: By Ethel Wilson. Reprinted by permission of the University of British Columbia Library.

Notes on Punctuation: From *Medusa and the Snail, More Notes of a Biology Watcher*, by Lewis Thomas. Copyright © 1979 by Lewis Thomas. Reprinted by permission of Viking Penguin, Inc.

PERIPETIA

The Creature from the Marsh: Loren Eiseley, from *The Night Country*. Copyright © 1966 Loren Eiseley. Reprinted with the permission of Charles Scribner's Sons.

Saturday Climbing: By W.D. Valgardson. Reprinted by permission of the author.

The Last Wife: From *The Tattooed Woman* by Marian Engel. Copyright © The Estate of Marian Engel, 1985. Reprinted by permission of Penguin Books Canada, Ltd.

Inland Beach: From *The Man Who Sold Prayers and Other Stories* by Margaret Creal. Reprinted by permission of the author.

Nursery Crimes: By Bergen Evans from *119 Years of the Atlantic* edited by Louise DeSaulniers. Reprinted by permission of Jean W. Evans. Published 1934.

Shakespeare in the Bush: By Laura Bohannan. With permission from *Natural History*, Vol. 75, No. 7; Copyright the American Museum of Natural History, 1966.

The Boat: From *The Lost Salt Gift of Blood* by Allistair MacLeod. Used by permission of The Canadian Publishers, McClelland and Stewart Limited, Toronto.

A Madness of Nature: By Franklin Russell. From New American Review. Published January, 1968.

Journalese as a Second Tongue: By John Leo. Copyright 1984 Time Inc. All rights reserved. Reprinted by permission from *Time*. Published February 6, 1984.

HEROES AND IDEALISTS

Mary Wollstonecraft: From *The Common Reader* by Virginia Woolf. Reprinted by permission of the Author's estate and the Hogarth Press. Published 1932.

The Blood of the Martyrs: From *The Selected Works of Stephen Vincent Benet* by Stephen Vincent Benet. Copyright 1936 by Stephen Vincent Benet. Reprinted by permission of Brandt & Brandt Literary Agents, Inc. By Special Permission Only.

Antaeus: Copyright © 1961, by Southern Methodist University Press (Southwest Review). Used by permission of the Borden Deal Family Trust, First Florida Bank, NA, Trustee.

Tin Lizzie: By John Dos Passos. Reprinted by permission of Elizabeth H. Dos Passos, Co-executor, Estate of John Dos Passos. Published 1936.

A Black View of Canada: By Mary Janigan from *Maclean's* Magazine, January 20, 1986. Reprinted by permission, Mary Janigan.

The Hallowe'en Party: © 1982 Miriam Waddington from *Summer at Lonely Beach and Other Stories*, Mosaic Press/Valley Editions 1982.

A Trip Abroad: From *The Medusa and the Snail, More Notes of a Biology Watcher*, by Lewis Thomas. Copyright © 1979 by Lewis Thomas. Reprinted by permission of Viking Penguin, Inc.

The Inventor of the Period: By K. Jason Sitewell. From *Saturday Review* Magazine, March 24, 1956.

THE URGE FOR DESTRUCTION

The Destructors: By Graham Greene from *Collected Stories*, published by William Heinemann, Ltd. & The Bodley Head, Ltd. Reprinted by permission of the Author's Agent, Laurence Pollinger Limited.

Clean Fun at Riverhead: From *The Kandy-Kolored Tangerine-Flake Streamline Baby* by Tom Wolfe. Copyright © 1963, 1964, 1965 by Tom Wolfe. Copyright © 1963, 1964, 1965 by New York Herald Tribune, Inc. Reprinted by permission of Farrar, Straus & Giroux, Inc.

The House on the Esplanade: By Anne Hébert (pp. 122 to 131) taken from *Stories by Canadian Women*, published by Oxford University Press. Reprinted by permission of Editions Du Seuil.

What Gets a Porcupines's Back Up?: Bruce Obee, a Vancouver Island outdoors writer. Reprinted by permission of Bruce Obee. Published Summer, 1985.

No News from Auschwitz: By A.M. Rosenthal. Copyright © 1958 by *The New York Times* Company. Reprinted by permission. Published August 31, 1958.

London, 1940: From *The Mulberry Tree: The Writings of Elizabeth Bowen*, edited by Hermoine Lee, published by Virago Press Ltd., 1986. Copyright © Elizabeth Bowen 1940.

The Drowned Giant: © 1964 by J.G. Ballard from the collection *The Terminal Beach* published by Victor Gollancz Ltd, London, and reproduced by permission of the author c/o Margaret Hanbury, 27 Walcot Square, London SE11.

History Lesson: By Arthur C. Clarke. Reprinted by permission of the author and the author's agents, Scott Meredith Literary Agency, Inc., 845 Third Avenue, New York, N.Y. 10022.

Will Someone Please Hiccup My Pat?: By William Spooner Donald. Reprinted by permission of the author.

THE POSSIBILITY OF ANYTHING

A Bolt of White Cloth: From *A Bolt of White Cloth* by Leon Rooke. Reprinted by permission of Stoddart Publishing Co. Limited, Toronto, Canada.

Northing: Section II of "Northing" from *Pilgrim at Tinker Creek* by Annie Dillard. Copyright © 1974 by Annie Dillard. Reprinted by permission of Harper & Row, Publishers, Inc.

Bio-Engineering Gone Wrong: Reprinted with permission of *Harrowsmith* Magazine. Copyright © 1977 Camden House Publishing Limited. Published June, 1977.

The Possibility of Evil: By Shirley Jackson. Copyright © 1965 by Stanley Edgar Hyman. Reprinted by permission of Brandt & Brandt, Inc.

Dance to the Piper: By Agnes deMille. By permission of the publisher, DA CAPO PRESS, New York, N.Y. Published 1952.

Thus I Refute Beelzy: Copyright 1940 by John Collier. Reprinted by permission of Harold Matson Company, Inc.

High Tech Can Mean Wealth and Jobs: By Stuart L. Smith. Reprinted from *The Toronto Star*, March 17, 1985. Copyright © Stuart L. Smith.

Skin: Copyright 1952 by Roald Dahl. Reprinted from *Someone Like You*, by Roald Dahl, by permission of Alfred A. Knopf, Inc.

The Oxford English Dictionary Awakens to a Computer's Kiss: By Martin Bronstein. Reprinted by permission of the author. From *The Globe and Mail*, Toronto. Published June 15, 1985.